A RICH AND FERTILE LAND

FOODS AND NATIONS is a new series from Reaktion that explores the history – and geography – of food. Books in the series reveal the hidden history behind the food eaten today in different countries and regions of the world, telling the story of how food production and consumption developed, and how they were influenced by the culinary practices of other places and peoples. Each book in the Foods and Nations series offers fascinating insights into the distinct flavours of a country and its culture.

Already published

Al Dente: A History of Food in Italy
Fabio Parasecoli

Beyond Bratwurst: A History of Food in Germany
Ursula Heinzelmann

Feasts and Fasts: A History of Food in India
Colleen Taylor Sen

Gifts of the Gods: A History of Food in Greece
Andrew and Rachel Dalby

Rice and Baguette: A History of Food in Vietnam
Vu Hong Lien

A Rich and Fertile Land: A History of Food in America
Bruce Kraig

A Rich and Fertile Land

A History of Food
in America

BRUCE KRAIG

REAKTION BOOKS

For Jan, Robert, Michael, Ted and his children in the hope that in the future they will live in a truly rich and fertile land for all.

Published by Reaktion Books Ltd
Unit 32, Waterside
44–48 Wharf Road
London N1 7UX, UK
www.reaktionbooks.co.uk

First published 2017
Copyright © Bruce Kraig 2017

Printed and bound in China by 1010 Printing International Ltd

A catalogue record for this book is available from the British Library

ISBN 978 1 78023 853 1

CONTENTS

INTRODUCTION

In 1893, Katherine Lee Bates, an English professor at Wellesley College in Cambridge, Massachusetts, had been teaching a summer course at Colorado College, in Colorado Springs.

She later said:

> It was then and there, as I was looking out over the sea-like expanse of fertile country spreading away so far under those ample skies, that the opening lines of the hymn [by Samuel Augustus Ward] floated into my mind. When we left Colorado Springs the four stanzas were penciled in my notebook, together with other memoranda, in verse and prose, of the trip.

Traveling by train across the United States through the wide prairies of the Midwest and visiting the great Columbian Exposition in Chicago reinforced her idea of her native land. First published in 1895, "America the Beautiful" has sometimes been suggested as a replacement for the difficult-to-sing "Star Spangled Banner" as the national anthem. The now familiar 1911 version reads:

> O beautiful, for spacious skies,
> For amber waves of grain,
> For purple mountain majesties
> Above the fruited plain!
> America! America! God shed His grace on thee,
> And crown thy good with brotherhood, from sea to shining sea.

"America the Beautiful" is a hymn to America's natural wonders and immense fertility. It is an image that remains in the American imagination, a country of unlimited agricultural abundance that retains much of its unspoiled wilderness. But the America of 1893 was at the hinge of changes that were transforming it into today's modern industrial state. The author was carried by railcars that were pulled by roaring, coal-fired locomotives. The machines were made from coke and iron ripped from once verdant hills and forged in the satanic mills of western Pennsylvania. Coal, steam, steel, and chemicals were the signs and muscles of progress.

America's cities were growing rapidly, the new immigrant populations working in sweatshops and jammed into ghettos. The Chicago Bates visited in 1893 had doubled in size to more than one million people during the previous decade, while New York City's population doubled to almost three and a half million by 1900. At the same time, the 43 percent of America's labor force working in agriculture in 1890 was reduced to 38 percent in 1900. Today, the march of progress has left only 2 percent of American workers on farms.

At the Columbian Exposition Bates saw a vast array of machines used in farming, the food processing industry, and for homes. She surely visited the Women's Building that showed not only the progress women had made over the ages, but all the new ways of thinking about food. It was here that Ellen Swallow Richards demonstrated the new science of dietetics and talked about the new Home Economics movement, complete with recipes for efficient, nutritious cookery. New methods of food preparation such as the all-electric kitchen first appeared at the Fair, creating an immediate demand for time-saving cooking methods. Bates also no doubt ate the samples given out by America's leading food processors, such as Heinz pickles, maybe putting one of the company's free pickle pins on her shirtwaist dress. She also likely sampled pancakes made by Aunt Jemima herself, the first personally represented brand name in America. In short, almost every element of modern America's food systems and ways of thinking about them were to be seen, some fully developed, others in embryonic form.

Across the vast country, America's abundant farms and ranches stretched from coast to coast. The produce of golden California was now being shipped by rail to eastern markets via Chicago, while that city became the world's greatest wheat shipper and meat butcher. But down on the farm the rhythms of life were much the same as in Colonial times. As Hamlin Garland wrote of his days on an Iowa farm in *Main-travelled Roads* (1891):

Threshing time was always a season of great trial to—the house-wife. To have a dozen men with the appetites of dragons to cook for was no small task for a couple of women, in addition to their other everyday duties. Preparations usually began the night before with a raid on a hen roost, for "biled chicken" formed the piece de resistance of the dinner. The table, enlarged by boards, filled the sitting room. Extra seats were made out of planks placed on chairs, and dishes were borrowed of neighbors who came for such aid, in their turn.

Potatoes were seized, cut in halves, sopped in gravy, and taken one, two! Corn cakes went into great jaws like coal into a steam engine. Knives in the right hand cut and scooped gravy up. Great, muscular, grimy, but wholesome fellows they were, feeding like ancient Norse, and capable of working like demons. They were deep in the process; half-hidden by steam from the potatoes and stew, in less than sixty seconds from their entrance.

Katherine Lee Bates would have recognized this kind of cooking and eating from visiting farms in western Massachusetts. Were she alive today, she might also see a form of it in many an American home and fast food restaurant. For nothing else than people of all social levels shoveling meat and potatoes down their gullets celebrates America, the land of limitless abundance. Looking at the agricultural landscapes from her train window and perhaps dining on the fruits of the land—steaks, fried chicken or chops, freshly baked bread and desserts—Ms. Bates could hardly have been expected to think of the long-term consequences of changes to the land that humans had wrought.

Are land and water infinitely giving? Human activity has so changed the planet that geologists now call the current era the Anthropocene. Dramatic climate change, destruction of millions of living species, water resources gravely imperiled, if not disappeared, have come about by food production systems, unrestrained urbanization, and war. With the world's food supply imperiled can we still think of abundance without limit? Or can science and technology, the tools by which people adapt to and change the ecosystems in which they live, salvage what is left of the natural world in which humans first found themselves not so long ago?

ONE

The Land

The "fruited plains" that Katherine Lee Bates exalted had only been planted with domesticated grains for about half a century when she saw them from her train window. The tracks themselves were only a quarter of a century old. What Bates saw and traveled along were overlays of the basic American geography and a seemingly stable climate. She marveled at what a great nation she lived in, a place with unlimited resources, unbounded possibilities for the people fortunate enough to live in it. "The people, perhaps," in Lewis Mumford's memorable take on Carl Sandberg's line, "the people, yes!"[1]

The United States of America is a vast land, stretching 3,000 miles across the North American continent and running more than 1,600 miles from the top of the Dakotas to the banks of the Rio Grande River on the south. It is a country that encompasses almost every climate and landscape that the Earth offers; New England alone has seven different ecological zones.[2] On the East Coast the land runs from the rock-bound coast of New England, along flat coastal lands of New Jersey and the estuary of the Chesapeake River, to the windswept sand dunes of North Carolina where the Wright Brothers flew the world's first airplane. Further south are the marshes and tidal swamps of South Carolina, where rice once flourished and drove a plantation economy. Down the continent lie the flatlands of Florida with its own wide subtropical wetlands, swamps, and thousand-mile-long coastlines along the Atlantic Ocean and Gulf of Mexico. Latterly "a sanitarium for Northern victims of consumption and nervous prostration," filled with retirement homes and resorts, its topography and climate was once both inviting and formidable to European conquest and settlement.[3]

To the west of coastal America, the land slopes upward into foothills that give into a continental barrier, the Appalachian Mountains. Once as high as the Himalayas, geological changes have caused the Appalachians to settle into a group of ranges whose highest peaks rise to over 6,000 ft in its southern parts. The whole system extends from the Canadian Maritimes, through Maine and interior New England, eastern New York State, most of Pennsylvania and West Virginia, part of Virginia, Kentucky, and Tennessee, the interiors of the Carolinas and down to northern Alabama. There are several large groupings and a number of smaller ones that are well known in American lore. These include the rugged Adirondacks of New York State (said to be geologically closer to the Canadian Laurentian chain), the Catskills (made famous by Washington Irving stories such as "Rip Van Winkle)", the Green, the White, the Poconos, the Black and the Blue Ridge (including the Bald and Smokys). Rivers cut through them, and mountain passes such as the Cumberland Gap allowed them to be traversed by later American settlers, such as the celebrated Daniel Boone. These mountains served as the physical backdrop for the first centuries of Euro- and African American history.

The western portion of the chain, called the Appalachian Plateau, has varied landforms, with fertile river valleys such as the Mohawk in New York State, the Allegheny and the northern sections of the Ohio in Pennsylvania. These and other Appalachian valleys, the Hudson and Connecticut among them, were major agricultural producers from the Colonial and Early National periods in American history. Most of them still are, as the Pennsylvania Dutch farm country in central Pennsylvania and apple and grape crops in New York State prove. At the same time, under the mountain country of Pennsylvania, West Virginia, and Kentucky lay riches, the coal that would have a profound effect on American history.

Off to the west, the plateau falls off, flattening into the rolling country of Ohio, and then opens into the enormous plains that cover the central part of the United States. In the south, a broad coastal plain covers Florida on the east, western areas around the Gulf of Mexico in Texas and north-eastern Mexico. Only the Interior Highlands, a plateau region known as the Ozark and Ouachita Mountains, centered on Missouri and Arkansas, interrupt the plains.[4] The product of continental plate tectonics, the Ozarks have distinct ecological zones with, later, unique American cultures.

It is the interior plains, or prairies, that America came to depend on for its food in the nineteenth and twentieth centuries. An enormous stretch of mostly flat savannah land starts with tall grass-filled lands in western Indiana and Illinois (called "the Prairie State"), runs to mid-grass territories from the Dakotas down to Texas and then short grass regions in

Male American bison, Wichita Mountains, Oklahoma.

Montana, Colorado, and parts of New Mexico and Texas. The western parts are usually called "the Great Plains," once home to immense herds of bison, white-tailed deer, and elk, while eastern prairies held more diverse environments, ranging from wetlands to dry, each with varied fauna and flora. Barring the Earth's curvature, anyone standing on the shores of Lake Michigan at Chicago could almost see Denver, Colorado, a thousand miles distant.

Prairie grasses, such as the big bluestem and switch grass, sink long interlacing roots in the deep fertile soils. When the first American farmers arrived, the whole prairie and Great Plains seemed to be a sea of grass. New technologies allowed farmers to cut the grasslands and the land proved to be among the world's richest agricultural soils, but at a cost. Today only about 1 percent of the pristine prairie grasslands remains, now preserved as a kind of living museum.

The prairies are bordered on the north by the Great Lakes. Five in number, Lakes Ontario, Erie, Huron, Michigan, and Superior comprise the world's largest freshwater system. Its watershed spans about 1,500 miles in length from New York State on the east, Ontario in Canada, and into Minnesota. Of immense economic importance in American history, the Lakes themselves have a number of complex micro-environments. Some are artificial—well-known examples being industrial, northern Illinois, Indiana, and Detroit, Michigan. Others, like the edges of northwestern

Michigan's Leelanau peninsula, which is perfect for blueberries, cherries, and wine grapes, are natural. Though much compromised by human intervention, the Great Lakes remain the continent's greatest resource—water for a warming planet.

From the Great Lakes complex comes the river system that drains the whole central part of the United States, the Mississippi. As Pare Lorentz puts it in Walt Whitman style:

From as far East as New York,
Down from the turkey ridges of the Alleghenies
Down from Minnesota, twenty five hundred miles,
The Mississippi River runs to the Gulf.

Carrying every drop of water, that flows down two-thirds the continent,
Carrying every brook and rill, rivulet and creek,
Carrying all the rivers that run down two-thirds the continent,
The Mississippi runs to the Gulf of Mexico.[5]

The Mississippi and its tributaries are the continent's arteries, offering both life-giving water and the means of human travel to every part of the country. As the Great River, in the Ojibway language, wends its way south from Lake Itasca in Minnesota, it picks up multiple tons of soil. Made brown by dirt, the "Big Muddy" debouches into the Gulf, depositing silt, year after year, to form a wide and ever shifting delta. It is here that the port of New Orleans was built by French settlers and it remains a major port—and sometimes the setting for natural and man-made disasters.

On the southern coastal plain a different history unfolded. The mixed pine and oak forests, wetlands, and coastlines hold the richest and most diverse plant communities in North America.[6] With the arrival of European and African Americans the grasslands were populated by cattle, north Florida being a large herding region. Forests were cut, to be replaced by cotton production in the early nineteenth century. Cotton was spread from east to west, from Georgia and South Carolina to Alabama and Mississippi, and then on, across Louisiana and Arkansas to Texas. The agricultural pattern was to use the land, and then when the soil was depleted to move further west. By the twentieth century wide swaths of the formerly rich southern land had been left barren of vegetation, leached of its nutrients, eroded, and nothing like the history of the eastern prairie lands.[7]

13

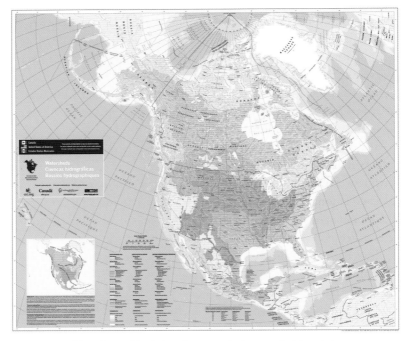

Map of main North American watersheds, post-glacial period.

In its far western expanse, the Great Plains turn into drier grasslands described by Pare Lorentz:

A high, treeless continent,
without rivers, without streams . . .
A country of high winds, and sun . . .
and of little rain . . .[8]

The Great Plains were home to some sixty million bison and almost equally large herds of an antelope species called pronghorn. By the later nineteenth century almost all the herds had been wiped out and the land set to the plow. Deep plowing set the scene of an environmental catastrophe called the Dust Bowl, a main element of the Great Depression of the 1930s, and perhaps being replicated in the early decades of the twenty-first century.

The dry, low rolling hills steadily rise up to a massive, snow-peaked mountain chain, the Rockies. When Meriwether Lewis and William Clark saw the northern parts of the chain on their famous expedition of discovery to the continent's west coast between 1804 and 1806, they were stunned by its scenic magnificence. This immense range runs from British

Columbia in Canada down to Texas. It is actually composed of a series of peaks, as high as 14,400 ft in Colorado, interspersed with lower mountains, plateaus, and basins. A watershed called the Continental Divide moves along the chain, from Alaska down through Mexico. All waters west of the divide flow into the Pacific Ocean including major rivers such as the Colorado and the mighty Columbia. Both have enormous economic importance to the American economy.

The eastern slope of the Rockies gives climatic protection for urban settlements such as Denver, Colorado. Across the mountains and the Continental Divide is a group of broad intermontane plateaus, the Colorado among them. It is a high and arid region, cut by rivers such as the Colorado and filled with geological wonders, the Grand Canyon and the Petrified Forest among them. It was here that the ancestral Puebloan peoples settled when the climate was wetter and eventually built the now famous monumental structures at Mesa Verde, Chaco Canyon, and other sites in the "Four Corners" region.

Further west are the mountains that delimit the extraordinarily varied environments of the Pacific coast states. The Klamath and Cascades descend from Canada, through Washington and Oregon, into northern California. Home to the highest peaks in the nation and active volcanoes, such as Mount St. Helens, and cut by major rivers, Oregon and Washington are broadly divided into dry plateau lands east of the mountains and wet, temperate coastal lands on the west. Washington, for instance, has America's only temperate rainforest, while the eastern area is given over to dry lands farming and cattle rearing. Southward is California where longitudinal mountains line the state. The Sierra Nevada range reaches along the eastern edge of the state, down to the Mojave Desert in the southeast. The Coastal Range rims the Pacific shore with smaller mountains such as the Transverse and Peninsular in the south. Between the mountains of the east and west is the great Central Valley. Fertile and well watered with an agreeable climate, the valley is America's food basket. In mostly dry southern California, depressions are the locations for cities—Los Angeles the largest—and irrigated agricultural regions, the foremost being the Imperial Valley near the Colorado River.

The newest states in the Union, Alaska and Hawaii, have climates and landforms all their own. The former is mainly a subarctic land, with the exception of the southern panhandle that juts out into the Bering Sea. Hawaii is an island chain. Located in the tropical Pacific Ocean, it could not be more different from Alaska. Although the islands are volcanic, there is considerable diversity in landscape and weather—in fact ten climatic groups—that range from urban Honolulu on Oahu to tropical jungle or deserts on barely inhabited islands. Hawaii's equally diverse produce, such as the pineapple and sugar cane, has long had roles in American food and had profound effects on the state's history.

Lands and climates in the past four centuries of European and African settlement in America have not stayed the same, nor have they over longer spans of geological time. Facts about changes over time, both long- and short-term, are not evident to a surprising number of Americans whose beliefs about the past are grounded in a literal interpretation of the Old Testament. For them, the Church of Ireland archbishop James Ussher's scholarly conclusion in 1650 that the world was created on the morning of October 23, 4004 BCE is literally true. There are some 25 Creationist museums in the United States, where people are depicted cavorting with pet dinosaurs.[9] A 2009 CBS News poll shows that 51 percent of Americans did not believe in human evolution.[10] Yet anywhere from 60 to 80 percent accept that climate change is happening in the early twenty-first century, though not necessarily through human activities.[11] These two inconsistent ideas are examples of strains of thought about the world and nature that run through American history and affect its foodways. For these religious believers, since God gave Adam dominion over the world, changing God's original creation is part of His plan. Presumably clearing the continent's forests, killing off whole animal and plant species, and even genetically modifying organisms are fine. It is the despised "secular humanists," with their acceptance of rational science, who have been interested in preserving natural environments and lessening the impact of human activities. Tensions of this kind run straight through American history up to the present day. Religious and political conservatives tend to want stability yet support private corporations' activities in changing foodstuffs and manipulating governmental policies, or lack of them. Liberals, who look to innovation as a means of creating the common good, are the leaders of the organic and sustainable food movement that looks backward to older farming practices. These are but some of the many paradoxes of life in America, a country where people like to think that ideologies do not drive actions, though in reality they affect everything that Americans do.

Throughout this book, we will explore how social-religious-political ideas held by the first European settlers in the New World shaped transformations of the land. The biblical templates underpinning Protestant communities of the sixteenth and seventeenth centuries, as one example, run through American culture and are seen not just in attitudes toward the land and Native peoples, but in foodways. The Thanksgiving myth can be interpreted in just such a way.

Things change, belief systems notwithstanding. And so, the story of America's food begins with an ending, the end of a geological era called the Pleistocene, or the last great Ice Age. For almost two million years the Earth has been subjected to periods of intense glaciation, interspersed with periods of glacial retreat and warming, called interstadials, and longer periods of warming called interglacials. These designations are not as simple as they might seem; climate changes over centuries and decades, one "era" spilling over into the next and sometimes reverting backward. Nor are they uniform, as today's global climate change shows. Warmer periods, like the Sangamonian, running some fifty thousand years, were warmer and wetter than today's climate in some places such as the American Midwest, but drier with wooded scrublands on the western side of the Rocky Mountains. And there were and are always many varied micro-environments.

The soils laid down by these geological processes in the American Midwest are the bases of later rich farmlands, but overlain with layer upon layer of glacially derived dust, called loess. The river systems were not the same as those familiar to us today. For instance, the Teays River system flowed northward through West Virginia to the early iteration of the Ohio River, cutting deep channels that are now steep valleys in that state. Other river systems like the Mahomet-Teays, the Ancient Iowa and Ancient Mississippi ran down from shrunken glaciers. They would be buried in the last and among the coldest of all glaciations.[12]

That last great glacial period in the northern hemisphere, the Wisconsin, lasted from about 110,000–75,000 BP to approximately 10,000 BP, with its cold maximum, called the Last Glacial Maximum, from roughly 25,000 to 18,000 BP. The huge Laurentide ice sheet, perhaps 2–3 miles thick, covered modern Canada, down to the northern parts of New York State, the Midwest and out across the Great Plains to the Rockies. The western extension of the great glaciers is called the Cordilleran ice sheet. Neither was to last as the ice sheets began their twelve-thousand-year retreat to the current—though changing—levels of world glaciation. The process was not continuous, cold snaps and warming trends causing interruptions along the way. With changing climates came changes in the land. One spectacular North American event was the rise and fall of Lake Agassiz. About eleven thousand years ago, as the glaciers melted, an immense lake—several lakes actually—formed over what is today southern Canada and today's northern Great Plains. Covering more than 150,000 square miles, with a

Tundra, Colorado. Landscape similar to that of the North American late Ice Age during the migrations of First Americans.

200,000-square-mile basin, this was the largest freshwater lake in history. Prevented from draining into Hudson Bay for several millennia, the ice dam finally broke eight thousand years ago. A massive surge of cold water flowed through the bay into the Atlantic Ocean, disrupting warm water flows from the Gulf of Mexico toward the Arctic, and changing weather patterns in Europe, southwest Asia and Africa for several hundred years. The event may have taken only a matter of days, just as a similar and perhaps related event occurred when the Black Sea broke through an ice barrier to meet the Mediterranean Sea. Some have suggested the Old World event was the inspiration for flood myths in Middle Eastern culture, including Noah's Ark. While interesting, the proposition is doubtful since the earliest flood tales appeared three thousand years after the event.[13]

Most of the modern landforms of the Holocene (modern post-Ice Age) era are results of the end days of the Pleistocene. The Holocene climate, our current era, is warmer, with different landscapes, climates, flora, and fauna. Melted glaciers and glacial lakes left behind the fertile plains and river valleys that supply a good deal of today's food crops. Modern climates are far more amenable to massive crop production, unlike the tundra lands of the previous age. The landscape and climates of the earlier period were critical to the American story in one other way: it was then that the first human beings arrived and settled.

The First Americans

Who the first humans to inhabit the Americas were and when they arrived are open questions among scholars of prehistory and laypeople interested in archeology. It is also a topic wrapped in politics and ideology among Native Americans (First Nations in Canada), some religious groups such as Mormons, and unrelated far-right-fringe racist organizations. The subject is important to the story of America's food for deeper reasons: how peoples interacted with the land and environments through which they passed and settled is a kind of model for later uses. For instance, were Paleoindians stewards of the land or not? Were later Indian peoples (for we know that European and African immigrants were not)? That question, in turn, leads to modern ideas about our food production systems and, deeper yet, Americans' ideas about nature itself from whence all sustenance comes.

There is no doubt that the first human Americans came from north Asia, most of them crossing over a land bridge that existed at the height of the last great glaciation period. As early as 1590 the Spanish Fray José de Acosta wrote that logically all Indians came from Asia and that ultimately all the peoples of the world were connected by land. Acosta and many after him believed in a monogenetic theory of humanity—all came ultimately from Adam whose offspring gave rise to the various "races" of Man.[14] In early nineteenth-century America there was a considerable literature on how and when ancient Hebrew (or sometimes Welsh) peoples came to the New World and founded the Indian nations. Biblical literalism, misinterpretation of languages, outright racism, and colonialism lay at the base of these ideas. It is within this religious environment that Joseph Smith, the founder of the Church of Jesus Christ of Latter-day Saints, developed his ideas of American Indians and the peopling of America (many, he claimed, came by boat in 600 BCE). A number of Mormons and fundamentalist Christians still wrestle with DNA and archeological evidence, but the idea that Indians were a "fallen race" was an important idea in American history, and a justification by Americans for taking Native people's productive lands.[15]

Interestingly, early French explorers, settlers and scholars had different ideas. As John MacIntosh writing in the 1840s points out, French writers of the early eighteenth century always believed that Indians came from Asia and were not related to ancient Hebrews at all. After going through various origin theories based on the Bible, MacIntosh uses empirical evidence stretching back to the Elizabethan scholar Edward Brerewood (*Enquiries Thouching the Diversity of Languages and Religions, through the Chief Parts of the World*, 1614), though one of his proofs was that indigenous Americans were possessed of "barbarous qualities" like the "Tartars of old." Using other accounts, MacIntosh thought that the immigrants from northeast Asia had come across the Bering Straits where there was some solid land.[16] By the later nineteenth century all but a few researchers had reached the same conclusion. The question remained of when the Americas were first settled, and exactly by whom.

Most scholars conclude that the Americas had no human beings in them until after about 20,000 BP at the earliest (there are carbon-14 dates earlier than this at sites such as Monte Verde in southern Chile, but these are not yet fully verified). The Last Glacial and Late Glacial Maximums created wide swaths of dry and often arid lands in regions that are today under water. One of these is the Bering Straits that separate Alaska from Siberia. Now called Beringia, the landmass is referred to as a bridge but was, in fact, a thousand-mile-wide stretch of dry land. During a lot of the period great glaciers covered it, but in the latter Late Glacial era one ice-free corridor led into northern Canada and another ran down the whole of the North and South American coasts. Dates for the coastal route are still problematic because the old coast was inundated by as much as 150 ft of meltwater at the end of the Ice Age. Small groups of hunter-gatherers migrated from eastern Asia into this unknown land, spread out and eventually peopled both continents. Just how spread out they were is attested by the fact that an estimated 330 languages were spoken in North America alone.

In 1932 Paleoindian artifacts were uncovered around Clovis, New Mexico. The diagnostic tools were beautifully made stone spear points characterized by "fluted" chipping and pressure removal of flakes. A few years earlier, generally similar stone tools had been found at Folsom, New Mexico. These were clearly the toolkits of big game hunters. Later, Folsom points were found amid the skeletons of bison, but Clovis points were found with mammoth bones. This fact implied that Clovis Culture preceded Folsom, because mammoths and a huge variety of large animals disappeared from North America at the end of the final ice age. Further archeological work proved this to be the case. Folsom culture was a regional development (on the Great Plains) of Clovis and dates to about 9000 BCE at the earliest.

For a long time, archaeologists thought that Clovis people were the first immigrants from Asia into the Americas. Later scientific data using carbon-14 put the dates of Clovis Culture at about 13,000–12,800 BP, or a roughly 250-year time span. The brief period (longer than the United States has existed as a political entity) is just at the time when glacial melting opened up passages in Beringia to the Americas.[17] Archeological finds of Clovis-style points are scattered across North America, the greatest variety being in the southeast United States. Some scholars speculate that the Clovis toolkit originated in this part of the country and not in the northwest or Alaska.[18] One

A Clovis Culture spear
point shows the splendid
artisanship that defines
the tradition.

reason for this conclusion is that the equipment of their assumed progenitors in Asia did not resemble the fluted spear points of Clovis and in recent years there has been a growing body of evidence for earlier tool traditions and settlements in the Americas.

The best evidence is that the first Americans originated among people who lived in northwest Asia during the less severe periods of the last ice age, some 21,000 BP. These were hunters and gatherers who ate whatever was available, large game and small, plants and roots. Their toolkits were composed of microliths of various sorts, among them scrapers and burins for preparation of hides. The land they lived upon was often tundra or some variation of it, but as they moved slowly eastward following melting ice, they fished in newly formed lakes and increasingly gathered plants for food and weaving. Roughly fifteen thousand years ago a group of people set up an encampment on a small creek in southern Chile where they ate game animals and gathered plants. One large hut, divided into individual rooms, was built with posts and woven wattles and had hearths inside it. The tools were chipped pebble tools much like those in other and later South American traditions. The site, called Monte Verde, is 10,000 miles from Beringia, so it seems clear that pre-Clovis peoples were in the Americas long before 13,000 BP. Monte Verde was a revelation to archeologists, but a recent excavation at Buttermilk Creek in Texas has revealed a pre-Clovis settlement underneath Clovis-era materials and dating to 15,500–13,200 BP. The blade technology looks like one that was adapted and perhaps became the famous Clovis projectile points.[19]

The reasons for discussing Paleoindians in the context of American food are several. One is the intrinsic interest in discovering origins of Native American peoples, a mystery that engrossed even the earliest Europeans in the New World. A large body of research into DNA in its several forms and other scientific evidence, including dentition, now shows places of origin, if not exact dates. The Native peoples belong to five mitochondrial (inherited from mothers) and two main NRY (male chomosomes) groups. These have been linked to people living in the southern Altai Mountains who may have arisen as separate groups twenty thousand or more years ago.[20]

Studies of tooth structures on modern and ancient people show close relations to peoples on both sides of the Bering Straits. The most recent research indicates that one main body of migrants entered North America— exactly when is still a question—with at least two smaller migrations likely afterward. The main migration may have been undertaken by small but related groups over time and likely accounts for different DNA groupings among Indian peoples. On the whole, however, the relationships among all are close because there was a "population bottleneck" in either Beringia or Alaska before wide dispersals across the Americas.[21] In a way the new data seems to justify the linguist Paul Greenberg's assertion that the many Indian languages descended from one mother tongue or group of them.[22]

One meaningful result of the genetic bottleneck and then isolation is that American Indian peoples lacked genetic diversity and thus immunities to many diseases endemic to Old World human populations at the time of contact in the early sixteenth century.[23] The effects of diseases upon New World peoples was catastrophic in every sense of the word. Depopulation was so great that, as William Cronon put it, the early European (and unwilling African) settlers of North America entered not virgin lands, but abandoned ones.[24]

A third reason for looking at the earliest Americans is to consider their adaptations to environments as templates for food production. How did small bands of hunter-gatherers change the land and life upon it? And how did food systems develop with rising populations and what effects did they have on later American foodways? The first question comes from the fact of Pleistocene extinctions. The first humans in the Americas encountered some 35 genera of animals that no longer exist. Among them were large ones such as mammoths, mastodons, giant sloths, and giant beavers and bears, and smaller types such as horses, camels (camelids remained viable in the Andes), sabertooth cats, dire wolves, and kinds of rabbits. All of these disappeared at the end of the Pleistocene and the beginning of the Holocene climatic period. With climate change came new environments and plants. What had been tundra became grasslands, while boreal forests turned deciduous, among many other changes. However, finds of Clovis projectile points among mammoth and mastodon bones led Paul Martin to speculate that perhaps these hunters had played a major role in killing off the megafauna, or at least the ones already in decline.[25] This theory led to major arguments within and outside the scholarly community. After much dispute and plenty of theorizing, the fact seems to be that Pleistocene fauna that were adapted to specific environments and conditions died out when those conditions changed. Other more generalized and adaptable genera survived and thrived, notably American bison.[26] Certainly animals were hunted but there could never have been enough people to have killed off thriving animal communities. Nor did people have the technology to do so; they did not have firearms, unlike later Americans who did, in fact, kill off whole species. Once rendered extinct, the horse was reintroduced from Europe by the Spaniards and became widespread in North America only after 1600. Today horses are so beloved that Americans are revolted at the thought of using them as human food.

An important, related issue arose in 1999 when Shepherd Krech III challenged a long-standing and deeply held American idea: that Indians were stewards of the land and vast changes occurred only when insensitive Europeans arrived on the scene.[27] Krech asked if some Indian peoples had so misused their environments that they destroyed, or at least helped to, their own food systems. Were food and environmental sustainability always practiced by Native peoples? Krech thought not and that, for various reasons known and unknown, Indians could and did cause serious damage to the lands in which they lived.

Though Krech's thesis, bolstered by examples,[28] has incensed some, there are two good reasons for examining it in relation to modern American food. One is the idea of sustainability. This is a main theme in

Petroglyphs

Lacking writing did not mean that early Native Americans were without symbolic systems to describe their world. Representations of spiritual ideas and quotidian life are found everywhere, from effigy mounds among pre-Columbian Woodland peoples to wood carvings (including the totem poles of the Pacific Northwest), drawings on buffalo hides, pottery decoration in the Southwest, and beading and embroidery on clothing and bags. Petroglyphs—rock carvings and paintings—are a large class of such images. Though best known from western areas, because of dry conditions and their location on cliff sides near settlements, they are found in many places across the continent. Among the symbols are food signs mainly in the form of hunting and corn. Along with rain symbols and perhaps territorial markers, these are the economic bases upon which people lived.

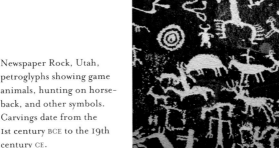

Newspaper Rock, Utah, petroglyphs showing game animals, hunting on horseback, and other symbols. Carvings date from the 1st century BCE to the 19th century CE.

twenty-first-century food preferences and, as a result, farming practices, and a romanticized idea of old Indian ways has been a model since at least the early nineteenth century. What books have expressed the idea of the "noble savage" better than James Fenimore Cooper's Leatherstocking novels?[29] Here were (mostly) noble people who lived simpler ways of life than the newly industrializing and money-hungry America. In this scenario they lived interactively with their natural ecological systems, using them lightly and in a sustaining way. As Cooper had it, one deer was taken at a

Walls that line Nine-Mile Canyon near Wellington, Utah, have been called the world's longest picture gallery. A loose grouping of peoples called the Fremont Culture occupied these dry lands from about 300 to 1250 CE. Originally hunter-gatherers, they established villages about 750 CE based on collecting local foods, hunting and raising corn. The imagery pecked into the canyon shows large or small herds of pronghorn sheep with men armed with bows and arrows standing at the perimeter. Other carvings show bison and hunters on the same panel. Excavations at Fremont sites show large numbers of pronghorn and some bison bones.

Changes over time in methods of food collecting and growing are evidenced by such indicators as bows and arrows, the atlatl (a form of throwing stick), and the horse. At the Jeffers Petroglyph Site in the southwest Minnesota prairies, thousands of images were laid over one another from at least 5000 BCE to about 1750 CE. Early ones are identified by animals alone, such as a club-footed bison. Others were made after about 500 CE, when the bow and arrow are commonly thought to have been introduced into North America. Near Canyonlands National Park in Utah is a spectacular petroglyph with a similarly long history. Amid pronghorns and bison are pictures of men riding horses shooting arrows at antelopes. Horses were not reintroduced to North America until the mid-sixteenth century, and the whole Great Plains horse–bison economic complex grew up only then.

time, only reverentially and only when needed. Earlier, Washington Irving satirized both this idea and the cupidity of Americans in his *Knickerbocker's History of New York*.[30] But the image of the forest primeval remains powerful in American popular culture and in ways of thinking about food.

A second reason for examining the work of Krech and others is to see what actually happened to Indian cultures and to examine modern trends in light of the past. One example is the coming of maize to North America. The domestication of the wild grasses called maize took a long time beginning about 7000 BCE until it became a staple of Central American civilizations and other kinds of socio-political organizations after about 2500 BCE, by which time the plant had been brought to the American southwest but not in the form we know today. Rather this was the Chapalote breed, genetically variable, that looks like modern popcorn.[31] Early maize was not a plant that could be relied upon for the sustenance of hunter-collector societies of the period and was, in fact, inferior in nutritional qualities to nuts and other seeded grasses. It lacks lycine and must be processed with lime and put together with foods that have necessary nutrients, beans and squash. Why did the peoples of the southwest plant it? Because it was xerophytic (resistant to drought) and when allowed to grow on its own could serve as a seasonal food to people moving seasonally. Maize was a way to "even out" a food supply that surely varied season to season (dry or wet) and year to year. That is exactly what modern farming is all about: ensuring reliable supplies of food year to year, decade by decade. Further, like wheat and other large seeded grasses corn does supply more food per plant than others. Farmers often say that their business is a gamble because weather and sometimes fickle markets can destroy their livelihood. No wonder farmers are interested in technologies—from seeds to machinery and chemistry—to ensure their success.

Maize was genetically manipulated by southwestern Indians to create new flour types. These had larger cobs and more kernels, were ground more easily into basic foodstuffs, and could be grown in different areas. As populations rose, people settled into smaller territories, forming villages and depending more on growing maize. By about 500 BCE beans

Corn in a modern farmers' market—the Native American staff of life.

Buffalo hunt on the southwestern plains, 1845, showing the importance of
bison and horses to native peoples of the vast American plains.

who remained hunter-gatherers might have practiced horticulture but
preferred not to. The main traditions were the Eastern Woodlands
(including the southeast), Prairie and Plains, Southwest, California
Coast, Northwest Coast, Northwestern Plateau, and Great Basin. Arctic
traditions are unique and not related to the main ones of the "Lower
48," as America south of the 49th parallel has often been called. None of
these survived the encounter with Europeans fully intact, though some
food traditions have been maintained or revived as signifiers of cultural
identity. Wild rice gathering among Indian peoples of Minnesota is one
such. Some foods and preparations passed into later American uses,
but on the whole, many food sources were lost. As Alfred Crosby puts
it, "The Columbian exchange has left us with not a richer but a more
impoverished genetic pool."[33]

The Native American peoples knew their environments intimately,
and from the Archaic Period (after 9000 BCE) onward gathered and
processed a broad range of plants and animals. In the Southwest Plains
and Great Basin, tubers such as biscuit roots and yampa (a *Perideridia*
in the parsley family) were gathered, dried and ground. In desert areas
agave plants served as both food and as fiber to be woven into clothing,
just as it was throughout Mexico into recent times. Marsh grasses such as

pickleweed (their seed pods look like small pickles) were also collected in season. Even more important were nuts. Piñon nuts have up to 24 percent protein; acorns contain 16 percent protein and 45 percent fat[34] and they can be stored for long periods of time. Nuts need a lot of processing, especially acorns, which have to be leached of their toxins with water baths. However, these and other nuts such as pecans and hickory in the Eastern Woodlands were major food supplies. Acorns are not eaten much today; many of the tubers are only eaten by small numbers of intrepid foragers, and most nuts are now grown commercially. Small numbers of hunter-collectors could flourish using broad forging strategies.

As mentioned above, maize entered the food system in the Southwest and over time came to be the major food, but only when added to other foods. Seeded plants such as chendopods of various kinds had long been collected and processed; maize was one such seed. Once dependent on maize, sedentarism in the form of villages became the way of life after about 200 CE. Maize mixed with beans (tepiary beans at first) and the third staple, squashes and pumpkins, also introduced from Mexico around the same time as maize, became the backbone of the Indian diet. Called the "three sisters" by peoples of the northeast, the three were planted together and grew symbiotically. Eventually, the "sisters" moved into the rest of the continent, reaching the East Coast after about 1300 CE. By the time of contact, there were about a thousand varieties of maize, a hundred types of beans, and several dozen kinds of squash raised by Native peoples throughout the continent.[35] Still, broad-range food collecting remained important in the southwest and elsewhere, for there were no domesticated animals, save turkeys from Mexico and dogs. Nor were there any but dogs among the other peoples of North America.

The Eastern Woodlands were rich in food resources. Deciduous forests, rivers, and temperate-to-warm climates, depending on latitude, produced plenty of wild food, including fish and shellfish. At the Archaic (post-4000 BCE) site of Koster on the Illinois River, archeologist Stuart Struever found a thriving community that exploited all that their ecological system offered. Nearby lakes provided large amounts of freshwater fish such as perch, carp, catfish, buffalo, lake chubsucker, pickerel, and pumpkinseed. Many thousands of mollusks were collected since the Illinois River had among the world's greatest concentrations of shellfish. The region was a flyway, allowing hunters to garner large numbers of birds such as ducks and geese, many to be smoked for winter eating. Seed from sumpweed, chenopods, and maygrass provided ample supplies for year-round eating when dried and stored. Nuts were equally important, black walnuts, pecans (*Carya illinoisensis*), and especially hickory nuts being collected in large numbers.[36] In short, Koster and a number of other contemporary near-sedentary sites show how much food was available to prehistoric peoples.

From Wisconsin in the north to the Appalachians, the Mississippi and Ohio Valleys, hundreds of earthworks dating to as early as 1000 BCE cover the land. The earliest, named after the Adena culture and the later Hopewell culture, are mortuary centers. One in Ohio is in the shape of a 1,348-ft-long serpent. Others, for example at the type site in Hopewell, Ohio, are up to 30 ft high, while one burial complex at Newark, Ohio, covers 4 square miles. For years archeologists thought that the Mound Builders were hunter-gatherers and marveled that peripatetic peoples could build such labor-intensive monuments. Modern research proves that Archaic cultures became sedentary and turned into complex Woodland period cultures. The central Mississippi River basin had become a center of independent plant domestication with perhaps some influences coming from the southwest and, ultimately, Mexico.

Hopewell sites (*c.* 200 BCE–400 CE) are located along riverways that are both food-intensive locations and trade routes; native copper ornaments, stone for tools, shell, and pipes were traded from the Gulf Coast to Ontario within these networks. Leaders were buried in wooden chambers within the mounds. It appears that they were in charge of the trade

Archaic American textbook image of Native American horticulture, Hopewell to Mississippian periods.

systems, though likely not food production. This similarity to the British barrows of the Neolithic and early Bronze Age indicates an apt parallel and likely a similar social system. The food base came from the Archaic period: oily seeds such as squash, sumpweed, and sunflower, starchy seeds like maygrass, amaranths, and chenopods, and plenty of nuts.[37] Tubers such as Jerusalem artichokes (also called sunchokes), groundnuts (not the African types or peanuts), King Solomon's seal, onions, asparagus, sorrel, wild turnips (not European ones) and types of lily were all eaten fresh or dried and pounded into flours. Many greens were also on the menu, of which mustards, purslane, watercress, ramps, and edible night-shades (*Solanum nigrum Americana*) are best known. Berries such as wild strawberries, chokeberries, huckleberries and, in the northern range, cran-berries were widely used, often as flavorings for dishes. Fruits, the likes of pawpaws, American persimmons, black cherries, American grapes, and American plums, were also consumed in season.[38] One estimate of the caloric potential of chenopod—goosefoot in this case— and marsh elder is that a field 70 m square (a little less than the size of a football field) planted with them could feed a household of ten people for six months.[39] Wild game and fish were also eaten as in ages past. Relatively large populations that could be mobilized to dig and build large mounds lived on what were domesticated wild grasses, but none of the plants are used today. Nor do modern Americans live on wild game, although somewhere between nine hundred thousand and one million deer are taken each year in the hunting season. Some have been commercialized, Jerusalem artichokes, mustard greens, watercress, and purslane (in Mexican communities mainly) being examples. Mainly, the rich varieties have been supplanted by narrower varieties of European plants, most of them raised for sale in markets.

The Eastern Woodlands cultures changed and reached their climax with the Mississippian culture that began about 1000 CE. By now, fully domesticated maize dominated the food base, though beans were increas-ingly used, especially after 1300 BCE. Nuts still provided important sources of proteins and oil, as did fish and, to a lesser extent, game animals. What makes Mississippian culture notable are the major population and political centers created by religious and political leaders. Cahokia, located above the American Bottoms across the great river from St. Louis, is the most famous of all the sites, though but one of several large ones. The Bottoms is a rich area of land alongside the river's floodplain that can produce a good deal of food but is subject to flooding. A short-cob twelve-to fourteen-row corn had appeared from the southeast in late Woodland times and by about

1000 CE was the major crop. Based on large-scale production apparently by family units, central Cahokia chiefs had dwellings and temples built on mounds that were grouped together into complexes. The largest is Monk's Mound, rising to 100 ft in height and covering 19 acres. It is the largest man-made structure in prehistoric North America, taking an estimated 370,000 man-days to build, albeit over the course of about three centuries. On it was likely a temple and probably a "palace-like" structure. Around the mound were houses for elites and a number of burial mounds, each with rich goods since the elites controlled long-distance trade in the same kinds of objects that the previous Hopewell peoples did. If these ceremonial mounds resembled Mexico then the comparison is apt, down to human sacrifice. It seems obvious that Mississippian chiefdoms were influenced by their Mexican counterparts (this was late Toltec times) via the Anasazi peoples of the southwest.[40] Cahokia declined around 1300, although another Mississippian center in Moundville, Alabama, lasted until about 1450 and the last of them, the Natchez, were described by French explorer Le Page du Pratz in 1720.[41] Understanding Mississippian food has resonance for modern American food production. Studies of skeletal remains of commoner Cahokians show that they suffered from poor nutrition brought on by a singular reliance on maize of the twelve- to fourteen-row type. Their average ages on death were 37 for men and 33 for women, with high infant mortality rates. From about 1200 to 1550 the climate entered a warmer Pacific Episode that saw considerable swings in seasonal weather. The prevailing maize was unable to cope with these changes and gave way to a new eight-row flint corn that was grown not along the Bottoms but inland to the east and west, away from the ceremonial center. The new corn was more resistant to droughts and to pests. Beans became increasingly popular, providing protein to diets, and were also grown far from the center of power. To the west, bison were increasing in numbers, the peoples of the prairie lands adapting their foodways to these abundant animals. In short, it seems that the Cahokian elites were conservative in their farming and, by not adapting to new realities, saw their populations drift away into new lands and new lifeways. Any political entity that relied so heavily on one food source or one mode of production was always in danger of decline or outright disaster, as the Irish potato famine tells us.[42]

The northeastern Indians described by James Fenimore Cooper lived in woodland environments, mainly in small social groupings, often organized into loose-knit tribes, but always small-scale farmers

Monk's Mound, illustration of 1887, a central structure in the
Mississippian chiefdom at Cahokia, Illinois.

and opportunistic food collectors, that is, knowing what food supplies
were available and when, but not limited to a small group of comest-
ibles. Seasonal menus are now popular among progressive-minded chefs
but they have nothing on the Native peoples of the northeast. Many
European commentators noted that villages moved seasonally. Coastal
peoples such as the Narragansetts of Massachusetts fished in the season
when their prey were running, hunted for game (as in the famous first
Thanksgiving story), gathered birds during migration season and eggs
at nesting time, and collected many greens (purslane always popular),
fruits, nuts, and berries. Where and when horticulture was practiced, it
was either within a seasonal pattern or the farmers used swidden techniques (often and misleadingly called slash-and-burn). As in times long
past, it was a way of evening out food supplies mainly gathered from the
wild. If times were hard, Indian peoples could expect to go hungry.[43]
The crops raised were the "three sisters" triad along with tobacco. These

were foods encountered by the early New England settlers who remarked on how abundant the crops were when planted in the Native fashion, corn and bean planted in a small mound of earth, the beans putting nitrates back into the soil, the corn stalks providing uprights for climbing bean vines. Incidentally, the famous story of Squanto teaching the first Pilgrims in Massachusetts to fertilize each hill with a fish may have been true only for a very local area where alewives might have run. It was not at all the case with the rest of New England or anywhere else because hauling fish inland would have been too much for people in a swidden horticulture system.[44] The Indian influence on early northeastern colonists can be seen in names and some preparations. The name "squash" comes from the Narragansett *askutasquash*, meaning something raw or uncooked, while the paradigmatic dish succotash, a stew of corn and beans, descends from *msickquatash*, or boiled corn. Succotash looked like European vegetable stews and so entered the American food inventory, to this day sold pre-prepared in frozen food sections of supermarkets.

Native peoples of the southeast (known later as the Five Civilized Tribes, among them Cherokee, Choctaw, and Creeks) also influenced European settlers. Farming was done on a larger scale among organized communities that were descendants of Mississippian-related cultures. Early visitors commented on large field systems, some a mile square, that produced the ubiquitous maize, beans, and squash. No plows existed,

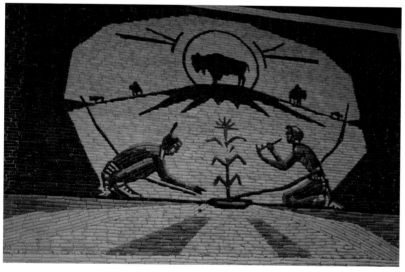

Mural made entirely of corncobs inside the Corn Palace in Mitchell, South Dakota, showing Native Americans with a corn stalk and bison rampant on the Great Plains.

35

only hoes and mattocks, as in the rest of the Americas. In the southern uplands, horticulture and hunting resembled the northeast and Midwest. Maize was boiled whole to become the paradigmatic hominy, the name hominy coming from the Powhatan word for maize. The word also means maize soaked in wood ash, a process that allows for absorption of vitamin B3. Without such processing, a diet dependent on maize leads to pellagra and actual malnutrition. Later in American history poor people living on unslaked corn suffered greatly, not having learned from their predecessors. Maize was ground into cakes, the ancestor of hominy grits and hoe cakes, while thickened stews looked like European and African preparations and were readily adapted by Old World immigrants.

Peoples of the West Coast lived almost entirely hunting and gathering lifeways, though what they ate depended on local ecologies. The best known and longest lasting—to the present day—are the peoples of the Pacific Northwest Coast running from northern California, north through Oregon to British Columbia. Peoples such as Kwakiutl (Kwakwaka'wakw), Tlingit, Haida (the great wood craftsmen whose art is widely known via totem poles, if nothing else), Chinook, and Salish lived in a dense biomass of temperate forests, rivers, and seacoast where wild foods were, and to some extent still are, readily available. Salmon and halibut are two of the major fish used, the name Chinook being applied to one salmon species. Great seasonal runs of fish provided enough protein for the year once processed by smoking and drying. Today, a number of tribes assert their rights to seasonal fishing and are in legal battles with state and federal authorities over enabling treaties signed in the nineteenth century. Berries of many kinds, greens and shoots were everywhere, forming the stable base for dense populations. Agriculture and problems associated with it were never a problem among these indigenous peoples.

California peoples varied as much as the environments do. The habitats of peoples living along the coast varied from the rich northern forests to the dry lands of southern California. Fish and shellfish were always central to diets, while plant and seed collection varied according to regions: piñons, cacti, and agave in the south, berries and acorns in the north. An inventory of peoples in the inland Sacramento River valley shows them eating soups, boiled ground seeds, fungi, birds, snails, shellfish, small mammals, fish, insects, nuts, and berries.[45] California as a whole has been transformed by modern agriculture, but today foragers try to emulate ancient gathering patterns even though these are not basic subsistence patterns for modern peoples. As in most other parts of North America, this has almost been changed into a commercial–industrial food system.

The indigenous peoples of the Americas north of the Rio Grande River offered what they knew about food production to the Old World immigrants, but their influence on mainstream American food and cookery is not as important as their neighbors in Central (Mexico included here) and South America. Popular literature and many a website tell us that Native

Powhatan village near Jamestown, 1585, drawing showing houses, gardens and ceremonial circle.

Native American Alcohol

One of the myths told by Euro-Americans about the Native peoples was that they were susceptible to alcoholic inebriation. The reasons given were that Native Americans did not have alcoholic beverages before Europeans arrived and that they do not have alcohol metabolizing enzymes. Neither seems to be true, but the deeply offensive pejorative "drunken Indian" runs through (white) American culture. Many North American peoples had mildly fermented drinks because fruit or grain left standing will naturally ferment. Native people used several kinds of alcoholic drinks ceremonially and usually in moderation. Mexican peoples had long fermented maguey juice, called pulque, and also made corn beers. Peoples of the American southwest Zuni, Yuman-speaking peoples, and Apaches made drinks from these and other fruits. Souian and southeastern peoples such as Creeks seem to have used corn for a mildly fermented drink that, as Thomas Ash reported in 1682, English settlers were already turning into whiskey. Northwestern peoples used the abundant forest berries. Some groups, however, such as the Plains Indians and the Hopi of the southwest, did not know alcohol at all. Evidence for genetic problems remains arguable.

Being convivial, Indian peoples joined in with the European settlers and travelers who drank huge amounts of alcohol. Beer and wine flowed at the first Plimoth Plantation Thanksgiving feast, since the Pilgrims brought 42 tuns of beer and 1,000 tuns of wine with them. Europeans, no matter how religious, drank mild "small beer" routinely instead of water. Distilled liquor gave rise to the "firewater" myth. Indian feasting customs with European guests and liquor led to drunkenness on all sides, only Native peoples were said not to be able to hold their liquor. Booze no doubt played a role when, under duress, Indian leaders signed away land in one-sided treaties. Though the myth remains, recent research shows that Native Americans have lower rates of alcoholism and are more moderate in drinking alcoholic beverages than other Americans.

Americans gave the world roughly 60 percent of its modern food crops, namely maize, potatoes, corn, manioc, chilies, most varieties of beans, blueberries (huckleberries), cranberries, and squash, of various kinds. With the possible exception of cucurbits such as pumpkins, and berries, these foods originated in the aforementioned Central and South America. That early European and African colonists of North America picked up some of these from Native North Americans is without doubt. Indians had hundreds of varieties of corn and beans, which, along with squashes, became staples of Colonial and later foodways. But hundreds of native food plants disappeared from the table upon encounter with Old World colonists. As for food animals and fish, they would have been eaten by the newcomers whether there were indigenous peoples or not. Nonetheless, the pumpkin pie that is so important to the American Thanksgiving is a fusion of native and imported plants, seasoning, and cookery.

What the old Indian peoples left—although "were driven from" is more like it—was the land. The colonists used the same lands and waterways as their predecessors and sometimes in the same ways. Major river valleys that had been avenues of trade, and along which ritual centers arose (as in Adena and Hopewell), would be the same, only later using barges and steamboats. Where land was especially fertile along rivers, population centers such as Cahokia appeared. One Cahokia site is underneath modern St. Louis. As mentioned, by no means all of the land left by Native peoples was virgin, but rather some had been abandoned. In the southeast, large tracts of forest had been cleared. Even in relatively infertile New England, swidden horticulture meant tree cutting and burning. Studies of ice cores in Greenland record the rates of carbon dioxide entering the atmosphere as a consequence of human activities over the last 2,000 years or more. Methane levels from burning forests and charcoal reached a high about 1450 CE and then dropped precipitously, not to return to the old high until about 1800.[46] William Ruddiman links this phenomenon to the catastrophic population decline among Native Americans across the New World brought on by epidemic diseases; no people, no burning.[47]

While new immigrants cut forests, exploited fisheries, dug mines in Minnesota, where Native peoples had plucked copper from hills and traded it widely to make ornaments, and took advantage of many other developments, they were following to a large degree the same adaptations that Indian peoples had. The immigrants, however, already possessed and developed technologies to truly transform the land. Technologies notwithstanding, Native American experiences should have taught the newcomers lessons in how to use land. Building an agricultural base on riverine sites that routinely flooded, or using land subject to drought in unsustainable ways, were lessons ignored or thought possible to overcome by technology. It was and is a gamble, sometimes leading to disasters of many kinds.

In recent years a growing movement to explore and revive old Native American foods and preparations has spread across North America, including Canada. Among the reasons for this as yet minor trend are cultural identity and a confluence of interest with "natural" foods and modern foragers. Foragers come in several varieties, from hunters who have always taken wild game for food to those for whom collecting is a culinary adventure and hobby. For instance, mushroom clubs abound in North America, their members enthusiastic hunters of the more than six hundred edible mushrooms that grow wild on the continent. No one who has ever sautéed in butter a freshly picked specimen of one of the nineteen morel mushroom varieties—Indians used animal fat or nut oil—will ever forget the flavor. More recent foragers have been part of an interest in sustainable food to be discussed in Chapter Nine.

Some are interested in the history of cooking and world cuisines, one of which should be American Indian. More to the point are Native Americans who see food traditions and cookery as important to cultural identity. An example is Northern Michigan University's "Decolonizing Diet Project," which is promoted by the claim "that there is a deep historical interconnectedness, or spiritual kinship, between Indigenous peoples and their traditional homelands that makes the act of eating indigenous plants and animals much more personal."[48] Native American culinary customs and technologies programs have been formed across the United States. Many of them are connected to "farm to fork" programs that are part of the sustainable food movement. In a limited way, the long historic line of human food collection and production extends down to the modern world. Whether the ideas and practices take deep root in an industrialized food world that feeds millions is problematic.

TWO

Colonial America

The word "Colonial" when uttered or shown to Americans usually summons up images of clothing and architecture: powdered perukes, knee breeches, tricorns, hooped skirt dresses, two-story brick houses, and spare but elegant wooden furniture. George Washington vies with the earlier Pilgrims of Plimoth Plantation for our affections, the former holding forth in a comfy tavern, the latter reverentially celebrating the first Thanksgiving with Indian "friends." Such scenes are the meat of popular visual art, retold over many years in school textbooks and children's literature and all the other means of American mythmaking. Without question, the two hundred and some years of America's Colonial existence constituted the founding period of the country's culture, crucially including food. Much of the early history is viewed through the lens of constructed mythology. John Bradford, the leader of the Plymouth colony in Massachusetts, may be the best-known figure of that story today, but the tale glosses over many a promoter of the exploitation and settlement of the American continent.

The conquest of the New World by Europeans and their usually reluctant African allies is a story, or rather stories, told many times over and from different perspectives. Two phrases have special meaning, New World and Colonial era or period. The first is a European term that was never applied to East or South Asia, areas that Europeans reached by ship at about the same time they encountered the Americas. "New" characterizes ideas that led to events and the consequences that flowed from human actions: travel to, exploitation, and settlement of places that were claimed to be empty of all that made for civilized life. William Shakespeare imagines Prospero's island as such in *The Tempest*. The brutish Caliban is often said to represent the Native peoples of the Americas.

Colonial has historical layers when glossed as "colonization" and "settlement." In its noun form, colonialism, the concept means something else, "enhanced aggressiveness and exploitation" and the domination by one group over others.[1] The first idea represents the early settlement of the Americas by Old World peoples. The second better describes what happened to Native peoples (including later Hispanics) and their land in the American west. Either way, except for the French for the most part, Europeans saw themselves as building civilization in empty or hostile territory. Yet history and human reproductive urges will out. A third layer of colonization can be called "creolization" and, more recently, "indigenization." Normally the term means people from the colonizing nation who settle in to their new homeland and give forth descendants of their own ethnic group. In common Latin American usage, as well as places like New Orleans with Spanish influence, the term 'creole' means something original to its local place. For instance, botanists and locals alike think that small round avocados that grow wild or semi-wild in parts of Mexico are the original version, hence creole. At the same time, people of mixed heritage or mixed cultures in New Orleans and the vicinity are often called Creole. So is its Euro-African–Caribbean–Amerindian cuisine.

Anyone who knows Roman history is familiar with the term "colonia." Coming from the word for farm or settlement, it meant a policy begun in the early Republic by which Roman farmers were granted land in newly acquired districts of Italy. By doing so, Romans "Romanized" Italy and later Europe. As Peter Martyr d'Anghiera, the first historian of the Spanish exploration and settlement of the Americas, put it: "Which thynge they [Christian Princes] myght easely brynge to passe by assignynge colonies to inhabite dyuers places of that hemispherie, in lyke maner as dyd the Romanes in prouinces newely subdued."[2] Americans are used to thinking of the Spanish explorers and conquistadors as a bunch of treasure-maddened sociopaths who ravaged the peoples they encountered. Some were nothing less than monsters—Francisco Pizarro and Hernando de Soto to mention but two, models in action if not name for the infamous Black Legend of Spanish cruelty that Protestant Europeans retailed to great effect. In reality the vast majority of Spaniards came to the new lands to settle and to create Christian political entities that were theoretically loyal to the Spanish crown. Most of these "conquistadors" were not soldiers but were entrepreneurs of middling social rank who invested in these expeditions in order to profit thereby.[3]

The first successful English colony at Jamestown, Virginia (founded 1607), differed only slightly in that it was envisioned as a settlement of craftsmen who were to manufacture such items as glass at much cheaper prices than could be had from English producers—the first but hardly the last offshoring of manufacturing. Of course, the nobles who went along looked for precious metals, but real wealth only came later with production of something more valuable, tobacco. Later, the wood of North America's primeval forests was even more valuable. Like the Spanish and later the French, the English settled in under forms of royal charter, followed by many more settlements in that century and those that followed. That means the colonies were English, meant for settlement, and were supposed to produce wealth for royal governments and private companies.

Four elements for the emergence of Colonial food stand out among others. One is the greatest (or most infamous) event in human history, the exchange of living organisms alien to the New and Old Worlds. A series of events, it has been called by the relatively mild term "the Columbian Exchange." Without it American and world food would be very different.[4]

The second comprises various beliefs. European settlers had fixed notions about taste, social status, ways of producing food, and health. Where and when the newcomers could establish their ideal food systems, they did. Ideas about social hierarchies dominated their thinking—save perhaps for some radical Protestant groups—and that meant food as well. English writers from at least the fourteenth century commented on the disparity between the food of the nobility and rich bourgeoisie and that of common folks. The poor widow of Geoffrey Chaucer's "The Nun's Priest's Tale," "Of poynaunt sauce hir neded never a deel. No deyntee morsel passed thurgh hir throte." Instead, like the peasants of William Langland's *Piers Plowman* and many others, "Hir bord was served moost with whit and blak, Milk and broun breed, in which she foond no lak." Translated to the seventeenth-century English colonies on the Chesapeake,

> the distribution of those foods played out the same way over the social hierarchy. People of higher status claimed English foods, by money or force. Their social inferiors either accepted Indian foods and the consequences of their changed diet or starved.[5]

The same held in Spanish America if not exactly in New France.

A third and perhaps most important feature of Colonial foods is ecology, meaning geography, landscapes, and climates. All played significant roles in what immigrant Europeans and Africans could plant and raise. Wheat, the most valued grain of all, could not be planted successfully everywhere, or at least enough to produce marketable surpluses. In these cases the Pennsylvania and New York Colonies with good fertile wheat land are sometimes called the "Bread Colonies." Down south the wetlands of South Carolina's low country were (and remain) ideal for Old World rice. Carolina rice was one leg of the plantation system and remains famous in American advertising, even though very little is grown there today. If the land did not conform to the colonists' ideals then the land would have to be changed. If climates challenged food production, then change the plants and animals to conform to them. The New World was and still is about transformation in every way imaginable.

Fourth, when circumstances such as local geography, climate, and demography did not permit full realization of the ideal foodstuffs to the colonists, then elements of creolization took root. Corn is one manifestation of the latter; wheat, cattle, and pigs embody Old World ideals. Before Europeans could implement their full complement of desired plants and animals, they had to adapt to some local food sources. The first would have been game animals and corn. Although privileged in Britain as the preserve of the nobility, deer were abundant in America. Indians and Englishmen alike ate them, most famously at the first Thanksgiving feast in 1622. Birds such as turkeys and pigeons, later prairie chickens, were also on the menu. By the eighteenth century and certainly the nineteenth, game birds such as grouse and pheasants were food of the genteel sporting class in the mother country. Not so in the rougher New World, where access to hunting remains open to almost all.

Native American turkey.

The Columbian Exchange

Alfred Crosby's *The Columbian Exchange: Biological and Cultural Consequences of 1492* (1972) opened a floodgate for studies about the course of human history after contact between living organisms of the Old and New Worlds.[6] As Crosby and many others have observed, North and South America had been separated from the other continents for around fifty million years by Columbus's time. Land links to Asia existed for geologically short time spans in the far northwestern corner of North America and even then it was during the Quaternary era when glaciation formed bridges across open waters. Over long periods of time, discrete ecosystems developed, declined, and developed again and again as climates and landforms changed. Living organisms adapted accordingly and formed any number of varied biomes across the globe. For instance, marsupials, which once represented a large bulk of mammalian life, lost out to more successful placental animals in the Old World and are no longer native to Europe, Africa, and Asia. In Australia, isolated from other continents for millions of years, they flourished and filled all the ecological niches that placental animals do on other continents.[7] Migrating birds and some insect species are exceptions. Birds perhaps helped plants migrate over oceans through their droppings (the grapevine may be one of them), but avians were and are minor agents of change despite their great numbers.

Since the triumph of the domestication of plants and animals in almost all parts of the globe, virtually all human foods come from manipulated plants, animals, fungi, and bacteria. The Old and New Worlds differed in the specifics but the ideas that lay behind the processes were the same—to produce as many calories and as much nutrition as possible from a given ecological setting (and to produce food that tasted good). Plants were and are generally the most efficient ways to do that, animals less so. Wheat, barley, rye, oats, chickpeas, lentils, sesame, rice, turnips, carrots, radish, brassicas such as broccoli and cauliflower, cabbage, onions, cucumbers, many mustards, rapeseed, olives, raspberries, various wine grapes, apples, peaches, cherries, apricots, pears, melons, citrus fruits, figs, sugar cane (which has a special place in world history), almonds, cumin, basil, coriander, and fermenting yeasts, among a host of others, came from various parts of the Old World. Wheat and barley were historically the first domesticated seeds, and wheat retained its prime culinary role among Europeans. Wheat grew well in New World climates such as the Middle Atlantic colonies and highland Mexico, later in the great American prairies and plains and the Argentine pampas. As the singular cash crop it was forcibly set upon these virgin lands, just as it had been in ancient Europe and Asia.[8]

New World domesticates upon which complex societies were built were passed down to the new colonial societies. In the English colonies these included corn (maize) and many kinds of beans, while in New Spain and Portuguese enclaves peppers, avocados, tomatoes, squash, cacao, vanilla, cassava, peanuts, potatoes, and sweet potatoes were adapted and spread across the globe. Of all these and other plants, corn, potatoes, and cassava were royalty and responsible for population growth wherever they became established. Corn can be grown almost anywhere. It produces many more bushels per bushel sown than wheat, as early European explorers observed. When translated to the rest of the world it replaced less productive millets in some places: northern Italian polenta and Romanian mamaliga are examples in Europe. In Africa corn became a main food crop especially in the eastern and southern regions, while in Asia it is heavily used as animal feed. Cassava took to the leached soils of western Africa and is now the number one supplier of carbohydrates in human diets. As for potatoes, there is a vast literature on the effects of potatoes on European populations. In an ironic twist of history, the plants that gave life to Native American civilizations did the same for Europeans whose populations rose and coalesced into powerful nations and empires.[9]

Not that the new crops were unmitigated blessings. Unless corn is soaked or mixed with lime or ash it lacks niacin and can contain harmful mycotoxins. People relying on unprocessed corn can suffer a debilitating and ultimately fatal disease, pellagra. In Ireland a soccer-pitch-sized field produced enough potatoes to feed a family of five for a year. But the "miracle" crop proved to be fatal. The Irish potato famine of the nineteenth century also struck the Low Countries, Germany and France, killing millions and wreaking major demographic changes in world history.

Where the Old and New Worlds differed in basic food production was in domesticated animals. Acts of bringing other kinds of animals into one's home—the literal meaning of domestication—were concomitant with bringing plants under human control. As archeologists of the Near Eastern Neolithic era have put it, early villages were wheat–barley and sheep–goat–cattle complexes; European primary farming villages were variations that included pigs. Early farmers were horticulturalists very much like Native Americans in the northeastern and Midwestern woodlands, only developing plow agriculture centuries later. When they migrated across Europe beginning in the late eighth millennium BCE, these pioneers brought with them

Florida "Cracker" cow and calf—an example of feral Southern cattle.

an already established relationship with their food animals. Long manipulated into usable forms, dogs, cattle, sheep, goats, and pigs were familiars that could be changed to suit local environmental or economic conditions. Other animals could be domesticated as well: geese and later chickens are examples. Except for dogs, North American Indians had nothing like these food and power sources (draft animals) and were thus at a disadvantage in the early years of European colonization.

Europeans and Africans (Euro-Africans) developed agricultural equilibrium systems in which animals, plants, and microorganisms lived together within their biotas.[10] Woods, meadows, gardens and plowed lands were balanced, ideally, with numbers of animals that a system could support. Domesticated animals were and are food banks in the sense that they turn vegetation inedible to humans into food. They return nutrients to the soils and can also be mobile. Like their Neolithic forebears, European colonists brought their food-producing organizations with them. Once set, they had a distinct caloric advantage over Native peoples because they had relatively stable production of animal proteins, fats, and hides. As Ralph Lane, who went on the first voyage of settlement to Roanoke, Virginia in 1584, wrote to his friend Richard Hakluyt, "To conclude, if Virginia had but horses and kine in some reasonable proportion, I dare assure my selfe being inhabited with English, no realme in Christendome were comparable to it."[11] Indian peoples knew nothing of these husbandry systems, though they quickly learned and adapted domesticated animals themselves where possible.

Taken out of their naturalized systems, environments created by humans, this triad of living organisms became invasive species with varieties of consequences to their new homes. In Alfred Crosby's memorable phrase, this was "ecological imperialism." Cattle set loose by Europeans ranged everywhere, feeding in clearings and expanding them by eating out forest undergrowth and forbs (non-seeding plants), trampling and eating Native people's crops, and moving into areas that later became cattle-raising country. Cattle adaptable to warm, humid conditions were brought to Florida by Spanish cattle ranchers in the sixteenth century. Along the Gulf Coast and in Florida's interior these "Cracker Cattle," "Pineywoods Cattle" or "Creoles" developed resistance to pests and diseases. Smaller than modern cattle (cows weigh about 600 lb), these animals were ranched extensively in large herds.[12] In contrast the famous longhorn cattle of Texas were cattle introduced by the Spanish into the drought-stressed environments of the American southwest. There they went feral, adapted to their environments, and grew exponentially large herd numbers. Moved up to the short-grass plains they competed successfully with American bison even though the native animals were much better adapted to their own environment. No other native grazers could compete with them, save for one other introduced ungulate, the horse.

Two domesticated animals say much about what happens when an organism enters territories that have few predators. Pigs appeared in the New World when Columbus brought eight of them with him to Hispaniola on his second voyage (1493–96). Lacking refrigeration, live animals were kept on board ocean-going vessels to be slaughtered on the spot. Pigs and

Wild (feral) American pigs.

goats were planted on islands, much like seeds, to reproduce and provide food for later explorers or settlers. Within a decade pigs were found on most Caribbean islands and on the North American continent. In Florida, Hernando de Soto's four-year expedition that began in 1539 brought pigs that went feral. They did the same in Spanish New Mexico and the English colony at Jamestown in 1607 (the English tried to corral their animals on a "Pig Island," but failed). Unlike modern husbandry practices, pigs (and cattle) were raised "extensively," a system in which animals were allowed to roam freely in woodlands near their settlements and thus fed themselves. They could be and were harvested in season—wintertime—or when needed. Pigs are forest-adapted animals, voracious omnivores who took to the American woodlands with gusto. They are highly intelligent, adaptable, fecund, fierce, and brave, and so spread across North America rapidly. With powerful snouts and teeth, pigs rooted up forests, ate out oyster beds in Massachusetts, ate Native Americans' corn and bean fields, and by the nineteenth century lived openly in American city streets. Even though large cats and wolves preyed upon pigs they were never enough to suppress feral or wild pig populations. Semi-wild or feral pigs were staples of Colonial tables, especially in the south where warmer climates made for more nutritious biomass; pigs flourish in all climates except the Arctic. The wild versions called "Razorbacks" from their spinal bristles are still in the American woods, some subject to human predation, but are often left to themselves. As of the early twenty-first century, an estimated five million wild pigs inhabited North American woodlands.[13]

Horses are the symbols of the Great Plains Indian peoples, but this was only from the seventeenth century. No horses existed in the Americas after the late Pleistocene era; no natives of the New World had ever seen one. Only camelids such as llamas and alpacas in western montane regions of South America were domesticated and none of these were ridden. Columbus brought horses with him to Hispaniola in 1493 to establish breeding stock. Donkeys (or burros) traveled on the same ships, animals which became the basic beast of burden in the Americas into the twentieth century. Hernán Cortés used sixteen of them on his expedition to Mexico in 1519; later in the sixteenth century Hernando de Soto (to Florida), Francisco Vasquez de Coronado, and Juan de Oñate also brought horses to the American southwest. Sturdy, smaller than the great draft animals of northern Europe, Spanish horses turned wild. They bred prolifically and evolved to adapt to the varied environments into which they migrated. The famed wild or feral mustangs of the southwest, some two million strong by 1900, were

Donkeys, Lancaster County, Nebraska, 1935.

direct descendants of the original Iberian breeds.[14] Settlers who were not of Spanish stock—English, French, Dutch, and Swedish—took their horses with them, beginning with the Jamestown and Boston establishments. By the later seventeenth century, horses (and donkeys) were everywhere.

Scholars such as Alfred Crosby have marked the horse and the burro-donkey as a kind of ecological imperialism that benefited Native peoples especially on the Great Plains.[15] Formerly sedentary or semi-sedentary Indian peoples adopted the horse as a means of transportation and food gathering as early as 1650. In a revolt beginning in 1680, Pueblo people seized Spanish horses, sheep, and cattle and became traders to other groups west of the Mississippi River, among them Apaches, Crow, Arapahoe, Blackfoot, Sioux, and Kiowas, who developed new societies based on buffalo hunting and pastoralism. The most powerful and fearsome of these were the Comanches; into the twentieth century American mothers in the southwest warned their children of them as they might bogeymen. They were the stuff of many a Western movie.

The new societies flourished, at least for about 170 years till they were destroyed by American aggression. But new studies of their economies, politics, and especially the ecologies of horse-centered cultures tell a different story:

> Intense horse herding, growing domestic horse herds, and large-scale trade proved too heavy for the grassland ecology, triggering a steep decline in bison numbers. Large domestic herds competed with bison for the limited riverine resources, depriving bison of

Wild (feral) horses in northern Nevada.

their means of winter survival and possibly transmitting deadly bovine diseases such as anthrax.[16]

Taken together with severe drought in the 1850s and massive slaughter for pelts and sport, the bison herds collapsed. So did Comanche populations, from about twenty thousand in 1820 to six thousand in the 1860s. Stories of unforeseen consequences fill the pages of the book of America's food. None, though, are as devastating as that of a third import to the New World, microorganisms.

Every human body is a world unto itself. Called the human microbiome by medical researchers, each one of us is inhabited with trillions of bacteria, fungi, and archaea.[17] The vast majority of them live symbiotically in the body, but some may not. Like invasive plants and animals that enter into a biome, so alien "germs" intrude upon human body systems and disrupt them even unto death. Euro-Africans carried such alien micro-passengers with them on their voyages to the Americas. While we have known about the effects of such organisms since Columbus's second voyage, the full impact and reasons for them were vividly brought to modern consciousness in the titles of Alfred Crosby's and Jared Diamond's books.[18]

In the Old World, domestication brought people closer to non-human animals than ever in the past. Hunter-gatherers/collectors simply could not get close enough to their prey, nor were domesticated dogs (at least as early as twenty thousand years ago) the household pets that they are today. Pathogens that lived within bovines or caprids crossed species boundaries in several places and then spread out across temperate zone farming communities.[19]

Where these original diseases originated is not clear, but Central Asia is often cited as the source for epidemics dating from at least the second century BCE to the fifteenth century. Modern versions of the process can be seen in avian flu epidemics that arise in massive Chinese chicken-raising operations.

The most significant diseases usually thought to have been brought to the New World are called "crowd diseases" from both human groupings and herd animals:

> diphtheria, influenza A, measles, mumps, pertussis, rotavirus, smallpox, tuberculosis). Three more probably reached us from apes (hepatitis B) or rodents (plague, typhus), and the other four (rubella, syphilis, tetanus, typhoid) came from still-unknown sources.[20]

Another culprit, malaria, can be identified in Europe from Roman times (China in the third millennium BCE and the Pharoah Tutankhamun of Egypt evidently had it) and was common in early modern England. Imperfectly drained lands in the east of the country left stagnant pools where disease-carrying mosquitos flourish. Called "ague," this mosquito-borne plasmodium (not a virus or bacteria) was brought to the Americas by Europeans in the sixteenth and seventeenth centuries. Some American mosquitos acquired the organisms and became vectors for further human infection. In like manner a viral disease called yellow fever apparently traveled to the Caribbean islands with enslaved Africans and from there caused large numbers of deaths in eighteenth- and nineteenth-century coastal cities such as Philadelphia and even Washington, DC (where one of Lincoln's assassination plotters died of it while in prison).[21]

Europeans knew a good deal about epidemics when they arrived in the Americas.[22] Diseases such as those mentioned above had become endemic or affected mainly children. Humans developed immunities to them over several generations. Even the horrific bubonic and pneumonic plagues of the fourteenth to seventeenth centuries today kill only about 50 percent of their hosts if untreated with antibiotics.[23] The social and economic effects of the great Old World pestilences were enormous. They lingered long in European culture and in the bodies of the immigrants.

Not having domesticated animals in most of the continents, having been long out of contact with the rest of humankind, and with a less diverse gene pool, Native American peoples had no immunities to malicious organisms. These tiny life-forms found unopposed feeding grounds in the native populations. The results were world-changing human population collapses. The subject has been widely discussed, but consensus opinion estimates deaths at up to 90 percent of infected people. Naturally these were higher among concentrated populations such as the Mexica's capital Tenochtitlan (now Mexico City), but less so in the more widely dispersed populations of North America. Nonetheless, massive destruction of peoples occurred on the continent from the seventeenth century to the nineteenth. Disease preceded conquest but immigrants were the disease vectors.

Whole peoples were wiped out, or close to it, but not all at once in North America. The dispersed and thinly populated Spanish settlements in the southwest left far less biological impact on Native peoples than the effect in the English colonies. Native peoples like the Powhatans in Virginia and Wampanoags on Cape Cod suffered losses at once. But it is likely that English enslaving and trading of Indians in Virginia and South Carolina set off the Great Southeastern Smallpox Epidemic in 1696.[24] Only new tribal confederations like the Cherokees and Creeks, who kept some distance from the English slavers (though some like the Choctaw participated in the system), survived in any numbers, albeit much smaller than in pre-contact times.[25] One effect of such losses was to bring in more labor, and specifically a labour force that might have some resistance to malaria, Africans. And thus ensued the slave trade.

Germs are equal opportunity feeders, and prey upon the weakest first. The earliest English colonists suffered grievously from the diseases that they brought with them. Jamestown was founded in 1607 on the James River in Virginia, and subsequent settlements further into the interior often suffered from "Bloody Flux," that is, dysentery and typhoid. Jamestown was located in a swamp where seawater backed up the river estuary from time to time. Human waste and animal wastes thrown into the river washed back into the drinking water, allowing Shigella and *Salmonella typhi* bacteria to pass into human bodies. That these bodies were malnourished only made the situation worse.[26] Of the roughly eight thousand colonists who arrived in Virginia between 1607 and 1625 only 1,218 survived. These are numbers that approach Native American mortality rates.

Beliefs

All peoples have sets of cultural ideas embedded in their minds from earliest years. Social distinctions are among the most deeply rooted of all, and of these caste and hierarchies have retained special power throughout the histories of complex societies. No Native American civilization was without them in some form and no Euro-African immigrant was, either. They are each expressed in what people raised, grew and ate (or desired to).

For Europeans of the sixteenth and seventeenth centuries, meats, refined wheat breads, and sugar-laced sweets were at the top of the culinary and social hierarchy. As Ferdinand Braudel showed in his magisterial works on European life and economies from 1400 to 1800, Europeans were truly carnivorous from the era of the Black Death to about 1550.[27] The fact that the royal guards of Henry VII were called "Beefeaters" and that English troops were called the same by their French enemies during a sporadic series of wars shows that soldiers ate lots of meat and that it had greater value than vegetable food.[28] But meat consumption declined dramatically in Europe at just the time of New World settlements, and especially in the Mediterranean. Beef was always of higher value than other meats, partly because of the expense of raising beef cattle with large appetites (horses even more so) and partly because cattle were farmers' main draft animals, and thus more valuable as work engines than food. When Spaniards released cattle in their new possessions, it was an act meant to supply conquistadors with the food that they thought they deserved.

Wheat was always prestigious grain in any period; it was the medieval peasant's cash crop. Refined flour's value lay in the labor it took to mill it, its pure white color, and ease to chew it. Certainly flavor and texture meant a good deal to diners. As for sugar, which had been introduced to Europe in the twelfth century, no peasant could afford it, at least until the development of the great sugar plantations of the Caribbean islands, along with slaves to work them. It is only fitting that Elizabeth I's blackened teeth were due to a surfeit of expensive sugar. By the later seventeenth and eighteenth centuries more people in a rising middling class could enjoy that privilege because of mass production.

The early colonists were no exception to the general European idea of elites, including the foods they wanted. Spanish conquistadors like Hernán Cortés and Hernando de Soto, among many others, came from minor noble families who knew their social station. Their acts (arrogance and cruelty among them) were intended to move them up the Spanish social scale and they meant to show it conspicuously. Sophie Coe's essay on a great feast put on by the viceroy in Mexico City in 1538, eighteen years after the conquest, shows a fantastical, thoroughly medieval multi-day feast for lords and ladies made up almost entirely of European meats and dainties.[29] Records of this feast and other written sources show

European colonizers in Mexico included in their diet ingredients that were common in Europe, such as beef, veal, pork, wine, oil, wheat, olives, onions, garlic, lettuce, radishes, parsley, carrots, eggplant, spinach, chickpeas, lentils, cauliflower, asparagus, melons, cantaloupes, squashes, cucumber, rice, citrus fruits, tea, and spices such as cinnamon, black pepper, and saffron.[30]

"Eating like an Indian" seems to have been a grievous insult, though the reality was actually different.

A compilation of material taken from Robert Beverley's *The History and Present State of Virginia* (1705) and John Lawson's *A New Voyage to Carolina* (1709), published in 1737 in a German translation by Samuel Jenner, has become known incorrectly as *William Byrd's Natural History of Virginia or The Newly Discovered Eden*. In promoting settlement in the backcountry of Virginia, it lists some 75 grains and vegetables, only nine or ten of which were native plants. Of fruits and berries in similar numbers, only a handful are native.[31] Lawson also disliked pork as being unhealthful—and perhaps as slave and Indian food—as he later said when writing about the swamplands of southern Virginia. New Englanders and colonists from other European nations thought similarly, though most of them were not exactly of the same aristocratic temperament that the Spanish supposedly had. English colonists in

William Byrd II of Westover, Virginia.

the south retained their old English status–family systems, while Dutch elites were mainly of the rich mercantile classes. New England's early settlers were Protestants of one radical stripe or another. Based on Calvinist and later some Anabaptist ideas, these people were far more socially leveled in their thinking and political structures. They would change over time, elites rising with the accumulation of money, but the old democratic spirit lived on, including in food—plain and closer to middle-class English than in other colonies. Where rigid social lines were set, in New England and elsewhere, was in attitudes towards Native peoples and Africans.

Americans have been schooled to think of Europeans with aristocratic leanings as being work averse. Jamestown is a famous example. Among the settlers in 1607 and later were "gentlemen" whose main interest was in finding gold, not planting the food necessary to stay alive. The Royally Chartered Virginia Company tried to recruit good working people but without much success. England was full of unemployed people, many kicked off their farmlands by enclosure, routinely called "sturdy beggars." John Smith, the expedition's leader, said that such people were mainly of the "'idle crue . . . of lascivious sonnes . . . bad servants . . . and ill husbands' who would 'rather starve for hunger than lay their hands to labour.'"[32] Starve they did, leading to John Smith's famous order to them to "work or die."

Still, gentlemen came and settled, as archeological work at the Shirley Hundred settlement of 1625 reveals the presence of Chinese pottery, delftware, and window glass. The rest of the settlement was composed of rough shacks with dirt floors. The southern pattern was set here and at places like Martin's Hundred.[33] Led by gentlefolk who would one day be the Famous Families of Virginia, if they survived the early years, the rest were masses of servants who lived in squalor. Food followed. Though tobacco brought the colony's cash, the Governor, Lord De La Warr, and, in his absence, Sir Thomas Dale, sent for wheat seeds and had them planted as widely as possible. The better folk, the budding planter class, could eat what they had in England, beef, white bread, sugar, and plenty of good Old World fruits and vegetables. The lesser people ate more like Indians: corn, hogs, and game.

Virginia elites constantly complained about lazy workers. So did other colonial leaders. Jacob Alrichs, who led New Sweden in what is today Delaware in the 1650s, said that many were rough people "as poor as worms and lazy withal."[34] In fact, idleness was the great Satan of colonial leaders everywhere. They were either reproducing their familiar societies or building new societies in new lands, so hard manual labor was necessary. Here is Peter Martyr d'Anghiera:

The story of the disorders, privations, and unrest, as told by Las Casas, Columbus, and others, makes cheerless reading; the misfortunes of the colonists were due to their inveterate idleness, their tyranny, which had alienated the good-will of the natives, and to the disillusionment that had dispersed their hope of speedily and easily won riches.[35]

Indians were placed in the same category of idleness. In the forest lands of the north, Europeans could not understand seasonality in Native people's eating patterns. In cold times they often went hungry for many days at a time or lived on the barest minimum food. As a result of several thousand years of experience, Indian peoples were far better equipped to deal with climatic and environmental disasters than Europeans. To the settlers, food had to be abundant; stomachs had to be constantly filled. That Native people did not appear to take advantage of the abundance the land had to offer seemed evidence of idleness or, in a word, barbarism.[36] Even Indian food production was uncivilized because it took so little effort. The corn–bean–squash triad seemed almost to grow themselves, not even needing fertilizing or weeding.

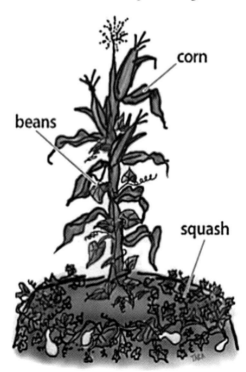

The three sisters: corn, beans, and squash.

As the Spanish chronicler Lopez de Gomara put it in 1552, "Nothing living escapes their gullet, and what is all the more amazing is that they eat such bugs and dirty animals when they have good bread and wine, fruit, fish and meat."[37] Knowing what was good for one's body and soul and not working hard to get food were marks of the uncivilized.

ENVIRONMENTS

The first English colonists had the misfortune to land in North America during what is called the "Little Ice Age." Not that the climatic disasters before and after the seventeenth century were confined to North America. To the contrary they were worldwide, but the Americas may have had a significant role in bringing them on. Swift reforestation of previously cleared lands seems to have sequestered so much atmospheric carbon that temperatures declined on average by a couple of degrees.[38] Like the fourteenth-century cold snap the results were unstable weather patterns in which bitter cold winters, cool and rain-filled summers alternated with occasional good weather, and all seasoned with violent unpredictable storms. At the same time some parts of the world experienced prolonged droughts. For pre-industrial economies that had few food reserves the effects were horrors of local starvation, famines, diet-deficiency diseases, plagues, and catastrophic wars throughout the seventeenth century.[39] The Thirty Years War (1618–48) might be the most infamous example of the great disorders of the age, when perhaps 40 percent of the population in German-speaking lands was killed and inexplicable weather led to mass fear and a revived witch craze.

Certainly American immigration was increased heavily by climatic events. In the British Isles, the Wars of the Three Kingdoms (including the English Civil War) probably killed 7 percent of the population:

> In addition, a series of failed harvests and a plague epidemic produced in Scotland a famine of which "the lyke had never heme seine in this kingdome heretofor, since it was a natione;" and "so great a dearth of corn [grain] as Ireland has not seen in our memory, and so cruel a famine, which has already killed thousands of the poorer sort . . ."[40]

Throughout the century, starving, unemployed people were forcibly rounded up and sent to the colonies where they suffered harsh indentured servitude. This was especially the way that labor was sent to the Chesapeake colonies. Many hapless victims simply did not survive either the voyage or their lives in America. Of those who did survive, a good number remained at the lowest levels of American society.

The same climatic problems affected the earliest English colonies in North America as well as the Spanish in the southwest and Mexico. In the latter areas massive droughts in the early seventeenth century killed uncounted newcomers, and large numbers of southwestern settlements were abandoned. Scientific analyses of the Chesapeake coastal regions from Virginia to North Carolina show that the aborted Roanoke Colony (the famous "Lost Colony") in 1587–90 and Jamestown were established during the worst droughts of an eight-hundred-year-long dry period.[41] At both places the English thought they could easily collect and grow the foods that were familiar to them and that marked them as civilized. Thomas Hariot, who went to Roanoke, said, "Of the grouth you need not to doubt: for barlie, oates and peaze, we haue seene proof of, not beeing purposely sowen but fallen casually in the worst sort of ground, and yet to be as faire as any we haue euer seene here in England."[42] It was not to be for quite a while.

Pigs and chickens flourished, another writer observed about the first Jamestown settlement, without people having to feed them. So did rats, humans' ever present companions, who ate much of the settlers' stored grain; rot and mold destroyed the rest. The climate and land were against them. So were the Indians, whom they antagonized by stealing their food and shooting them. Consequently, the Powhatans besieged Jamestown and forced its inhabitants to starve. A contemporary report of cannibalism was confirmed when the unearthed skeleton of a fourteen- or fifteen-year-old girl was examined in 2013. After death she had been expertly butchered, her brains and innards consumed as well as her flesh. She is a symbol for the awful era in which she lived and died.[43]

New England fared better, though not by much. The story of Plimoth Plantation is a well-established part of American historical and folk traditions. In 1621, 102 passengers with thirty crewmen set out from Leiden in the Netherlands with a stop in England, ostensibly bound for Virginia. In fact they landed on Cape Cod in November 1621. As the first governor, William Bradford, said, the ground was too frozen to dig and the passengers so weakened by hunger and disease that little was done to build the kind of English town that they had imagined.[44] About half the party died in the first winter. Since their provisions were low and rotting, only maize provided by local Wampanoag people saved the remainder. Wampanoags and

Highly idealized illustration of Squanto meeting with pilgrims at Plimoth Plantation.

others nearby had suffered epidemic disease brought by English fishermen in 1616–19, leaving vacant cornfields and open lands for the immigrants. Bradford claimed that his people had landed in a wilderness, but clearly he did not understand Indian food-raising practices and that so many of them had been killed by European-borne microbes.

The Plymouth colonists were helped by a Native American named Squanto or Tisquantum who had been enslaved by Spaniards and later worked on English ships. Fluent in English, he brokered peace between the colonists and his own people. The story Bradford tells that Squanto taught the colonists the "Indian way" to plant corn by placing fish on each hill as fertilizer has long since been dismissed as alien to Native practices; it was, in fact, a European technique and wasteful of both energy and fish protein.[45] Squanto is also central to the story of the first Thanksgiving held likely in the summer of 1622 and with only half the original company present. Only four women were left alive to cook and serve the participants. The main features were some biscuits made from the small stores of precious wheat flour left and lots of wild game and fish.

The new New Englanders immediately tried planting their own preferred crops. As Bradford says, "Some English seed they sew, as wheat and pease, but it came not to good, eather by the badnes of the seed, or latenes of the season, or both, or some other defecte." The Cape Cod region was not the most fertile soil, nor was the later Massachusetts Bay Colony centered on Boston nor did the cold climate help. Cattle and pigs fared well enough; shellfish, fish, root crops, native beans and corn all appeared on New England menus. But the ecological costs were high. Replacing Indian patterns of forest cutting, planting fields, and fallowing for long periods with monoculture with fields close to one another led to crop failures throughout the seventeenth century. Since fields were not burned, insect pests flourished to live upon field and orchards. Worse yet, a fungus or "blast" called black stem rust (*Puccinia graminis*) was transported from Europe to American wheat and rye fields by the 1660s. It is hosted by the European barberry, a weed brought along by the colonists and accidentally spread across the landscape. The rust devastated New England's grain production, leaving wheat to be the main cash crop of the Middle Atlantic colonies and Virginia to the south. In the mercantile economies of the North American colonies, production centers and trade among them and abroad were the emerging order.

Indian peoples did not think in terms of global markets, so food and other natural resources were not commoditized. They had no full-scale market or monetary system, but Europeans did, and Native Americans learned about these quickly enough. The land had to be changed to accommodate the new order. In Central and South America indigenous civilizations had been built on massive changes such as irrigation systems. Spaniards amplified the process in the early sixteenth century, when

> the mechanical transformation of landscape undertook by engineers in the pay of the Spanish empire in Potosi and the central Valley of Mexico were as extraordinary as those dreamed up by the knight of the House of Salomon, including the creation of artificial lakes and rivers to power mills to crush silver ores and the cutting of sluices through massive mountains to drain the city of Mexico.[46]

Europeans in all the Americas cut down forests at great rates, built mills and dams, and planted single crops. By doing so, large and small ecosystems—in fact entire biomes—were changed. Forest clearance in New England was widespread for cropping and to produce charcoal and potash for industrial uses. As William Cronon points out, forests are efficient at producing nutrient-rich soils, as Native cultivators well knew, but cutting trees and burning them destroys soils faster than any other methods. If market conditions demanded certain products, whether grain or potash,

Thanksgiving Feasts

Of all holidays save Christmas, none are as food-centered as Thanksgiving. Like Independence Day it was invented as a political symbol of national unity and loaded with mythologies having to do with family and the nation as family. Sitting down at a table massively loaded with native food reifies Americans' sense of place in the world. It has become, though, a commercialized holiday using factory-farmed animals and sealed with a quasi-religious practice, televised American football games, making it all the more modern American.

Americans have been taught that the feast descends from a first one held in 1621 by the 53 (out of 101) grateful survivors of the first New England colony at Plimoth Plantation. In the three brief contemporary sources, no date is given save for after the corn harvest and we learn that wild deer and various fowls, including turkeys, were served. Thanksgiving was a local fest celebrated sporadically in some New England towns, including a December 1769 recreation at Plimoth. The Continental Congress had a day of thanksgiving in 1777 and George Washington proclaimed November 26, 1789 in honor of the ratification of the constitution by (almost) all the states. Big feasts were hardly mentioned.

The Thanksgiving feast as a national holiday exists because of Sarah Josepha Hale's long campaign to make it so. Born in New Hampshire in 1788, she was literary-minded and when widowed at age 34 she turned to writing to support her five children. Her first novel *Northwood* (1827) was a success and launched her career as an author and literary "Editress," as she called herself, of the most popular women's magazine of the nineteenth century, *Godey's Ladies Book*. The novel contains the first description of an ideal New England Thanksgiving dinner. Duck and geese stand with roasted sirloin of beef, flanked with leg of pork and loin of mutton, all surrounded by myriad bowls of gravy, pickled condiments, and vegetables, and for follow-up pudding and pies. At the head of the table sat the roasted turkey, "and well did it become its lordly station, sending forth the rich odor of its savory stuffing, and finely covered with the froth of the basting." Puddings and pumpkin pie were all on the menu.

This early description of a family banquet set the tone for most other writing about a Thanksgiving festival set in early New England. Hale increasingly wrote about making the day a national holiday in response to the deepening national political crises of the 1840s and '50s. Could not the nation reconcile its differences like a family celebration? she reasoned. Other magazine and newspaper editors took up the cause, but war broke out anyway. From the war's beginning, Hale had urged a reluctant President Lincoln to declare a national holiday—and the feast it implied. After two years of defeat and stalemate, Union victories at Gettysburg and Vicksburg brought President Lincoln around. In October 1863 he formally declared Thanksgiving a national holiday.

Sarah Josepha Hale popularized not only the groaning board dinner, but the turkey at the center. The wild American fowl was fast disappearing from the eastern United States due to hunting and especially loss of habitat from farming. Farmers discovered that improved domesticated turkeys such as the Bronze were easy to breed and were much liked by consumers. In setting the turkey at the center of the meal—as compared to mutton, for example—she helped create the market for farm-raised fowl. Today Bronzes are heritage breeds, bearing only a resemblance to the universal mass-produced turkeys found everywhere.

then forests would be devastated.[47] After all, there were so many of them, the new Americans thought.

By the early eighteenth century whole sections of New England's lands had been turned to hard unworkable soils. The tobacco planted in Virginia and later cotton throughout the South leached soil nutrients to such an extent that planters moved on and on to new soils in the west. The long-term results were ecologically and politically dire. The Swedish naturalist Pehr Kalm, who visited North America from 1748 to 1751, reported that bird populations had suffered drastic declines within a generation of his visit.[48] The first century of settlement destruction of natural habitats and mass slaughter had done its work. The process is ongoing in American history.

CREOLIZATION

The first place to consider creolization is New Spain. It was there that a greater degree of genetic intermixing took place beginning with Hernán Cortés, who fathered two children with his Native American mistress and translator La Malinche. Food follows genes in the sense that with few Spanish women available to run households and train cooks, native foods entered Spanish-American diets from the start. The preferred Mediterranean diet brought across the ocean included bread made from wheat, grapes, and olives. These foods were crucial in establishing Spanish cultural identity. Wheat and wine had an important religious place as holy wafers in the Catholic Mass, and hidalgos ate what cultural dictates suggested. Where wheat was not available, in hot, humid climates especially, then mixtures of grains would be used.[49] Early Spanish writers often praised maize for its fecundity and multiple uses, while at the same time saying that it was food preferred for the great body of Indians or people of mixed race—the lower orders.[50]

Nevertheless necessity leads to familiarity and even eating pleasure. Spaniards who lacked wheaten products ate corn as tortillas, mushes, and puddings, liquefied as atole, plantains and local fruits such as tunas (cactus fruits, alias prickly pears) in the north when they had to. They might have added dried meats while on the road, so a kind of rough creole cuisine was formed.[51] It certainly was in another way. in the gardens of Spain, where New World tomatoes and chilies were transformed into the bases of the modern versions.

It would seem that the well-known mixture of Mediterranean (in its medieval and early modern forms) and Native American foods and techniques that we know as Mexican cuisine came from the bottom up.

George Catlin, 1847 illustration of René-Robert Cavelier, Sieur de La Salle, meeting Native Americans in the Lower Mississippi Valley in 1680.

Humbler Spaniards who intermarried with local women, or who lived in the new towns and villages as workers, artisans, and small-scale merchants, certainly ate many more native foods than the elites. Pottery evidence on the ground in Mexican cities indicates as much.[52] However, the most celebrated example of mixed, or creolized, cuisine came from the upper classes, *mole poblano*. The dish was supposedly invented at the convent of Santa Rosa in Puebla about 1680 by Sor Andrea de la Asunción, of Spanish origin, and Indigenous nuns who worked with her for a visiting grandee. *Molli* is the Nahua word for "sauce," specifically made with dried chilies and thickened with ground nuts or seeds. There were numerous kinds of such sauces made in Mexico when the Spanish arrived. The now classic *mole poblano* from the state of Puebla and its region is made with native turkey, three kinds of dried chilies, lard, onions, garlic, almonds, raisins, cloves, cinnamon, coriander seeds, anise, sesame seeds, ground cumin, shredded tortilla or sweet cookie, tomato, and bitter chocolate at the end. All of these are boiled together and the sauce then cooked down until thick and somewhat hot-sweet. The ingredients mix native and European, indeed worldwide, ingredients using techniques familiar to cooks on both sides of the Atlantic in the sixteenth and seventeenth centuries.

However, Rachel Laudan and Jeffery Pilcher have argued persuasively, on the basis of contemporary cookery books and other materials, that Colonial Mexico had two caste-bound cuisines. One was Spanish, based on wheat bread and old-fashioned heavily spiced meats, the other far more mestizo with corn at its base. Only with a surge of Mexican nationalism in the nineteenth century, and especially after the Revolution of 1910, was *mole poblano* made into a symbol of Mexican culinary nationalism. Though the Sor Juana story is likely a myth, the dish remains a model of idealized creolization.[53]

The English differed from Spanish and Portuguese America because the colonists discouraged intermixing with Native Americans and brought European women with them. They cooked. Many American culinary historians consider a small book of recipes published by Amelia Simmons in 1796 (more on her later) to be the first American cookery book because it contains American ingredients married to British culinary practices.[54] Simmons's recipes call for maize (still called Indian meal), pumpkins, and cranberries among others. Thomas Hariot, John Smith, and William Bradford among the earliest Englishmen in America would have readily taken to these dishes, but other early colonists did so only out of necessity. All three spoke of the abundance of native American foods and how well people could fare upon them. Hariot declared that "Indian corne yields 200 London bushels while in England wheat yields 40 . . . Plus one man can in 24 hours of labor produce enough to last 12 months."[55] Maize had good commercial value and could sustain sturdy English folk if they would but eat it. Smith talked about the abundance of deer and sturgeon at Jamestown before the Starving Time of 1609–10, and these colonists certainly ate what maize they could get from the Indians when hunger overcame their prejudices. Bradford also spoke about wild game, fish and shellfish, and maize as subsistence food, though he yearned for butter, cattle, sugar, and wheaten bread. All three men might be seen as propagandists for settlement, as indeed they were, because once maize reached Europe it was destined to be food for poor backcountry folks and food animals.

But food comes where one can get it. A British writer styling himself Ebenezer Cook published a well-known satirical poem on Colonial life called *The Sot-weed Factor*, meaning someone who grew and brokered tobacco. At the planter's table, after drinking as much (hard) cider as he wished, Cook says this:

> While Pon and Milk, with Mush well stoar'd,
> In Wooden Dishes grac'd the Board;
> With Homine and Syder-pap,
> (Which scarce a hungry dog wou'd lap)

Sweetcorn boiling in a pot, still the preferred method among corn farmers.

Well stuff'd with Fat from Bacon fry'd,
Or with Mollossus dulcify'd.[56]

Pon(e) (small cakes), mush (hasty pudding), and hominy (or samp) are all based on pounded or ground maize. What Cook means is that, though the planter may have land and presumably money, he is still a rude Colonial, and thus comical. But there is truth in the food itself because it was made of native seed made with European ingredients—apple cider, bacon fat, and molasses—in ways that were familiar to Native Americans and Europeans alike. The corn dishes were made in European styles by mixing in milk, butter, and sugar. Milk and butter came from domesticated cows kept by established farmers. Sugar or molasses was the great import from the Caribbean, part of the trade system that was normal to the Americas by the later seventeenth century. Like a *mole poblano*, made with imported spices but in British style, samp and hasty pudding represent northern creolization.

Nonetheless, important as these dishes were to making an "American" cuisine, these were vernacular dishes and more or less class-bound.[57] Nor was the corn produced in the same way as that used at least by Native peoples of New England. No patches were cut out of nutrient-rich forests, then left to fallow. Instead, corn came to be grown as a commoditized crop in larger cleared fields, sent to powered gristmills and then sold cheaply. Thus was a pattern set for America's food and the way that it was and is produced.

Nineteenth-century Thanksgiving Menus

Big food is only natural for a holiday that celebrates all the good that comes from the American cornucopia. Thanksgiving dinners follow fashions but no matter the economic straits the ideal remains a nineteenth-century-style spread. The Mother of the Feast herself, Sarah Josepha Hale, printed two recipes in her 1839 *The Good Housekeeper*, saying that mince pie made with cow tongue is necessary to the holiday meal, while true Yankee pumpkin pie, with ginger to make it authentic, is good for digestion. Turkey is a centerpiece with the crop filled, unlike the modern method of body cavity and neck stuffing. If more gravy is required, then Hale's directions for dredging a turkey in flour and boiling it would do the trick. A major feast is assumed.

By the end of the century, menus contrived to make Hale's feast in *Northwood* look like small potatoes. One such feast was a Thanksgiving Dinner for Mrs. John A. Logan reported in Adelaide Hollingsworth's 1893 *Columbia Cook Book* (published the previous year in Philadelphia and redone for Chicago's World's Columbian Exposition):

> The grand dinner or feast at 2:00 was characterized by abundance and deliciousness of each article was rarely entrusted entirely to domestics, vegetable soups came first. Roast beef, sweet potatoes, baked squash, and hot slaw making the next course, followed by turkey or goose that had been hung before a log fire until it was brown as a bun . . . The drippings were always caught in a pan set underneath and carefully dipped with a spoon and poured over the turkey fowl which, cooked in this way, is most delicious. The dressing was prepared by mixing bread crumbs with the liquor in which giblets had been boiled, seasoned with butter, pepper and salt and

sometimes sage and browned in an oven. Cranberry or apple sauce, fried sausage cakes, white potatoes that had been mashed and seasoned with milk, butter, pepper and salt, placed in a earthenware dish, then browned in an oven, were served with the goose or turkey. Next was a game course of prairie chicken, venison, or wild duck, with lettuce, pickled peaches, cucumbers, and beets, furnishing abundant relish. Indian and plum puddings, pumpkin, apple, and mince pies, with plenty of sweet cider, supplied an abundant dessert. Coffee, tea, with the accompaniment of real pound cake and doughnuts, completed a feast for the gods.

Over the course of the next century, two world wars, the Great Depression, and healthy eating advocates worked to change menus. In 2015 the Food Network cable channel suggested the following dishes made by several of its presenters for a classic Thanksgiving:

Squash Soup, Turkey with Stuffing, Velvety Mashed Potatoes, Green Bean Casserole, Glazed Carrots, Cranberry Sauce, Cast-Iron Skillet Cornbread and Pumpkin Pie. The ingredients of each dish are fresh, the recipes use plenty of herbs, the results lighter and more flavorful than many,

Nonetheless, at Thanksgiving time across America people buy huge frozen genetically modified turkeys that are nothing like their wild (intelligent) progenitors, bags and boxes of ready-to-use bread or cornbread stuffing mixes, canned cranberry sauce, frozen vegetables, and canned pumpkin filling to go with pre-made piecrusts for the feast.

THREE

Immigrants: The Things They Brought with Them and Found

In 1802 the eminent French naturalist François-André Michaux set out on a journey to the western regions of the still new American Republic. His father, André, had done the same before him. Michaux *père* was an even more distinguished botanist than his son, a man who had risen from humble farming origins to being the French government's (royal at first, revolutionary later) emissary in its quest to bring new species of trees back for a major reforesting project. As part of his mission and because of his curiosity about all floras, Michaux *père* traveled to the then western territory of Kentucky and into the Carolinas from 1793 to 1796. Michaux *fils*, also working for the French government, went further still beyond the Allegheny mountain chain, down the Ohio River to Kentucky, Tennessee, South and North Carolina, and back to New Jersey where his father had established an experimental garden in 1785.[1]

The Michaux journals are classic accounts of what the United States was like in the generation after the American Revolution. While not fully comprehensive studies of botany and agriculture, they tell readers a good deal about settlements, farming, and commerce in the rapidly developing interior of the country. For instance, François-André reports this:

> Near the town of Marietta are the remains of several Indian fortifications. When they were discovered, they were full of trees of the same nature as those of the neighbouring forests, some of which were upwards of three feet diameter. These trees have been hewn down, and the ground is now almost entirely cultivated with Indian corn.

Settled by people from around Boston, Massachusetts, Marietta was the first permanent American settlement in what was then the Northwest Territories (1788). Its location at the junction of the Muskingum and Ohio Rivers allowed it to become an important trade center with connections as far away as the West Indies. Today it is a small town of about fourteen thousand, having been superseded by Cincinnati, some 200 miles down the Ohio River.[2]

These "pioneer" European-American settlers were led by the Revolutionary War general Rufus Putnam. A surveyor and millwright, Putnam with a group of friends formed a private company to buy a huge tract of land from the United States government and plant settlements in it. The final price for the Ohio tract was 8 cents an acre. With land at premium prices in their home area and relatively poor soils for the kind of farming that they wanted to do, the west beckoned many young men and their families. They first had to deal with Native peoples whose land it really was and they did so in successful military campaigns (led by the famous general "Mad" Anthony Wayne).

One might suppose that the economy of the new settlement was like that of earlier New England or upland Appalachia, basically subsistence or frontier farming with surpluses going to local or regional markets. Not so.

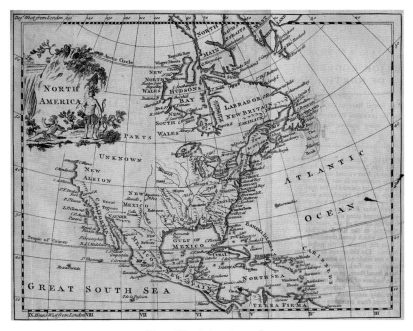

Map of North America, 1767.

View of St. Louis from South of Chouteau's Lake, 1840. The still-undeveloped interior of the
United States, on a meander of the Mississippi River.

Michaux wrote throughout his journal about the kind of agriculture the
newcomers wanted, commercial crops for sale in both wider internal and
external markets. The ancient trees grew not on fortifications, but on the
great burial mounds of the Hopewellian peoples, which had to be cleared for
their main cash crops, corn and hogs, and wheat with salt collected nearby.
Up and down the interior rivers great and small, American settlements
were set up for such farming. Crops flowed to the newly rising cities such
as Cincinnati, Louisville, and St. Louis, and down to the port city of New
Orleans. There the produce was sent to the Caribbean islands to be used in
a transatlantic trade that included slaves.

Land hunger led many to move on and on further and further west,
there to exploit the land. In this way American settlements moved across
the new western lands of today's Midwest and the South. By the mid-
nineteenth century Americans had spilled out over the Mississippi into the
plains and as far as the Pacific Coast. The economics remained the same,
creating settlement and farming patterns that met the economic desires of
the settlers. Besides feeding themselves, the ultimate goals were to produce
maximum quantities and turn produce into commodities for cash. As for
land and water, the environment, these were issues that could hardly be considered by most of these entrepreneurs.

Commercial agriculture did not happen all at once. A longer story lies
beneath Michaux's visit to the new Marietta in 1802, for, in a way, Marietta
mirrored the early immigrant experience. First, a group of Boston area families with English roots made their way into the wilderness to recreate their

own hometowns, their familiar societies. Second, the newcomers had or developed technologies that allowed them to exploit their local resources to the maximum extent that they were able. Third, they were not alone, since Michaux says alongside them were Germans newly arrived in American or only a generation removed from immigration from Europe. French settlers, most of whom proved to be unsuccessful, were also in the mix. Each group might have had differences in language, religious affiliations, attitudes toward life, and perhaps foodways as Michaux said. Nonetheless, by this time in American history, all shared the same regard for commerce and commodity production. That economic engine remains the same to the present day despite many social and political movements meant to modify or even end it.

For America before the twentieth century, immigration took two main forms. One was internal, the people Michaux found in Ohio who were already absorbed into what can be conceived of as a fairly common American culture. The Putnam family and their friends had long roots in New England where the original stock of migrants from the British Isles had risen from about 21,000 in 1640 to a million in 1800.[3] Most of the Ohio Germans had come from Pennsylvania, where the elder Michaux described them as, even when newly arrived, prospering, and though German, acclimated to American ways.

Newly arrived Germans and many more groups were external migrants who were not yet absorbed into the local versions of American culture. An example is the numbers of Scots-Irish or Highland Scots who came to the interior regions of Pennsylvania in the early eighteenth century and who clashed with Quaker leaders about everything from treatment of Indians to ways of worship. The same story runs throughout the rest of American history. The overwhelming numbers of immigrants to North America in the seventeenth and eighteenth centuries came from the British Isles. Great Britain was not yet a unitary nation state (regional nationalists would say that it still is not), so the immigrants could hardly be expected to have the exact same cultures. To some scholars such as David Hackett Fischer, British regional cultures, including foodways, established four major competing cultural zones in American life.[4] To others, the early patterns are far more complicated and not nearly so neat.

Fischer proposed that the foodways—Virginia, New England, Pennsylvania–Delaware, and the backcountry of the Appalachians and their foothills—were discrete and based on the regions from which most of the settlers came. For instance, Virginians mainly hailed from southwestern England, where frying and simmering were main cooking styles and the dishes were spicier than other traditions. New England was Puritan and "puritanical" in its food styles and, as in eastern coastal England, much given to baking. The middle colonies, whose founding Quakers came mainly from the Midlands, were not interested in class-conscious foods and were fond of boiling, simmering, cheeses, puddings, and similar hearty fare. The northerners, Scots, and Scots-Irish who immigrated from the poor soils of the northwestern slice of the British Isles, boiled and fried their foods, ate oats and rye, made whiskey, and when the original ingredients were not available used corn—corn liquor replaced whiskey and corn grits were once oat dishes. As have others before and after, Fischer also suggests that American regional dialects and accents come from the same disparate sources.

Albion's Seed has been heavily criticized in many ways, not least for its description of foodways as making inaccurate if well-intentioned generalizations. Bernard Bailyn shows that the New England colonists were not exclusively East Anglian but came from a broad swath of the country from as far away as Yorkshire and the West Country. That they were mainly Puritans, or at least nonconformist Protestants, does make them a kind of cohesive group, but only to a point and not for more than two generations. The twenty families led by the "Imperious" minister Ezekiel Rogers, who left Rowley in Yorkshire's East Riding to found another village of the same name near Boston in 1639, set up a village in an archaic, inward-looking style. Neighboring Ipswich, filled with East Anglians, was quite different since it was immediately part of an international trade system.[5] Nor did the two sets of villagers speak the same English, as anyone who is familiar with Yorkshire dialects knows. One might even doubt that they cooked the same way, given their varying access to trade goods and social outlooks. But necessity bred new creolized foodways.

As it happens, food elaborated in New England over time as it did in other colonies. As mentioned before, European fruits and vegetables colonized North America where conditions were favorable. As the anonymous author of the highly influential book *American Husbandry* (1775) says, New England's climate had become more temperate by his time due to forest clearance, and temperatures were a main factor in farming (an early version of the forest-clearing-as-climate-change-catalyst theory).[6] Contrary to most opinion, New England's lands were not all poor rock-strewn specimens but good soils were to be found in river valleys such as the Connecticut, along the coasts, and on the western borders adjoining New York. Here and elsewhere corn was the main crop, yielding upwards of 25–30 bushels of grain for each peck (4 pecks per bushel) sown; richer soils in New York produced 50 bushels per peck. Corn does exhaust the land, so crops had to be rotated or lands left fallow for several years. European clover had been imported and widely planted as a nitrogen-fixing crop for fallow fields and good for grazing cattle. Dairies were numerous, as were livestock from cattle to pigs and sheep. Wheat was the preferred crop, but blight made it all but impossible to grow. *American Husbandry* says that barley and rye are poor crops, not valued in England, but raised in these colonies out of necessity. Naturally fisheries played a large role in the New England economy, with exports of dried fish a major source of income. So was forestry, with ongoing and considerable land clearance programs even in mountain regions of the interior. The author comments favorably on land-holding patterns that featured many small to medium farmers who might live comfortably enough on their holdings. Labor was scarce and dear because almost anyone who desired to could get land for their own farms. Yet, a generation after 1775, groups of people moved out of New England for richer lands some 700 miles away, along the Ohio River. The process was similar to what brought many a Briton to the Americas in the first place.

Obviously conditions in 1775 were not the same as a century earlier. Then food provisions had been precarious, especially when food stored over the winter had run low before the spring planting. In a classic essay, Sarah F. McMahon shows that in the eighteenth century country people changed their food habits and production systems. They did so for two reasons: smaller farm yields and smaller land-holdings, and access to markets where farm products could be sold and new ones purchased. As a result the compositions of meals changed and cookery practices did as well.[7] Because wheat was often blighted, breads made from cornmeal and rye became staples: the famous "rye 'n' injun" (later taken by settlers to the great prairies). Contrary to some modern commentators, corn was not disliked by New Englanders but was much enjoyed as cakes, in puddings, and as vegetable preparations (succotash a prime example of the latter). Cookery book recipes, starting with the first American one, Amelia Simmons's *American Cookery* (1796), illustrate the pleasures of corn.[8] Reliable meat supplies were established in the same period, as were dairy products. English peas, as in "pease porridge," once the staple, gave way to other legumes, namely beans that were boiled and baked into the canonical New England dish. While that may seem plain, international trade brought the molasses that is always an ingredient, often the more the better. Vegetables also changed as kitchen gardens increased in size and diversity. Cabbages, carrots, turnips, various squashes, and many greens appeared as accompaniments on tables. As in many a traditional farm, poultry were raised as part of the kitchen garden complex, again varying diets with meat and eggs. Orchards sprouted throughout the colonies, apples and peaches being favored fruits. Apples, mainly of English stock such as pippins, proliferated so that apple cider was a staple beverage, along with beer made from barley and hops. If cider fermented into an alcoholic beverage, so much the better or worse, since the rate of alcoholism in the new Republic was staggering. By the late eighteenth century spices, pepper sauces, coffee, chocolate, and a host of other once exotic ingredients were in circulation even in rural New England. Boston was not alone in its cosmopolitan fare, nor were the other regions in the new Republic.

Far from adopting a cuisine of plain boiled foods out of necessity, New Englanders had developed sophisticated palates and cooking techniques using English and American ingredients during the course of the eighteenth century. And they still preferred wheat products. Kelly O'Leary points out

Cover of the first edition of Amelia Simmons's cookery book.

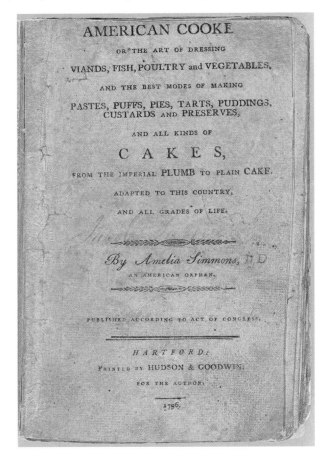

AMERICAN COOKE

OR THE ART OF DRESSING

VIANDS, FISH, POULTRY and VEGETABLES,

AND THE BEST MODES OF MAKING

PASTES, PUFFS, PIES, TARTS, PUDDINGS,
CUSTARDS AND PRESERVES,

AND ALL KINDS OF

C A K E S,

FROM THE IMPERIAL PLUMB TO PLAIN CAKE.

ADAPTED TO THIS COUNTRY,

AND ALL GRADES OF LIFE.

By Amelia Simmons,

AN AMERICAN ORPHAN.

PUBLISHED ACCORDING TO ACT OF CONGRESS,

HARTFORD:

PRINTED BY HUDSON & GOODWIN,

FOR THE AUTHOR.

1796.

George Washington's Beer Recipe

George Washington made beer on his plantation, only it was not the kind of beer sold today. It uses the commonly available molasses that came from the Caribbean from the sugar-slave trade. The recipe is from a manuscript held by the New York Public Library.

> Take a large Sifter full of Bran Hops to your Taste—Boil these 3 hours. Then strain out 30 Gall. into a Cooler put in 3 Gallons Molasses while the Beer is scalding hot or rather drain the molasses into the Cooler. Strain the Beer on it while boiling hot let this stand til it is little more than Blood warm. Then put in a quart of Yeast if the weather is very cold cover it over with a Blanket. Let it work in the Cooler 24 hours then put it into the Cask. Leave the Bung open til it is almost done work-ing—Bottle it that day Week it was Brewed.

Presumably when drinking his brew with others he observed the rules of etiquette that he had kept since copying them out at the age of sixteen: "Drink not too leisurely nor yet too hastily. Before and after drinking wipe your lips breath not then or ever with too great a noise, for its uncivil." And "Drink not nor talk with your mouth full."

---

that the reasons were not related to the wish to define social status or even show social distinctions on the part of a rising middle class as in Europe. Nor, as some suggest, did the Pilgrims and Puritan founders prefer wheat to corn because of the latter's association with feared and despised Indians. Rather, it was the grain itself and what could be made from it. Wheat has more nutrients than rye, barley or oats and, once the wheat germ was removed, resisted spoilage more than the others, especially oats (weevils were and remain another matter).[9] Processed wheat was available to many more English cooks by the seventeenth century and home cooks were accus-tomed to making pies and cakes of many kinds. They also made lighter raised breads, though in towns these were bought from bakeshops. Cookbooks

Ripe wheat, the
American cash crop.

of the period such as Gervase Markham's *Countrey Contentments, or, The English Huswife* (1615 and many editions thereafter) or Thomas Dawson's *The Good Huswifes Jewell* (1596) and others all discuss cakes and pies. From the preference for wheaten products flowed technical innovations in milling, hearths and ovens, leavenings, and more. No matter how prevalent corn and other grains might have been across North America, wheaten bread, cakes, and pies were always at the heart of a woman's culinary arts.

Simmons's three recipes for a classic preparation show the English traditions transferred and transformed. The author evidently came from New York's Hudson Valley but the recipes are classic New England dishes. These are baked versions of hasty pudding, a dish made by adding corn meal to boiling water or milk with butter and optional molasses.

A Nice Indian Pudding.

No. 1. 3 pints scalded milk, 7 spoons fine Indian meal, stir well together while hot, let stand till cooled; add 7 eggs, half pound raisins, 4 ounces butter, spice and sugar, bake one and half hour.

No. 2. 3 pints scalded milk to one pint meal salted; cool, add 2 eggs, 4 ounces butter, sugar or molasses and spice q: s: it will require two and half hours baking.

No. 3. Salt a pint of meal, wet with one quart milk, sweeten and put into a strong cloth, brass or bell metal vessel, stone or earthen pot, secure from wet and boil 12 hours.

The recipes show how much local ecology had changed in the course of a century and a half. Eggs came from chickens kept on small farms usually close to or in garden plots (surely predators such as wolves had been eliminated). Or they were purchased from neighbors in town and village markets. Dairy products were common ingredients produced by a family's own cows or purchased locally. Molasses, always important in New England cuisine, and sugar were brought in the overseas trade with the West Indies, while spices such as mace and cinnamon came from much further quarters of the world. New England and the nearby colonies (later states) were no longer the raw "wilderness" that the early European settlers found; instead it was a land tamed.

This 18th-century painting by Pehr Hilleström shows a maid taking soup from a pot in an open hearth, typical of cookery before the advent of iron stoves.

Nonetheless, there is something to be said for supposing that peoples immigrating to new lands looked for what was most familiar to them and their ways of living. It is a truism that eighteenth-century Germans from the southern Palatinate sought out certain landforms, climate, and alkaline soils, identified by the kinds of trees growing in the area, in their new Pennsylvania home.[10] Presumably alkaline soils meant that they wanted irrigable meadowlands for cattle since these were a main source of agricultural production in the homeland. The same can be said for later immigrants such as the nineteenth-century Bohemians in Willa Cather's novels to whom the rolling Nebraska country looked familiar.[11] That can extend to urban areas as well. Studies of eighteenth-century immigration to Pennsylvania show that, as the century wore on, more and more German and Irish immigrants were in trades rather than being farmers (though a substantial number of single German men and women were "Redemptioners," indentured servants who had to work for a set period of time to pay for their passage). For them Philadelphia and its surroundings was a natural environment. But land to the west and south of Philadelphia beckoned.[12]

Before the American Revolution the largest ethnic groups of European immigrants in Colonial North America were from German lands. By 1790 German-speakers numbered anywhere from 65,000 to 100,000 out of a total population of about four million. Many more would arrive in the mid-nineteenth century from various regions of the homelands, but the earliest were mainly from the Palatinate or Pfalz. Because William Penn, the founder of the Pennsylvania colony, was a Quaker who took the tenets of his religion seriously, he invited his co-religionist German Quakers and Mennonites to settle near Philadelphia in 1683.[13] Germantown, Pennsylvania, became the distribution center for other Germans to follow. Although Mennonites and Amish are the most famous, most Germans were Lutheran or Reformed. For land-hungry and poor farm families, Pennsylvania seemed to be a godsend even if many owed years of labor for their passages.

In 1750, a half century before Michaux *fils*'s journey to the American interior, a German schoolteacher from the kingdom of Württemberg traveled with four hundred migrants to Pennsylvania. Upon returning to his homeland, Gottlieb Mittelberger wrote an account as a warning to fellow Germans of the treacherous ways of greedy immigration agents and the hard lives to follow. However negative his early impressions were, the latter part of the journal is a fulsome and personal account of life among the Pennsylvania Germans. The land was fat and fertile:

Provisions are cheap in Pennsylvania, but everything that is manu-factured and brought into the country is three or four times as dear [costly] as in Germany. Wood, salt and sugar excepted. Otherwise we can purchase in Germany as much with one florin as here with 4 or 5 florins. Nevertheless, the people live well, especially on all sorts of grain, which thrives very well because the soil is wild and fat. They grow chiefly rye, wheat, barley, oats, buckwheat, corn, flax, hemp, fruit, cabbage and turnips. They also have good cattle, fast horses, and many bees. The sheep, which are larger than the German ones, have generally two lambs a year. Hogs and poultry, especially turkeys, are raised by almost everybody. In this country the chickens are not put in houses by night, nor are they looked after, but they sit summer and winter upon the trees near the houses. Every evening many a tree is so full of chickens that the boughs bend beneath them. The poultry is in no danger from beasts of prey, because every plantation owner has a big dog, if not more, at large around his house.[14]

Mittelberger also says that meat was cheap: "Even in the humblest and poorest houses in this country there is no meal without meat, and no one eats the bread without butter or cheese, although the bread is as good as with us. It is very annoying, however, that nothing but salt meat is eaten in summer, and rarely fresh meat."[15] His description of the Philadelphia market must have left quite an impression on his German readers because it describes abundances of cheap meat, seafood, produce, and grain but also spices, tea, coffee, and sugar from across the globe in this seaport city.

Because Germans came in family groups to a far greater degree than the British, women retained their cooking traditions. Much has been written about Pennsylvania Dutch cookery (a corruption of Deutsch and not the tourist fare of Lancaster County, Pennsylvania). Mittelberger was among the first observers: "The English know little or nothing of soup eating; bread and butter and cheese are always their dessert, and because sugar, tea and coffee, are very cheap, they drink coffee and the like 2 or 3 times daily." The most popular cookbooks in the colonies, Eliza Smith's *The Compleat Housewife: Or, Accomplish'd Gentlewoman's Companion* (1727) and Hannah Glasse's *The Art of Cookery Made Plain and Easy* (1747), have plenty of soup and pottage recipes.[16] In fact the 1739 edition of Smith's book opens with a crawfish or lobster soup. Mittelberger's comment implies that British diners did not eat soups with thick slices of bread as did Germans. None of Glasse's recipes call for dumplings to be put in soups (most dumplings were sweet) or for noodles. William Woys Weaver notes that dumplings of several kinds were expected in German cookery books of the period.[17] The Palatinate is famed for hearty dishes including liver dumplings, horseradish, and the one dish that Weaver says distinguished Germans from English, sauerkraut. These were the beginnings of the German influence on Anglo-American cuisine.

Being French, André Michaux obviously looked for his brethren during his travels. Going down river to Gallipolis, he found

> about sixty log-houses, most of which being uninhabited, are falling into ruins; the rest are occupied by Frenchmen, who breathe out a miserable existence. Two only among them appear to enjoy the smallest ray of comfort: the one keeps an inn, and distills brandy from peaches, which he sends to Kentucky, or sells it at a tolerable advantage . . . [It] is not that the French are less persevering and industrious than the Americans and Germans; it is that among those who departed for Scioto not a tenth part were fit for the toils they were destined to endure.[18]

Almost every commentator on the settlements of the trans-Appalachian interior had similar impressions of French inhabitants of the regions including those in early New Orleans. Partly these are due to the social class of settlers that the French government sent to their colonies and also to the fact that so many other French lived in the "wilderness" while engaged in the fur trade. That was not the case in Acadia, now Canada's Maritime Provinces, where some fifteen thousand French colonists established thriving farms and worked the lucrative fishing industry.

Jacques Cartier, a Breton explorer, began France's formal entry into North America in 1534. His attempt at establishing a colony failed, as did all others until 1605 when Port Royal in Acadia, modern Nova Scotia, was set up by Samuel de Champlain and colleagues. One of the great figures of early European colonization, Champlain befriended Indian tribes, traded iron implements and founded the village of Quebec. Actually small fisheries had been established on the Canadian coasts a generation previously for drying and salting codfish. Newfoundland's Grand Banks had been European fishing grounds since the fifteenth century, the fish processed into *bacalao* and sent to Mediterranean countries. The famous explorers Father Jacques Marquette, Louis Jolliet, and René-Robert Cavelier de La Salle all paddled their birchbark canoes into the Great Lakes and then on to the Mississippi. In the early 1680s Cavelier de La Salle set up a string of small forts along the great river—later to be cities such as Peoria, Illinois, and Memphis, Tennessee—while claiming the whole valley for France under the name Louisiane. No magnet for mass migration, the colony was to be a commercial venture for trade primarily in furs and later foodstuffs.

Early French reports always included food, as did all the other European correspondents. Entertained at a council of the Illinois near the mouth of the Wisconsin River in 1673, Marquette described being served bowls of cooked cornmeal (Sagamité), followed by the greatest treat and a high compliment, baked whole dog (which the Frenchmen refused to eat), then followed by "fat and tender cuts of buffalo meat."[19] Dog and corn were offered by peoples up and down the river, when they were available. The cooking methods were boiling for corn and broiling on hot coals for meat. This was hardly a cuisine suitable for French nobility such as La Salle, but he adapted. In the settled parts of New France European transformations of flora and fauna were in effect. Father Pierre François Xavier de Charlevoix was sent on a royal commission in 1713 to survey regions of Acadia that had been lost to the British in war. Writing about Cape Breton Island he noted: "Fruits, especially apples, vegetables, wheat and all other grains necessary for subsistence; hemp and flax are less abundant, but of as good a quality as in Canada."

The American beaver.

He also commented: "All the domestic animals, horses, cattle, swine, sheep, goats and poultry, find abundant food. Hunting and fishing can maintain the inhabitants a good part of the year." But deer and elk, which were once abundant, had become rare.[20]

Clearly the inhabitants of the island, Quebec, and the settled lands between were not unsuccessful agriculturalists. Other French immigrants did fail in food production, as in early New Orleans, or were not interested in changing the land. The latter were fur trappers and traders, the famous *coureurs des bois*. In response to the highly lucrative fur trade that the French crown tried to monopolize, young Frenchmen beginning in the seventeenth century went into the forests of North America to trap, trade, and sell pelts. They were single entrepreneurs who had to live by stamina and wits. *Coureurs* lived among Native peoples, serving as intermediaries between them and Colonials, between animal hunters and shippers. Considerable numbers of young men seem to have engaged in this trade. By one estimate eight hundred out of a thousand settlers in 1693 New France took off for the woods to make their fortunes. The most famous, Pierre-Esprit Radisson and Médard des Groseilliers (Médard de Chouart, Sieur des Groseilliers), were among the founders of Canada's great trading entity, the Hudson's Bay Company in 1670. Apart from the impact that *coureurs* and everyone else had on the American environment—the near extermination of beavers—these men of the woods became romanticized by novelists, thus becoming part of American folklore. Natty Bumppo, the hero of James Fenimore Cooper's *Leatherstocking Tales* (*The Last of the Mohicans* the most famous of them), though not a beaver hunter, had many *coureur* features in him. Cooper places his hero, at the end of life, in a wilderness far from the sounds of men's axes felling trees, and speaking of conservation of the wilderness in the 1840s.[21] Many a folklore figure would follow, from Davy Crockett to Mountain Men of the Rockies.

In culinary terms the best-known French settlement lay at the Mississippi River's delta, New Orleans. St. Louis, 670 miles upstream, was second. La Salle in his expeditions looked in vain for the specific mouth of the river as it flowed into the Gulf of Mexico. Because of the extraordinary amount of silt carried by the river waters, plus tides and storms, the Delta is a complex and ever-changing mass of channels. After failed attempts at finding a suitable spot for what could and would be a port city, in 1718 Governor Baptiste Le Moyne, Sieur de Bienville, began work on a planned city. Or rather, convicts and slaves began digging and diking the muddy channels to create a new town environment. French planters were interested in export crops such as indigo and rice, so food production for the settlers was neglected. For them

Alfred Jacob Miller, *The Trapper's Bride*, 1858–9, showing intermarriage between Native
Americans and (usually) French voyageurs from the 17th to 19th centuries. Their children,
metis, were important figures in the interior part of the continent's early settlement.

food was wild game, including fish and shellfish, and they imported salted
pork, beef, salt, corn, and fresh produce from the upriver St. Louis region.[22]

In his travels to Louisiana from 1801 to 1803, François-Marie Perrin du
Lac was far more impressed with St. Louis than Louisiana. In neighboring
St. Charles he observed fine meadows and that the "lands which are better
cultivated, produce corn [wheat], barley, maize, potatoes, in a word, every
necessary for man or beast."[23] Another writer contrasted the salubrious climate and lands of St. Louis with New Orleans: "those great vast plains and
those low swampy lands, such as are seen at New Orleans, are not there,
but instead magnificent hills and pleasant valleys," full of trees and grapevines. People in St. Louis were healthier, their streets not filled with standing
water, and morally purer.[24] Later in the nineteenth century St. Louis lost its
French language and culture as English-speaking Americans, Germans in
large numbers, and other ethnic groups occupied the city, but its environs
remained good agricultural land.

Rice was a key to the southern Louisiana colony because the wide wetlands were conducive to rice cultivation. As Christopher Morris observes, rice was part of French culinary culture at the time, the plant being grown in the Camargue. French and English cookery books, Amelia Simmons as an example, had rice recipes, but mainly for puddings, that is, thickened sweet dishes. It was not a replacement for wheat to French elites, for whom bread was their preference and a mark of social status. In letters to the royally chartered company that set up his plantation, Bienville asked that enough flour, brandy, wine, and butter (made from bear grease) among others be sent to keep the colony going for four years or more. That is what French diners of aristocratic tastes—and that was who the founders were—expected. Early on, rice (and corn) was for Native peoples, slaves, and poor whites. However, necessity bred new food practices and rice eventually became a staple of classic Creole cookery.[25]

Rice was an export crop, necessitating changes in the land, population, and foodways. In order to make rice fields, cypress forests in the vicinity were cut down. Since trees held floodwaters, more and more labor had to be diverted to levees and ditches. Rice changed the ecology of the Delta.[26] In the 1820s some six thousand African slaves were brought to Louisiana to do the necessary work. Many of them were from lowland West Africa where rice was grown and consumed; they knew not just farming but culinary uses of rice as well. Because New Orleans and Louisiana never had a large French population and many were not farmers, authorities tried in vain to bring in other groups such as Germans as settlers. Only when Spain

George Caleb Bingham, *The Jolly Boatman on the Mississippi River*, 1847.

was handed control of Louisiana in 1763 as a result of France's loss in the French and Indian War (also called King George's War, 1754–63) did New Orleans begin to attract a greater diversity of people. Among them were other French-speakers expelled from Canadian Acadia during the French and Indian War. Scattered across the English and French New World colonies, many families naturally came to Louisiana. They did not find a French paradise and so settled in other parts of southeastern Louisiana, especially in watery bayou country. They intermixed with Native peoples, Scots-Irish, Germans, Yankees, and others, yet retained their general name, Cajuns. Their culture and language is distinctive, though their famous cuisine is in many ways close to New Orleans Creole.

Spaniards, West Africans, Europeans of various origins, and Native peoples met together in what was becoming a large trade center. A distinctive Creole cuisine grew up based on the now acceptable rice, fish, shellfish, crustaceans, fresh produce such as tomatoes, peppers, and greens, and one central ingredient, okra. Called *gombo* in West African languages, gumbo came to mean a variety of highly flavored stews combining meats and vegetables cooked in a single pot. The earliest reference to the name dates to 1803, by then clearly a well-established preparation.[27] One dish symbolizes how rice was internalized in New Orleans cookery, jambalaya. It is a version of paella that may have been devised by Spanish cooks, but among its many variations are those made with local game and plenty of spices. It, too, has an African flavor. In the nineteenth century, Louisiana cookery slowly made its way to the rest of North America where it retains a unique historical and cultural cachet distinctive from any others. That it was the product of less than successful colonial programs, environmental destruction, and unintended ethnic mixing makes it all the more interesting.

Neither Michaux made it to Louisiana, but they both journeyed to the South, the younger across Kentucky, down to Tennessee and into the Carolinas, from where he embarked by ship back to New York. As soon as he crossed into the South, François-André set eyes on slaves of African descent. As noted above reguarding Louisiana, Africans played a large role in agriculture and food. The same held throughout the South once they became household servants and cooks. Importation of Africans to North America and the roots of slavery began in 1619 in Virginia. No matter the discussion about whether the first were bondsmen on indenture with freedom at the end of the term, it was obvious from experiences in South America that Africans would become slaves. Slavery is a voluminously discussed subject and with good reason, since the effects last down to the present day. The main cause for enslaving peoples in one form or another—Africans were not the only ones—was the need for labor. In labor-intensive, pre-industrial economies muscle power and human skills had not been replaced by machines. Colonial landowners in the North complained about high wages because labor was so scarce. But slaves could be cheap:

> Through the whole of the low country the agricultural labours are performed by negro slaves, and the major part of the planters employ them to drag the plough; they conceive the land is better cultivated, and calculate besides that in the course of a year a horse, for food and looking after, costs ten times more than a negro, the annual expense of which does not exceed fifteen dollars . . . I shall abstain from any reflexion concerning this, as the opinion of many people is fixed.[28]

How much back-breaking labor slaves in the low country near Savannah had to do was accounted by Johann Martin Boltzius, a German Lutheran minister who came to the new colony of Georgia. An opponent of slavery, Bolzius was appalled at the never-ending work slaves had to do. In his commentary he says that during winter months slaves did household work. Also to feed themselves they were given "as much land as they could handle," where they planted

> corn, potatoes, tobacco, peanuts, water and sugar melons, pumpkins, bottle pumpkins (sweet ones and stinking ones which are used as milk and drink vessels and for other things) . . . Their food is nothing but Indian corn, beans, pounded rice, potatoes, pumpkins. If the master wishes, he gives them a little meat when he slaughters. They have nothing but water to drink.[29]

Other commentators described greater varieties of foods. Alexander Falconbridge was a surgeon on slave ships running to Africa between 1780 and 1787. As a result he became an abolitionist. In an account of his service Falconbridge said that on board ship during the infamous Middle Passage slaves ate

> horse-beans, boiled to the consistence of a pulp; of boiled yams and rice, and sometimes of a small quantity of beef or pork. The latter are frequently taken from the provisions laid in for the sailors. They

sometimes make use of a sauce, composed of palm-oil, mixed with flour, water, and pepper, which the sailors call "slabber-sauce." Yams are the favourite food of the Eboc, or Bight negroes, and rice or Corn, of those from the Gold and Windward Coast; each preferring the produce of their native soil.[30]

Falconbridge says that in their homelands, the captives ate vegetables, grains and meats. Robert L. Hall suggests that women cooked while en route and that once in America they sought to recreate the cuisines that they knew.[31] Some used plants transferred from Africa such as cowpeas, pigeon peas, okra, hot peppers, and even the caricatured watermelon. Other ingredients were local and familiar to Africans because they either resembled plants they knew or were New World crops that had been transmitted to their native lands in the sixteenth century, mainly by Portuguese merchants. Peanuts, corn, and peppers were among them. The slave diet could be more diverse than at first glance, depending on local conditions.

In order to work as hard as Boltzius says slaves did, they had to have sufficient calories. He says that slaves had their own garden and were permitted to sell produce in local markets. Chickens and eggs, wild game, and fish were all available to these agricultural workers but these foods varied from region to region, even plantation to plantation. Despite Michaux's claim that in the low country slaves were less valuable than horses, the fact is that by the Civil War most of southern slaveholders' wealth was in the slaves they held. Therefore workers had to have enough calories to carry out the heavy manual labor required of them. There is much controversy about the amount and quality of the food people in bondage had. It was monotonous, high in carbohydrates, but also had more fresh vegetables (hence vitamins) in season than might be expected from a corn and bits-of-hog diet. Of the twelve million or so people forcibly sent from Africa to the Americas, about three hundred thousand ended up in the United States. By 1860 that number had increased to almost four million and little of that by importation, since a slave trade ban had been in effect since 1808. Natural increase must have had at least enough food to support it in general. Again, that does not mean that all enslaved people were fully healthy since conditions varied greatly.

Domestic cooks who worked in plantation houses took their knowledge into those kitchens and created much of the canon of southern cookery. Though much of this process took place after the Civil War, when African American cooks were hired and thus professional, what they knew and practiced came from long roots. Free black women had long been famous for public cookery in places like New Orleans, Charleston, Philadelphia, and other cities. In the late eighteenth century they sold preparations ranging from pepper pots to fine candies. As such these entrepreneurs helped establish a roster of preparations that would create regional southern cuisines.[32]

Among the other ethnic groups André Michaux mentions in his travels east of the Alleghenies and down to South Carolina were French and Africans, as discussed above. He did not mention Dutch or Scandinavian settlers because only a few made it west of the Alleghenies in 1802 (many more would come later in the century). Of the two the Dutch had a greater impact on American foodways and American history in general. Dutch colonies began as a mercantile venture when the newly formed (1602) Dutch East India Company was chartered as a monopoly to explore shorter routes to the East Asian spicelands. The company sent an experienced English captain named Henry Hudson to round Scandinavia and Russia, but he ended up 5,000 miles off course across the Atlantic Ocean. In 1609 Hudson and his *Halve Maen* explored the river that today bears his name. He reported: "This is the finest land for cultivation that ever in my life I have set foot upon, and it also abounds in trees."[33] The river and bay that he explored became the base for the New Netherlands. Hudson also knew that the New World was super-rich in fur-bearing animals since French merchants had been trading with Native peoples for them and he himself had conducted a raid in Nova

Plowing by a slave or new-made freedman, using a simple ox-drawn share and moldboard plow.

New Amsterdam (New York) as a Dutch settlement at the bottom of Manhattan
in the 17th century.

Scotia to get them. For the Dutch East India Company, their plantation was
about furs and perhaps fish in the great transatlantic trade. But the settlers
turned it into a full-fledged colony.[34]

In 1624 the Dutch West India Company took over the project settling
Protestant Flemish families on Manhattan Island and sending families up
the river to Fort Orange near modern Albany. Peter Minuit, the governor,
purchased lands, including Manhattan, from the Native peoples with trade
goods, not with beads as the embellished legends have it, but iron kettles,
axes, hoes, blankets, and other manufactured implements novel to the recipi-
ents. The tiny village of New Amsterdam (270 souls at first, not more than
three thousand by 1664) always had Company-appointed governors, but
many free citizens, of varied religious persuasions, were settled on nearby
Long Island and to the north. Land further north along the Hudson was
parceled out to great landowning families called patroons who leased sections to farmers in sharecropping schemes. Most of these farmers were
actually English since the Dutch-speaking population was always small in a
heterogeneous colony—perhaps eight thousand by the time the British took
over in 1664. "Dutch" did not imply completely Dutch culture or language
or even foodways.

The best-known contemporary description of New Netherlands is Adriaen van der Donck's *A Description of the New Netherlands* (1655). Exploring the "North River" (later the Hudson River), Van der Donck described not just the land but the potential uses of it. Meadows, he observed, resemble those of the Netherlands perfect for diking, with rich grass for cattle. Great trees can be cut, especially nut trees whose wood was suitable for mill parts and would not run out for a hundred years. In addition to some twenty native fruits and nuts, Van der Donck described those transplanted from the Old World, such as the ubiquitous apples and pears. Horses, pigs, cattle, and sheep were imported, the cattle from nearby New England where breeds had been acclimated to living outdoors. Contrary to European practices, livestock were not wintered in barns but left outside. Hay was left out for cattle, but pigs fended for themselves in nearby woodlands. American pigs were less fat than Netherlandish ones for obvious reasons. As for many other European visitors, Michaux among them, such apparent disregard for animal welfare was shocking and set down to "American ways."[35]

Gardens were filled with European imports. On New Amsterdam's *bouwereijn*, or farmland, and in other places carrots, lettuces, cabbages, parsnips, beets, spinach, radishes, cress, onions, leeks, artichokes, asparagus, and many herbs such as sorrel, dill, thyme, hissop, laurel, tarragon, and marjoram were grown. Old World peas (much used as in traditional northwest European cookery), New World beans, pumpkins, squashes, and melons were used commonly. As for grains, cleared fields were for wheat, rye, barley, oats, and buckwheat; only the second planting of buckwheat would produce much since finches ate so much of the first crop. Wheat was the prime grain for bread and pastries, though rye breads were very common. And Van der Donck noted with approval that corn was grown everywhere and much enjoyed.

During the seventeenth-century Anglo-Dutch wars for empire, New Netherlands was seized by the British and renamed for King Charles II's brother, the Duke of York, in 1664. Still Old Dutch families were powerful in the colony for the next fifty years until they were assimilated into Anglo-American culture. Place names remain in New York and New Jersey as reminders of them: Brooklyn, the Bronx, the Oranges, Rensselaer (a reminder of the longest-lived patroonship near Albany), and even Yonkers, named for Van der Donck, are all part of New York's history and its folklore. One particular name is a reminder of the cultural mix that New Netherlands-New York was: Franklin Delano Roosevelt, an English personal name, a Huguenot middle name (from the four hundred or so French Huguenot families in the colony) and a Dutch surname.

By 1819 "Old Dutch" had become embedded into New York folk-lore. Some of their dishes remain in America's lexicon such as "Cookies, pancakes, waffles, wafers, donuts, pretzels, and coleslaw."[36] The inimitable Washington Irving was largely responsible for both when he decided that doughnuts should be the characteristic food:

> Sometimes the table was graced with immense apple-pies, or sau-cers full of preserved peaches and pears; but it was always sure to boast an enormous dish of balls of sweetened dough, fried in hog's fat, and called doughnuts, or olykoeks—a delicious kind of cake, at present scarce known in this city, except in genuine Dutch families.[37]

Irving's first literary triumph, *The Sketch Book of Geoffrey Crayon, Gent*, created the everlasting image of Dutch America. His stories "Rip Van Winkle" and "The Legend of Sleepy Hollow" are enduring classics. In the latter, Irving gives an idealized picture of Dutch fare:

> The pedagogue's [Ichabod Crane] mouth watered as he looked upon this sumptuous promise of luxurious winter fare. In his devouring mind's eye, he pictured to himself every roasting-pig running about with a pudding in his belly, and an apple in his mouth; the pigeons were snugly put to bed in a comfortable pie, and tucked in with a coverlet of crust; the geese were swimming in their own gravy; and the ducks pairing cosily in dishes, like snug married couples, with a decent competency of onion sauce. In the porkers he saw carved out the future sleek side of bacon, and juicy relishing ham; not a turkey but he beheld daintily trussed up, with its gizzard under its wing, and, peradventure, a necklace of savory sausages; and even bright chanticleer himself lay sprawling on his back, in a side dish, with uplifted claws, as if craving that quarter which his chivalrous spirit disdained to ask while living.
>
> As the enraptured Ichabod fancied all this, and as he rolled his great green eyes over the fat meadow lands, the rich fields of wheat, of rye, of buckwheat, and Indian corn, and the orchards burdened with ruddy fruit, which surrounded the warm

George Washington's Whiskey

Americans from the Colonial to early national periods drank about three times as much alcohol as modern Americans: seven gallons a year compared to a little over two in 2015. Beer and cider were the most common drinks, wine was available for finer tastes and purses such as Thomas Jefferson's, and distilled liquors were everywhere. Beer was simply made by malting grains or corn kernels to turn starches to sugars, boiling them and then allowing natural yeasts to create mildly alcoholic beers. Once apples became widespread, cider was easily made by crushing, saving the juice and allowing it to ferment naturally—the longer it sits the stronger it gets. Rum made from molasses was the most popular of all the distillates in Colonial North America. The best were imported from Caribbean islands, but Americans, especially New Englanders, made it themselves at the rate of more than a half-million gallons per year. That was to change with the Revolutionary War's disruption of British trade and growing nationalism. With so much corn and grain available, Americans, especially of Scottish and Irish origin, turned to cheap, locally made distilled liquors. The closest modern equivalent would be grain alcohol, alias moonshine.

tenement of Van Tassel, his heart yearned after the damsel who was to inherit these domains, and his imagination expanded with the idea, how they might be readily turned into cash, and the money invested in immense tracts of wild land, and shingle palaces in the wilderness. Nay, his busy fancy already realized his hopes, and presented to him the blooming Katrina, with a whole family of children, mounted on the top of a wagon loaded with household trumpery, with pots and kettles dangling beneath; and he beheld himself bestriding a pacing mare, with a colt at her heels, setting out for Kentucky, Tennessee,—or the Lord knows where![38]

George Washington made beer using grain and molasses according to a recipe in his journals. He also made a lot of whiskey. Despite his scientific farming methods and fairly profitable gristmill and fisheries on the Potomac River, Washington was chronically in debt. He knew that grains, especially corn, which would not fetch high prices in the market, could be turned into a profitable product. As president he had suppressed a revolt in the Pennsylvania back country by farmers who had refused to pay an excise tax on just such liquor—the famous Whiskey Rebellion. Washington's farm manager James Anderson was a Scot who grew up on a farm near Edinburgh and knew a good deal about distillation. Anderson oversaw the construction of stills at Mount Vernon that within a year produced nearly 11,000 gallons, which were sold to an eventual customer base that numbered 270.

Whiskey neat or mixed with water became an everyday beverage for Americans, especially in the developing western regions. Charles Woodmason, who traveled to rural North Carolina in 1768, reported that mothers gave their babies diluted spirits regularly. Whiskey or what passed for it was matched only by cider in a republic that in the first half of the nineteenth century had an estimated 50 percent rate of alcoholism.

Two themes run through this tale of the ignoble Ichabod. One is that a country has been transformed into a land of plenty. This is not the land of rich potential that the earliest European immigrants wondered at, but one that has been subjected to orderly development; order out of chaos. Virtually all visitors' journals to inland America thought the same, and, of all the people they met, the most admired were German farmers. Coming into Ligonier, Pennsylvania, on the way to Pittsburgh, for example, François-André Michaux saw this:

The houses are much larger, and most of them have two rooms. The land better cultivated, the enclosures better formed, prove clearly it is a German settlement. With them everything announces ease, the fruit of their assiduity to labour.

They assist each other in their harvests, live happy among themselves, always speak German, and preserve, as much as possible, the customs of their ancestors, formerly from Europe. They live much better than the American descendants of the English, Scotch, and Irish. They are not so much addicted to spirituous liquors, and have not that wandering mind which often, for the slightest motive, prompts them to emigrate several hundred miles, in hopes of finding a more fertile soil.[39]

Another traveler, the distinguished scholar and Unitarian minister Thaddeus Mason Harris, said that hard work and sobriety made for a strong family and community. By German customs Harris would have meant food as well, likely plain and lots of it. Harris found similar life habits down the Ohio River in and around Marietta, where he found fields well laid out with good fencing and thrifty people who had apple and peach orchards. He even liked the good brandy made from the fruits. What a contrast to the Virginians:

The industrious habits and neat improvements of the people on the west side of the river, are strikingly contrasted with those on the east. Here, in Ohio, they are intelligent, industrious, and thriving; there, on the back skirts of Virginia, ignorant, lazy, and poor.

I had often heard a degrading character of the Back settlers; and had now an opportunity of seeing it exhibited. The abundance of wild game allures them to be huntsmen. They not only find sport in this pursuit, but supply of provisions, together with considerable profit from the peltry. They neglect, of course, the cultivation of the land. They acquire rough and savage manners. Sloth and independence are prominent traits in their character; to indulge the former is their principal enjoyment, and to protect the latter their chief ambition.[40]

No Natty Bumppo fan, no woodland romantic the Reverend Harris. He was really talking about the second thread in American thought, personal liberty, an ability to move off into a limitless wilderness and create one's own life. The idea runs strong and it was a major way that the continent was developed: first pioneers, then orderly development. The reality was that pioneers were elements in a money economy. What they did was first clear the land of Indians and trees and other obstacles, then sell the land for a profit and move on to make more profits. Liberty could and did mean rampant speculation, economic cycles of boom and bust. That is exactly what Irving has Ichabod dream about, along with his food fantasies.

One more of Harris's comments was a foreshadowing of what was to come, yet another theme in American history and culture:

> Another cause of the difference may be that, in the back counties of Virginia, every planter depends upon his negroes for the cultivation of his lands; but in the State of Ohio, where slavery is not allowed, every farmer tills his ground himself. To all this may be added, that most of the "Back-wood's men," as they are called, are emigrants from foreign countries, but the State of Ohio was settled by people from New-England, the region of Industry, Economy, and steady habits.[41]

The Virginians were crude and lazy and dependent on slaves for labor. Many were rough immigrants—Scots and Irish, no doubt—who were nothing like the community-minded virtuous people of the North. The contrast was a powerful image in the North that ran up to a great war and long thereafter.

FOUR

Technology and Land

Weapon shapely, naked, wan!
Head from the mother's bowels drawn!
Wooded flesh and metal bone! limb only one, and lip only one!
Gray-blue leaf by red-heat grown! helve produced from a little seed sown!
Resting the grass amid and upon,
To be lean'd, and to lean on.

. . . The axe leaps!
The solid forest gives fluid utterances;
They tumble forth, they rise and form . . .
Walt Whitman, 'The Song of the Broad-axe' (1856)[1]

American democracy's poet, Walt Whitman, sang his paean to the rise of his country's power and glory through the hard work of its peoples. From the forests, from the field, from the barren lands where coal and iron lay, America was developed. The land would be chopped and torn, reformed, and made productive by its strong people. So Whitman thought and so too did most of the people he addressed beginning with the publication of the first edition of *Leaves of Grass* in 1855. Americans and European travelers thought much the same fifty years earlier.

What Whitman said in free verse is that exploitation of environments has preconditions, namely having the tools to do so. The Europeans arrived with ideas about what they wanted and used their technology to carry them out. Because conditions in the New World differed considerably from the Old, technology changed, and so did ideas. As ever in human history, the will to change everything from material technology to social and political systems had to exist before actions were carried out. Regarding tools, the objects by which physical changes were made, some were to be used directly by hand, others were complex constructions using either natural power or, later, combustion-driven technology. Whitman's axes (operated by human muscle), mills, and farm machinery that used animal power and later water and wind spread across the continent from the beginning of colonization. Canals, flatboats, steamboats, roads, and railroads were also critical instruments of expansion without which there would not have been anything like a United States of America or its food systems.

Social technology intertwined with material culture in complex ways and was driven by economic ideas. In the late seventeenth century the English-speaking world was set on a new economic course, consumerism. As one historian has put it: "It is often forgotten that industrial revolution was, to a large extent, founded on the sales of humble products to very large markets—the beer of London, the buckles and buttons of Birmingham, the knives and forks of Sheffield, the cups and saucers of Staffordshire, the cheap cottons of Lancashire."[2] American colonists took to the new consumerism with alacrity, importing huge numbers of English goods during the eighteenth century.[3] Studies of household inventories and archeological excavations of Colonial domestic sites usually turn up quantities of decorative English pottery, pewter vessels, dining utensils, and more (in archeology, privies are ripe sites for exploration).

Among Americans this meant making and selling goods themselves, even foodstuffs, in markets great and small for money. In this system, buying and selling land (and people) was critical to turning land into farm and pasture. That each of these physical and human technologies came into the hands of specialists was an inevitable sorting by talent, luck, and often ruthlessness. Inventors worked on new devices or improved old ones in myriad ways. For instance, scientists with varying degrees of education worked on improving fields and animals from the early nineteenth century onward. Some real estate speculators created entities to buy and sell land (a good number of them failing), while business people set up manufacturing and trading companies. Business, commerce, and development infused every aspect of American life, from society to politics and cultural values. Naturally, food from ground and water, to processing, to plate, was at the base and connected to everything that happened.

As an example of culture and economics coming together, scrawny-necked and physically weak Ichabod Crane had a fantasy of a manor in the

Kentucky borderlands bought with his wife's wealth. No laborer he. Had he ever got there, the poor fellow would have been in for a shock. Here is François-André Michaux once again:

> However, it was not politic of the speculators, who sold land at five shillings an acre, which at that time was not worth one in America, to acquaint those whom they induced to purchase that they would be obliged, for the two first years, to have an axe in their hands nine hours a day; or that a good wood-cutter, having nothing but his hands, would be sooner at his ease on those fertile borders, but which he must, in the first place, clear, than he who, arriving there with two or three hundred guineas in his purse, is unaccustomed to such kind of labour.[4]

First comes hard work, then the reward, and all depended upon tools.

BEAVERS

At the very start of colonizing American land clearance there was animal removal, beginning with a rodent. When Anglo-French colonization of North America began in the seventeenth century the continent held some sixty to eighty million beavers (*Castor canadensis*). Hardly anyone does not know that beavers are aquatic animals and that they dam streams by chewing down small trees (also their food) and construct their lodges. There is a voluminous literature on the beaver ecology past and present. Perhaps most surprising is the likelihood that beavers had a large role in floodplain development (by cutting channels) in post-glacial North America just as they did and still do with wetlands.[5] In constructing ponds that silt up after about a decade of use they create ecological microzones for varieties of flora and fauna. These are also incubators for nearby forest regeneration and, once abandoned, the resulting "beaver meadows" supply significant amounts of nitrogen-rich water to the forests. Beavers rival humans as shapers of ecological systems.

Unfortunately for these large rodents, they have magnificent coats that were perfect for clothing, especially certain kinds of hats that had become fashionable in Europe after about 1620. Once European beavers had been virtually wiped out, American beaver pelts came onto the world market. Furs were a mainspring of French settlements and the ongoing romantic vision of voyageurs in the great wildernesses. Beaver had long

The American Beaver and His Works. A beaver dam showing its effects on a landscape.

been hunted by Native peoples for their pelts; as a food source they were secondary. Indeed though edible after some preparation, beaver meat, especially tails, has not been as popular a comestible as in the European Middle Ages. Native peoples were amazed at what they could get for furs. One is reported to have said with some irony, "The Beaver makes everything perfectly well . . . it makes kettles, swords, knives, bread; in short, it makes everything."[6] Hatchets made into the famous tomahawks were prized possessions. Desire for trade goods along with major social changes impelled Indian peoples to hunt fur-bearing animals with an intensity never seen before. The wish to dominate the fur trade drove Iroquoians, who had long before formed a confederation and were known for fierce warfare, to engage in wars with other peoples, namely Algonquins. Called the "Beaver Wars," by the late seventeenth century these were particularly brutal, causing peoples to flee from almost the whole Ohio region. Animal populations suffered as well, so that instead of Native peoples only killing what they needed, now whole areas were cleared. By the end of the eighteenth century beaver populations had declined dramatically in Iroquois and Algonquin regions.[7]

Indian peoples using spears and simple traps could kill only so many beavers. In the mid-eighteenth century more lethal metal traps and rifles really destroyed the beaver. European metal technology combined with commerce had catastrophic effects on Indian peoples whose ways of life were completely changed, to say nothing of beavers that were almost driven to extinction in the eastern and Midwestern regions of America. The biotas that beavers created were not mourned by American farmers. While farmers liked meadows for grazing, wetlands were to be drained for agriculture; beavers were (and in some places still are) considered pests. That beavers now flourish in many parts of the United States is only due to conservation and repopulation efforts begun in the twentieth century.

AXES

As David Nye put it, "The axe, the mill, the canal, the railroad, and the dam stand at the center of stories about how European-Americans naturalized their claim to various regions of the United States."[8] Plows, reapers, harrows, seed drills, and other implements were and remain parts of the technological complex. Of all the tools the most celebrated, not only by Walt Whitman but by many others, was seemingly the simplest, the iron or steel axe. As Nye claims, Americans had something of an axe cult since it was the tool that civilized the new lands.[9] The first European colonists brought wood-cutting tools with them, among them several types of axes. One was a short-handled, wide-bladed implement with no poll (or back), which can be described as a hatchet. Several types of these were widely traded to American Indians, who treated them as treasured objects. Not that the stone hatchets already in use were that much inferior to metal for cutting small trees.[10] Iron tools were better because they could be resharpened more easily than flint and were less brittle. Besides, iron axes were prestige items that gave status to those who owned them. The famous tomahawk with a longer poll was developed by Native peoples, though made by Colonial blacksmiths for trade, specifically the business of beaver pelts.

During the course of the eighteenth century what came to be called the "felling axe" was developed in America by numbers of anonymous American craftsmen.[11] This looks like the standard depiction of the woodsman's axe. Slim in design with a slightly widened cutting edge, it has a balanced poll that is flattened for such tasks as hammering. With its slightly curved wooden handles—there were many designs—developed for maximum leverage, it was perfect for cutting larger trees. Other axes were invented or developed from European models in America for specific purposes such as rail splitting and hewing. The famous double-bitted axe that looked like the ancient Minoan ritual double-axe appeared in the 1850s and became the standard logger's tool in the Pacific Northwest. In short, local smiths and later companies created dozens upon dozens of axes well into the twentieth century. Axes in hand, pioneers entered the great American forests, created clearings for houses and farms and thus began the long road toward America's settlement patterns and food production systems.

TOOLS AND HOUSEHOLD INVENTORIES

Any inventory of Colonial and later American rural households (and only in the twentieth century did the majority of them became urban) lists iron tools used for operating farms. Axes were one, but there were others. In 1629 the Puritan minister Francis Higginson wrote in his diary that any settler in the new Massachusetts Bay colony should have:

> Tooles. 1 Broad Howe. 1 Broad Axe. 1 Narrow Howe. 1 Felling
> Axe. 1 Steele Handsawe. 1 Gimblet. 1 Whipsawe. 1 Hatchet.
> 1 Hammer. 2 Frowes. 1 Shouell. 1 Hand-Bill. 1 Spade. 1
> Grindstone. 1 Augres. 1 Pickaxe. 4 Chissels. Nayles of all sorts.
> 2 Percers stocked.

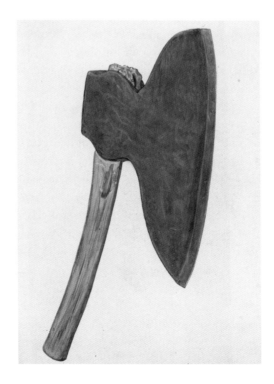

Pioneer broadaxe.

Houshold implements.
1 Iron pot. 1 Spit. 1 Kettel. Wooden Platters. 1 Frying pan. Dishes. 1 Gridiron. Spoons. 2 Skellets. Trenchers.[12]

Upon his death in 1684, Samuel Parker, Sr of Bridgwater's estate included:

an Iron Crow; 2 smale Iron wedges, two old whipe sawes & a sett of hookes [&] boxes, two old plow Shares & 3 old Coulters, s3 quarters of a hundred of Iron, a paire of fetters 3s and a paire of scales and waites 2s, one brod axe, 1 Narrow axe a Ring staple and Clearises, an old spad and pronges & other Iron Lumber.[13]

Similar inventories of farm households are found throughout North America from the settlement period into the twentieth century. What farm does not have shovels, axes, pickaxes, sharpening stones, and the like? As the eighteenth century progressed, tools changed to meet the food demands of the market and as farmers from different ethnic backgrounds exchanged ideas. In a comparative study of farm inventories of York, Pennsylvania, and the New Jersey communities of Burlington and Hunterdon, Judith McGaw found significant differences between the two at first and then convergence.[14] As noted earlier, visitors to America commented favorably on the efficiency and quality of German farmers. York, in Lancaster County, was heavily German (it is the original center of Pennsylvania Dutch settlements), with a 68 percent German population in 1782.[15] Not far away to the east were many more Welsh, English, and Scots-Irish, while Burlington had few German settlers. What neatness meant to observers was more intensive agriculture by using manure, careful crop rotations, and husbanding of wood resources, with consequently higher crop yields. Soil types did not matter as much as the traditional practices that settlers brought with them. McGaw found that earlier German households in York had dung forks, dung shovels, and dung hooks, but by 1774 almost all farms, no matter the ethnicity, had them. Up to 80 percent of York farmers used grubbing and weeding hoes. Weeding hoes were used extensively in gardens and for corn growing, while grubbing hoes mean more intensive cultivation of root crops. Potatoes and turnips were most often mentioned in contemporary accounts as being important crops for home consumption and for sale in local stores and markets. A number of York farmers also used harvesting cradles (multi-tined scythes that better collected the grain stalks) because wheat was the main cash crop, though barley, rye, oats, and buckwheat were also grown. Pennsylvania was wheat country and by late in the century so was Hunterdon.

Other products on these diversified farms included flax, hemp, apples, cherries, and the hay critical to maintenance of farm animals. Billhooks, dairying equipment (butter churns for example), and cider mills all reflect such products. So do wagons. Large wagons heavily reinforced with iron strappings and metal-shod wheels became features of the areas west of Philadelphia beginning about the 1750s. Philadelphians called them Conestoga wagons. Often drawn by four horses or bullocks, these were more numerous in the richer lands of Lancaster County, meaning that they were used to carry heavy sacks of grain to market.[16] The Conestoga is the wagon always seen in pictures of pioneer farmers heading west across the continent to the Pacific Ocean. No movie Western would be without them. Yet it is appropriate that the most famous wagon makers were the Studebaker family, later to make distinctive automobiles in South Bend, Indiana, since their name means "fine flour baker" in Low German.

Cooking gear also reflected traditional and ethnic metal production. McGaw's study shows that the women in York used the then modern iron kettles rather than the old-style brass ones that remained in Burlington. The Germans of Lancaster County used iron stoves in far greater numbers than their British counterparts in New Jersey. Iron stoves with cooking plates had appeared earlier in the century in Europe, but British cooks tended to retain the old open hearth cookery that is so often replicated in historic living history museums and is beloved of those who recreate Colonial cookery. Lancaster County women did cook in hearths since iron trammels, hot racks, and pot hooks abound in household inventories, but it would seem only reluctantly since, where families could afford them, iron stoves were preferred. Either British cooks were resistant to change for cultural reasons, or because of personal cooking preferences, or poverty, or they were too far from places where stove plates were cast; America was a big country with scattered settlements.

One more difference between German and English settlers was the powdering tub. These were literally tubs used to salt meats and likely vegetables. Everyone knew the importance of salt for meat preservation, but Germans came with culinary traditions using salted cabbage, or sauerkraut. Inventories of York and Hunterdon's German families in the 1770s exclusively have powdering tubs and processing tools such as paddles.[17] Pickling was long established in English culinary practices. Hannah Glasse has many recipes for pickled vegetables, though not cabbage. German sauerkraut and the related Dutch coleslaw became naturalized in the next century, that is, they became elements in standard American fare and were often made by farm families.

One of the lessons of sauerkraut is that culinary practices were changing along with assimilation. Potatoes were not necessarily associated with Germans in the eighteenth century, but rather with Scots-Irish and Irish whose homeland had long been consuming these tubers. Introduced to New Hampshire in 1719, they spread across the colonies especially in

Steel pots on an open fire.

areas where these groups settled.[18] In the Pennsylvania and New Jersey communities mentioned here they were planted alongside turnips and often in rotations. The reason was to fix nitrogen but also because potatoes were becoming standard features of the American diet, no matter the ethnic origins. Amelia Simmons, or at least the Hartford, Connecticut, transcriber of the first edition of *American Cookery* in 1796, tells us about several types of potatoes, the best soils for them, and how best to prepare them for cooking. She (or he) then looks to Irish cultivation practices as the best way to raise good mealy potatoes. Every cookery book of every type then included potato recipes. The specialized hoes of the Germans in Lancaster County in the 1770s replicated the hoes used in Ireland. It is an instance of practical application to growing what was essentially a new naturalized American food.

The foregoing about tools and household inventories in Pennsylvania and New Jersey tell us about processes in American history and its food. First European farmers had to clear the land by felling forests, something that English farmers had not needed to do since the Middle Ages. They needed tools to do it and new ways of crop production. Corn, for instance, did not require plowed open fields, at least until modern means of production permitted it. European crops were planted right away, but the cash crop, wheat, produced only 10 bushels per acres, about half the yield in England. German farmers farmed more intensively, but the British moved onto new lands—extensive farming—because they needed to produce more for the emerging commercial market. In Pennsylvania, farmers also sold barley to Philadelphia's brewers, oats for the city's horses, and flax and hemp to town rope- and cloth-makers. Naturally, that means more tools to keep cutting forests and building anew.

One of the significant things in McGaw's study is the fact that settlers who moved west from their old centers tended to have newer and better tools. Iron kettles versus brass ones, as mentioned above, newer hoes and cradles, and cookstoves were all indicators of what can only be seen as demand for newer and better tools. Better transportation became a greater priority, hence better wagons, new roads, and use of waterways expanded. As so often happens, demands of the periphery drove changes in ideas. Americans in general looked to innovations to improve their economic and social conditions and were willing to leave their long-time homes and ways of life to do it. Again, American ideas were extensive in another sense of the word.

IRON

Tools made for a prosperous man, and men (mostly) made the tools. Iron was the normal material, as the Parker inventory shows, but steel was the most desirable. For instance, early iron axes were made better by the blacksmith setting a thin steel bar into the cutting edge before hammering it into place and tempering it. The edge remained sharp longer and took to sharpening better. Repairs could be effected in the same way. Though scarce at first, once the technology of steel-making was perfected, American civilization, as it was often called, moved across the land. Whitman enthused, "The main shapes arise! / Shapes of Democracy, total—result of centuries."[19]

The British Parliament encouraged American production in the Iron Act of 1750 by removing import duties on pig and later bar iron. William Byrd II, on visiting Virginia mines and smelters in the 1730s, learned that "our iron from the plantations sold for less than that made in England, though it was generally reckoned much better."[20] The problem for American colonists was that they were not permitted to make tools such as knives, sickles, even machinery that made nails. Under the rubrics of the Navigation Acts, many specific rules and duties were imposed for the benefit of British manufactures. Colonists needed farm tools in large numbers and as cheaply as possible, thus laws were widely evaded and eventually the Revolution ended them for Americans. The first step was developing iron and steel technology.

Kemble Coal & Iron Company, Riddlesburg Works, Riddlesburg, Bedford County, Pennsylvania. The earliest buildings date to 1807, at the start of the Industrial Revolution.

In the seventeenth century Europeans made three kinds of iron: wrought iron, cast iron, and steel.[21] The iron-making technology brought to the colonies had not much changed from the Middle Ages, though that period saw gradual improvements in amounts of production using different fluxes and water mills.[22] First, one had to get pure iron from the raw iron ore, the earliest way using a bloom smelter. Ore was melted in a small furnace with burning charcoal and perhaps some flux like shell or lime using bellows to blow in oxygen. Bloomeries could be made quickly and ad hoc using only a few people. One of the great medieval innovations, the blast furnace, produced far greater amounts of iron. These were tall, enclosed furnaces that were continuously stoked and oxygenated by more and larger bellows. When married to water mills bellows could intensify heat and thus drive out more impurities in the iron while instilling some carbon.

After smelting, molten iron was allowed to flow out into a depression in the ground with channels running from it. Because the main body with rivulets resembled a sow with piglets, the result was and remains "pig iron." Pig iron could be made into cast iron or further processed into more ductile (flexible) material. Cast iron meant the iron being melted and then poured into molds. The cauldrons, pans, pots, and later stoves of early American cookery were all made this way. Cast iron is fairly brittle, but nonetheless because of the lower costs it was and remains widely used because pans made from it retain heat and distribute it evenly depending on the quality of the iron). Cast iron could also be used for agricultural implements; plowshares were routinely made of it in the eighteenth and early nineteenth centuries. Vermont inventor Thaddeus Fairbanks opened an ironworks in 1823 making cast iron plows and stoves and eventually morphing into the great engine and industrial parts company, Fairbanks Morse & Co. of Chicago. Brittle cast iron plowshares broke, especially on stony soils, but were still widely used because easily replaced and cheap interchangeable parts were developed early in the nineteenth century.[23] Cast iron would give way to John Deere's steel plows slowly, beginning in the 1830s.

Wrought iron was most desired in earlier periods for tools and armor. It is more malleable than cast iron and so can be beaten into shapes more easily. From the Middle Ages to the eighteenth century the finery forge was the best way to make wrought iron. Pig iron was remelted using charcoal and beaten with hammers to drive out the slag, or impurities. It was then formed into bars for further processing. Bars were the primary shape for ease of transport and sales to smiths, but hoops for barrels and wheels were commonly made. Plating was also important, an example being the early ironclad ships such as the Civil War *Monitor* and *Merrimack*, which were covered in wrought iron sheeting. Hammering was done by hand, but water-powered hammer mills were widely used for larger production. The trouble was that water mills had to be near swiftly flowing streams and these were not always where the iron ore was. The process also used a lot of what proved to be a finite resource, charcoal.

England began to suffer a timber crisis in the sixteenth century. There were many reasons for it, including topography and demand for cleared agricultural and pastoral land. The demand for charcoal for use in metallurgy was another.[24] Coal was an obvious substitute as a carbon source for iron-making, but in the seventeenth century it was only used by brewers in Derbyshire to heat their wart before brewing and later to dry hops. Brewers learned to create coke from coal (thus driving out noxious sulfur) by cooking it down for a long time, in much the same way that charcoal was made from wood. Not until the late 1740s was coke used to make wrought iron by the remarkable Darby family of Coalbrookdale in Shropshire, the place where Abraham Darby III built the world's first cast iron bridge over the River Severn in 1781 as a testament to the rising technology of coke and iron.[25]

Although large amounts of iron could be produced in these older ways, in 1781 Henry Cort patented the puddling process that increased volumes of wrought and cast iron.[26] Iron made the early industrial revolution, including the revolution in agriculture and food processing, possible; steel brought it to full flower. A mixture of iron and specific amounts of carbon, steel is flexible, durable and made into cutting tools amenable to sharpening. Early steels were hard to make and limited in production. Large-scale production of steel began in Sheffield, England, when clockmaker Benjamin Huntsman, who needed flexible steel for movements and springs, began producing crucible steel in the 1740s. By 1800 mills in the Sheffield area made 90 percent of British steel and half the world's total production.[27] Henry Bessemer changed everything. His technique was to place iron and flux in "converters" (basically closed tanks), melt everything over very high heat, and force air into the chambers to drive out impurities. Converters could be scaled up to immense size, the great cauldrons of molten iron often pictured in photographs and films. Bessemer patented his process in 1855 and it was brought to the United States soon thereafter. Although pirated by some, engineer Alexander Holley became Bessemer's agent in America, improved the original designs and built the earliest plants in the hemisphere. More than one place is named Bessemer as a result. Now precision machinery and even more efficient implements were springs of American industry and agriculture.

Where Francis Higginson's and Samuel Parker's iron tools came from is integral to the story of America's agriculture and food transformations. The first English colonists included blacksmiths and iron makers. Blast furnaces with finer forges were set up in Virginia in 1621 and Massachusetts in 1647.[28] They failed, the former because Indians killed everyone, so part-time makers set up simple bloomeries across the colonies from which smiths made all kinds of implements. "Forge" place names remain along the eastern seaboard colonies, though the original purposes are long forgotten. These remained in rural communities into the mid-nineteenth century, and yet by the early eighteenth century English iron-making practices had spread across the colonies. William Byrd II described a larger-scale smelting process and the cost.

> That the properest wood for that purpose was that of oily kind, such as pine, walnut, hickory, oak, and in short all that yields cones, nuts, or acorns. That two miles square of wood, would supply a moderate furnace; so that what you fell first may have time to grow up again to a proper bigness (which must be four inches over) by that time the rest is cut down. He [Mr. Chiswell, an ironmaster] told me farther, that one hundred and twenty slaves, including women, were necessary to carry on all the business of an iron work, and the more Virginians amongst them the better; though in that number he comprehended carters, colliers, and those that planted the corn. That if there should be much carting, it would require one thousand six hundred barrels of corn yearly to support the people, and the cattle employed.[29]

Iron was easily found, though of varying quality, and critically so was wood. In Europe iron made with charcoal was reckoned to be better than that made with coal even after the coking process had been invented. Hundreds of charcoal iron foundries remained in Ohio and Pennsylvania in the 1860s and even a few as late as the 1940s.[30] America had forests in abundance, the famous "forest primeval" in Henry Wadsworth Longfellow's epic poem of 1847 *Evangeline, A Tale of Acadie*. And all the forests were waiting to be cut by the axes made from the iron and steel. In an age of wood, from houses to mills, to ships (a large percentage of British shipping was made in the colonies or from American wood), the forests provided foundational resources.

Just as England's Black Country was developing in the Midlands—likely named for soot from mining and factories—so was America's version. Large-scale mining and smelting transformed landscapes and rivers in eastern Pennsylvania, western New Jersey, and famously around a rising Pittsburgh. In an environmental irony, catastrophic diseases killed off most of America's Native peoples, thus increasing forests. Forests fueled the new European-type economies and over the course of two centuries forests old and regrown were cut again with grievous economic and social consequences. An example is the Mississippi River valley, where clear cutting of forest in the later nineteenth and early twentieth centuries led to massive flooding of the great river. Another is the cotton-land South, the cultivation of which devastated lands cleared of forests. An extensive cotton growing system had political consequences that led to the American Civil War. However, large-scale replanting for land reclamation and the creation of national parks and forests, beginning in the early twentieth century, has stabilized United States forest at about 33 percent of its landmass. That is roughly three-quarters of the total in 1630, though primeval forests are only a small portion of the total. Iron tools cut the forests and iron tools remade many of them.

Byrd's description tells about production of materials and food in his time and in the future. First, is the amount of labor needed to run even a modest iron-making operation. Not only were there the people actually making the metal but they needed support personnel. These were specialized, carters, colliers (miners), farmers, and iron makers. As Byrd says, everyone had to be fed adequately to get work out of them. Although one might suppose that slave labor was free, it was not to the plantation owners, who carefully calculated all costs of food, clothing, and housing, no matter how crude. (Byrd was horrified at how poorly clothed the slaves were yet how healthy they seemed to be.) Setting up and running an ironworks was a large investment, so they had to be built and assessed as commercial enterprises. Visiting another ironworks Byrd observed:

> The use of it is to melt his sow [pig] iron, in order to cast it into sundry utensils, such as backs for chimneys, andirons, fenders, plates for hearths, pots, mortars, rollers for gardeners, skillets, boxes for cart wheels; and many other things, which, one with another, can be afforded at twenty shillings a ton, and delivered at people's own homes.[31]

Home and garden gear delivered to people's homes sounds very modern.

Costs included replanting trees, from fast-growing pines to much slower oaks, and food production. Corn meant agricultural land cultivated by tools made from the self-same iron. At about 100 lb per barrel of corn, that meant 16,000 lb of corn or the product of 160 acres of land. What might appear to be a circular, self-sustaining system is actually not, because the iron and charcoal were finite resources. If furnaces were to be maintained over many years, the raw materials would eventually have to be brought in from further afield. As the land in Byrd's Virginia was made into plantations, land costs rose, so getting more woodland was not easy or cheap. As a result, establishments like these eventually disappeared in favor of places where iron ore and charcoal (and later coal) could be more easily obtained or had by cheap transportation. Pittsburgh, for instance, at the junction of the Monongahela, Allegheny, and Ohio rivers, became synonymous with iron and later steel making by the 1840s. Doing so was an integral part of Americans' belief system: if resources are to be had, move on to get them; the continent and its riches were theirs.

One cannot but take note of food practices in this context. Byrd mentions dinners he had throughout his survey of southern Virginia and northern North Carolina. Just before his description of Mr. Chiswell's iron furnace, he talks about a wonderful meal with a fat deer as the centerpiece. Venison, buffalo, beef, fish, and fowl were all consumed along the way. When in towns, roast beef and chicken pie were boarding house delights. Byrd knew good food and, interested in gardens, he knew herbs, fruits, and vegetables well. Had he lived beyond 1744, he might have sat at table with a distant cousin, Mary Randolph. She was the author of one of the great early cookery books, *The Virginia House-wife* (1824). From a prominent plantation-owning family, Randolph comes from the tradition of elite cookery, though not by professional chefs—she does not cite her contemporary, Carême, for example. Meat preparations such as boiled turkey with oyster sauce, ragout of breast of veal, fricando of beef, and a complex white sauce for fowls, among others, are examples of hearty rich cuisine. Interestingly, Randolph, who spent her last years in Richmond, Virginia, and Washington, DC, wrote out recipes for African–West Indian based dishes such as gumbo, okra, and pepper pot, and foreign creations that include curry and Spanish olla. Vegetables are also prominent, including an early version of broccoli. Desserts such as custards, puddings, cakes, and pies are prominent. So is bread: "When you find a barrel of flour, a good one . . . "[32]

Corn

New technologies eventually led to massive production. There are few other foods as iconically American as corn on the cob. In October of every year for more than a century past, the town of Carmi located on the Little Wabash River near the Illinois–Indiana border holds its corn festival. Stacks, pyramids of fresh corn on the cob slathered with butter, maybe some flavored with Mexican-style spices, are gnawed by revelers. The featured dish is "corn chowder," a stew of fresh sweetcorn named for the New Englanders who settled the town. It is one of numerous festivals held across America's corn belt (mainly the Midwest) in honor of the crop upon which their farms, towns, and villages were built. Getting to these festivals, visitors drive through miles of corn (and now soybean) fields. Along the edges are small signs such as "Pioneer Hi-Bred" or "DuPont Pioneer" or a winged ear of corn named "De Kalb" among many others. Despite the classic corn-eating imagery almost none of this corn goes into the corn chowder or directly into human mouths, but instead into animal feeding troughs, fuel-making machinery, oil mills, and corn syrup extractors. Of the 14 billion bushels harvested in the United States in 2015, only 1 percent is sweetcorn—corn on the cob. The rest is field corn for industrial uses at home and for export, and most of it is hybrid of one sort or another.

Serious hybridization began when agronomists in the Midwest saw that feed animals needed higher protein and other nutrient levels in their feed corn. Beginning around 1908, scientists at land grant agricultural universities, such as

When she and her husband lost their money and plantation, Mary opened a famous boardinghouse. Flour was no longer made from wheat grown on the plantation, but was now store-bought. That is, in the 1820s wheat was grown elsewhere, perhaps in Pennsylvania or northern Maryland, from where it was milled and shipped in barrels to shops in cities and towns in the eastern part of the Republic. *The Virginia House-wife* was highly influential in American domestic cookery since it was widely

Illinois and Iowa State, began the process of selecting desirable seeds by planting crop after crop of row corn for inbreeding and later cross-breeding. Most labor-intensive of all was detasseling, removing the silken tassels (the sexual organs) of one row so that the plants will be pollinated by another, thus producing hybrids. It was all laborious work that only became mechanized in the 1970s. Crop yields improved slightly to about 25 bushels per acre until Henry A. Wallace of Iowa, the founder of the Pioneer Hi-Bred company, Secretary of Agriculture in the Franklin Delano Roosevelt administration and Vice President from 1941 to 1945, persuaded farmers to be more scientific about choosing hybrids. Yields zoomed to 40 bushels an acre. Private companies and schools of agriculture have worked together ever since to raise yields to about 180 bushels and, in the wet summer year of 2016, a bumper crop that reached 200 bushels an acre. Some innovations are through constant experiments with hybridization, others from transgenic work (genetically modified organisms). Far from the folksy corn festivals, corn production is as industrialized as food production gets. Animal feed in one form or another takes up about 47 percent of the crop, 30 percent is made into ethanol for automobile fuel, almost 6 percent goes to sweeteners such as high fructose corn syrup, alcoholic beverages such as beer and liquor (bourbon the most famous) take up 1 percent, and only 1.5 percent is made into breakfast cereals. Of these, cornflakes, invented by John Harvey Kellogg, is the best known. Whether animal feed and ethanol are the most efficient ways to use corn remains a contentious issue.

read and copied in other manuals. There was a new world of commerce in which it appeared. Though many a housewife raised their own food they had long been able to buy spices, even curry powder, in local shops. Most of them may have had laying hens—the amounts of eggs used in baking were prodigious—but they bought sugar and flour. What Mrs. Randolph thought of this we cannot say, but her husband David Randolph invested in coal and iron mines and had a reputation as an inventor. Perhaps Mrs.

Randolph's cast-iron pans, cauldrons, skillets, tongs, and wrought iron fireplace accessories might have been made in a foundry supplied by her husband's mines. Iron and steel, mills, mines, canals, and soon railroads changed everything; America was becoming industrialized and its food commercialized.

SMITHS

Although the Colonial American metal-producing industries accounted for one-seventh of the world's production in 1776 (much of it in Pennsylvania and New Jersey), factory production did not come all at once.[33] Until only a generation or two ago, American schoolchildren heard or had to learn a poem that memorably begins:

> Under a spreading chestnut-tree
> The village smithy stands;
> The smith, a mighty man is he,
> With large and sinewy hands;
> And the muscles of his brawny arms
> Are strong as iron bands.[34]

Blacksmiths were indispensable to the local economies from the start of European settlement. They were vital to the communities being

Blacksmith at work in a John Deere shop, 1930s.

The John Deere 1838 steel plow.

established further and further west and south toward the Mississippi in the early decades of the nineteenth century. Longfellow's model was a smith long settled in Cambridge, Massachusetts, in 1840; in fact, years later local schoolchildren gave him a chair made from the very chestnut tree in the poem. Blacksmiths made and repaired almost everything needed for households and farming. As David Nye found, in 1845 a South Carolina textile mill owner complained that due to lack of investment "the state's roads were in poor repair, its farmers poorly provided with blacksmiths and agricultural implements, and its citizens underemployed."[35] That means farm tools ranging from axes to shovels, rakes, sickles, scythes, plows, harrows, wheel bands, axles, harnesses, horseshoes—in short, everything used to create income from food products—depended on blacksmiths being at hand.

Blacksmiths were tinkerers, inventors who worked closely with farmers and other craftsmen. Many of the wide variety of axes developed during the eighteenth and nineteenth centuries were created by blacksmiths in response to local conditions. Solving immediate problems was a key element in the evolution of farming equipment. After the War of 1812 ended in 1815 (a stalemate with the British and Canadians and their Indian allies), advances in farming technology took off. Although books and journals were published in some numbers and agricultural societies were established, most of the changes came from farmers and allied blacksmiths in the field.[36] Knowledge of new techniques developed by practical application, trial and error was spread by word of mouth, smith to smith. They were part and parcel of an enduring American myth: "Yankee Ingenuity."[37]

Blacksmiths as the nation's toolmakers would pass into history, to become objects of nostalgic poetry and images. Mechanized production took their places as primary producers. The axe is an example. In 1826 Samuel W. and David C. Collins founded an axe-making company in Canton, Connecticut. The Farmington River provided power to their mill and local high-quality ores the iron and steel. Their employee Elisha Root invented a metal-shaving machine to avoid time-consuming hand grinding; new furnaces and tempering techniques were developed to create high-quality products. The axes were "uniform results at low cost, ensuring that pioneers could attack uniform tracts of geometrically laid out lots with an identical tool."[38] By the time Samuel Collins died in 1871 the company had produced fifteen million axes that were sold across the United States. There is perhaps no better way to see the trajectory of the American food industry than to observe that John Deere, a native Vermonter who moved to Illinois in 1836, was a blacksmith who repaired and made tools in the village of Grand Detour. There Deere invented a steel plow, literally the plow that broke the prairies and later the plains. America's commercial agricultural system now began.

MILLS

General Rufus Putnam, who led the foundation of Marietta, Ohio, was not only a surveyor but had also worked in his Massachusetts hometown as a millwright. Almost every early American town, village, or plantation had at least one mill; cities had many. Most were for food processing, others after the mid-eighteenth century were both for food and sawing lumber. If one were to make breads, cakes, and biscuits then grains had to be processed. In the case of corn that could mean soaking and grinding or allowing kernels to dry and then grinding them. For wheat, barley, and rye, grains had to be ground dry, then the chaff winnowed out and, in the case of wheat, the flour was bolted (filtered through screens or cloths, usually by hand, to remove unwanted "impurities"). In all cases, mills required mechanical knowledge and blacksmith skills to build them. Metal gudgeons used to reduce friction and wear on the end of shafts attached to the main wheel had to be made from the best wrought iron. Mills needed plenty of upkeep since parts wore out frequently. Numerous commentaries about communities link smiths and millers together as critical to economic success.

European colonists set up mills of various kinds from the start based on designs that they knew, designs that had been developed from antiquity

through the Middle Ages. The simplest water mills involved placing a vertical shaft with blades on it horizontally in a stream. Sets of millstones were
set above the shaft and grain fed into the stones for grinding. Called a Norse
mill, many a small village without sufficient water power used these. Vertical
water wheels—the picturesque Ferris wheel type—were more technologically advanced though as old as vertical mills. Here a large vertical wheel with
paddles with a horizontal axle through it was attached to a vertical shaft by
gearing. Although power was lost by transferring energy from the axle to
the shaft, it was more efficient than other kinds depending on how much
water passed over the wheel. Two major types of waterwheels appeared in
the Americas, the undershot and an overshot mill. In the first type water
passed under the wheel at its normal flow. These are not as powerful as
overshot wheels but cheaper to build and adequate in really swift streams.
Overshot mills meant constructing a dam and pond above the wheel and
then allowing pent-up, narrowly channeled water into the paddles. The
weight of the water drives the wheel with some force, perhaps double the
horsepower of an undershot wheel. Because of the force needed to cut
lumber most sawmills were overshots. The waterwheels that seem to be features on nostalgic depictions of rural landscapes were anything but; instead
they were symbols of land and river transformation. Now in place of beaver
dams with their small ecosystems there were millponds, millraces, and dams
to make them work.[39]

Mills on the Black River, 1818–29.

In the backcountry to which population increasingly flowed after the Revolutionary War, and especially to the Midwest after 1815, mills of various types were usually local and small. Horsemills were the dry land version of this kind of mill, only instead of water running through blades a draft animal walked in a circle around the vertical shaft to which grindstones were attached. Where water and wind were not feasible sources of power, muscle had to do. At least this method produced more flour with less effort than human-powered querns (usually women), and even querns were better than simple grinding stones and stone rubbers. Before much wheat could be planted, before enough forest could be chopped down and before the long grass prairies were cut, corn was the primary crop. Gristmills appeared everywhere, some horse- or, where possible, water-powered. The grits and corn flour from which johnnycake, hoe cakes, and other versions of cornbread were made came from the local mills. When the early settlers of the Ohio and other Midwestern river valleys sent their hogs and corn down the rivers to the Mississippi and ultimately to New Orleans, their cornmeal was ground in these mills. Even later in the nineteenth century when gristmills ramped up to economies of scale, local establishments remained to serve local communities.[40]

Windmills are similar in design to the vertical waterwheel and may have been modeled on them. The classic Dutch windmill, developed over several hundred years, is the familiar sail-powered setup with a horizontal axle attached by gears to a vertical shaft. The top part of the structure can be turned to face into the wind. Much later, in 1854, a Connecticut machinist named Daniel Halladay devised a steel-bladed windmill that was geared to the up and down motion required of a water pump. His patented device cleverly incorporated a piston system that slowed the sail's action, thus regulating the amount of water to be pumped. These were so successful, especially with Midwestern and western farmers, that Halladay's U.S. Wind Engine & Pump Company moved to Illinois, closer to its customer base, in 1857. By the 1880s it was the largest such company in the world. Used extensively in cattle feeding operations, no depiction of a western farm, as in the movie *The Wizard of Oz*, is without one of these windmills.[41]

Virginia's first wind-powered corn mill appeared in 1621 and by "1649 there were 5 water mills, 4 windmills, and a great number of horse-and-hand mills."[42] That was for a population estimated at 18,000 and was not enough to keep up with demand. Plimoth Plantation had a watermill by 1636, while in the Dutch colonies in New York and New Jersey windmills remained in use for many years. In areas where wheat production was an

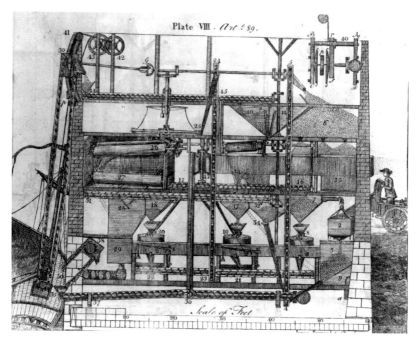

Oliver Evans's automated grain mill design for the works at Brandywine, Pennsylvania.

important part of economies mills were abundant. In 1800, Pennsylvania's Chester County, one of America's "Bread Colonies," had two hundred mills in an area of 20 by 30 miles. The whole state with 430,000 people had two thousand mills.[43] Pennsylvania produced fine white flour of the kind called for by Mrs. Randolph for her fancy baking. The flour could equally have come from Baltimore, where merchant millers flourished after the Revolution. Merchant millers were literally that, larger-scale producers who milled and sold grain in the commercial market. Baltimore's merchants, like New York's and Philadelphia's, sold hundreds of thousands of barrels overseas and supplied America's growing industrial cities.[44] Mrs. Randolph's cookery book was to be at the edge of America's food production revolution.

What made merchant milling really take off were the innovations of a mechanic of genius born in 1755, Oliver Evans. Milling was hard work and the results were not always uniform, as Mrs. Randolph says about barrels of flour. Most mills were two-story structures. Bags of grain or corn were hauled up to the top floor either carried by "sack boys" or by pulleys. The contents were poured in a chute that funneled the grain into the whirling millstones, where it was ground. Channels cut into the stones moved the ground matter outward to a wooden structure surrounding the stones, which then funneled the grain into a bin beneath them. Depending on the quality and speed of the millstones, there were varying amounts of bran and grit in the flour. The impurities were removed by bolting. Making finer flour meant removing not just the unwanted bran but the nutritious germ, because leaving the germ led to rancidity since it contained oils. Finer flour was bolted more than once and was the most highly prized.[45]

Hard wheat was more difficult to mill because the exterior husk was just as the name says, hard. Soft wheats were easier to process, though that is a relative term because milling itself was not easy. As for wheats, those such as the modern winter and spring hard reds were not in the Colonial grain inventory; they would come later, accompanied by new milling technologies. Rather, soft English wheats were the rule. Hard wheats have higher protein and gluten contents than soft varieties, so are much preferred for making bread in the modern era. Durum wheat is for pastas, but was not much grown in the United States before 1900. Soft wheats were and remain the choice for flatbreads, biscuits, pancakes, and the like. Colonial and post-colonial cookery books have bread recipes but not nearly so many as for sweet baking. Whether that was a function of the flour available at the time or the fact that sweet baking has always been the home cook's art is a question.

Milling was labor intensive, often backbreaking with all the lifting and bending, and dangerous because heavy millstones had to be regularly cleared on hot "middling" produced from grinding. Oliver Evans changed everything. A native of Delaware, Evans first worked on the most complex machines of his time, spinning frames and jennys. Working with his two miller brothers in Maryland, he decided to try automating the milling system. After seven years of trial and error he was able to build a model plant near Newark, Delaware, in 1784. The worst tasks of milling were automated, from moving grain by using a bucket system (much like that used in later mines and steel mills) to grain spreading and cooling, grinding more efficiently, and bolting. After resistance from traditional millers, the Ellicott family mill on the Patapsco River was rebuilt using the Evans system. The results were astounding. Making 32 barrels of flour a day while paying out $4,875 in annual wages reduced the cost of flour by 50 cents per barrel and saved a total of $32,500 ($808,000 in modern dollars).

When the u.s. Patent Office was established in 1790, Evans's mill design was the third patent given. Not long afterward the large milling concerns along Pennsylvania's Brandywine River adopted Evans's designs and the mills spread across the eastern United States. As Andrew Smith notes, the towns along the new Erie Canal all had these large mills, which were much taller than the old ones, to process local grain produced locally and from trade along a waterway that was critical to the nation's development.[46]

Evans went on to invent a high-pressure steam engine that revolutionized steam power, and later a fantastical mobile dredging machine that resembled an amphibious car. Evans worked with ideas that were being fully developed during his time. One was what Brooke Hindle called "the

The Mechanic.

JULY, 1834.

[For the Mechanic.]
STEAM-CARRIAGES.

[Evans' Steam-Engines. See page 196.]

HAVING traced the steam-engine from its first invention to the successful application of its power for the purpose of navigation, by Fulton, it now remains for us to continue the subject, by a brief history of its application to land-carriages on common roads, and its superior advantages on railways. Two individuals, in particular, are claimants for the honor of this invention, both of whom also claim the invention of steam-boats ; but as all claims to the invention

17

Oliver Evans's steam-powered amphibious vehicle design.

exhilaration of early American technology," the drive among so many early inventors to invent new things, to mechanically improve everything possible. Everything was done to fulfill potentials "simply because the potentials existed."[47] The potential for the new republic was the continent that Americans could overspread. With the beginnings of mass production and internal colonization, that meant using any and all resources available—to change everything because it was there to change. In a new rising consumer society, lower prices for everything including food was high on people's list of desires, though often at greater cost than they knew.

FIVE

Old Hickory's Big Cheese

The meadow was finely diversified by groves and clumps of trees, so happily dispersed, that they seemed as if set out by the hand of art . . . The whole had the appearance of a broad beautiful tract of pasture land, on the highly ornamented estate of some gentleman farmer, with his cattle grazing about the lawns and meadows.

Washington Irving, *A Tour on the Prairies* (1832)[1]

America's first internationally famous writer, Washington Irving, spent many years living in England and Spain (in the latter country as a diplomat). While living in London, his popular collection of short stories *The Sketch Book of Geoffrey Crayon, Gent.* was published by John Murray (the same publisher used by his friend Sir Walter Scott) and at the same time in his native New York. This is the collection with his most famous stories, "Rip Van Winkle" and "The Legend of Sleepy Hollow," among others. Unlike his great early satire, *A History of New-York from the Beginning of the World to the End of the Dutch Dynasty, by Diedrich Knickerbocker* (1809), and comedic as they are, these tales were well within the Romantic literary and visual arts canon. In America the Hudson River School of landscape painters pioneered by Thomas Cole showed dramatic landscapes of the wilderness. Cole exalted mountains and waterfalls, often in the dim lights of dawn or dusk, or in stormy weather, somewhat in the manner of England's J.M.W. Turner. American contemporaries such as George Inness, influenced by the great English landscape painter John Constable and the French Barbizon School, portrayed more bucolic scenes in which well-tended fields and placid cattle were common themes.[2]

In 1832 Irving had just returned from Europe and apparently was anxious to show American readers that he was one of them. Being a cultivated man, and famous raconteur, Irving knew the art world well. When he decided to see the American interior and meet with Native Americans who lived in a more "natural" state, images of his more tamed New York and Europe cannot have been far from his mind's eye. He wrote about broken, gullied country, the stuff of a Cole painting, as he traveled up the Arkansas River into what is today Oklahoma. It was the magnificent prairies that really captured him. While witnessing this "wild" bison land untouched by the plow and occupied by "uncivilized" Indians (actually Irving was always sympathetic to Native peoples), he imagined the land in its potential state: an estate.[3]

The estate was satirized by the great actor and impresario David Garrick and George Colman the elder in their play *The Clandestine Marriage* (1766). As Mr. Sterling described to Lord Ogleby, it was formed thus:

> The chief pleasure of a country house is to make improvements, you know, my Lord. I spare no expence, not I. This is quite another-guess sort of a place than it was when I first took it, my Lord. We were surrounded with trees. I cut down above fifty to make the lawn before the house, and let in the wind and the sun—smack-smooth—as you see.

Lord Ogleby was then offered a "sullabub warm from the cow."[4] Amusing as an overdone estate built by a comical parvenu was to English audiences of the time, this kind of tamed landscape was in the minds of English visitors to America in the first half of the nineteenth century.

English estates were also farms of an orderly kind, part of a rural economy that had been shifting from arable to grassland since the fifteenth century. Most Americans, Ichabod Crane notwithstanding, saw themselves as farmers, not country squires. Other things were at work, one of them the reality of pioneer farming. Charles Dickens, traveling by steamboat down the Ohio River in 1842, saw this near Big Grave Creek, an ancient Indian burial mound, in what is now Moundsville, West Virginia:

> At lengthened intervals a log cabin, with its little space of cleared land about it, nestles under a rising ground, and sends its thread of blue smoke curling up into the sky. It stands in the corner of the poor field of wheat which is full of great unsightly stumps, like earthy butchers'-blocks. Sometimes the ground is only just now cleared: the felled trees lying yet upon the soil: and the log-house only this morning begun. As we pass this clearing, the settler leans upon his axe or hammer, and looks wistfully at the people from

Washington Irving, celebrated author and inventor of fake folklore.

the world. The children creep out of the temporary hut, which is like a gipsy tent upon the ground, and clap their hands and shout.[5]

Dickens greatly disliked rough American ways, implicitly comparing Irving's imagined estate of which he approved to the real America that he saw.

Yet this rough clearing was improved land in the 1840s and was so long before that. To have an "improved" estate or farm, people had to have an idea about what progress was, though not every American had the same notion. No matter the dissident philosophies, a general consensus about what was to be done had always been there in American life: to wrest riches from the earth by whatever means necessary and using (Yankee) ingenuity to do it. The argument was just how to organize development of resources. From the 1790s to the 1860s, three generations at most, America underwent massive economic and social transformations. The process has been given a dramatic name, the Market Revolution. In terms of food production and technologies, it was the first of three linked "revolutions": the first from about 1790 or 1812 to 1860, the second as a result of the Civil War begun in 1861, and a third after about 1920 and further ramped up after the Second World War. Each was an amplification of the original, and all show major ideas that run through American life.

The term "Market Revolution" has several meanings. In one sense it means the remarkable change in America from pre-industrial localized economies to an industrialized and commercial system. Technical inventions that mechanized labor made these changes possible, notably John Deere's steel plow, Cyrus McCormick's reaper, Eli Whitney's cotton gin (although many better gins were actually to follow) and, most important, interchangeable parts, attributed to Whitney and Samuel Colt, for machines. Machinery made factories possible and with them came new forms of wage labor and new classes of Americans. Transportation systems were transformed with new canals, steamboats, railroads, and improved roads built almost everywhere. The market was regional, national, and international. In a money economy capital is necessary to make the system work, so banks became ever more important. With their lending practices came uncontrolled land speculation followed by boom-and-bust periods in roughly twenty-year cycles: the first notable one was in 1819. As Ralph Waldo Emerson wrote in 1839, "This invasion of Nature by Trade with its Money, its Credit, its Steam, its Railroad, threatens to upset the balance of man, & establish a new Universal Monarchy more tyrannical than Babylon or Rome."[6]

The term has taken on political and social meaning, especially with the publication of Charles Sellers's magisterial study *The Market Revolution: Jacksonian America, 1815–1846*.[7] Sellers explained how commercial agriculture as a dominant means of present-day food production meant the triumph of capitalism. Emerson succinctly states that this is not just an economic system but the social and political orders that arose from it. Three stages of the farm economy marked the change. Early pre-industrial or subsistence farming, milling, and the like was done for local communities by neighbors. Second, payments for goods and services with moneys of various kinds were long established in cities and towns along the coasts like Philadelphia and even on the interior rivers. The places were already linked to wide commercial networks. Backcountry farmers were pulled into commercial markets around 1815. Finally, the process accelerated until all economic activities became monetized: "the use-value world" of the subsistence farmer had been almost entirely supplanted by the "market world" within which Americans have lived ever since.[8]

Assuming that pure subsistence farming was the standard means of raising food, it would have been like the farms seen in Chapter Three, a world that gave rise to Amelia Simmons's recipes. In 1821 Englishman William Hall, traveling to his new home in Albion, Illinois, near the Wabash River, came across an old friend of his from England. Mr. Bishop had settled four miles from Pittsburgh. Bishop's estate was a half-mile of arable land along the Allegheny River:

> there are also great plenty of Pheasants Woodcocks & Partridges
> & some Turkeys he raises & makes almost everything he uses,
> his Woods afford him plenty of Maple Sugar [sold in markets for
> 4–6 cents a pound], his Sheep Wool which after being spun in
> the Family is manufactured into Cloth in the neighbourhood but
> for hardly any part of his produce can he obtain money which is
> very scarce in every part of America.[9]

Scarce money in 1821 was the result of the Bank Panic of 1819 and collapsing prices for American food and cotton, which Hall never noted. What caught his attention were lands that could have been made into "Villas" with glorious vistas and "smooth" landscapes. The hills around Pittsburgh were one location but spoiled by "smoke of the Houses & Manufactories prevented by the neighbouring hills from ascending beats down upon the Place & renders it the most disagreeable [*sic*] place of residence imaginable."[10]

Hall encountered something different en route to his new homestead. He stopped at Harmonie in Indiana (now called New Harmony), a German Pietist community founded by Johann Georg Rapp in 1814. The town was already thriving as the "Plain around it is the most fertile soil imaginable, & quite level & finely adapted for Cultivation they have also good artificial Meadows on the River [it had once been a beaver meadow]." Hall reported that "they have a Steam engine which drive a flour Mill, Cotton & Woolen factories & a sett of Grindstones, A Tannery, Distillery, Brewery,

Hat makers, Tinners, Turners &c a fine Blacksmiths shop with six forges, Wheelers Shop, very extensive Brick Yard, Carpenters, Masion & all mechanics workshop."[11] All of this had been accomplished within six years and was based on an earlier successful Harmony Society community called Economy, near Pittsburgh. Although these settlers were not doing large-scale monocropping for export, they were fully into forms of commercial food production.

Further into the backcountry of Illinois, Daniel Harmon Brush's life was on a similar path. As told in his 1888 memoir about life in southern Illinois, his family migrated from its poor Vermont farm to the Illinois River town of Bluffton in 1820 when Brush was seven years old. After a terrible bout of "fever 'n ager" (fever and ague, perhaps malaria, which was widespread among the river bottom communities—William Hall's family had the same affliction), the family worked the land as best they could. Like others in the small community they lived on what they could raise, hunt and gather in the woods and streams (lots of wild berries, persimmons, pawpaws), and barter. Once, the family was so hungry and weak from illness that they fell upon some ripe corn growing nearby:

> we could not grate as much meal day by day as would make as much pone and mush as we all wanted to eat. Nothing in my remembrance before or since has tasted so good as the bread and the mush thus acquired, nor do I forget the bootless hankering for more.[12]

A few years later, in his early teens Brush recalled having had to take the family corn on the sturdy horse his father had brought from Vermont 10 miles distant to the only gristmill in the vicinity. His memory of it, sixty years later, was

> getting home with the meal late in the evening, half frozen and hungry . . . but if a good mother had for her boy a cozy nook by a huge log fire and a warm supper of nice things, with perhaps a roasted prairie chicken or tender quail, hot and luscious, to satisfy the appetite on his return, the discomforts of the day would not long be remembered."[13]

A hundred and fifty years later, these very same dishes appeared on tables of the region's hunters and farmers. The old prairies are long gone

Karl Bodmer, view of the utopian community New Harmony, Indiana, on the Wabash River, 1839.

but there are still forests and streams. Older cooks and cookery books talk about wild berries and greens, and recipes for the same wild game including opossum, raccoon, muskrat, squirrel, deer, turkeys, and the now rare prairie chickens roasted with strips of lard. Catfish were in every stream to be "hogged," meaning taken by hand and often cooked right on the spot. Corn was and remained a staple, including ashcakes, hoecakes, corn pone, corn mush, and a host of other variations of cornmeal. The Brushes ate pokeweed salad, wild leeks, flagroot, Jerusalem artichokes, wild mushrooms, and many others that the original Native American knew well. It is a fading feast, as modern community cookbooks tell us, as thoroughly saturated as they are with food from major manufacturers. Even now some usually have a few old-time recipes that the early settlers of the interior rivers and prairies would recognize.[14]

At thirteen Brush wanted an education but did not have money for a school book and so:

> Pecans and hickory nuts abounded in the river woods. The trees were large in trunk, and of great height. Men would cut them down with axes and then assisted by the children gather the nuts, each retaining all he could pick up. Bushels were taken.[15]

131

Appalling as it may be that whole trees were cut just to get their nuts, that is how the land was used and young Brush learned the lesson. The young lad swapped his share for a Webster's Spelling book, thus beginning his school learning, a career in commerce and for-profit land development, and later the law. By the early 1830s, he owned a general store and was taking hogs specially raised for export and corn down to New Orleans by steamboat. In the next decade he moved further south to the new town of Murphysboro on the Big Muddy River, the better to take wheat, corn, and hogs down the great river. In 1852, he was a founder of the city of Carbondale as a center for the new Illinois Central railroad. The town was a depot where nearby farmers could load wheat, then fetching excellent prices, and carry fruit from the many orchards 320+ miles to Chicago. If anyone represents a shift from subsistence to commerce it was Daniel Harmon Brush and others like him in the American interior. Although not a farmer, Abraham Lincoln, living not too far away, was one who shared these ideas.

Across the great river in Missouri a similar society of small-scale farmers and shopkeepers was being established in the 1820 and '30s. Gottfried Duden, a German immigrant to the Missouri River area west of St. Louis, wrote a journal that is filled with enthusiasm about the prospects of settling in his part of the emerging Midwest. The land was cheap and fertile and every farmer tried to be as self-sufficient as possible.[16] His region of the state had another compelling feature, access to the Missouri River and its easy navigation to the Mississippi. No farm was ever truly self-sufficient and as settlements grew a network of trade developed to supply goods that could not be made at home. Where would coffee, tea, sugar, molasses, spices, decent cloth (much preferred to homespun), cookware, china, and tools come from if not from merchants who were supplied by river boats? Itinerant merchants on horseback were the first to reach the backcountry settlements and soon general stores were established in every settlement and town. At the local level farm women played a significant role in any family's income. Many sold eggs, beef, salt pork, chickens and turkeys, tallow, beeswax, butter, and cheeses. Making these took considerable time and effort, but they were necessary, even if they only sold for credit at the store. Since money was needed to buy goods, farmers like those at Harmonie and Blufton produced food for subsistence and more for sale down the river to larger markets. Richard L. Bushman has called these "composite farms" and makes the case that they were the origins of America's commercial farming industries.[17]

View of Cairo, Illinois, at the junction of the Ohio and Mississippi Rivers, 1854–7.

Here is what the Massachusetts-born minister Timothy Flint said about the commercial activity he saw in the Mississippi valley:

> From Kentucky, pork, flour, whiskey, hemp, tobacco, bagging, and bale-rope. From Tennessee there are the same articles, together with great quantities of cotton. From Missouri and Illinois, cattle and horses, the same articles generally as from Ohio, together with peltry and lead from Missouri. Some boats are loaded with corn in the ear and in bulk; others with barrels of apples and potatoes. Some have loads of cider, and what they call "cider, royal," or cider that has been strengthened by boiling or freezing. There are dried fruits, every kind of spirits manufactured in these regions, and in short, the products of the ingenuity and agriculture of the whole upper country of the west. They have come from regions, thousands of miles apart. They have floated to a common point of union.[18]

Except for small religious groups such as the Amish of Pennsylvania, America was settled and exploited by people who were caught up in world trade networks and therefore knew well about commerce, money, and forms of capitalism. The long-standing slave trade in return for cotton, molasses, wood, and other raw materials is an example. From the 1750s,

Europe was unable to feed itself and relied increasingly upon American wheat, flour, beef, and pork. As wheat prices rose in response, more farmers at ever greater distances from the market discovered that they could profitably enlarge their marketable surplus despite the high cost of transportation. Between 1772 and 1819, the profitable wagoning distance for wheat doubled to over one hundred miles. A wheat exporting belt spread from the lower Connecticut to the lower James and inland to Virginia's lower Shenandoah valley.[19]

There was very good reason for Oliver Evans to invent new high-volume flour mills and for the millers of the Brandywine to build them. The continental interior after the War of 1812 was fully opened to American settlement—after crushing the Native peoples—and before long was filled with entrepreneurial types such as Mr. Brush who farmed for cash.

Composite farming became more specialized in the early to mid-nineteenth century, starting with the eastern states. Wheat in New York State and Pennsylvania was a major cash crop, as it was almost everywhere, and Pennsylvania was the largest producer of hay in the nation. In the age of horsepower, hay production was crucial to keeping an economy going. In Vermont and Massachusetts, wheat yields declined, farmers migrated westward where soils were far better and those who remained turned to sheep and cattle rearing on their upland farms. Dairy products became more important, with cheese a specialty from the 1840s to the present day. As American cities grew, composite farmers sold produce to them either directly in markets or through wholesalers. Boston, as an example, grew from 25,000 in 1800 to 178,000 in 1860. Direct-to-customer open air markets, such as the Haymarket (1830) and Faneuil Hall Market, supplied urban dwellers at reasonable costs. American cities in the nineteenth century and into the twentieth were urban cores ringed with small composite farms. These mostly disappeared under urban sprawl in the twentieth century.

The American south also underwent a "Market Revolution" that magnified social differences. Cotton, tobacco, rice, and indigo (the latter two on the Carolinas coast) were always export crops. They were the prime ingredients for a slave-worked plantation system that developed in the American south in the seventeenth century. The plantation model was imported from the Caribbean sugar colonies, especially Barbados. Owners and slaves came to South Carolina where new estates were established complete with harsh slave codes. Meanwhile in the backcountry, from the piney woods and Gulf Coast flatlands, up into Appalachia, small farmers were far more like the early settlers of the Midwest. The foods mentioned above in southern Illinois and Indiana applied to much of Tennessee, Kentucky, and further south along the Mississippi River. In many ways it was closer to the diets of the enslaved peoples. Plantation food differed considerably from both in preparation and quality.

There has been some debate about whether the slave system would have withered away in the South; Thomas Jefferson thought that it would and George Washington manumitted his slaves upon his death in 1799.[20] Popular history has it that the plantation system we know from popular culture, such as the repellent novel and film *Gone with the Wind*, was revived by the invention and patenting by Eli Whitney of the revolutionary saw cotton gin (gin being short for "engine") in 1794. Cotton production for export boomed; by 1820 about 60 percent of all cotton used in the British textile industry came from the American south. Cotton drew the south fully into the commercial system. In reality, there were earlier versions of cotton processing machinery called roller gins. Southern planters had experimented with them throughout the eighteenth century, even harnessing windmills to larger ones.[21] They also introduced new varieties of long staple cotton from the southwest and Mexico called "upland cotton."

Eli Whitney's first cotton gin.

Cider and Champaigne: Election of 1840

The presidential campaign of 1840 has been described as the
first carnival campaign, the first drunken election and the first
modern election campaign. All are true. Martin Van Buren's
presidency began under the cloud of a great depression in 1837
as a result of his predecessor Andrew Jackson's intemperate
economic policies. People were angry over unemployment that
they blamed on elites and were incensed that Van Buren seemed
indifferent to their plight. The opposition Whig party settled
on William Henry Harrison, a member of Congress from near
Cincinnati. Their strategy was to portray Harrison as a down-
home man of the people from rural America, as opposed to
the supposedly snobby insider, Van Buren. Harrison lived in a
log cabin, they said, and drank hard cider just like "real folks."
Newspapers in that era were organs of political parties; the
first issue of the Ohio Whig paper, the *Log Cabin*, pictured what
was supposed to be Harrison's cabin complete with a barrel of
cider in front of it. Van Buren, they claimed, dined on fancy
French food at the White House, with oysters on the menu
every day, eaten with golden spoons. The "Golden Spoon
Oration" in the House of Representatives by Pennsylvania
congressman Charles Ogle described what he considered to be
the excesses of Van Buren's administration—taking three days
to do it. He called the White House a "Presidential Palace,"
that outdid even "the grand saloons at Buckingham Palace."
Upon the President's table stood turtle soup, roasted capons
and duck with fancy sauces, pâtés and foie gras, complex desserts and, horror of horrors, champagne. No, said Ogle, Van

Variations were developed by experimentation in the different ecological
niches of the south. The result was a nearly universally grown high-yield
cotton that could be grown in most locales from drier uplands to humid
lowlands.[22] Plantation owners who developed the new cotton varieties
were entrepreneurs who worked for large-scale commercial production in
a planned rational way and they intended to expand their cotton domains
across the new lands to the west. The labor was provided by slaves of

Buren was not a true American because he never dined upon hog and hominy or settled down to fried meat and gravy and hard cider. Harrison, Americans were told, did.

Not for the first or last time, lies filled the air. Harrison was not a county bumpkin but instead the educated scion of a distinguished Virginia family. Raised in wealth, he had been made secretary of the Northwest Territory in 1798 and governor of the Indiana Territory (1801–12). There he fought a skirmish with the Indian leader Tecumseh in 1811, which battle gave him his election nickname and famous slogan: "Tippecanoe and Tyler, Too." His Ohio mansion, not a log cabin, sat amid fields in which he took an active interest. Like Jefferson and Washington before him, Harrison was interested in agricultural improvement. But his election handlers would have none of the country gentleman. Instead they put on a raucous campaign holding huge rallies of as many as sixty thousand people. Aside from the hoopla attendant upon supporters rolling logs from town to town and also a 10-ft-tall ball made of paper and tin, the campaign served barrel upon barrel of hard cider and bottles of whiskey. So popular was the log cabin theme that the Philadelphia distillery E. C. Booz created log cabin bottles for the grand parties. Log-rolling, getting the ball rolling and booze (an older Dutch word reinforced by the distiller) became parts of the American vocabulary. More important, for the first time food became the marker of social class, an ongoing cultural symbol to be played upon by politicians and marketers ever since.

African origin and descent who were treated as machines that powered the system. Slavery was never going to disappear because it was too profitable and because of the social system that made it seem indispensable to the masters.[23]

Food and farming have always been tied to politics. Farming economics alone was and remains a driver of political decision making and arguments about policies. Until 1900 agriculture was the United States' main exports, never less than 75 percent of the total. Much of the export trade was in cotton, close to 60 percent by 1860. With a dramatically increasing population, from about 4 million in 1790 (90 percent of them in farming) to 76 million in 1900, America's internal market became more valuable than its exports. Who owned the land and what was done with it lay at the heart of economic cycles and sociopolitical conflicts. Sellers's *The Market Revolution* is really about politics based on agricultural production and centered in the presidency of Andrew Jackson. As he said, contentiously and maybe better applied to the early twentieth century, "democracy was born in tension with capitalism, and not as its natural and legitimizing political expression."[24]

In standard American histories two main political parties express this tension. The Federalists, later Whigs, are seen as the business or capitalist party. They called for ordered progress toward building a new nation with governmental action to aid business and individuals. The nation would be one of neat fields and meadows linked by canals and new railroads with industrial towns at end points. In political terms progress was to be guided by business elites and later corporations, that is, people whose accumulated wealth allowed them to build estates—and splendid urban mansions. The Republican-Democrats, later the plain Democratic Party, were a party of democratic revolution where individuals could make their own self-governing communities. Although founded by an aristocratic slave owner, Thomas Jefferson, they became the party of often rowdy central-government-averse people, the pioneer farmers of the west, the small (mostly non-slave owning) landholders in the South, and the laboring folks in the new factory towns of the northeast. Improvement for them meant something else: the freedom to do as they chose no matter how disordered the economic and physical landscape. Though a grossly simplified description (for instance, the great slaveholders of the South were Democrats who feared intrusion by federal government on their economic "rights"), this tension runs through American history in many forms. In a way, the modern sustainable farming movement is a reaction to commodity, meaning capitalist, farming, a deliberate return to what is seen as "democratic" values though often cloaked in terms of health and environmental issues.

Food has always been a way to express political opinions and ideologies. Metaphors and images are common but so is physical food itself. Republican-Democrats often depicted Whigs as dining at elaborately set tables eating dishes loaded with fancy sauces and even with forks. Good old yeoman farmers and laborers made do with cornbread, plainly roasted meats, plenty of apple cider, and cheese. Cheeses, very big cheeses, were edible symbols of sociopolitical differences among Americans. On New Year's Day 1802 a wagon pulled up to the door of the White House bearing a present for President Thomas Jefferson. It was the world's largest cheese, 4 ft across, 18 in. high and weighing 135 lb. It had been made in the late summer of 1801 by the women of Cheshire, a small community in the western backcountry of Massachusetts. Led by a charismatic preacher named John Leland, these were Baptists resolutely opposed to the hierarchical religious and political establishment of Massachusetts, so they set to work to celebrate the electoral victory of the more populist Republican-Democratic Party. The milk of nine hundred cows was turned into curd which was put into a huge vat set on a cider press, salted, then turned in the Cheddar style into a big block of cheese. So large was the creation and so poor were the roads that it could only be moved by sleds over snow and ice in wintertime. It went down the Hudson River by boat to New York City where it was viewed by throngs of people, then to Baltimore and on to Washington, DC. Jefferson stood in the doorway welcoming this rare thing and was pleased by the message attached to it:

> The Cheese was not made by his Lordship, for his sacred Majesty; nor with a view to gain dignified titles or lucrative offices; but by the personal labour of free-born farmers (without a single slave to assist) for an elective President of a free people . . . Sir, we had some thought of impressing some significant inscription on the Cheese; but we have found such inconveniency in stamps on paper, that we chose to send it in a plain Republican form.[25]

Jefferson's Federalist opponents ridiculed the cheese in their newspapers, calling it a "Mammoth" cheese that would soon be filled with maggots and that only Republican-Democratic rats would eat (since there is no special record of the cheese, presumably that is what happened to a lot of it). One satirical poem said, "Their cow-born monster [was fit] for a nobler use, Than just to stuff the Presidential sack."[26] "Mammoth" was meant as a joke because Jefferson was a famous naturalist who had argued with European colleagues that American fauna were larger (and presumably better) than Old World ones. Only the year before with Jefferson's help the bones of a mammoth had been unearthed and put on display at Charles Willson Peale's Museum, America's first natural history museum. One wit in western Massachusetts proposed that the ladies of Lenox, Massachusetts make a mammoth apple pie, 15 ft across and 4,800 lb in

weight, to accompany the colossal cheese: "the Apple Pye ought therefore to weigh at least forty-eight hundred as Mr. Jefferson, unless he has
a Mammoth appetite for Cheese, will want four pounds of Pye to one of
Cheese."[27] Inadvertently perhaps, the opposition press had hit on an ever
compelling American idea, bigness as better in every way.

The party of the people took up the theme with gusto in more than
one way. In the spring of 1804 the official baker of the Navy prepared a
Mammoth Loaf of bread said to accompany the last of the great cheese.
Dressed to the nines, the Navy bakers carried it into the Capitol where it
was set in a Senate committee room. Plenty of roast beef, whiskey, and hard
cider were on hand. Jefferson, usually seen as an effete diner and dressed in
a plain old coat, mingled with a large crowd of ordinary people. As a critic
said, they were "people of all classes & colors from the President of the
United States to the meanest vilest Virginia slave." The President pulled
out a pocket knife, sliced off a hunk of beef and bread and ate them on the
spot, washed down with liquor. The "mob" merrily joined in and spent the
rest of the day partying. The event was part of the administration's campaign to raise money for the Navy to fight the infamous Barbary pirates,
but it was a populist celebration and a rude one at that.[28]

Thirty years later, the purported populist president supreme, Andrew
Jackson, whose nickname was Old Hickory for his toughness, was also
the recipient of a great cheese. At the end of his second term in office on
New Year's Day 1836, Jackson was presented with an even bigger cheese
than Jefferson's: 2 ft thick, 11 ft in circumference, and weighing 1,400 lb.
Col. Thomas S. Meacham, a prosperous dairy farmer with lands in Salt
Creek near Lake Ontario and north of Syracuse, New York, created it in the
summer of 1835. He also made several 750 lb cheeses for prominent political
leaders. Local citizens at Meacham's suggestion made the cheese a gift from
"the whole people of the State of New York." It was so big that a special vat
using 24 staves, representing each state in the Union, was made to carry
it. Meacham, a colonel in the War of 1812, was a Whig, not a Democratic
supporter of Jackson, but he was a patriot. On the cheese was a banner
12 ft long and 7 ft wide, handsomely painted with the motto: "The National
Belt: The Union it must be Preserved." Twenty-four gold stars and a dedi-
cation to President Andrew Jackson followed. Not lacking ego, Jackson was
pleased if for no other reason than the phrase about the Union was his own
toast (one of 24) given at the White House Jefferson Day dinner in 1830.[29]

Accompanied by a grand procession, the cheese (and its smaller
fellows) was sent by boat down Lake Ontario to Oswego, thence by the

Andrew Jackson in a formal heroic political pose.

decade-old Erie Canal down to New York City. In cities along the way, the grand creation was admired by throngs who cheered the patriotic sentiment on the banner, as was done in the great city itself. From there, the Mammoth was taken by boat to Philadelphia, then to Baltimore and finally up the Potomac River to Washington where the President accepted it and offered up bottles of wine from the White House cellar.[30] The cheese sat in the vestibule until February 22, 1837 when on George Washington's birthday the White House was opened to the public for the last levee (party). A large crowd from across the social spectrum came to take and eat whatever portions of the now very ripe cheese they wanted. One writer described coming to the threshold to encounter "an atmosphere, to which the mephitic gases over Avernus must be faint and innocuous." The dense crowd stood around the "fragrant gift" without even a cracker or drink and within two hours had consumed all but a tiny portion left for the President.[31] The stench of rotted cheese remained in the White House for some months, requiring all the drapes and furniture aired out and the walls whitewashed to remove "an odor which is pleasant only when there is not much of it." Bigness has its downsides.

The mammoth cheeses were embodiments of emerging American ideas and the politics that arose from them. Jefferson's cheese was made by supporters of his ideas of personal liberty, equality of opportunity, and national union in a time of political conflicts. Jackson's Bank War against rich men who ran the nation's early (and private) central banking system in alliance with the Whig-led government was one of them. The longer-standing clash was between the slave-owning plantation owners of the South who ran their political systems and northern free farmers, entrepreneurial manufacturers, and social reformers. The North feared southern secession, something they had threatened in 1832. Jackson promised military action against South Carolina, hence his support by the nationalistic Col. Meacham and others. It was as if to say literally one big cheese, one great nation, but made by America's "humble members of society—the farmers, mechanics, and laborers," as Jackson put it. Too bad his sympathies, or at least antipathy for moneyed elites, did not extend to African American slaves or Native Americans.

The propaganda around Jackson was that he was a man of the common people, a product of the backwoods, rough and ready, just as his White House events supposedly were. Although he was poor as a youth, Jackson became a country gentleman and lawyer whose home, The Hermitage, in Nashville in the then still frontier state of Tennessee was nothing less than an estate with rolling lawns and pleasant gardens. Like other Southern plantation owners, he was a businessman and slave owner who raised cotton and wheat for an external market.[32] After his death, his heir Andrew Jackson, Jr. (his nephew by marriage) cut back on the cotton in favor of a more market-stable cash cow: dairy. In 1850 the Hermitage produced 1,000 lb of butter, and likely cheese as well.[33]

Just as Jackson embodies contradictions in American ideas, so his taste in food reflects ongoing themes and tensions. His preference seems to have been a mélange of common foods of the country South—some African-Caribbean influenced such as rice and beans (hoppin' john)—corn cakes and the like, and high-class European-influenced preparations. The same combination could be found in many upscale hotel dining rooms such as

The great cheese levee at Andrew Jackson's White House event.

the Briggs House in still raw Chicago, with plainly cooked meats (and few vegetables) appearing alongside such dishes as Quail Pie French Style on a Pedestal, and Bread of Fat Goose Livers, à la Richelieu washed down with good French and German wines.[34]

Jackson's White House dinners were as refined as any of his day yet sprinkled with down-home dishes: "Spiced round of tenderloin with mini biscuits and jezebel sauce; hot water corn cakes with caramelized onions & squash relish, roasted lamb chops with rosemary, hoppin' John, cheese and grapes, benne wafers, floating islands and mini-custard tarts." He had a French chef, a good stock of French wines and had the finest French china and silver available, all set forth by a full staff of slave servants.[35] Since Thomas Jefferson's day White House meals had become rituals of status identity. President James Madison's brilliant wife, Dolley, put on elaborate French-inspired dinners for guests who were honored to attend. On February 20, 1804 a congressman, the Reverend Manasseh Cutler of Connecticut, found unfamiliar dishes at the President's table:

> An excellent dinner. The round of beef of which the Soup was made called "Bouilli." It had in the dish spices and Garlic kind, and a rich gravy . . . The Dessert good; much as usual [perhaps ice

cream for which Mrs. Madison was famous] except two dishes which appeared like Apple pie, in the form of the half of a Muskmelon, the flat side down, tops creased deep, and the color a dark brown.[36]

Bouilli was likely boeuf à la mode, not the modern French and Creole boiled dish, while the dessert resembles a steamed or baked pudding perhaps made with molasses. Jackson might have loved some country dishes but made by trained professional chefs. Their cookery was used as symbols of power and as such shows how food was layered, from the haute cuisine of the elites to the humble fare of Jackson's slaves and the vast majority of working Americans.[37] The White House was and is an estate with a famous manicured sward.

There is considerable literature on Andrew Jackson and the era to which his name has been attached. Studies picture him as the most "democratic" of presidents, who followed Jeffersonian principles that the majority of citizens should have control of their own lives and political systems. Others think him a rank opportunist, a humbug and much worse.[38] As mentioned, Jacksonian America was the era of the Market Revolution when food production was just beginning its journey to mass production by fully capitalist businesses. Most farmers were commodity producers or, like Jackson, semi-capitalists. Farmers of the era sold their commodity crops to middlemen who in turn either processed the food or sold it in markets. When farmers hired help, or perhaps used slave labor, they became semi-capitalists, or in American terms, "self-made men." Plantations were different, certainly businesses interested in profit but more like ancient Roman *latifundia*.[39] Perhaps this is what Jackson meant when he wrote: "Equality of talents, of education, or of wealth can not be produced by human institutions. In the full enjoyment of the gifts of Heaven and the fruits of superior industry, economy, and virtue, every man is equally entitled to protection by law."[40]

American's egalitarian ideals had to be displayed in public even if not self-consciously and even if not in reality. The impressive cheese processions were one form of food-related presentation, public dining another. Histories of American food and culture almost always discuss early American dining habits as seen by European visitors. These are amusing tales, some worth repeating if for no other reason than to show that deep in Americans' cultural heart coarse food and rude dining mean authenticity.

Back in 1768, Charles Woodmason, an Anglican minister, traveled into the backcountry of North Carolina intending to minister to the stubbornly independent Scots-Irish Presbyterians who had settled the region. What he found disgusted him. Wooden trenchers and wooden mugs, accompanied by hunting or scalping knives and big spoons, provided table settings, tables themselves rough wooden trestles. There were only two meals a day, breakfast and midday, but the food, "and their Provisions I could not touch—All the Cookery of these People being exceeding filthy, and most execrable." Everything was washed down with corn liquor; even children were given it with a little sugar. He met a poor woman in the Waxaw District (Andrew Jackson's native region; he was born the year before Woodmason's visit) who offered hospitality:

> having nor made what could be called a Meal for some days—
> Nothing but Indian Corn Meal to be had Bacon and Eggs in
> some Places—No Butter, Rice, or Milk—As for Tea and Coffee
> they know it not. These people are all from Ireland, and live
> wholly on Butter, Milk, Clabber [the fresh ancestor of cheese]
> and what in England is given to the Hogs and Dogs.[41]

Not that these folks made a display of dining rusticity; they were just poor. Even if there was more food by the early nineteenth century,

"Hillbilly Hot Dogs," Cabell County, West Virginia—affectionately derisory image of the backcountry Appalachian folk described by Charles Woodmason.

ordinary Americans ate it in much the same ways as the old Carolinians. In 1827 Frances (Fannie) Trollope, the later well-known English author and mother of a more famous one (Anthony Trollope), came to America seeking her fortune as an hotelier in Cincinnati. On the steamship going up the Mississippi from New Orleans, she soon discovered a carpet made filthy with spittle and wrote, "Let no one who wishes to receive agreeable impressions of American manners, commence their travels in a Mississippi steam boat; for myself, it is with all sincerity I declare, that I would infinitely prefer sharing the apartment of a party of well conditioned pigs to the being confined to its cabin." Food was often not much better: hard venison and peach sauce, and hung beef, chipped up raw, were ubiquitous.[42]

Trollope was an astute observer of people and attitudes, only more blunt than her contemporary Jane Austen. At another dinner event she noted:

> The total want of all the usual courtesies of the table, the voracious rapidity with which the viands were seized and devoured, the strange uncouth phrases and pronunciation; the loathsome spitting, from the contamination of which it was absolutely impossible to protect our dresses; the frightful manner of feeding with their knives, till the whole blade seemed to enter into the mouth; and the still more frightful manner of cleaning the teeth afterwards with a pocket knife, soon forced us to feel that we were not surrounded by the generals, colonels, and majors of the old world; and that the dinner hour was to be anything rather than an hour of enjoyment.[43]

Like others, Mrs. Trollope was appalled by the speed with which Americans ate. Captain James Edward Alexander of the 42nd Royal Highlanders, visiting Andrew Jackson's adopted hometown Nashville in 1831, reported:

> No ceremony was used; each man helped himself with his own knife and fork, and reached across his neighbour to secure a fancied *morceau*. Bones were picked with both hands; knives were drawn through the teeth with the edge to the lips; the scalding mocha and souchong were poured into saucers to expedite the cooling ... Beefsteaks, apple tart and fish, were seen on the same plate the one moment, and had disappeared the next![44]

Contemporary cartoon of Mrs. Frances Trollope with three of her children in Cincinnati, 1832.

"Diners bolted their food 'as if it were their last meal,' then arose from the table, and 'Wiping their mouths with the heel of their hand,' strode into the bar for a drink and a plug of chewing tobacco."[45]

Superstar author Charles Dickens travelled to America in 1842 to meet his adoring admirers. On a canal boat to Pittsburgh:

> everybody sat down to the tea, coffee, bread, butter, salmon, shad, liver, steak, potatoes, pickles, ham, chops, black-puddings, and sausages, all over again. Some were fond of compounding this variety, and having it all on their plates at once. As each gentle-man got through his own personal amount of tea, coffee, bread, butter, salmon, shad, liver, steak, potatoes, pickles, ham, chops, black-puddings, and sausages, he rose up and walked off.

Earlier he had met one of these passengers: "'Will you try,' said my opposite neighbour, handing me a dish of potatoes, broken up in milk and butter, 'will you try some of these fixings?'"[46]

Common Americans ate plain food quickly and without polite table conversation. Cultivated Britons expected long meals with wine, witty repartee, and mixed company. Mrs. Trollope remarked on a meal she had with the better sort in Cincinnati at a Washington Day ball. A large room was filled with elegantly dressed men and beautiful young women. One

Beer

If cheese and cider were common fare, so was beer. Beers of various strengthes were widely made and consumed, often as a substitute for polluted water. Americans consume about 640 million gallons of beer each year. Almost 90 percent of it is made by eleven breweries, making beer a model for what happens when a comestible is subject to industrialization and modern business systems. Most early beers were made by tavern owners or at home using whatever ingredients were available. Others, for example in New Amsterdam, later New York, were Dutch- and English-style ales. German immigrants began brewing early in the nineteenth century: the oldest continuous brewery is that founded by David G. Yuengling in 1829 in Pottsville, Pennsylvania. A new kind of German beer appeared in the 1840s, made by John Wagner in Philadelphia and Adam Lemp in St. Louis, soon followed by the still existing F. & M. Schaefer Brewing Company in New York in 1842. Lighter, sparkling brews called pilsner (from the Bohemian town of Pizeň where it was invented) that used hops and special yeasts became popular after the Civil War, many of them made by German and other central European immigrants. Anheuser-Busch in St. Louis, Pabst, Schlitz, Blatz and Miller in Milwaukee, Stroh's in Detroit, and Coors of Colorado all date to the period. By 1873 there were more than four thousand brewers in the country. Despite the influx of beer-drinking European immigrants from the 1880s to 1920, the number of breweries declined as large breweries figured out ways to ship refrigerated beers, bought up smaller makers, or commissioned local breweries to make their beers. Consolidation lowered brewery numbers to about 1,500.

Prohibition damaged but did not kill beer-making; about 750 operations were left intact. Americans drank it up, especially after the Second World War when production soared. Canned beer became widespread and with it local brewery numbers nosedived. National and regional advertising for canned beer by big breweries blotted out locals because they could not compete on price. A few remained in business because of their perceived quality, including Rolling Rock in Pennsylvania, Wisconsin's Leinenkugel (now owned by Miller-Coors) and Steven's Point, and Anchor Brewing in San Francisco. By the 1970s, American consumers were beginning to receive European beers and had drunk them in Europe and in Mexico. Founded mainly by Germans, Mexican beers were higher quality than American national brands. Like the growing appreciation for fine wines, a segment of the American drinking public wanted more flavorful beers: the common epithet for national beers was "brewed through a horse." Anchor Steam beer, followed by the first microbrewery, New Albion in Sonoma, California, in 1973, set off the microbrewery movement. In the forty years since, microbreweries, brewpubs, and small- to medium-scale breweries have sprung up across the country: of the 3,400 beer and ale makers now operating, about 1,900 are small craft breweries. Most use traditional ingredients such as malted barley and hops, creating different styles of beer such as wheat-based products, and often vary flavorings to distinguish themselves. As tastes change, especially among younger beer drinkers, so have styles. Heavily hopped India Pale Ales are particularly popular, a beverage that no long-time Budweiser or Miller Lite drinker would touch. Despite craft breweries' large numbers and growing customer base, the big brewers still dominate the market as their low prices and penchant for buying up smaller breweries rolls on.

particular lovely whom Trollope had met previously at a prestigious private school was absent. Asking her host why this bright young person who attended the same school as the society ladies was missing, she was told: "'You do not yet understand our aristocracy,' he replied; 'the family of Miss C. are mechanics . . . He [her father] is a mechanic; he assists in making the articles he sells; the others call themselves merchants.'"[47] The same ordinary people Jackson addressed who lived by the manual arts were deemed lesser than those who dealt in goods and money in this class-conscious society. Jackson knew his voters well.

And it was a masculine world, for at the ball the gentlemen retired to a bounteous table in another room,

> while the poor ladies had each a plate put into their hands . . . shortly afterward servants appeared, bearing trays of sweetmeats, cakes, and creams. The fair creatures then sat down on a row of chairs placed round the walls, and each making a table of her knees, began eating her sweet, but sad and sulky repast. The effect was extremely comical.[48]

For this pioneering feminist and anti-slavery advocate (her books on the subject influenced Harriet Beecher Stowe's incendiary *Uncle Tom's Cabin*), lacking the leavening effects of women, men were self-absorbed, gloomy, and devoid of conversational skills. Americans were, in short, uncivilized, crass, and above all mercenary. In a much repeated quote the French visitor Alexis de Tocqueville, whose study of American government and ideas *Democracy in America* (1835–40) remains relevant today, said, "As one digs deeper into the national character of the Americans, one sees that they have sought the value of everything in this world only in the answer to this single question: how much money will it bring in?"[49]

In such a world, what does dining mean except to fill a belly and to make one ready to do business? Frances Trollope and other writers did not like Americans in general not just because of their personal habits but for their attitudes. She wondered that if they

> were indeed the true patriots they call themselves, they would surely not incrust themselves in the hard, dry, stubborn persuasion, that they are the first and best of the human race, that nothing is to be learned but what they are able to teach, and that nothing is worth having which they do not possess.[50]

This is the certainty of the Jacksonians, perhaps an inkling as to Americans' long attachment to rude food. The swells, snobs, the Cincinnati (and elsewhere) merchants might dine daintily, like ladies perhaps, but real Americans did it their way, the only way. It is an idea with a long life in American culture.

Mammoth cheese says something about the food of the common folks and the changing market economy. From the Colonial period well into the nineteenth century cheese was made in farmhouses by women, just as it had been in England and the Netherlands, where American cheese techniques originated. Cheeses are mentioned frequently in writings, not as a privileged food but as accompaniments to meals or snacks while working or traveling. As a drollery, a group of New York literary lights led by James Fenimore Cooper formed a lunch group in 1824 called the Bread and Cheese Club. What that meant was humble feed for not so humble writers. It also referred to the popular notion of quaint old Dutchmen who were well known for eating bread and Dutch cheese on their stoops. As for cheese, anyone up for membership who found cheese on his plate was rejected. Such was cheese's reputation at the time. In the club's first two years, they met at "the restaurant of Abigail Jones, a popular colored cook of the city, whose establishment was located at 300 Broadway."[51] Jones was listed in city directories until 1828 as a pastry cook. Like cheese, baking was women's work.

In composite farming cheese making was a sideline to most farmers' main activities but an increasingly valuable asset to a family income. As in the Missouri examples, women raised poultry and sold eggs in nearby markets, doing the same for butter and cheeses. Early products were inconsistent because milk production was seasonal, cows did not produce a great deal of milk, and techniques such as making good rennet were not always observed. By the nineteenth century American cheeses were being named by English style along with using better techniques.[52] Cheshire was initially the popular style, superseded by what would become the mainstay of American cheeses, Cheddar. A scalded, salted and pressed cheese, Cheddar kept better than Cheshire and so was transportable not only to Washington, DC, but by ship to the Caribbean and England. Cheese making, still in women's hands, shifted from New England to New York, Pennsylvania, and Ohio in the first third of the nineteenth century for ecological reasons: better grasslands, more open meadows, more and better cows—presenting bucolic scenes as on English estates, but with the women farmers more like those in a painting by Jean-François Millet.

Van Camp's Pork and Beans advertisement using the "Old Dutch New York" image created by Washington Irving for commercial purposes, early 20th century.

By the Jacksonian era American cheesemakers were making roughly 100 million lb of cheese a year. It was hard work, again women's work.[53] Agricultural publications often gave directions for cheese making. The *Genesee Farmer and Gardener's Journal* of 1835 discusses every phase of farmhouse cheese making, starting with what time of year to milk, its quality and the proper temperature for the task. It also has directions for the rennet used to curdle the milk: calves' stomach with its digestive juices, here mixed with sweet herbs, bottled and so storable in a cool place for about a year. Once the raw cheese was mixed with yellow annatto coloring, it was placed in a tight hoop and pressed under 200-lb weights. The cheese was rubbed with salt and covered, sometimes with lard but by this time with cloths. Each cheese had to be turned and rubbed four times a day to keep mold from growing.[54] The yellow coloring caused American cheeses exported to Britain (as land restriction made dairy farming less viable there) to be called "yellow cheese." In the United States these now generic Cheddars were simply called "American" cheese. Small cheeses could be handled by one or two women and mammoth cheeses by a whole town full of people, but what of the 500-lb cheeses awarded prizes at the Genesee Fair in 1854?[55]

That prize was given to Jesse Williams who lived in nearby Oneida County, New York. Williams had an idea that if he and neighboring farmers pooled their milk they could produce more cheese that was both cheaper and, if in one facility, better. In 1851, he began buying milk and making what turned out to be prize-winning products. Williams is usually credited with beginning the first cheese factory. That is not exactly the case since farmers in the 1840s as far away as Wisconsin were described as having cheese factories. What Williams did was to divorce cheese-making functions from the farmhouse and individual family. Working in something like manufacturing buildings he was able to make considerable quantities using specialized labor. In 1860 Williams produced almost 100,000 lb of cheese. In the process, he had become a semi-capitalist as had others in the Market Revolution.

Humble though it was, cheap cheese was one of the many food products that transformed the new American mass market. Williams and others like him recognized the driving economic principle: make it fast, make a lot of it, and sell it as cheaply as possible. In the case of cheese, women lost their artisanal roles as cheesemakers as the business came to be dominated by men. The same can be said for other foods as well. No matter what the final result, food had to come from farms and in order to have abundance the land and animals upon it had to be transformed.

SIX

Grass and Animals

One of my nooks is south of the barn, and here I am sitting now, on a log,
still basking in the sun, shielded from the wind. Near me are the cattle,
feeding on corn-stalks. Occasionally a cow or the young bull (how handsome
and bold he is!) scratches and munches the far end of the log on which I
sit. The fresh milky odor is quite perceptible, also the perfume of hay from
the barn. The perpetual rustle of dry corn-stalks, the low sough of the
wind round the barn gables, the grunting of pigs, the distant whistle of a
locomotive, and occasional crowing of chanticleers, are the sounds.

Walt Whitman, *Specimen Days*[1]

Walt Whitman liked cattle, at least the image of cattle grazing in
green and pleasant fields. Of Jean-François Millet's painting
Watering the Cow he wrote that he would never forget the simple evening scene.[2] Cattle and grass were bound together in Whitman's poetry
because they were literally and metaphorically life and death. Cattle ate
grass, manured it, died; their bodies were absorbed into the earth and
this was life renewed.[3] What he did not talk about in his epic *Leaves of
Grass* was what cattle and grass were really in terms of American agriculture, American food, and changes in the land. Bucolic imagery glossed
over long-running transformations in farming, for in Whitman's lifetime
(1819–1892) food production was being transformed from farmhouse to
factory. Whitman, a vegetarian, may never have thought about how
American's hunger for meat was satisfied, if ever it was, or where all the
presidents' cheeses came from.

Cattle have always been at the center of meat and dairy production.
Pigs, poultry, and, to a lesser extent, sheep are major meat sources as well.
From the later nineteenth century, however, pork came to be viewed almost

everywhere as a food of the lower classes both urban and rural. Although widely consumed across all social classes, it was suspect as unclean in the way that it was grown, as a vector of disease, and cheap. The latter was an alloyed virtue in many a cookery manual. That pork was widely consumed by poor African Americans at a time when beef consumption was on the rise among white Americans, along with pure milk and cheese, surely had a role in the prejudice.[4] Perhaps the inhumane treatment of pigs once production was industrialized was a result of such attitudes.

The impact of cattle in the Americas can be considered in several ways. Cows were an invasive species into the biosystem, though Europeans preferred to call them introduced animals. Like all invasive creatures they spread into whatever environmental niches allowed or were created for them. The scrawny feral cattle of the South adapted to local foods available to them, and cattle in the southwest did the same. Cows changed landscapes mainly by having humans change the vegetation to better suit them. As an example, in 1846 upper New York State farmers sent 34,535,000 lb of cheese down the Erie Canal to eastern port cities. At about 10 lb of cheese per 100 pounds of milk, that means American farmers produced more than 345 million lb of milk. This figure does not include the many backcountry farms

"Then Came the Cattle High Plains," showing how cattle replaced bison on the grasslands, from *The Plow that Broke the Plains*.

that were not counted in agricultural surveys.[5] Cows in many parts of the South gave only 1 or 2 quarts of milk per day. "In Maryland the name 'Five Pints' was bestowed on a cow, apparently as a title of honor, on account of her yield of milk."[6] Northern farmers were more advanced than Southern ones because they had urban markets in which to sell. But everyone knew that to give more milk and/or meat, cows needed better food, and that meant planting the best grass, forbs, and grains for the purpose.

Cattle convert cellulose to protein that is edible by humans and other predators. They were not the only grazers critically important to Europeans. As the story of Hernán Cortés's conquest of Mexico and the subsequent development of Latin American societies shows, the horse was central to the colonizing process. The same held for North America for the same reasons. As Vaclav Smil put it, "Energy is the only universal currency: It must be transformed to get anything done."[7] Europeans had animals for traction and transportation; Native peoples did not, at least at first. Until the invention of steam and internal combustion engines, animal power was the only means by which most aspects of American agriculture developed. The term horsepower is still applied to engines as a reminder of animal muscle as the real power on the land.

Though they live together on farms and on the western cattle ranges, cattle and horses do not have the same feeding behaviors. With a thick pad rather than upper teeth, cattle eat with their tongues, wrapping them around vegetation and pulling it out of the ground; they have been described as lawnmower feeders. Their four-chambered stomachs are marvels of processing that can digest almost any roughage, from sweet grasses to woody growth. However, not all vegetation is good for them. Farmers past and present know what makes them fat and happy and what makes them sick. Johnsongrass (*Sorghum halepense*) is a case in point. A Mediterranean native, it was accidentally imported to South Carolina after the Revolutionary war when Thomas Means brought back a sack of hemp (widely grown in the United States before it was effectively banned in the twentieth century) from Egypt with "Egyptian" or "Means" grass in it. It was widely planted in the South as a forage grass popularized by Alabama planter Colonel William Johnson, who spread it after 1840 and whose name is now attached to it. Cattle love it, but when hit with frost or when wilted the grass produces hydrogen cyanide, which can poison cattle and horses when eaten in large amounts. Every state and federal agricultural agency considers johnsongrass to be a noxious invasive weed that should be extirpated. Like some other immigrants, it is a highly successful plant that is found everywhere, from vacant land to river margins, to vegetable patches. Old-time farmers in Southern regions will say a bit hesitantly that they like it because if not "spoiled" their animals do well on it.

Johnsongrass is closely related to sorghum (*Sorghum bicolor*), or milo in American usage. It, too, is a dry lands plant that evolved in warm climates,

Johnsongrass (*Sorghum halepense*).

likely in Africa. There it is widely consumed as a staple grain. It may have been brought to America by African slaves, though its commercial uses date to the mid-nineteenth century. In places like Tennessee, Kentucky, and southern Indiana, sorghum syrup replaced molasses and corn sweeteners at various times but is now a "heritage" product. In other parts of the South and southwest, such as the southern Great Plains, milo became a major crop for fodder (with care because like johnsongrass the leaves contain prussic acid) and especially for its grain. Once cracked—cows have a hard time digesting its waxy outer hull—it is a good substitute for corn as feed. Milo is the third largest crop in the United States, itself the world's second producer.[8] Sorghum is one of those plants that have been moved latitudinally across the globe and later genetically adapted to wider climatic zones.

Horses are "nibblers," pickier eaters that, when in rich pastures, bite off vegetation they like with their teeth, leaving the rest as patches and clumps. They need more protein-rich food than cattle because they lack the cow's ability to produce amino acids necessary for good nutrition. Although an 1,100 lb horse will eat about 22 lb of hay per day (versus 24 lb for a 1,400 pound cow), it is more expensive to feed horses. Being grazers, sheep eat short grasses, preferring forbs and weeds to grass.[9] Their goat relatives are browsers that eat taller grasses, bark, twigs, vines including poison ivy—in short, anything that is head high. Cattle and horses are happy in lowland pastures or plains, while caprids thrive in the uplands to which their ancestors and modern wild relatives are adapted. Each of these species affected local environments. For instance in the mid-nineteenth century sheep farming took hold in the Kentucky uplands, which became the nation's main wool-producing area before sheep were taken to the Great Plains. To this day, the signature heritage dish made at festivals in parts of that state is mutton burgoo (or Brunswick stew, a dish normally made with mixed meats, especially squirrel).

Cattle and horses were the prized animals of European Americans. Upon setting their farm animals on the new land, European colonists saw immediately that native grasses in the northeast did not provide the kind of nourishment required for large and healthy stock. Native annual grasses in the north such as wild rye and broomstraw were destroyed because cattle ate the seeds before they had time to reproduce by wintering over. Cattle also trampled on delicate perennials and so both they and horses had to feed free range on poor or even poisonous vegetation.[10] As early as the seventeenth century European colonists brought seeds for feed plants with them. When the new fodder plants did not work, farmers adapted them to land and climate by continuously experimenting with plant genetics. They did the same with their animals and in so doing created the kind of domesticated landscapes that Whitman and other "improvers" liked and needed. Some of the changes were accidental, but most were not. Whether supplying neighbors in early villages or semi- or fully commercial enterprises, the goal was as much production as possible with the greatest efficiency. Agricultural improvers such as George Washington and Thomas Jefferson experimented with many kinds of grasses on their plantations to increase farm production. As discussed previously, the market drove changes in the land and everything on it.

GRASS

Any American who looks out of their windows at a grassy suburban lawn, urban park or even grassy strip along a sidewalk sees a domesticated landscape. Any golf course is a model of what in science-fiction-speak is called terraforming. Gazing from their automobile windows as they zoom along interstate highways through farm country, most Americans have no idea that they are looking at modified landscapes with botanies totally transformed from their original post-glacial states. Overpasses, bridges, and concrete speak of radically altered lands. In summer travelers might be delighted to see fields filled with crops or stands of blue cornflowers along roadsides, but the flowers too are European imports. For every change in flora, fauna, and land, for every species for the presumed human good, there are unintended consequences: invasive plants and creatures. The response is to do battle with further innovations, mainly chemical and biological. And for every effort to eradicate them, plants and animals adapt themselves through natural selection. It is a never ending struggle, one based almost entirely on Americans' food preferences and food systems, and on aesthetics.

Some ten thousand species of grass categorized into six or seven hundred genera populate the earth. One group, the Pooideae, brought to the temperate zones of North America, originated in parallel zones of the Old World of which are "such familiar species as wheat (Triticum), barley (Hordeum), rye (Secale), and oats (Avena), as well as most north temperate lawn and pasture grasses [the Pao genus including meadow grasses and blue grasses]."[11] These are all cool-weather grasses from Eurasia adapted to native micro-environments and later naturalized in the Americas. Bermuda grass (*Cynodon dactylon*) seems to have been accidentally imported by ship to the American south where it naturalized quickly in latitudes parallel to its native areas. Although considered an invasive plant, it became widespread as fodder and is common on golf courses.[12] Rice and sugar cane (from two different tropical genera) were two other food plants from southern latitudes brought to the American south. Other grasses such as panics, on the other hand, had early pre-human global distributions and include both Old World millets and the native switchgrass that dominated the original American prairies. Wild ryes were and remain widespread in all regions save for the High Plains.

From long experience in Europe, where grasses and leguminous plants such as clover were widely used by the seventeenth century, American farmers understood that they had to colonize the land with new fodder crops. Grasses were not selectively bred for maximum nutrients per acre until well into the twentieth century. Rather, in the typical American style of rarely farming intensively by using fertilizers and crop rotation, early farmers introduced grasses and legumes and allowed them to propagate on their own.[13] In the Massachusetts colonies clover, lucerne (alfalfa), and timothy were widespread by the early eighteenth century. So were a number of other "weeds" such as dandelion (*Taraxacum officinale*) and common plantain (*Plantago major*), also known as Englishman's foot. Both seem to have been deliberately planted as food and medicinal plants. Dandelion is packed with vitamins and is also a diuretic, hence a vernacular name "piss flower." Both are unwanted weeds in modern lawns, though young dandelion leaves are widely eaten in rural areas and dandelion wine has been an American home-made product from early days.

Clover (genus *Trifolium*) is a leguminous plant related to peas. One of the plants that made the agricultural revolution in Europe, beginning in the sixteenth century, clover was well known as animal feed. Because of nitrogen-fixing bacteria that live at the plant's roots, clover was known as a replenisher of exhausted soils. Of its three hundred or so species, the three most commonly sown in America were white or Dutch clover, red clover, and crimson varieties. These are all cool-weather plants that grow in compacted soils; the biennial red clover in particular flourishes in poor land. In the first of his pioneering works on scientific agricultural methods, "Essays upon Field Husbandry" (1748–59), the Connecticut lawyer and clergyman Jared Eliot discussed the role of red clover as a lifesaver for denuded soils and meadowlands.[14] Farmers were more interested in fat food animals than land reclamation so Eliot's ideas were mostly ignored for some years. These three clovers have different characteristics; crimson is good as an annual cover crop, and white is better able to tolerate warmer weather conditions. Planted widely and spreading on their own, crimson and white clovers are attractive to pollinating insects, and thus major contributors to honey production in the Americas. Like the plants they harvest, honeybees are yet another immigrant to the New World. But like dandelions, clovers are often considered as weeds in American lawns and so subject to eradication by chemical means, to the detriment of beneficial insects.

Timothy grass (*Phleum pratense*) is a bunch grass (meaning it grows in clumps) named for Timothy Hanson, a New England farmer who developed the seed as a commercial proposition probably in the 1720s. He claimed to have discovered it in France, but this common European perennial was known in New England as herd or hurd grass earlier in that century. Hanson traveled down the coastal colonies touting its benefits and selling seed as cattle fodder. Like so many ideas in early America, Hanson's drew upon biblical authority. Americans have always had a peculiar penchant for mixing religion and commerce: in his 1773 journal, which he "speaked out to a kindful schoole teacher lady," he cited Genesis: "And God said, Let the Earth bring forth grass and herb-yielding seed. And it was so. And God saw that it was good."[15] Timothy grass was a commercial success because it is excellent fodder for cattle and horses. Many of the rolled bales of hay that dot rural America at haying season are composed of it, among other nutritious grasses. Originally a cool-weather grass, timothy grows in warmer, though not drought-prone, climates and has been adapted to other landscapes. Modern genetically developed strains, including rust-resistant Climax, Colt, and the premium Horizon (developed in Hokkaido, Japan), have populated most of the cattle-rearing uplands of Colorado and the Great Plains.

Other important immigrant grasses include orchardgrass (*Dactylis glomerata*), now as widely used as timothy because it is more heat resistant, and fescues. Fescues (*Festuca*) are cool-weather perennials that comprise a genus of about a hundred varieties. It is likely that fescues arrived in North America before 1800, though they were not widely sown as fodder until the end of that century. Today some 35 million acres are sown with varieties of it. Most fescues grow well in deep, fertile soils, where they produce excellent hay. The earliest one was called meadow fescue; other names such as sheep fescue and chewing fescue show what good feedstuffs they are. The commonly used version is tall fescue, which thrives on heavy, compacted soils and does well in irrigated lands. Since California, Washington State, Oregon, Montana, and Wyoming have a good deal of irrigated land, created

Soybeans

A rotational crop became one of the nation's leading exports. During summer to early autumn, the open Midwestern farm fields are green. Acres upon acres are covered in corn but alongside the tall plants, almost equally, are low, deep green plants that most people hardly think about, much less think about as all-American food: soybeans. Yet the United States is the world's leading grower and exporter of soybeans to the tune of almost 4 billion bushels a year grown on almost 80 million acres of land. Unknown to most, soy products are ingredients in dozens upon dozens of everyday American foods.

Before the 1920s, the native Asian soybean was hardly known in the United States. First planted in 1765, it was a minor crop used as a forage crop, a rotational crop for corn, because it is a plant whose bacteria fix nitrogen. Scientific studies especially during and after the Second World War led to its development for oils and animal feeds. The benefits of soybean production using research and new technologies were so obvious that by 1956 the

by dams built in the earlier twentieth century, it is not surprising that most fescue seed varieties are grown there.

Tall fescue traditionally had two cultivars, Alta and Kentucky 31. Alta is particularly adaptable to the dry summers of eastern Oregon and Washington State. Kentucky 31 was discovered in a valley in that state in 1931 where it remained green all winter. In 1943 it was released to the public; it remains popular because its deep roots stabilized soils, hence it was widely planted in American Dust Bowl regions. Kentucky 31 grows in southern latitudes and makes fine lawn grass.[16] Unfortunately it is not always healthful for cattle and horses, which can come down with various ailments, one of which, fescue foot, means animals loosing hoofs. After research across the globe, scientists discovered in the 1970s and '80s that a fungal endophyte in tall fescue and some rye grasses was responsible for poisoning livestock. The fungus is not a parasite but instead a symbiote that helps the plant survive

U.S. had become the world leader in soybean production. Today 90 percent of American oilseed production comes from soybeans, from the bottle of vegetable oil on a grocer's shelf to deep fryers in fast food restaurants. Soy meal or extruded soy is a meat extender used in products from sausages to Betty Crocker's "Hamburger Helper," introduced in the 1970s. It is also a meat analogue in a variety of brand iterations. Soy lecithin, oil, and protein are in numerous foods, among them breakfast cereals and drinks, cookies, crackers, soups, dog and cat food, peanut butters, candy, margarines, salad dressings, sauces for meats, and many frozen and fresh entrees sold in supermarkets.

It is hard be free of some soy product, even if one wanted to, in everyday American food. A growing number of consumers would like to renounce conventional soy products because roughly 95 percent of the crop is genetically engineered. Introduced by Monsanto in 1995, engineered soybeans were made to resist the glyphosate herbicide used in the company's Roundup. Whether such modifications affect human health is an ongoing controversy but the technology permitted major increases in crop production. For farmers and corporations that export so much product, that is the clinching argument.

in environmentally stressful conditions. Researchers concluded that the reason for this form of ergot in Kentucky 31 was that it is not competitive with other grasses but was planted for economic and aesthetic reasons.[17] As with other introduced species, unintended consequences arose to create new problems. Today plant biologists have developed new non-toxic fescues such as Kentucky 32, keeping fescue as the nation's leading fodder crop.

The most famous fodder grass is Kentucky bluegrass (*Poa pratensis*): it is the nickname for the state, a region famous for its horses. Bluegrass may have been brought by French explorers in the seventeenth century and early English settlers. It spread down from the northeast along waterways so that by 1800 it was common in watered regions with the right soils. As Lewis Gray put it, "Bluegrass was the magical pasture grass of the limestone lands of the Valley, West Virginia, Kentucky, and the Nashville Basin. In some of these areas it was sown in the midst of woodlands."[18] Today it is one of the most popular lawn and fodder grasses, much of the seed commercially produced in Oregon and Washington State.

In the far west from Mexico to California, Spanish colonists brought Mediterranean plants along with cattle and horses. Some were deliberate, others fellow travelers now regarded as weeds. Along with vegetables and fruits came clovers, thistles, wild oats, bromes, European rye – some ninety weeds in all. As Alfred Crosby put it, once cattle ate native grasses out and trampled the land, aggressive weeds found their opportunities.[19] California, with its fragile mountain chaparral biomes (meaning drought-resistant and heath plants), was especially susceptible to invasive species. In the mid-twentieth century more than 60 percent of California's wild plants were invaders. Redstem filaree (*Erodium cicutarium*) or cranegrass is one example. A plant in the geranium family with lovely small flowers, it spreads on denuded ground and is drought resistant. It likes fertile soils even better and produces huge quantities of small seeds that outcompete food plants such as wheat, beans, and peas. Cattle and horses love redstem filaree but it does harbor fungi that are harmful to food plants and, because it accumulates nitrogen, can be slightly poisonous to the cattle or horses that gobble it up when they can. Gardeners root it out, but like so many other weeds it is widespread in fodder fields and meadows.

America's pioneer environmentalist George P. Marsh wondered what it was in Old World weeds (like redstem filaree) that gave them adaptive advantages over native plants. He speculated that human changes in landscapes were a key to the process.[20] Other plants, he knew, had to be

Lone antelope on the Laramie Plains, a high grassland south of Laramie, Wyoming.

nurtured in order to flourish; that is just what people did while dramatically changing the landscape, as Marsh keenly observed. Lucerne or alfalfa
was one of these. *Medicago sativa*, a member of the pea family, is the oldest
named fodder and silage crop whose use by humans runs back at least ten
thousand years.[21] It is high in protein, good for dairy cattle and, within
limits, for horses. It is a dry climate plant whose roots run deeper into the
earth for water than other grasses. It is not surprising that it grew prolifically in the Spanish colonies. Today 18 million acres of the cattle-rearing
Argentine pampas is covered in it and it is found in many cow pastures in
Mexico. Alfalfa was brought to California during Gold Rush days in the
1850s where it flourished in dry soils. Since numerous horses and mules
were needed in the mining and other mineral industries this was a perfect
crop. One of America's most famous product brands is 20 Mule Team
Borax, which literally describes what entrepreneur William T. Coleman
devised to get 10-ton loads of borax out of California's Mojave Desert
in the 1880s. Alfalfa grown in lightly irrigated lands of the later named
Lucerne Valley made this possible.[22]

Though much desired by farmers in the east and Midwest, alfalfa was
not so successful since it could not withstand cold winters. In 1857, German
immigrant Wendelin Grimm sowed alfalfa seed ("*ewiger Klee*," everlasting
clover) on his Carver County, Minnesota, farm. It failed save for a few
plants. Undeterred, he saved seeds from these plants and replanted them.
The seeds of the next year's survivors were then saved, some sold to neighbors, and so it went for the next half century until southern Minnesota
became the only place where the now naturalized alfalfa grew well. In 1903
United States Assistant Secretary of Agriculture Willet M. Hays, who had
seen this alfalfa while a professor at the Minnesota Agricultural Experiment,
named the variety Grimm and worked to spread it across the nation's northern tier. At about the same time Professor Niels Hansen, from the South
Dakota Agricultural Experiment Station, was sent by the U.S. Department
of Agriculture to Central Asia to find alfalfa strains that could withstand
cold weather. His Turkestan breeds were planted in Nebraska and, when the
brutal winter of 1898–9 killed vast numbers of plants, Hansen's Turkestan
variety survived. Later expeditions to Kashmir and Peru brought disease-
resistant versions to the United States where they have been further
developed. Today's modified alfalfas can fix nitrogen not only in the soil by
their symbiotic bacteria but from the air as well. Anyone traveling through
American farm country will see fields of yellow flowers, alfalfa flowers turned
yellow from nitrogen absorption. Some alfalfas can break down herbicides

and petroleum compounds, thus decontaminating soils. As a result of plant breeding, roughly 58 percent of all hay comes from various alfalfas.[23]

The drylands High Plains that run from Manitoba down the 100th meridian to Texas have a romance about them. Tourism photographs and movies show wide rolling grasslands populated by cattle herds and herders astride their horses, that is, authentic cinema cowboy country. The region is remote from urban America, the old buffalo country where one might expect more native plants to remain. As a major cattle-raising region, that is not the case because of fodder needs. Instead native cool grasses such as native wheatgrasses, bromes, switchgrass, native ryes, bluestems, and gramas are interspersed with introduced orchard grass, Russian wild rye, and Siberian wheatgrass among numerous variants as well as alfalfas. Not one of these, native or introduced, is "pure" but all have been genetically modified to fit the particular climate and soils of the High Plains. Careful rotation of grasses and cattle movement are attempts to keep the land from becoming once again the Dust Bowl of the 1930s.[24] However, once lands have been disturbed and planted with desirable crops the way is open for other immigrants.

Spotted knapweed, saltcedar, Russian knapweed, purple loosestrife, musk thistle, diffuse knapweed, Dalmatian toadflax, Canada thistle, absinth wormwood, yellow toadflax, and leafy spurge are all "noxious" weeds that affect the Plains. Most drive out desired plants. Some, like saltcedar (*Tamarix spp.*), were Eurasian ornamentals that escaped from nurseries in the nineteenth century. The low tree sucks up prodigious amounts of water in drylands and leaves salt deposits. It stresses other plants, its seeds have no nutritional value for wildlife, and it is difficult to eradicate.[25] The accidentally introduced leafy spurge (*Euphorbia esula L.*) is another major problem across the American west, the High Plains included. It has several versions, the most common of which came from Russia with food plant seeds in the 1890s. Leafy spurge has long roots that are hard to extract and it grows prolifically. Cattle and horses will eat it but often become ill, horses losing hair and hoof material when stepping in it. Where it is unchecked, land values have decreased as much as 90 percent. Efforts to eliminate leafy spurge and other such weeds vary from insects that eat the plant to herbicides. One natural solution is another alien creature, the caprid. Goats and sheep eat leafy spurge with gusto and no ill effects (except to pass some seeds in their excrement). In experiments, eight years of continuous grazing on infested plots reduced the plant to almost zero. Left alone the plots resumed their weed densities within two years.[26] More caprids on the land would help but inventories of sheep and goats have been in steady decline from the 1960s, when Americans ate more than 4 lb of lamb a year to the 1 lb of 2011.[27] Beef is and always has been prime eating, with pigs and chickens as the second choices.

ANIMALS

American cookbooks have hardly ever spoken about animal feeds, much less grass. There have always been plenty of recipes for meats, most of them from domestic animals. Both fat meats and animals fats themselves are discussed directly and indirectly since candle making using beef tallow was part of a housewife's duties. How to get fat on animals was left to farmers. Lydia Maria Child's classic *The Frugal Housewife* (1829) is one example of many. All subsequent editions, renamed after 1832 as *The American Frugal Housewife*, have illustrations of food animals naming the cuts taken from each part of the animal. Taken from much older crude woodcuts, the mutton, pork, veal and beef diagrams bear generally the same names as those in current use, with some exceptions. Sirloin is spelled "Sir Loin," which gives rise to some fanciful etymological speculation about the part's origins (it is French, meaning above the loin, and not a nobleman's title).[28] The sheep, pig, calf, and bull (Child calls it an ox) depicted are certainly the correct species but they have only a resemblance, as Olmstead and Rhode say, to their descendants in the mid-twentieth century. The later creatures were "far more productive and manageable in the tamer and more confined environments they inhabited."[29]

Child's pig is long legged and leaner than the fat hogs seen today. It is closer to the feral pigs and wild razorbacks that lived in forests against which early farm fields were set, as well as the pigs that cohabited with people in America's nineteenth-century cities. The sheep is leaner, and the bull, though substantial, is smaller and long-horned, rather than the newly developing shorthorn breeds that became dominant. In Child's time (she died in 1880), great changes were made to the animals set onto American farms and ranges. The reasons for manipulating animal genomes, or breeding, were and remain the same to this day: to maximize the amount of product of desirable kinds to meet market demands or what speculative farmers thought these might be. Uniformity of breed for expected outcome such as meat and fat yields or milk are the same idea as in manufacturing, that is, standardization allows for predictability, efficiency, and maximum profit on investment. Unlike some high-value manufacturing, in farming economies more is better. It has been said, more grass and grains, more animals.

Although dedicated to using every bit of an animal in cookery for economy's sake, *The American Frugal Housewife* speaks to the kinds and qualities of meats available to cooks in the early to mid-nineteenth century. Even though meat grading was introduced only in 1917, cooks knew what they wanted. Lettice Bryan's *The Kentucky Housewife* (1839) describes what that is: "in choosing beef, be particular to select such as has a lively open grain, an oily smoothness, a carnation color and white hard suet. These signs are always present with good beef."[30] Bryan's cookery is more elaborate than Child's advice—there are no set recipes, just advice on how to cook various dishes—since it derives from the southern tradition exemplified by Mrs. Randolph's *The Virginia House-wife*. Tougher cuts of meat are stewed, boiled, minced, or slowly roasted. Lard appears in beef cookery often. For both, roasts are larded, something not often done in modern American cooking, and in Bryan's recipes melted lard is used in lots of other preparations. Perhaps it is no wonder that the illustration of a pig and its cuts in Bryan's book is fatter than in Child's. The textures and flavors of fats were clearly favored in meat dishes, implying that well-marbled, tender beef was desired but not always available for most cooks. As Child says, rump meat is tough and chewy so perhaps people would eat less of it. That is as much a commentary on the state of Americans' teeth as on frugality.

Genetic manipulation and fitting animals into appropriate environments was the means. Pigs and poultry can be changed more rapidly than cattle because they breed more prolifically and faster than cattle. Cows gestate for nine months and usually give birth to one calf, unlike pigs that birth twice a year with litters of eight piglets (up to ten in recent years due to genetic alterations). Cattle may have been slower to develop but doing so was an imperative because of demand for products, from milk to meat, to leather and as draft animals. The famous Conestoga wagons that carried settlers across the American continent to the west were drawn not so much by horses or mules, but by cattle. On the other hand in America as in England, by 1800 horses largely came to supplant cattle as plow beasts, thus allowing the latter to be fattened for earlier slaughtering; four years rather than ten years for draft animals. Among the reasons for the changes were food preferences among a rising population. From populations of 2.5 million in 1776, to 5.3 million in 1800 and 23 million in 1850, demand for beef and meat (other than horse and mule) in general rose dramatically.

Meat cuts chart from
Lydia Maria Child,
*The American Frugal
Housewife* (1838).

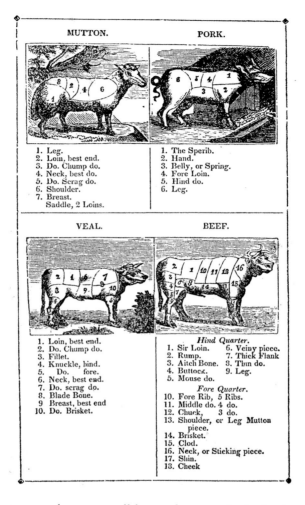

Eighteenth-century cattle were small by modern standards. In the middle of the century regional breeds were well known. Larger cattle such as those from Devon, Durham, and Hereford weighed about 1,000 lb on average, half the size of modern versions.[31] Meat cattle in the uplands of Wales and Scotland seem to have averaged 500 to 600 lb, though Ayrshires were larger and fine milkers. Even the now popular Anguses were small and in transition from middle-horn to short-horned cattle. Mendelian genetics had not yet been discovered but in the 1760s and '70s Robert Bakewell of Leicestershire began breeding for specific traits. Best to best including incest were among his techniques in producing reliable results, namely uniform animals of specific types. He did not understand recessive genes so that when breeding for a red coat or a beast with more meat and less bone, he might also have bred for mulefoot or deformed vertebra. Nonetheless, other breeders in England followed suit and prominent American agricultural improvers experimented with breeding. Among them were George Washington, Thomas Jefferson, James Madison, Henry Clay, Daniel Webster, the ugly apologist for slavery John C. Calhoun, and even Andrew Jackson's bête noire, Nicholas Biddle.[32] As in England these experimenters were the landed elite who had the money to do so. Only after the middle of the nineteenth century would scientific breeding become democratized by farming organizations and new land grant universities.

Most of the modern American cattle breeds originated in Britain, though later English dairy breeds such as Jersey and Guernsey cows were derived from Norman and Breton French prototypes. Early in the nineteenth century Bakewell's and others' "improved" breeds were being introduced into the eastern United States. Farmers such as Robert Patterson and John S. Skinner of Baltimore imported short-horned Devon bulls, some of which were put on common lands for public use as studs. Since bulls aggressively collect harems, performing this service no doubt pleased them. By the 1830s Devon stock had been introduced to Massachusetts, Vermont, Ohio, South Carolina, and New York.[33] Durham cattle that had been developed in northern England early in the century were also shipped in. Because they fattened so well they became even more popular than others. With few exceptions these new breeds did not possess the long curved horns of their ancient aurochs ancestors but lesser ones, hence their generic name, shorthorns.[34]

Of all shorthorns, the Hereford is perhaps the best known. Typically white-faced, the type was developed in the late eighteenth and nineteenth centuries as a local variation of generic shorthorns. They are well muscled, efficient at grazing, and adaptable to varied climates (though not dry ones) and are good milkers. Pure-bred Herefords appeared as early as 1817, but were brought in great numbers after the Civil War by Midwestern speculators in beef production and by British investors in western Plains ranches.[35] From 1846 to 1887 the rapidly transforming Illinois prairies received the greatest numbers and trans-Mississippi Iowa, Kansas, and Nebraska took large numbers. Herefords thrived in the upper Great Plains because they could withstand winter cold and could feed on varieties of forages. They were also highly successful as cross-breeders with the naturalized American Texas longhorn.

Black Angus beef has become a significant brand in late twentieth- and early twenty-first-century America. Aberdeen Angus cattle were developed in the eponymous region of Scotland in the late eighteenth and early nineteenth centuries; the official herd book was established in 1862. Anguses are naturally polled with glossy black coats, pleasant tempered, resist harsh climates, and mature early. Anguses are said to yield more boneless meat and higher quality than other cattle, including Hereford bull–Angus cow crosses, which live longer and are more efficient at calf production. Red Angus is a slight genetic variation of the Black that has become more widely raised since it was developed in the 1950s. Reds are gentler and more insect resistant than Blacks. What makes Angus so good to carnivorous humans is that they yield fine marbled meat. Marbling quality is determined by the amount of fat globules in a ribeye cut from the twelfth to thirteenth rib of the animal. So successful has the Certified Black Angus campaign been that cattle with black hides, Angus or otherwise, make up about 63 percent of American beef herds (that number likely includes dairy Holsteins). Black means quality, the advertising people might say, though as one rancher says, when you eat a steak do you care what color the hide was?

There is a truism in cattle history: shorthorns in the east and north, longhorns in the southwest. Along with the small feral cattle of the American southeast, the Texas longhorn was an early naturalized American. Unlike their Southern cousins they are ensconced in American folk culture because of the romance of cattle drives. After the Civil War, cowboy literature boomed as dime novelists such as Ned Buntline sold highly exaggerated tales of heroes and villains by the many thousands. Owen Wister's

Prize bull, New York state, 1852.

novel *The Virginian* (1902) and his friend Frederic Remington's paintings and sculptures of the Old West remain landmarks of American culture. The newly emerging cinema industry made horse operas even more popular, with cowboys, cattle drives, gunfights, damsels in distress, and scenic images of the west (at least around Los Angeles for the cheaply made ones) being familiar subjects. Andy Adams (1859–1935), a former cowboy, and Joseph McCoy (1837–1915) both wrote about the hard realities of the long drives and cowboy life from the 1860s into the 1880s. Anyone who has seen Howard Hawks's great Western movie *Red River* (1948) will get the influences of both authors in it.

The recent decoding of Texas longhorn DNA shows how hybridization works to allow animals to adapt to new environments. Texas longhorns, like other New World breeds, are feral, having been let loose by Spanish settlers in Mexico and the American southwest in the sixteenth century. Longhorns are highly resistant to drought and to a tick-borne disease called "cattle tick fever" (*babesia*, a protozoa that had been introduced from Europe). As one might expect, longhorns are leaner than the beef and dairy cattle that were being developed in Europe. The reason for their adaptation was that the southern European cattle already had genes from Asian cattle (*Bos indicus*, such as the Brahman) via Africa sometime before their migration to America. Over the course of "between 80 and 200 generations of predominantly natural selection, as opposed to the human-mediated artificial selection of Old World breeding programs," these hardy cattle became longhorns.[36] The famed Texas writer J. Frank Dobie described them as:

> Tall, bony, coarse-headed, coarse-haired, flat-sided, thin-flanked, some of them grotesquely narrow-hipped, some with bodies so long that their backs swayed, big ears carved into outlandish designs... But however they appeared, with their steel hoofs, their long legs, their staglike muscles, their thick skins, their powerful horns, they could walk the roughest ground, cross the widest deserts, climb the highest mountains, swim the widest rivers, fight off the fiercest bands of wolves, endure hunger, cold, thirst and punishment as few beasts of the earth have ever shown themselves capable of enduring. On the prairies they could run like antelopes; in the thickets of thorn and tangle they could break their way with the agility of panthers. They could rustle in drouth or snow, smell out pasturage leagues away, live—without talking about the matter—like true captains of their own souls and bodies.[37]

Ben Steele, *Cowboy with Lariat*, 2004, sketch.

Joseph McCoy wrote of the realities of cattle drives in the 1860s and
'70s. The famous western cattle drives were not new inventions. From early
in the nineteenth century farmers in the developing Midwest needed to
get their cattle to the eastern markets and the newly developing cities in
their regions. Rich cattle-feeding areas such as the Scioto River in Ohio, the
Kentucky bluegrass lands, and the Sangamon in Illinois were raising cattle
in ever larger numbers. Farmers up and down the Ohio River realized that
they could stuff cattle with good grasses and corn, thus fattening them faster
for the market. From 1800 to 1850 there were, for example, hundreds of
cattle drives from the new town of Marietta, Ohio, to the headwaters of the
Potomac River destined for Baltimore and Philadelphia. Chicago, chartered
in 1837, had become a major cattle transshipment town by 1846 for animals
raised by regional corn farmers. The trails were remembered for the clouds of
dust raised by walking herds following natural trans-montane routes to the
east. The Cumberland Road, later the National Highway (now Route 40),
ran from the head of the Potomac River all the way to Illinois's early capital,
Vandalia. The modern Pennsylvania Turnpike from north of Philadelphia
to Pittsburgh and beyond to Ohio is another route. In fact a good number
of modern roads throughout the eastern sections of the Midwest were old
cattle trails. No cowboys ran them and herds may have numbered under one
hundred, but the idea was the same: get fat cattle to market.[38]

The Texas cattle business boomed in the 1840s and '50s. Gold discovered in California created a rush of people to the state and a demand for
beef. Texas cattle were walked up through the dry southern California country to the north. They were also driven north to Kansas and then Missouri
in large numbers. Tick fever, terrible droughts in the 1860s that devastated

Ben Steele, *Cattle on High Plains*, 2002, sketch.

cattle stock, and the Civil War interrupted the overland trade. Longhorn populations recovered, the demand for western beef grew apace. In 1867 Joseph McCoy saw how critical railroads had been in moving materiel during the war. He built a stockyard in Abilene, Kansas, to receive cattle brought up from Texas along the Chisholm Trail. As McCoy said, 35,000 head were taken in and transshipped by rail to the newly built Chicago Stockyards. Places like Dodge City at the end of the Santa Fe Trail grew into towns where lawmen such as Wyatt Earp and Bat Masterson shot their way into American legend via dime novels, movies and television. What the shows and novels do not say is that the food these characters ate likely made for their dyspeptic temperaments, as a song apparently composed about the Apex Boarding House in southern Utah suggests:

> The coffee has the dropsy, the tea it has the grippe.
> The butter was consumptive, and the slapjacks they had fits;
> The beef was strong as jubilant; it walked upon the floor,
> The spuds got on their dignity and rolled right out the door.
> The pudding had the jimjams; the pies was in disguise.
> The beans came to the table with five hundred thousand flies.
> The hash was simply murdered, just as hard as dobe mud.
> We howl, we wail, our muscles fail on Baxter's awful grub.[39]

The food made by chuck wagon cooks has also been romanticized in popular media and numerous cookbooks. The reality on the dusty cow roads and from filthy wagon kitchens differed, as Dobie said:

> They fried their steaks. They roasted ribs and joints on the open fire. They jerked quantities of meat and ate the sun-dried—often sun baked—jerky raw, cooked it a little more on coals, or stewed it. Onions or garlic and—when possible to obtain—Irish potatoes helped the stew; native red peppers made it just right.[40]

Jerky beef, lots of beans, biscuits, and plenty of extra-strong long boiled coffee made the menu more complete.

More than culinary disasters were at hand. Texas cattle sold to farmers in central Illinois bore fever-spreading ticks. Within a few months whole herds of local cattle died from the disease. Tick fever continued to plague western cattle to the point where the state of Kansas banned any Texas cattle in 1884. By then the northern and central plains were well stocked with cattle.[41] Not that the improved cattle did not suffer as well. The droughts of the 1860s killed hundreds of thousands of California cattle since they were not adapted to such conditions, while improved cattle including longhorn mixture were

Chuck wagon line, Montana, 1910.

virtually exterminated on the Great Plains during the brutal winters of 1883 and 1884. Cattle ranching and driving was nothing like the movies, but rather ongoing battles by farmers with disease and environmental catastrophes. Organization of operations in the manner of industrialization was required to ensure cheap beef for American tables.

Meanwhile, longhorns were being bred out or simply killed into extinction. As McCoy wrote in 1874, longhorn cows were being bred with Durham cattle to create animals that would fatten better and faster than their dams. *Red River* is about the first cattle drive up the Chisholm Trail. Shot in 1946 to 1947, the cattle shown in it are not longhorns but mainly white-faced Herefords. By 1910, few of the once millions-strong longhorn herds remained. That pure longhorns still exist and are raised in all fifty states is due to a group of conservationists in the early twentieth century. The efforts to save longhorns were based on the pioneering conservation work of William Temple Hornaday, Director of the New York Zoological Society, and his friend President Theodore Roosevelt. A naturalist and taxidermist for the United States National Museum in Washington, DC, Hornaday traveled to Montana in 1884 where he saw the last remaining American bison and became determined to save them. Of about forty million bison living on the Great Plains in 1830, only 1,300 were left according to Hornaday's 1888 survey. Most had been murdered by hunters for sport and many killed in an attempt to deprive Plains Indians of their livelihood since the United States was at war with many Plains tribes. Besides, killing off bison opened the land to the desired beef cattle. Hornaday and Roosevelt were founding members of the American Bison Society, which placed animals in wildlife preserves under the care of the federal agencies. Bison began to flourish in these preserves as Hornaday happily observed in his book, *Our Vanishing Wild Life: Its Extermination and Preservation*.[42] Of the half million bison alive today, only about thirty thousand are pure-bred wild animals that live in preserves; domesticated bison raised for meat have cattle genes in them.

One of these newly created preserves is the Wichita Mountains Wildlife Refuge in Oklahoma, created in 1901. Pairs of breeding bison were sent there in 1907, as Hornaday wished, but he never mentioned longhorns in his conservation work. In 1927 a congressional act paid for thirty surviving pure longhorns to be brought to the refuge at the urging of William Drummond, a conservationist-minded forest ranger. There they flourished and the seven families of cattle are the basis for most of the quarter of a million longhorns bred in the United States. The story of bison and longhorn

Longhorn, Texas.

conservation, along with other species such as the endangered sage grouse or prairie chicken, is one of the consequences of American appetites and the business of providing for them.

Dairy cattle have a similar if not so romanticized history as beef cattle. Presidents Jefferson and Jackson's big cheeses required lots of milk, and that, in turn, impelled farmers to look for more productive cows in terms of quantity of liquid and quality, meaning butterfat content. The latter was and remains important, as any cookery and household book shows in its butter-laden recipes. Early cattle in the northeastern regions of Colonial America were whatever unimproved animals settlers brought with them. Dutch colonists in New York and New Jersey seem to have had what are the ancestors of Friesian and Friesian-Holstein cattle. Because the Netherlands had long since made cheese production a key element of its national economy, presumably Dutch cattle were better producers; there are no statistics. Most early American cows used so much energy for traction-plowing and wagon hauling, their milk production was low. Improved breeds were introduced in the late eighteenth century, mainly products of Bakewell and other breeders' labors. Called milking shorthorns (or shorthorn Durhams) because they did give more milk than the often scrawny old cattle, most of these early imports were also used as general-purpose animals.

More productive dairy cattle were imported around the turn of the nineteenth century as founders of the first dairy industry. In eastern states, especially in regions where soils were poor for market crops such as wheat, dairying became an economic necessity from the third decade of the nineteenth century onward. Midwestern states followed in the decades after the Civil War. Ayrshires were among the founding breeds. Hailing from the southeast region of Scotland, Ayrshires could cope with hilly country and when fed on good pasture could produce more than 6,000 lb of liquid at 3.9 percent butterfat content per milking season.[43] At about the same time in the 1840s, Pennsylvania cattle were estimated to furnish 2,500 lb per season.[44] Ayrshires were spread across the country as other types of registered breed cattle were brought in.

In 1815 Baltimore dealers began importing Alderneys from Britain's Channel Islands. Likely these were Guernseys, the name by which they are now known, but Jerseys are related to them. American farmers noted the golden color of Alderney/Guernsey milk (from the carotene in it) and how rich in butterfat it was (4.5 percent). The famous banker Nicholas Biddle settled several of them on his Pennsylvania farm in 1840; in 1850 Jerseys were shipped to Connecticut and the great orator Daniel Webster's farm in Massachusetts. Guernseys and Jerseys are smaller than other dairy cattle, weighing about 1,000 lb, but more efficient milkers as well as producing milk with higher butterfat content than the other popular dairy cows.[45] Jerseys in particular are well liked because of their gentle nature (the bulls are notoriously aggressive) and lovely faces. In 1936 the milk and glue company Borden, Inc. created an advertising campaign featuring a cheery soft-eyed Jersey named Elsie. She, her later husband Elmer (Elmer's Glue

George Catlin, *Expedition Encamped on a Texas Prairie. April 1686*, 1847–8.

is the company named for him), and their children Beulah, Beauregard, Larabee, and Lobelia became icons of American advertising. Incidentally, Lobelia was the name of the first real Elsie who appeared at the New York World's Fair in 1939. Like so many other industrialized food products that use animals to their utmost potential until worn out or killed, Elsie was a charming façade.

Brown Swiss were really twelve alpine breeds from various Swiss alpine regions. They were bred together into a uniform race in the early nineteenth century and adapted to their environments. Sturdy, with strong builds and feet and disease resistant, they could withstand cold winters and high altitudes. All Swiss browns in the United States descend from the original shipment of 25 bulls and 140 cows in 1869. At about 1,300 lb these sweet-tempered cows produce about 21,000 lb of milk at 4 percent butterfat per cycle. Like Jerseys, these cattle are prized by artisanal cheesemakers for their butterfat, and the cheese made from it is often labeled with the breed name.

Ninety percent of American milk is supplied by the Holstein. Called Friesians or Friesian-Holsteins in their native Low Countries, they are simply called Holsteins in America. They average about 1,500 lb and are prodigious milk makers that average 28,000 lb per cycle. The lower butterfat content at 2.5–3.6 percent is compensated by the sheer amount of milk. Of the original Holsteins, the largest number of imports ran from 1852 to 1905, some 7,757 in all, when European shipping was stopped because of foot-and-mouth disease. Of the nine million dairy cattle in the United States, 90 percent are Holsteins or of Holstein descent, most of them from these original imports. Modern artificial insemination techniques mean that one bull can produce five to twenty thousand daughters in a year. This kind of breeding has narrowed the Holstein gene pool, making for some worries about the future of the type. Nonetheless the familiar black and white— sometimes red and white—animals are the symbols of milk production.

The state of Wisconsin, nicknamed the Dairy State, is awash in Holstein iconography as befits a place with 10,290 dairy farms and 1.3 million dairy cows.[46] Wisconsin is America's leading cheese producer, the fourth largest in the world including the rest of the United States' production—the world leader at around 12 billion lb per year. But this was not always the case; the state's commercial dairy industry began as the result of ecological disaster. Immigrants from New England and New York began expansive settlements in southeastern Wisconsin after the War of 1812 where they planted their main cash crop, wheat. The soils are thin, sitting atop essentially glacial moraine, and easily eroded. Without many cattle to provide fertilizer, and not using sod-building plants in rotation, regional soils deteriorated after years of heavy wheat planting. By 1850 a number of farms were abandoned to be bought up by new immigrants from Germany and Scandinavia. As always they were better farmers than their Yankee predecessors and also interested in dairying. Agricultural experts began to advocate for dairying based on the booming cheese industry in New York State. In 1861 Alanson Slaughter of Orange County opened what is thought to be the first creamery and butter factory.[47] Led by William Dempster Hoard, an agricultural journalist (his publication *Hoard's Dairyman* is still in business) and later the state's governor, dairying began in earnest. In 1864 New Yorker Chester Hazen built the first cheese factory in Fond du Lac County, in 1872 Hoard formed the Wisconsin Dairymen's Association, and in 1881 the University of Wisconsin's new Agricultural College began work in the field. By the 1880s Wisconsin's cheeses were being shipped across the nation on refrigerated railway cars, at the same time that Chicago's meat and California's produce was.[48]

Wisconsin was not alone in shifting from wheat to dairy. In the 1880s, Minnesota and northern Iowa also joined in because of declining land fertility. Farmers in both states found butter more profitable than cheese. What made the nineteenth-century dairy industry go were more highly productive cows—shorthorns at first, followed by some Jerseys and then lots of Holsteins—and better rearing, pasturing, and barn feeding practices.[49] For instance, the average milking season increased from 237 days in 1850 to 300 in 1910 (it is 305 now). Machines made for more hay and silage, and better grasses made for more milk. Improvements meant that average milk production went from about 2,300 lb to 3,570 in 1910.[50] Although dairying and cheese production was becoming industrialized, the factories had to collect milk from a number of local farms. In 1940, 4,663,431 American farms had dairy cows, with an average of five per farm. By 2000 that number was down to 105,250 farms holding 88 head each.[51]

In each of these areas the soils were thin and then plowed over, without regard to local ecology, to meet American food demand or at least entrepreneur farmers' notion of what it was. After all, there was always land to the west. These transformed lands would be converted yet again to more intensive farming using the "best practices" of the time. Walt Whitman's bucolic reverie was not of some wilderness but of a land changed by humans: it seemed good to him. More was to come, more that he may not have liked.

SEVEN

The Rise of Machines

Since winter I had seen very little of Ántonia. She was out in the fields from sunup until sundown. If I rode over to see her where she was ploughing, she stopped at the end of a row to chat for a moment, then gripped her plough-handles, clucked to her team, and waded on down the furrow, making me feel that she was now grown up and had no time for me.

Willa Cather, *My Ántonia*[1]

With the introduction of agriculture mankind entered upon a long period of meanness, misery, and madness, from which they are only now being freed by the beneficent operation of the machine.

Bertrand Russell, *The Conquest of Happiness*[2]

In her great song to rural and small town life on the Nebraska prairies, *My Ántonia*, Willa Cather describes the hard life of newly immigrated Czech farmers in the 1880s and '90s. Only fifteen years old, Ántonia Shimerda "kept her sleeves rolled up all day, and her arms and throat were burned as brown as a sailor's. Her neck came up strongly out of her shoulders, like the bole of a tree out of the turf. One sees that draught-horse neck among the peasant women in all old countries." She says to her friend and the novel's narrator: "'Jim, you ask Jake how much he ploughed to-day. I don't want that Jake get more done in one day than me. I want we have very much corn this fall.'"

At the same time that Ántonia and her family plowed the rich lands of southern Nebraska, Hamlin Garland wrote of his years in Wisconsin and Iowa, a region called the Middle Border:

Gift of the Grangers, 1880. An idealized depiction by the first American farm organization on the theme of farmers feeding the nation.

It is a phase of life passed away. The "check-rowing automatic corn-planter and coverer" has taken the place of the girls and boys with aprons and hoes. With a long knotted cable and a machine, one man now drives a team into the field and plants and covers eighteen acres a day . . .

Those whose recollections extend over a term of twenty years have seen many changes in the implements of haying; from the old-fashioned scythe and rake to the patent-geared-self-lifting-adjustable-front-cut-meadow-king mowing-machine, and the self-dumping spring-tooth horse-rake. Indeed there are even more wonderful inventions in the field. These changes are marvelous in themselves, to say nothing of the changes in human thought which necessarily accompany them.[3]

Ántonia and her family worked the land by hand and horse. The technique of horse- or ox-drawn plowing had not changed in America since early European colonization. But food production was changing because in the period covered by both writers the country had long been undergoing revolutions in the means of production. Innovations in materials and manufacturing transformed tools, and steam (and later gasoline engine) power was being applied to the ever-more sophisticated machinery. All the innovations in tools, plants, and animals, all the immense work of changing the land for agricultural production were the basis for these technological leaps that are often called "the first agricultural revolution" (the second would come after 1940). There is much discussion of how and why such changes took place, that is, what drove innovation in technologies. For instance, was it the farmers' drive to produce ever more because of the existence of the money-run marketplace? Did farmers move to commodity-level production of certain crops that were in demand, such as wheat, corn, cattle, or cotton? Perhaps demand for foods of all kinds came from

Sod house, North Dakota, 1937.

the enormous immigration beginning in the 1840s that drove production. Others have theorized that new machines in themselves led innovative people to create new devices or improve old ones, a take on the old Yankee ingenuity theme. Whatever the theories of how and why the revolution on the land took place, but one thing is certain: as Garland said, changes in human thought worked together with technology to create new relationships in American food from producer to consumer, from the field to the table. All was becoming systematized, more like machines.

The agricultural historian Deborah Fitzgerald, discussing the post-1940 shift in farming, expanded on Garland's theme. A modern farmer who adopted a tractor "tacitly adopts a whole host of other practices and entered into a new set of relationships."[4] Ranging from banking and finance to mechanics, fuel suppliers, and buyers of farming products, each of these has long chains of connection to each other and to other entities. Fuel, for instance, has long supply lines that stretch across the globe. Such interconnections are different from the American subsistence farmers of the early Colonial period and even different from those who worked in the emerging markets of the early nineteenth century but the precedents were there all along.

Ántonia might not have known that her plowing was actually made possible by a line of agricultural improvers running back into the Colonial period. Her device of toil may have borne the name of one of them, John Deere. Today John Deere is a massive international corporation headquartered in Moline, Illinois. There, the company has displays devoted to its history and a good number of current and vintage machines ranging from tractors, plows, and combines to lawnmowers. One building is filled with tractors, some antiques, some newer, loaned by individual farmers to the company. Many seem nondescript but to the curators they are the highlight of the museum. Tour the facility and a curator might stop at a tractor and point out a gadget attached to the front. "That," they will say, "was not a standard issue company device. It was invented by a farmer to clear small shrubs on a piece of land that ordinary machinery could not reach." Winches, springs, all sorts of homemade bits and pieces are the curators' prized possessions. What they show, the John Deere people say, is the ingenuity that farmers have always had to cope with the tricky business of working the land. Standardized implements are the base but adaptation is critical, perhaps in the same way that a standard recipe is almost always adapted by the cook to meet the conditions of their kitchen and taste. In an industrializing food system the machine metaphor for production in the field, factory, and at home only goes so far.

John Deere is an American legend told many times in somewhat different forms. He has been characterized as the lone inventor beloved in American folklore, a pioneer in the business of agriculture, and a transforming visionary; "the man who made bread cheap," as one saying goes. In fact he was a Yankee tinkerer who knew how to adapt and expand existing technologies. Born in 1804 in Rutland, Vermont, he became a blacksmith. In 1836 his business failed and Deere took his family to the newly opening prairielands of Grand Detour, Illinois, a village on the Rock River. Since he repaired farm tools, Deere saw that the plowshares used on the tall grass prairies were inadequate to the task. A gift of the last glaciation, it was and remains some of the world's richest farmland but it is thick and requires draining. Plows of the day could hardly cut through the deeply rooted intertwining prairie grasses and, when cut, the deep humus clung to the unpolished cast- or wrought-iron tools like pure clay on a shovel. By happenstance, Deere was visiting a friend who owned a sawmill where he noticed a saw blade with damaged teeth. No one knows the kind of steel from which it was made, likely the primitive blister variety since new steel-making technologies were just in the offing, but it could be sharpened and polished. Almost as important, Deere gave it just the right curve to turn soil correctly after lots of experimentation. The result was a plow blade attached to the larger wrought-iron share that "scoured" the furrows and did not need constant cleaning.[5] This was literally a plow that broke the prairies, though not the only one.

The plows were initially expensive for farmers at about $10 each, and Deere sold only ten plows by 1839. Over the next few years his sales increased to four hundred by 1843. In that year the small company moved to Moline on the Mississippi River where access to coal and new steel-making operations in St. Louis was available. He soon switched to a Pittsburgh steel maker whose products were as good as the steel he had originally imported from Sheffield, England. The newly founded Chicago and Rock Island Railroad linked Moline to Chicago in 1854 and thus Deere had access to national markets. In 1859, at the edge of the Civil War, the company made fifteen thousand plows. Although not the nation's first (the first patent dates to 1844), Deere introduced a wheeled sulky plow in 1863. With the driver seated, a three-horse team now pulled a heavier plow that could work heavy soils more efficiently and faster than the standard walking plows. A multi-ganged plow patented by the company in 1867 was even better for open flatlands; instead of one plowshare there were two, spaced to work two rows instead of one. That meant a farmer who

Farmer with a two-mule team cultivating cotton in the South, 1947. Already archaic in the mid-20th century, this kind of farming has disappeared.

invested in the new device could work roughly five times the acreage per day of the old one. Better mechanisms allowed expansion of farmland across the developing American west.

Efficiency, especially versus cost, was John Deere's sales pitch and was in fact the case. It had to be, because his was one of 420 plow companies in business in the 1860s. The Scottish immigrant James Oliver's "Chilled Plows," made in South Bend, Indiana, were so called because of a manufacturing process in which the outer edges of a cast plow were made smooth and hard by chilling (actually in hot water) the surfaces quickly while the inner core remained a softer grade of iron. These plows resisted breakage and were initially cheaper than all-steel products. Oliver Chilled Plows were made for all kinds of terrains from southern cotton fields to narrow vineyards in Germany. By 1900, it was one of the largest manufacturers in the world and produced three hundred thousand plows a year.[6] James Oliver, John Deere, Nourse in Massachusetts, Case in Wisconsin, and many others depended on the application of new technologies and production ideas.

No better examples exist than Cyrus Hall McCormick and his rival Obed Hussey. New plows, new seed drills made by many companies including John Deere, and new harrowers created conditions for growing crops.

Harvesting them quickly and without grain loss was always a problem. Long-handled scythes and the ancient sickle were traditional harvesting tools brought from the Old World. The grain cradle, first patented in the late eighteenth century, began to appear in American farms. It is a scythe to which long teeth are attached. When the reaper cuts the grasses, the stalks are laid upon the teeth and can then be set down for bundling without the worker having to stop and bend down at each cutting. The job usually took two or more workers to bundle and tie the stalks and some grains were shattered in the process, but experienced hands harvested more, as much as 2 acres (0.8 ha) a day.[7] Machines would make the process much quicker with fewer losses.

Inventors across the world worked on the problem. Robert Boyce patented a reaper in Britain in 1800 but it never made its way to the United States, nor did the Scot Patrick Bell's never-patented device. Maine native Obed Hussey, who had been a sailor and creator of corn husking machinery, devised and patented a mechanical harvester in 1833. A cutting bar containing long hand-forged steel teeth was set on a platform and geared so that when drawn by horse team across a field the stalks were automatically

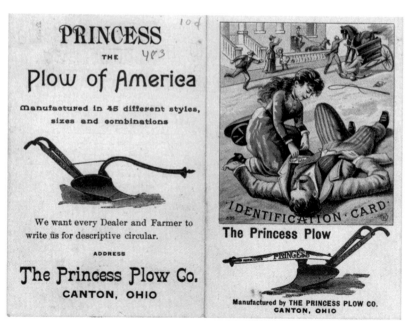

Advertisement for the Princess Plow Company of Canton, Ohio, *c.* 1890. Notice the "45 different styles" of equipment the company sold. This is a promotional piece that includes a personal identification card in case of emergency, an early example of the species.

Santa Fe Railroad, grain elevators.

laid down onto the platform. The system worked well enough for Hussey to begin manufacturing in Cincinnati, Ohio, among other places.[8] Hussey was a serious, stubborn man who insisted upon using only his own ideas about machinery and business. By 1858 he was driven out of business by McCormick, even though his machines were preferred in areas such as the South "as less liable to get out of order, and, if slightly damaged, more readily repaired by the slave blacksmith on the farm."[9]

Cyrus McCormick was a native of Virginia's Shenandoah Valley where broad fields stretched under the Blue Ridge Mountains and cotton was not the main cash crop. McCormick's father had worked on a reaper since about 1815, but his son fulfilled the vision of a labor-saving machine in 1831. Much like Hussey's, this had a cutting bar with steel blades set onto a frame with horses walking alongside it, only McCormick's gearing was better if more complicated to repair. Young McCormick did not patent his mechanical reaper until 1834. Hussey and McCormick became bitter business rivals in the 1840s and '50s, when lawsuits on patent infringement flew like chaff in the wind. McCormick was a better businessman who knew that constant improvements were the key to business success. Over the years, he bought up other companies' patents and created his own innovations. He also knew his market. Realizing that the smaller farms east of the Appalachians would not buy expensive machines—his reaper sold for more than $100, about $3,000 in 2015 money—he looked to the west. Expensive as that was, the prospect of a two-man crew cutting 12 acres per day was attractive to farmers and to other manufacturers. In 1847, McCormick partnered with the Gray and Warner foundry in the new city of Chicago where his production took off. With a new factory, rebuilt on an even larger scale after the Great Fire of 1871, production was centralized rather than licensed out as other manufacturers did. Constant improvements led to new machines with a single operator sitting at the back of the team and cutter, and a rake that left bundles of stalks on the ground. Combines that reaped, bundled, and tied followed to further revolutionize grain production.[10]

Besides McCormick a number of other companies sprang up in the 1840s and '50s to meet growing demand for harvesting. Mowing machines for cutting forage, or hay makers, appeared when William F. Ketchum of Buffalo, New York, patented a simple mower in 1844, followed by Cyrenus Wheeler, Jr.'s 1854 mower, later called the Cayuga Chief. As these inventors imply, New York State became a center for grass-cutting technology because heavy wheat-growing from the later eighteenth century was depleting soils in many areas.[11] Fodder for dairy and beef cattle has always been important and in the age of horsepower was critical to the working of the American economy. Dozens and dozens of companies made reapers and mowers in all parts of the country. Northern Ohio became a major production center as was Illinois, where McCormick had seventeen competitors,

The McCormick Twine Binder, advertisement, 1884.

Modern grass cutter for making hay.

notably the J. H. Manny company of Freeport, whose machines rivaled McCormick's in quality. By 1859 an estimated 73,000 machines were in use west of the Alleghenies, harvesting 70 percent of the wheat crop of 173 million bushels of wheat. Even that large number worked out at 5.6 lb (2.5 kg) of wheat per person in the United States in 1860, so evidently the major cash food crop of farmers was unevenly spread or a lot of wheat was not counted by government harvest estimates. Thirty years later new wheat species, expansion of acreage in new territories, and transportation systems allowed for almost 10 lb (4.5 kg) of wheat per capita.[12]

The number of reaping and mowing machines sold mushroomed to 250,000 during the Civil War (1861–5) largely because of the demands of war.[13] All contemporaries say that lack of manpower due to army service and the necessity of feeding troops and workers at home were further factors impelling farmers to use labor-saving mechanisms. Prior to the Civil War, supply requirements for allied troops fighting in the Crimean War (1853–6) far across the world from American farms led to a minor boom in the export grain business; foreign wars paved the way for the great war at home. During the war Union armies numbered about two million and Confederate troop numbers are estimated at about one-and-a-half million, at most, all soldiers raised from a total population of 31 million that included almost four million slaves. Using modern harvesting machinery made sense (and lots of money for manufacturers) because the numbers of man-hours needed to harvest an acre of wheat declined from 40 in 1800 to 23 in 1840 and 12 in 1880. Though yields in the last year were somewhat lower than in 1840, due to declining fertility in the northeast, the Midwest more than made up for the loss. Since new plows and harvesters could do more work, cultivated acreage for food and fodder crops expanded especially in the north. The 173 million bushels of wheat in 1859 grew to 287 million by 1869. Those numbers increased over the rest of the century and as a result wholesale prices for wheat dropped from a high of $2.60 per bushel in 1866 to 62 cents in 1900. Corn, oats, and barley followed similar trajectories, with prices halved by century's end. The same process worked for meat as well after the war.[14] Although not always good for farmers, the drop in prices made more food available to America's rising and increasingly urban population.

Machines are systems and no modern machines can exist without machine parts that can be used interchangeably. That, in turn, depends on mechanisms to work metals "accurately and economically."[15] The process began in mid-eighteenth-century England centered on metalworking lathes for the manufacture of steam engines and for boring cannons. Boulton and Watt's steam engines would not have been successful without precision parts working together. Of all the inventors the brilliant Henry Maudslay (1771–1831) is considered to be the father of the machine tool industry. His screw-cutting lathe made standard screw and nut-and-bolt sizes possible, and together with a metal hole-punching machine and bench micrometer laid the foundations for precision interchangeable parts.

Americans took to the idea of interchangeability so avidly that in the nineteenth century it was called "The American System," or sometimes "weapons system." Eli Whitney of cotton gin fame is usually associated with the idea, not for the gin but for weaponry. In 1812 he sought a government contract for muskets, saying that he wanted to "to make the same parts of different guns, as the locks, for example, as much like each other as the successive impressions of a copper-plate engraving." In fact Whitney was not alone in the movement to make standardized replaceable parts. Simeon North, like Whitney a Connecticut man, invented the metal milling machine and with it made pistols. James H. Hall of Maine, who worked at the Harpers Ferry Armory (now West Virginia) on breech-loading guns, was also a pioneer in building the industry.[16] Samuel Colt invented his famed revolver pistol in 1836 and after initial skepticism by the Army eventually sold thousands during the Mexican War in 1846. His new factory in Hartford, Connecticut, was modeled on Whitney's as were many other manufacturers who followed, from sewing machines to later bicycles and farm machinery. Without well-made gears, for instance, the wheels of industry would not have run.[17]

Agricultural machines were powered by muscle, human and animal. The factories of the nineteenth century initially used water power, hence the early concentration in New England with its swift-flowing rivers. Horses and mules were preferred in agriculture because the amount of energy output they provide per unit of feeding (meaning calories needed to function) is equivalent to as many as thirteen field hands.[18] The United States had almost five million horses and mules, providing 70 percent of all horsepower in 1850, and 8.7 million in 1860 providing more than 62 percent of all horsepower.[19] Railroads and steamboats rapidly became the means of long-distance travel but equines were used heavily for short-haul transportation in cities and rural areas. That 1,600-lb draft horses excrete perhaps 50 lb or more of manure and 20 lb of urine every day is why American cities were filthy with it—as in 150,000 horses in 1900 New York City. Horses were treated abominably, their lifespans perhaps four years, and dead horse carcasses littered the streets of American cities. Horses were treated like machines in the great social mechanism that was the city. Everyone knew about the problem, especially when considering food brought into cities and eaten on the street, but, until motorized transport, horses were necessary. Another downside of horses is that they need a lot of feed, to say nothing of other care. In 1900 the 16.5 million working animals required 74 million acres of small grain and hay to feed them. Horses and mules ate a quarter of the total 308 million acres of farmed land.[20]

Innovation was at hand, based on the new metal technologies and power sources. Steam, used for railroads and ships, spilled over into farming. In the 1830s, stationary steam engines were in use, notably for cotton gins in the South. Eli Whitney's original invention was manually powered but his patents were appropriated by local planters who adapted them to steam power. Moving an engine from location to location was one thing, but making something like a steam plow was soon recognized as desirable because of increasing production from harvesting machines in the wide lands of the west. Though horses were widely used for harvesting machines, they had other drawbacks: exhaustion, injuries due to improper harnessing, uneven pulling power because walking speeds varied, and often broken gears as a result. Steam engines had none of these defects. Joseph Fawkes of Lancaster, Pennsylvania, demonstrated the first successful plow in 1853. When he showed his improved machine at the 1858 Illinois State fair in Centralia the press was ecstatic, one journal declaring that "The steam-plow is a success and Fawkes is immortal!"[21] The machine could pull eight plows at 4 miles per hour,

Harvesting grain with horse-powered reapers that cut 200 acres daily, California, *c.* 1890.

encompassing 4 acres in one hour. The test was on dry baked prairie land, but when tested on wet soils the 10-ton behemoth's iron rollers sank into the mud and reality set in. Fawkes did not have enough capital to continue improvements and went bankrupt. It was a start, and improved engines were introduced quickly by such manufacturers as J. I. Case in Racine, Wisconsin, McCormick, Allis-Chalmers, and a dozen others in the Midwest, Pennsylvania, and New York.

The Civil War drove expansion of farmland, and railroads carried foodstuffs to processing centers. Transcontinental railroads, the first completed in 1869, opened California, the western prairies such as Nebraska, and the Great Plains to farming. Bigger planting and harvesting mechanisms were adapted to the lands. So called Bonanza farms were constructed on the short grass prairies centered in the Red River Valley. Portable, if very large and heavy, steam engines that could get to a field came early to this area and to California's fertile valleys. Most were attached to threshing machines in the field by belts, though by late in the century there were full-scale steam tractors attached to full combines. These were effective: "Dr. Hugh Glenn, who owned 66,000 acres of land in the Sacramento Valley,

Steam tractor plowing, California, 1912.

in 1880 used 6 steam engines, 60 headers, and 180 header boxes to harvest and thresh his million-bushel crop of wheat."[22]

Further mobility was the next step. Russell & Co. of Massillon, Ohio, developed a self-steered engine in 1882 and the tractor was born. A new kind of farm specialist called a thresherman operated the steam engines. Since farmers usually could not afford a several-thousand-dollar machine, they hired threshermen at harvest time. As *The American Thresherman* (in print from 1898) shows, these were owner-entrepreneurs who worked in teams stoking the boilers (wood and straw in early models, coal in later ones), keeping the leather belts in order and moving the levers of power—and powerful they are, as anyone who sees these mammoth multi-tonned machines in the field at state fairs and threshermen's gatherings will say, often in awe.

The age of steam power in farming passed with the widespread adoption of the internal combustion engine. The earliest gasoline- and kerosene-burning engines were sold in the United States as early as the 1880s when the German inventor Nikolaus Otto's engine appeared. Their fuel depended on the new petroleum industry, which began commercially in 1859 in western Pennsylvania. Advertisements in farm journals such as *The Prairie Farmer* and *The American Thresherman* claimed that these had the advantage of eliminating boiler explosions, fire damage, water leakage, and delays and used cheap fuel.[23] These were large machines that resembled their steam-powered forebears and many were used in the same way as stationary engines for belt-driven machinery.[24] The familiar modern light tractor appeared when Henry Ford introduced his Fordson in 1916. Based on his concept of the Model T automobile, to sell at the lowest cost possible to create a larger market, by the later 1920s, 70 percent of American tractors were his products. Manufacturers such as Allis-Chalmers, Case, Deere, and International Harvester (the former McCormick) joined in to create a competitive market. Nonetheless by 1930 there were only nine hundred thousand tractors and one million gas engines on America's six million farms. Progress was uneven, with northern and western farms more technologically advanced than many in the South.[25]

Like living organisms, changes in one system lead to changes in other related ones. The considerable discussion about this idea ranges from plants (weeds, for instance) to machines. The application of new technologies to farming was related to changes in metallurgy and energy sources applied to cloth manufacture, weaponry, and transportation. Ideas and production techniques then moved to other aspects of food production. Milling, as discussed previously, was crucial to getting grain products to wide markets. At the St. Anthony Falls at Minnesota's Twin Cities, water-powered milling concerns grew beginning in the 1840s. Millers such as Cadwallader

Steam engine tractor at an American Thresherman show.

Case Steam Engine Separator advertisement, c. 1900. Case was a major agricultural machinery manufacturer, famous for its tractors. Merged with other companies, the brand name has disappeared but its tractors appear at agricultural shows regularly.

Washburn and Charles Pillsbury built large mills to process the immense output of the Bonanza farms on the Great Plains. In 1885,

> The twenty six flouring mills . . . on both sides of the river below the falls . . . consumed last year 24,000,000 bushels of wheat and made 5,450,163 barrels of flour, an amount more than sufficient to supply with bread the entire population of the city of New York . . . [T]he wheat demanded for the daily consumption of the mills requires for its transportation 266 cars, or a solid train of a mile and three-quarters in length, and . . . to move the daily product of flour and mill-stuff there are required 328 cars and 16 locomotives, or more than two miles of solid train.[26]

That was only the beginning because technology was changing.

Techniques using hot air for removing middlings, the unwanted dark chaff from ground grain, were introduced, followed by new porcelain and steel rollers that gradually pulverized the flour, thus mixing gluten and starch thoroughly. The result was a white flour that was thought to be the world's best for bread. The wheats used were high-gluten hard reds that were well adapted to the northern lands. The white flour, unspeckled by chaff, was highly desirable to consumers who increasingly disdained coarser flours, even if some retained their basic nutrients. By 1900, Twin Cities mills produced one-quarter of America's flour. The dominance would not last because steam-powered mills appeared in Kansas City near the Kansas and Nebraska wheat fields, but Pillsbury and General Mills (Gold Medal flour), the successor of Washburn and Crosby, remain major brands.

Crop production in open lands changed the American landscape. Anyone passing through the American countryside will see grain silos and elevators standing like fingers pointed to the sky. The increasing amounts of grain being produced for the commercial market had to be stored before shipping to distant parts of the country. Buffalo was the shipping center for the Great Lakes and the terminus of the Erie Canal. It was here that an entrepreneur named Joseph Dart created the first successful elevator in 1842. Based on Oliver Evans's original designs, buckets hauled grain to the top of large bins and then dumped it; unlike Evans's, however, Dart's were steam-powered. "Huge skyscraper warehouses" holding massive quantities of grain appeared in in this and other cities along trade routes. By 1845 his elevators could store 100,000 bushels of grain. Chicago became the greatest of all, by 1861 handling 50 million bushels annually in its steam-powered elevators along the slow-flowing Chicago River. Several still stand, including the abandoned concrete Santa Fe Grain Elevator, built in 1906, which could store almost a half-million bushels and processed 75,000 bushels per hour.[27] One technology that grew out of grain shipping remains a core Chicago business: the grading system for wheat that is still used today and a grain exchange, founded in 1848, that stands as the nation's central futures market.

Farm fields with haystacks.

The transformation of American agriculture was done by innovative people working with machines in a kind of evolutionary feedback system, as mentioned. The reasons that impelled change have been much discussed especially in light of seminal work done by Yujiro Hayami and Vernon W. Ruttan. Using a term from economic theory, induced innovation, they argued that agricultural advances did not come primarily from outside sources, inventors thinking up new machines, but from the needs of farmers themselves. The authors thought that scarcity, especially of labor, caused farmers to ask for innovations that could produce more and cheaper because less labor was needed.[28] Certainly contemporaries all marveled at how much new plows, tillers, seed drills, harvesters, silos, and more worked to produce more. However, Ruttan also thought that government policies were a powerful external input to innovation, citing war as a chief example. If the model is applied to actual cookery, then the instructions in almost all nineteenth- and early twentieth-century manuals for economical preparations paved the way for labor-saving devices. Advertising for new products from stoves to pans, washing machines, and gadgets all boast of efficiency and speed. Over the course of the twentieth and early twenty-first centuries that is exactly what happened; think frozen entrees, microwave ovens, or food processors.

Like the cooking gadgets of today, so many new machines were available by the early twentieth century that farmers of means became consumers as well as suppliers. In an ironic comment on consumerism and the machine metaphor, Edgar Lee Masters's invented epitaph for Abel Melveny reads:

I bought every kind of machine that's known—

Grinders, shellers, planters, mowers,
Mills and rakes and ploughs and threshers—
And all of them stood in the rain and sun,
Getting rusted, warped and battered,
For I had no sheds to store them in,
And no use for most of them . . .
I saw myself as a good machine
That Life had never used.[29]

Acknowledging how important the idea of induced innovation is, Olmstead and Rhode in *Creating Abundance* show that mechanical improvements alone were not responsible for America's agricultural advancement. Genetic experiments were just as crucial and began even earlier in time. Farmers from the beginning looked for optimal plants and certainly manipulated them by selective breeding. In 1880s Ohio there were some eleven different types of wheat being grown as experiments, to say nothing of a huge variety of apples developed in the nineteenth century (some seven hundred at least) for cider and for eating. All studies of American farm production show that actual yield per acre of wheat did not increase much for the century after the introduction of the Deere plow and McCormick's harvester. The same can be said for cotton which, in fact, declined in productivity after the Civil War. Modern wheat yields of 40 or so bushels per acre as opposed to 15 came as a result of modern chemicals after the Second World War. Absent heavy fertilization, the only way farmers could increase the amounts of grain or cotton was by opening new arable lands, hence all the machines. Replacing horses with tractors freed up land needed to feed them so it could instead be used for human food crops. On the other hand, fewer horses meant less horse manure for fertilizing fields and gardens, but such techniques of intensive farming were not in the general American scheme except in certain locales. Extensive rather than intensive farming was the American pattern and that came with grievous problems over time.

Perhaps the best example of the argument about genetics and machinery, or lack of it—and one with the most pernicious effects—is cotton. Prior to 1806 cotton was confined to coastal areas of the South and the lower Mississippi Valley. Eli Whitney's cotton gin, patented in 1794, made the industry possible because it mechanized the tedious task of picking seeds from the sticky Sea Isle or Green Seed cottons grown at the time. Cotton production increased greatly but intensive labor was still needed for picking; mechanized pickers only came into use during and after the Second World War. In 1806, a Natchez planter named Walter Burling saw high-quality cotton plants in Mexico and smuggled out some seeds. Experiments with seeds followed, leading to a plant whose lint hung out of the boll for easy picking and with high production values. Whereas workers could harvest up to 100 lb a day of older types, they could collect several hundred pounds of the Mexican Highland breeds. Other improved breeds followed.[30] The new cotton was adapted to the rich alluvial lands of the South but it was also grown in the less fertile upland soils. By the 1830s, cotton boomed, going from some seven hundred thousand bales to two and one-half million in 1850. By 1860 the American South supplied roughly 75 percent of the world's cotton.[31] England's mills hummed to the strings of Southern cotton, but at what a cost.

Though some cotton was grown in the Carolina Piedmont regions in the antebellum period, the Southern tier states were the Cotton Belt. It was here in the warm climates that the large monoculture plantations were located and where the majority of agricultural laborers, African American slaves, worked. Cotton is hard on the land, needing a good deal of fertilization to maintain production in fields devoted to it. It is a disputed truism that the agricultural practices of Southern planters were to use land until it wore out and then move on. The need for new cotton lands is usually given as a reason for the conflict between North and South over the western lands newly opened to American settlement in the 1840s and '50s. The pre-Civil War bloody conflict between free farmers and slave owners in these states was the cause of "Bleeding Kansas" and the career of abolitionist John Brown. Of course, ideology played a decisive role in the fight.

Visitors like Frederick Law Olmsted and some Southerners alike commented on how much Southern land had been rendered useless and abandoned by poor farming practices and cotton growing. The planters knew about fertilizers since commercial fertilizers such as marl, lime, and guano shipped from Peru had been available from the 1830s. Improving lands was a topic discussed in American agricultural societies from early in the century.[32] But Southern planters rarely used fertilizers outside of animal dung for gardens. An argument has been made that there was fertile land available within the South for cotton, and cotton production increased greatly in the decade between 1850 and 1860 in the cotton states. But the fact remains that much land in the red clay lands of Georgia, southern Alabama, and Mississippi had been ruined. Plantation owners wanted to have more western lands such as California (it remained a free state). Given the lands and climate, most of the South was not conducive to commodity food production like the Midwest. Cattle did not thrive, insects and fungi decimated crops; cotton boll caterpillars were plagues even before the infamous boll weevil. The population was smaller than the North and scattered. Out of some twelve and one-half million people only about one-half million people were urban dwellers.[33] Nor were the railroad systems as developed as in the North.

And then there was the slave system. Energy for producing cotton, rice, and sugar came from human beings. Of the almost four million African American slaves some 60 percent were forced to work in cotton fields. The more cotton fields, the higher the production demands, the more slaves were needed. Southern planters often complained of lack of experienced labor but they did not look to machinery save for gins and railroads. Induced innovation does not work well for an archaic manorial system. Depleted lands had something to do with this as states like Virginia with tobacco-ravaged lands came to rely on breeding human beings for sale to the labor-hungry plantations of the South. With more than a million people sold at auction, the term "sold down the river" has real meaning.

Scholars have debated slave diets for many years. While slaves may have been treated like machines, since plantation incomes depended on them they had to have been fed enough to work effectively. That slaves worked under the threat of violence is indisputable. Workloads varied from industry to industry and also depended upon seasonal planting and harvesting. Estimates are that between 4,000 and 4,500 calories or more per day were needed for men harvesting. Women and children needed less, yet almost 60 percent of all cotton before the war (and by sharecroppers after it) was picked by women and children.[34] Slaves were given staple rations amounting to about 3–4 lb of pork per week, rations of cornmeal, and dried beans. Much of the pork was raised in the marginal farming area of the South and was imported from the Midwest down the Mississippi and Ohio Rivers. Fat pork contains 650–800 calories per pound, so it is obvious that slaves ate more legumes and vegetables than meat, unless they were able to hunt for squirrels, raccoons, opossums, and fish. Slaves ate from the garden plots that many were given, as well. Whether all enslaved people were fed enough calories is debatable. What is not in question is that the work requirements of women and cooking practices available to them did not allow for healthful meals. Vitamins and minerals were often leached from fresh ingredients and frying was the order when enough fat was available. Nor was fancy baking on any slave laboring family's menu. Vitamin deficiency diseases were common well into the twentieth century. Not that poor whites had much better diets, but for them it was some consolation that they were not chattel slaves.[35]

Systematized manufacturing with interchangeable parts changed agriculture. The same ideas eventually penetrated into the home, where work was perhaps more unrelenting than on the farm. As Andrew F. Smith has noted, there was an explosion of printed cookbooks after the Civil War, all of them giving instructions on how to make desirable and economical dishes for one's family. None of these were intended for slaves and poor folks but for women in middling rank families who may have had servants.

Cookery practices were at the consumer end of the emerging production system. In 1851 Angelina Maria Lorraine Collins published Indiana's first cookbook. A native of Virginia, her Methodist and abolitionist family moved north when she was young. After marriage to James Collins, a lawyer and politician, she settled in New Albany across the Ohio River

Local Foods

American food was on the way to nationalization but local foodways remained and are still found. Locavorism usually means collecting and eating fresh produce and meats from a specific local area, typically no more than 100 miles from the source. It can also mean dishes created and served in, or at least attached to, certain communities and regions. Some of these are so well known as cultural identifiers that they have become embedded in local tourism. Usually made by local eateries, the list is long, including: Cornish pasties (that may not be truly Cornish as advertised), served in Michigan's Upper Peninsula and western Wisconsin; cudighi, an Italian-American sandwich composed of sausage, mozzarella cheese, and tomato sauce, also from the Upper Peninsula; she-crab soup in coastal South Carolina; Maryland crab cakes; Wisconsin fish boils; New Mexico Hatch chili tacos; Indian tacos in northwest Nebraska and the Great Plains; New England lobster rolls dipped in butter; New Orleans muffuletta and Po'Boy sandwiches; California fish tacos; Texas and Oklahoma chicken fried steak; pork tenderloin sandwiches in a belt running from middle Indiana through Illinois and into Iowa; and poke, a Hawaiian raw fish, tomato, and onion salad that has gained recent national attention through newspaper and magazine articles.

Some local dishes have become more commercialized through local chain restaurants, such as Cincinnati Chili, a commercialized food served in a number of outlets. Nebraska's Bierock (from the Volga German-Russian pirok) or Runza is a pasty made with ground meat, cabbage, and onions that has become somewhat commercial through a restaurant chain of the same name, but is often made at local restaurants and at home. Iowa loose meat sandwiches are widely sold in the state and nearby areas by Maid-Rite, another small chain specializing in a regional dish. It seems unlikely, though, that these and other foods will become national in the manner of Chicago deep dish pizza or Philadelphia cheese steaks.

from Louisville, Kentucky, and 120 miles from Cincinnati. Her fame as a hostess and cook led to *Mrs. Collins' Table Receipts: Adapted to Western Housewifery.*[36] The book was dedicated to ladies, homemakers, who lived in "The West." In Mrs. Collins's time what we call the Midwest was still "the west" with its implications as a land occupied by rustics. The earliest "Midwestern" book, Philomelia Ann Maria Antoinette Hardin's *Every Body's Cook and Receipt Book* (1842), is similar in outlook and language. The author's forceful language, as in "In the first place, (take no offence, madam!) it is highly necessary that your vessel should be perfectly clean)," seems directed to such a readership. To the contrary, this and regional cookbooks to follow were meant for women of middling rank who lived in the rising towns and cities, not farm women who, like Willa Cather's Shimerdas, were exhausted by the grind of daily chores and lack of labor-saving devices. As Andrew F. Smith points out in his introduction to *The Centennial Buckeye Cook Book* (1876), the famous and much reprinted and revised community cookbook from Marysville, Ohio, many recipes are the same as or descend from popular English authors such as Susannah Carter and the American Amelia Simmons.[37] Beef à la mode recipes, for instance, vary in cookery books over the century mainly in seasonings, not cooking method.

Western Housewifery has a recipe, unusual for the time, for what was the brand new West, "California Soup." The recipe calls for taking 10 lb of beef bone, breaking it and gently boiling for ten hours, straining and then cooking down into a gelatin. "Put it away in small dry vessels, or, if you wish to preserve it more than six months, in bladders, such as are used for German sausages." Or the gelatin cubes can be air dried until solid and then reconstituted with water. Here is a unique dried soup preparation and an early mention of German, meaning ethnic, cookery. It was first published in 1851, only three years after the American conquest of California from Mexico, two years after the beginning of the Gold Rush, and a year after California became a state. Mrs. Collins certainly saw steamboats filled with passengers going to California moving down the Ohio River toward St. Louis, and then up the Missouri to St. Joseph where their overland journey would begin. With them went culinary skills, recipes, and farming technologies.

Ten years later Mrs. T.J.V. Owen of Springfield, Illinois, published a community cookbook consisting of recipes from local cooks who were obviously friends; a Mrs. Hurst endorsed the book and lent a half-dozen recipes.[38] In her preface, Mrs. Owen says, "I have been careful of preserving all well-tried receipts, and in collecting such as, in my own judgment and the judgment and experience of my friends, would reach the necessities of

Odd Local Foods

Some American preparations are so local that they have not achieved the status of "iconic local" foods. As in earlier periods before the nationalization of much of American food, some come from the immediate area in which they exist. Murder Point oysters from Alabama's Gulf Coast are an example. Others are invented and considered to be odd because they are either unusual combinations of ingredients, have tastes outside ordinary American food, or have unique names. No matter which of these apply, they do represent local flavors and food cultures. Among them are rabbit hash from a Kentucky district of the same name along the Ohio River. The community received its name in the 1870s, presumably from a dish that might or might not have been made from rabbit that was served to river boatmen. It is not served at the hamlet's famous general store or to the place's mayors who, since 1998, have been dogs.

Some dishes are in the Big Sandwich class. Invented in Hilo, Hawaii, the Loco Moco is composed of a meat patty covered in a fried egg and brown sauce. The Louisville, Kentucky, Hot Brown is an open-faced turkey and bacon sandwich covered in Mornay sauce, then broiled until browned. Also dating to the 1920s, the Horseshoe from Springfield, Illinois, is two ground beef disks on white toast, covered in French fries and then coated in a cheesy Welsh rarebit sauce. The original had ham slices, but hamburgers became more popular after the Second World War. Found on Chicago's South Side is the Jim (or Gym) Shoe made of corned beef, roast beef, and gyros meat in a submarine bun with melted cheese, or tzatziki, giardiniera, and lettuce and tomatoes. In the Twin Cities of Minneapolis and St. Paul, Minnesota, the Juicy Lucy is two hamburgers with American cheese between them on a bun with varieties of toppings. Of all such giant dishes the Garbage Plate of Rochester, New York, stands out. Invented by Nick Tahou's restaurant, it is a layered dish with baked beans or macaroni salad together with French fries topped with hamburger, cheeseburger, hot dogs, Italian sausage, fried fish, fried ham, eggs, grilled cheese, onions, and a Coney sauce. Iterations vary in the region, but the concept of mounds of food is the same.

Other unique foods include: St. Louis pizza, a thin crust covered in a local processed cheese made with liquid smoke called Provel; Cincinnati Goetta, pork or beef mixed with oats made into a loaf and then fried in fat; Chislic (from shash-lik) in South Dakota, squares of lamb or beef skewered; Rocky Mountain Oysters or Prairie Oysters in the Great Plains and Colorado, bull or bison testicles battered and deep-fried; and Massachusetts and Rhode Island Stuffies, a clam shell heaped with chopped clam, sausage, herbs, and breadcrumbs. Most local of all is Snook, Texas, with a population of about five hundred: here chicken-fried bacon was invented and fifty thousand people descend each year for a monster Texas chili fest.

all who may desire a good practical receipt book." Likely the future president Abraham Lincoln dined upon some of these dishes during his days in Springfield from 1837 to 1861. As might be expected, many recipes resemble Mrs. Collins's, from bread baking using homemade yeast to corndodgers and using corn meal for quick breads and as a vegetable. One such is the redoubtable succotash, which made its way west from New England. Both books call for dried and soaked beans cooked in plentiful water for long periods of time, together with corncobs from which the kernels have been cut, with fresh corn added for fifteen minutes at the end and seasoned with butter and pepper. Sweetcorn grew locally and was easily available, while beans could be local or purchased. Butter was indispensable in many recipes and black pepper was always available from grocers. Mrs. Collins called her dish à la Tecumseh in honor of the famous Native American war leader. "This is a real

Western dish, and is very easily made." Since Lincoln grew up impoverished in southern Indiana no doubt he knew such simple dishes well.

What is different in these books aside from the more rural quality of *Western Housewifery*—the recipe for forcemeat balls calls for grinding veal and cow udder in a mortar—is in cooking equipment. Boiling, baking, and frying are in each book's repertoires but Collins's recipes look closer to hearth cookery than to stove cookery. That might be expected from dishes that descend from the eighteenth century, but all cooking is adapted by practical cooks to the means at hand. The earlier book instructs cooks to roast potatoes in a tin oven or cheese toaster (a toasting griddle) and "do not put them too near the fire." The 1871 book says: "bake in a quick oven, according to their size . . . Let the oven have a good heat, and do not open any more than necessary to turn them."

Cast iron stoves had been available in various forms since the previous century, beginning with the Franklin stove. By the 1830s various designs from step stoves to larger multi-plate stoves existed, made locally by numerous foundries. Early stoves were wood-fueled but as cheaper coal came onto the market it became a preferred source. Mrs. Owen discusses where to place coals in an oven for maximum economy.[39] At the time of *Western Housewifery* nearby Louisville had perhaps ten foundries that made stoves, such as J. S. Lithgow's Eagle Foundry, James Bridgeford's Louisville Stove and Grate Company, and Fischer, Leaf & Co. Access to Kentucky's ample coal deposits (begun in the 1820s) made Louisville and Covington up the Ohio River near Cincinnati natural places for foundries. The companies also made cookware and there were specialty rolling mills that made plate and tinned pots and ovens; almost all cookery books mentioned the importance of such pots for braising and making stews. Among the products were tea kettles and spiders. Cast iron kettles could be hung over open fires and with their flat bottoms set on flat ranges. Spiders were deep lidded cast-iron pans with legs made to be set among coals in a hearth. While they could be adapted to stoves with removable plates, by the 1850s they were more likely to be sold for outdoor cooking, such as by people moving in wagons to the west. *Western Housewifery* stands at the point when homes in the west were adapting recipes and techniques to modern technology, something that was well underway in the states east of the Appalachians.[40]

Thirty years later in 1881, another Illinois community cookbook shows the transition from local food sourcing to wider production circles. *The Illinois Cook Book* was compiled for the Grace Episcopal Church of Paris, Illinois. An agricultural center of about four thousand people at the

Historic stove, mid-19th century, Historic Bishop Hill village, Illinois.

time, Paris is set in the flat prairie lands of central Illinois near the Wabash River.[41] That it was integrated into the emerging American commercial network is seen in the recipe collection. Two recipes for "Dolly Varden Cake" (named for a character in Charles Dickens's *Barnaby Rudge*), the au courant fashion style among upper-crust ladies, show the national connections to small town America.[42] A dozen recipes for oysters that had to be imported from the East Coast and were de rigueur for upscale and holiday dining in the century form a chapter. Though many recipes look like earlier preparations—yeast for instance is to be made from hops and not yet the commercial kind—the kitchen inventory recommended for the home cook is more modern. A wide range of tinware including bakeware, a clothes boiler and ham boiler, and cups for measuring by volumes stand by such ironware as porcelain-coated tea kettles, gem pans, griddles, and waffle irons. Listed in the inventory are an egg beater and a can opener. Rotary egg beaters that resemble modern ones appeared by the 1850s but they are not apparent in recipes for beating eggs in the earlier books.[43] The can opener could have been a lever type invented in England in the 1850s (now commonly found as a blade in fancy Swiss Army knives), or the new rotary device invented by William Lyman in 1870.[44] In either case, by the 1880s homemakers in the middle of the United States were using canned goods. *The Illinois Cook Book* has recipes for home canning, as did most others of its kind up to the present day, but a can opener means commercially made products by companies outside the immediate area. New technologies developed during the Civil War made mass canning at reasonable costs a large business, though not for all products.[45] Perhaps the opener was used for the more prestigious canned oysters that came from the booming industry centered in Baltimore: the city went from producing 1 ton of oysters to 80 tons in 1868 and about 15 million by the 1880s.[46] It is not surprising that restaurants like the Boston Oyster House in Chicago were famous for these bivalve treats.

Sarah Heston Tyson Rorer's famous *Philadelphia Cook Book* stands almost at the end of the nineteenth-century process of changes in food production and technology.[47] Mrs. Rorer (1849–1937) was perhaps the most famous culinary authority of her era and one of the pioneers of scientific nutrition education in America.[48] Her Philadelphia Cooking School lessons and lectures, sometimes to thousands of attendees, were the basis for her 1886 book. In it she extolled simple, presumably healthy cookery using fresh ingredients—though still boiling vegetables for longer than today: the then little-known broccoli, for instance, appears with directions to boil for twenty minutes and serve with a cream sauce. Clear explanations of why various cooking methods work mark some of the differences with previous books. *The Illinois Cook Book*, for instance, gives no cooking directions for most dishes. To make the same beef soup as *Western Housewifery*, Rorer discusses albumen and fibrin and a phantom substance called osmazome that gives aroma to meat dishes and might be the modern umami. A frequent direction is to set the stock pot at the back of the range to simmer. Canned goods are taken for granted; yeast might be made at home or bought in cakes at a store. Her beef à la mode was a more elaborate preparation than others using forcemeat for larding and calling for an oven temperature of 220°F, which implies the use of an oven thermometer, something she advised stove makers to set into their products.

The *Philadelphia Cook Book* recipes are a wonderful compendium of dishes that represent the range of nineteenth-century American rural and urban cookery. For instance, "mango" is a term usually used for sweet peppers but also for peaches and melons in all the books mentioned here. The outer casing is soaked and stuffed with finely shredded cabbage laced with mace, allspice, mustard seeds or horseradish, perhaps sugar, and then set in vinegar to steep. This dish represents a whole range of spiced pickled products made at home, from sauerkraut to pickles, chow-chow, and catsups. Making these was a routine job for women on farms and in small towns across America well into the twentieth century, even when canned and jarred commercial products were available. That would change after the Second World War, when canning became more a hobby than a necessity.

Mrs. Rorer's audiences were often urban, though her popular books and pamphlets were read across the nation. Her tables of weights and measures, use of thermometers, knowledge of pan placement in an age before gas and electric stoves with accurate temperature controls, and assumption of ingredients that could be purchased at retail shops, speaks to an age when rational division of tasks and mechanisms began to replace the old intuitive methods of cookery. The kitchen mirrored what was taking place on the farm and in new food factories.

At least that held for families of middling rank. For the immigrant Shimerdas in Nebraska and for farm women across America, labor-saving machinery was slower in coming to the home. Not until electric motors were attached in equipment such as washing machines around 1900, and not until rural America was more fully electrified in the 1920s and '30s, was women's ceaseless round of labor ameliorated.[49] Here is Hamlin Garland on the less than idyllic life of farm women: "Sallow, weazened, old before their time, with a dull, patient, hopeless look on their faces; condemned to a life of littleness and vacuity, occupied in running from stove to pantry, from cradle to frying-pan."[50] His description of meals made for farm workers such as his

Late 19th-century coal stove, Mascoutah, Illinois Historical Society.

A. A. Knoke, homestead with corn, Montana, 1910.

ox-strong uncle were massive amounts of meat, chicken legs sucked through in one go, heaps of potatoes, maybe some string beans and corn in season, all followed by pie or cake and lots of coffee. All of it gobbled in minutes so that, at least in harvest season, no time was lost. It was three massive meals a day, every day, every year. Only on Sundays or holidays could women show their better cooking skills, especially with desserts. Willa Cather's old Mrs. Shimerda labors in her kitchen thusly:

> As I sat waiting for the hour when Ambrosch and Ántonia would return from the fields, I watched Mrs. Shimerda at her work. She took from the oven a coffee-cake which she wanted to keep warm for supper, and wrapped it in a quilt stuffed with feathers. I have seen her put even a roast goose in this quilt to keep it hot. When the neighbours were there building the new house, they saw her do this, and the story got abroad that the Shimerdas kept their food in their featherbeds.[51]

None of Mrs. Rorer's fancies for them.

EIGHT

What We Ate and Why (to 1945)

His exertions made him hungry, and entering a small eating-house he
ordered a cup of coffee and a beefsteak. To this he added a couple of rolls.
This was quite a luxurious breakfast for Dick, and more expensive than he
was accustomed to indulge himself with . . . Total__25 cts.
Horatio Alger Jr., *Ragged Dick; or Street Life in New York with
the Boot Blacks* (1868)[1]

Fresh Shrimp Cocktail, Served with Lemon, Our Special Cocktail Sauce,
And Saltine Crackers with Butter. Gulf of Mexico Shrimp, strictly fresh and
full of minerals and vitamins of the sea__ .45

Famous Triangle Specialty—Generous a la Carte Portion—Delicious
Spaghetti a la Toffenetti, with Rich Meat Sauce and Grated Parmesan
Cheese__ .35

Slenderella Salad, Made with Non-Fattening Mineral Oil
Chicken a la King on Toast, French Fried Potatoes and Green Peas. Truly a
dish fit for a king. It is rich and tasty and full of chicken__ .65
Excerpt from a Toffenetti's Triangle Restaurant menu, Chicago and New York, 1945

During the span between Ragged Dick's "expensive" breakfast and
the items on Toffenetti's menu, America's food changed considerably. The process was evolutionary and ended up as a revolution. While
the basic foods were much the same, how they were produced, processed,
marketed, and sold was not. Technologies developed with increasing
velocity from plows to mills, reapers, and bailers, from horse to steam
locomotives to internal combustion, and from fireplaces to coal and
then gas and electric stoves. Chemistry—nitrogen fertilizer a prime

example—and genetics made for new variations in plant and animals. Production of staples such as meats became increasingly mechanized and thus systematized. Science entered the kitchen and, like mechanical devices made with perfectly fitting interchangeable parts, recipes by experts gave precise directions for perfect results using both old ingredients and new modified foodstuffs. The new "pure white" degermed wheat flour, leavenings, canned, and later frozen products were among the many innovations. Scientific advances led to new ways of measuring human (and animal) nutrition, indeed a whole new professional field, home economics. Several generations of American women (boys were not usually permitted in these classes until late in the twentieth century) well remembered their required grade and high school home economics classes, often putting what they learned about modern products and cookery to use in their own homes.

None of a host of changes happened by accident or on its own. Rather, they were essential parts of America's social and economic transformations during the two to three generations between the end of the Civil War and the beginning of the Second World War. Much occurred during the latter third of the nineteenth century, a period often referred to by the title of a novel by Mark Twain and Charles Dudley Warner, *The Gilded Age* (1873). Reviled by many, then and now, as a time when robber barons like Jay Gould, Andrew Carnegie, and John D. Rockefeller became immensely wealthy while their workers barely got by or starved, it was the time when America's industries were rationalized into coherent bureaucratized business and production systems. Standardized rail widths and timetables, agreed upon by railroad executives and instituted on November 18, 1883, are an example of change that was critical to the flow of goods. Some changes came from the utility of new improved production that, when applied to food, made more of it available at lower costs to consumers. Others were from newly introduced and marketed foods, such as imported bananas and hydrogenated fats replacing lard and suet for frying and baking. That so many changes came from trusts (vertical and horizontal monopolies), and at the cost of so much misery for workers, seemed to many Americans the price to be paid for progress (else they would not have voted for conservative presidents). Not everything was set by the marketplace. From the Civil War to the present, federal and state government policies changed much about America's food. The Homestead Act and the Morrill Act establishing land grant colleges, passed in Abraham Lincoln's administration, permitted both the development of western lands and the model for basic research in agriculture that lives on today. Later, food policies such as crop supports created during the Great Depression of the 1930s formed the basis of modern agricultural business, for better or worse.

New mouths to feed drove agricultural expansion and distribution systems. Between 1880 and 1930 roughly 27 million "new immigrants" came to the United States, joining the ten million "old immigrants" who had arrived between 1820 and 1880. Most of the new ones were east and south Europeans who largely settled in and around the rising cities, while some went to farms in the hinterlands. Huge numbers of immigrants took urban jobs ranging from factories to peddling. Farmers like Willa Cather's Bohemian Shimerda family in Nebraska entered the national food-producing system by selling their crops in the marketplace. In the southwest, Mexicans became the labor backbone of the farming industry. All of them ate foods from home, many of which, over time, entered the mainstream of America's food. Just as in species evolution, these foods became naturalized in their new environments, thus deserving hyphenated labels such as Tex-Mex or Italian-American.

Not that the changes moved as a uniform wave across a continent-spanning nation. Depending on place and people, environments and economies, new ways came swiftly or slowly. It has been said that electrification took about fifty years to be fully implemented from Thomas Edison's first distribution system in 1882. By 1935, about 90 percent of the nation had electric lights, but only federal government action through the Rural Electrification Act of 1935 brought electricity (and telephone service) to almost all rural areas by 1970.[2] Fast food chains founded on hamburgers began in the 1920s, notably White Castle in Wichita, Kansas, in 1921. Its success and that of its many imitators, such as White Tower, Royal Castle, White Palace, and A&W, meant that hamburger stands and drive-ins could be found in numerous cities and good-sized towns by the 1930s.[3] None of these, though, were as massive or ubiquitous as modern chains such as McDonald's. The creation of the national road system, funded as a national defense initiative, in the 1950s speeded the creation of America's corporate fast food industry. Founded in 1955, McDonald's had seven hundred restaurants across the nation within a decade.[4] Many more fast food chains followed, as did massive consolidated food-producing corporations that reached into every nook and cranny of American society.

Mark Twain's Feast

What did Americans eat in the pre-Second World War period and why? Almost every foreign visitor from the nineteenth century to the present has been amazed at the volume of food available and served in eating establishments. From restaurants to food stores and on home tables, extolled in magazines, newspapers, and cooking classes, Americans took for granted that more than abundant food would be set before them. Both foreign and domestic travelers to a greater degree than previously also noticed regional and local differences in foods set before them. One of the best descriptions of rich abundant American food in several iterations comes from a travelogue, only not across the United States but within Europe, Mark Twain's 1880 book *A Tramp Abroad*.[5] Modern gastronomes relish the items on this imagined menu because they are the substance of a diminished and now reviving interest in American *terroir*.

Twain and his friend Harris, actually the Reverend Joseph Twichell, decided to take a walking tour into the Alps. Breakfasts are mentioned throughout, Twain telling his readers that coffee and beefsteak were the usual simple American breakfast. Europeans, he remarked disdainfully, knew nothing about coffee and the beef was awful. Like many a traveler to distant lands before and since, he dreamed about returning home for real American food, meals that he expected to find immediately upon setting foot on native soil. Twain's roster of American food has been discussed many times.[6] One reason is that the list looks like a description of an American cuisine in its regional variations. It has elements of both but with a pronounced Southern flavor, as one might expect from a nineteenth-century Missourian. Standard American recipes familiar from cookery manuals and within the minds of home cooks entered Twain's food dream: baked apples with cream, American toast (presumably a form of today's French toast) with clear maple syrup, Saratoga potatoes, broiled chicken, American style, mashed potatoes with catsup, boiled potatoes in their skins, and new potatoes, minus the skins. The catalogue holds various vegetables, legumes and gourds, some native American, others naturalized, from asparagus to butter beans, string beans, lettuce, squash, and pumpkin. He loved sweets and cream, so desserts that one thinks of as truly American appear, including apple dumplings, with real cream, apple pie, apple fritters, peach pie, American mince pie, pumpkin pie, squash pie, and "All sorts of American pastry."[7] American pastries, he declared, were better than German and Swiss varieties, even though European pastry

Cartoon of "Mark Twain at Work" on *A Tramp Abroad*.

chefs had long been working in America's restaurants and bakeries such as Delmonico's in New York and Henrici's Viennese Cafe in Chicago. One might suppose that Twain was overcome with nostalgia and culinary nationalism, but being who he was the list was followed by some amusing mock recipes. This one resembles a modern toaster pastry fresh in its sealed package from the factory:

Take a sufficiency of water and a sufficiency of flour, and construct a bullet-proof dough. Work this into the form of a disk, with the edges turned up some three-fourths of an inch. Toughen and kiln-dry it a couple of days in a mild but unvarying temperature. Construct a cover for this redoubt in the same way and of the same material. Fill with stewed dried apples; aggravate with cloves, lemon-peel, and slabs of citron; add two portions of New Orleans sugar, then solder on the lid and set in a safe place till it petrifies. Serve cold at breakfast and invite your enemy.

Other dishes were locally sourced, most prepared in specific style: a kind of locavorism from a time before fully nationalized food systems.[8] They reflect Twain's travels up and down the great river and throughout the nation; he had lived in northern California as a young man and settled in Connecticut. The dishes are a virtual ecological history of the country. For instance, "Philadelphia Terapin soup" [*sic*] was made from the Diamondback terrapins of the Delmarva peninsula, which are now so reduced in numbers by hunting that they are protected by law. The once abundant San Francisco mussels from the Bay were steamed, in the style of the city's many Italian fishermen. Twain then names some more, like oysters from the Chesapeake, a regional animal that was distributed nationally. More dreamed-of delights, though, were not:

Oysters roasted in shell—Northern style.
Soft-shell crabs.
Connecticut shad.
Baltimore perch.
Brook trout, from Sierra Nevadas.
Lake trout, from Tahoe.
Sheep-head and croakers, from New Orleans.
Black bass from the [lower] Mississippi . . .
Canvas-back-duck, from Baltimore.
Prairie liens [Prairie chickens, a kind of grouse], from Illinois.
Missouri partridges, broiled.

Even hot buckwheat cakes were regional because the cool-weather grass was widely used as cover crop in the northern states, not much in the South.

Twain once declared that no one north of the Mason–Dixon Line knew how to make fried chicken. He meant by that an identifiable regional Southern style that he knew from his Missouri boyhood on the Mississippi River. He used "Southern style" to identify cookery from both the Southern hog-and-hominy and plantation cooking traditions:

Fried chicken, Southern style,
Hot biscuits, Southern style . . .
Hot wheat-bread, Southern style . . .
Bacon and greens, Southern style . . .
Early rose potatoes, roasted in the ashes, Southern style, served hot . . .
Hot corn-pone, with chitlings, Southern style.
Hot hoe-cake, Southern style.
Hot egg-bread, Southern style.
Hot light-bread, Southern style.

Apple puffs, Southern style, and peach cobbler, Southern style, are variations of standard American apple dumplings and baked fruit dishes. Hot corn-pone with chitterlings, or chitlins (pig intestines), Southern style is surely among the most famous dishes in the repertoire now called "soul food." Considering Twain's sympathies and outrage at slavery, as his great novel *Huckleberry Finn* shows, he meant this as an African American dish. It is likely that Twain did not consider Southern dishes as a distinct cuisine or as a form of regional or sectional, to use an antebellum phrase, patriotism. But in its varied styles informed by race and class, it was already distinctive.

And then there was big food: roast turkey, Thanksgiving style, cranberry sauce (a northern berry not yet available in the South), porterhouse steak, and American roast beef were all to be served in large portions:

A mighty porterhouse steak an inch and a half thick, hot and sputtering from the griddle; dusted with fragrant pepper; enriched with little melting bits of butter of the most unimpeachable freshness and genuineness; the precious juices of the meat trickling out and joining the gravy, archipelagoed with mushrooms; a township or two of tender, yellowish fat gracing an outlying district of this ample county of beefsteak; the long white bone which divides the sirloin from the tenderloin still in its place; and imagine that the angel also adds a great cup of American coffee.[9]

The Mississippi Room, Elmira, New York, 1958. The dishes are hardly Mark Twain's idea of American feasting. He did spend time in Elmira but at a different hotel.

The steak, properly cut and aged, is currently served in America's many steakhouses. The juices and lots of gravy are the symbols of Americans' idea of their food and identity, big food in the land of plenty.

Most of the list in *A Tramp Abroad* look like dishes served in American restaurants (the Museum of the City of New York has a photograph of Twain dining in Delmonico's in 1905), the mighty steak a prime example. From early in the nineteenth century restaurants and hotel dining rooms served stunning numbers of dishes—thirty, forty, even hundreds of dishes. Many around the country modeled themselves on Delmonico's, including menu items in sometimes fractured French. In 1830, Swiss brothers John and Peter Delmonico opened what became arguably America's premier restaurant into the twentieth century (it started as a cafe in 1827). A good example of the kind of menu offered is one from April 18, 1899 in both English and French versions and containing 411 items.[10] The structure is similar to many others, starting with oysters served on the half shell or as soup oyster soup or clam soup, always followed by numerous fish dishes, ready-made beef steak, roast lamb, and other heavy meats, followed by entrees including Pigeon with Peas, Vol au Vent, Financière, Sweetbread, Neapolitan Style, and Terrapin (Maryland or Baltimore). The separate roast category contains fowl of all kinds, plover, duckling, squab chicken, chicken, squab, red head duck, canvas back duck, ruddy duck, and mallard duck. Most, if not all, of these were locally sourced. In the Midwest, where game was common on fancy menus,

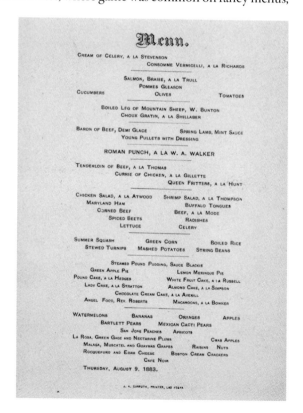

Dinner for Boston Commandery, Knights Templar, and Ladies [Held By] The Montezuma [At] Las Vegas, Hot Springs, Nm (Hotel), 1883. Note the elaborate, grand buffet-style menu.

prairie chicken (*Tympanuchus cupido*) was an everyday dish until the first third of the twentieth century, when the bird had been hunted to the verge of extinction.[11] Some vegetables were seasonal such as new asparagus and fresh green beans, while cauliflower, sweet peppers, eggplant, green and French peas, green beans, spinach, stewed tomatoes (as in Twain's list), and braised celery were likely imports from California or Florida. The same was likely for celery, once ubiquitous as a cooked vegetable and even more so as an appetizer on restaurant menus until the 1960s. Eight potato preparations and, as customary at the time, Macaroni, Italienne or Parisienne appear in the vegetables category with nary a sign of modern greens such as broccoli, spinach, or kale. Desserts were just as numerous with Nesselrode, the restaurant staple Charlotte Russe and a long list of cream pastries, ice creams, and fruit preparations as treats. Imported French and German wines from the best wine-producing regions were not only on Delmonico's menu but on others across the continent beginning early in the century. Finding Mosel and good Bordeaux and Rhône wines on hotel menus in the new city of Chicago in the 1840s, when its streets were mere mud patches, is surprising.

Quotidian Cuisine

Whether the actual cookery in many a would-be grand eatery was up to classic standards is a question. During 1882 and 1883, Major William Shepherd, one of a group of English travelers and ranching entrepreneurs, spent twenty months on the Great Plains living rough among cowboys and sheep herders (some of whom were Basques). In his vividly written book, Shepherd commented on this phenomenon saying that outside of New York City, American cuisine was less than stellar:

> even in first-class hotels, the liberal *menus*, with the choice of twenty dishes where in Europe you find but two or three, so often extolled, are the most laughable take-in; each small article on the table is enumerated, while many of the dishes are repetitions—for instance, under broiled and fried you will find the same chops, steaks, and fish spun out into a dozen items. *Relishes* will head various sauces, pickles, and vinegars; eight or ten different shapes of bread are specified; the same for preparations of eggs. Potatoes, boiled meats, cold meats, vegetables, each give an opening for more names . . . but the materials, in my estimation, left much to be desired for improvement—at least, I thought so,

until my opinions were completely upset by being told that "We Americans never can find anything fit to eat abroad." Then I humbled myself, and recognized the good sense of the proverb "*de gustibus*," for we need only refer to French authors for an opinion on English cookery.[12]

Dining on rich and voluminous amounts of food made by professional chefs, stars in their times, is emblematic of America's Gilded Age. It is no wonder that provincial restaurateurs would imitate the style of their culinary (and social) models if not having the substance. American advertising was already mining this lode of American desire. It still is when television advertisements for chain "family" restaurants such as Olive Garden show beautifully photographed heaping dishes glistening with buttery sauces that claim some connection to fine Italian cuisine. The theme was, and remains, abundance.

The eminent historian David Potter sparked an ongoing discussion about the meaning of American abundance in his 1954 book *People of Plenty*. Writing after the Second World War, when the United States sent huge amounts of food to the stricken nations of Europe and Japan under the Marshall Plan, Potter thought that unlike the Old World, America's material wealth came from its limitless natural and human resources. Rather than a "zero sum" economy, where one class or group grew wealthy at the expense of another, the country could provide equitably for all under capitalism.[13] That idea, with or without capitalism, was deeply rooted in American culture, at least until the twenty-first century. Agricultural expansion to every corner of the nation and Mark Twain's massive steaks are an expression of it. So are McDonald's Big Macs, which appear later in the nation's food transformation. Potter's book does not really address the processes that made for culinary changes: his book was not about food in any case. As the Toffenetti menu items above illustrate, these included more disposable income for a rising, largely urban, middle class who shopped for more abundant consumer goods, the very people who ate there. What people bought more and more after the turn of the twentieth century were commodified things, from clothing to toasters and automobiles. So was the restaurant's food, the shrimp not hand caught but netted by trawlers that worked the Gulf waters. Once a regional dish as Twain might have eaten in New Orleans, shrimp was now middle-class fare made into a standard restaurant and party dish complete with factory-made crackers and spicy red sauce. On "Slenderella Salad" hangs many a

ready-made fashionable dress because it is one of "the exemplars of consumption, models for imitation and emulation provided increasingly by
the media of mass communication."[14] As Shepherd says later, of culinary
life among the unlettered herders:

> In every art of civilization there is a descending scale; and while
> east of the Missouri the bottom of culinary talent is still a long
> way off, a thin leathery fried steak and a piece of stringy lamb will
> smile as dainties after a course of doughy rolls and coarse bacon.

Stringy meat or fast indifferent cooking was not confined to the west or
backcountry America. Shepherd did not explore every part of the country,
certainly not the sharecroppers of the south, factory workers of urban
America, or Hispanic farmers of the southwest or upcountry Appalachia,
and so did not report on their often poor fare. But he did observe, as many
visitors before him, that "habit may make a people prefer fried meat, hot
bread raised with baking powder, and a cup of tea or coffee as the staple
of their dinner." Habit was one thing, money another, for American meals
eaten both at home and in public dining establishments were determined
by class: money in one's pocket mattered.

Such is the steak and coffee to which Ragged Dick treated himself
after an early morning of rustling up nickels on the city streets. Normally
the shoeshine boy ate at a place on Ann Street:

> On this street was a small, cheap restaurant, where for five cents
> Dick could get a cup of coffee, and for ten cents more, a plate of
> beef-steak with a plate of bread thrown in . . . Neither the coffee
> nor the steak were as good as can be bought at Delmonico's;
> but then it is very doubtful whether, in the present state of his
> wardrobe, Dick would have been received at that aristocratic res-
> taurant, even if his means had admitted of paying the high prices
> there charged.

Specifically, that meant 6 cents on Ann Street and 50 cents at Delmonico's.[15]
Dick's cut-rate dining place was one of the city's many "beef and__"
(usually beans) restaurants such as Hitchcock's and Dolan's on Park Row,
only a short walk away, that served dime meals to not only the impecu-
nious but even Mark Twain and his peers.[16] They were the equivalent of
today's quick service outlets.

RAGGED DICK SERIES
BY HORATIO ALGER, JR.

RAGGED DICK

In Horatio Alger's best, most realistic novel, fourteen-year-old Dick Hunter is a poor shoeshine boy, dressed in second- and third-hand clothes but clever, honest, hardworking, generous to his friends, working on lower Manhattan's streets in the mid-nineteenth century. Through his good character he becomes friendly with people of higher station in life who educate him. Then, as the result of a heroic act of rescue, he is taken into a business firm by a grateful wealthy industrialist. Calling himself Richard Hunter, he enters middle-class respectability through a job in his benefactor's office. Alger knew well how impoverished working boys lived through his lifetime spent aiding them. Alger is more famous in modern popular mythology than in readership because his young adult novels are repetitive and didactic: it has been said that if you've read one, you've read them all. Contrary to the myth of "rags to riches," their single theme is that deserving young men rise into the urban middle classes or in some cases a comfortable rural life (*Phil the Fiddler*, 1872). In almost every case a good dinner seals the hero's ascent.

URBAN FARE

Public and private dining followed similar paths. In America's mushrooming cities a new middle class rose between the extremes of wealth and poverty, albeit slowly. The term "middle class" is as much an idea of social status as it is real personal and family income. They were and are the "have-somewhats," in Studs Terkel's memorable phrase. Usually associated with urban life, the middle class meant professionals such as physicians, lawyers, new management personnel who operated businesses, some better-paid clerical workers, and small business owners. Take lawyers, for example. The United States had 40,736 of them in 1880; by 1900 there were 114,640 lawyers, or one for every 254 Americans.[17] Surprisingly, that is more per capita than the 1.2 million for 323.5 million people in 2015. In 1900 the average middling income stood at about $750 a year.[18] Laboring people who made up the vast bulk of the American public brought home around $450 on average, with lesser-skilled workers and public school teachers getting as little as $325.[19] Since 43 percent of their expenses went to food and almost all the rest was spent on clothing and housing, there was little disposable income except for professionals, such as lawyers and managers/business owners, that is, the perhaps 15 percent of Americans who made $1,100–1,500 a year or more. Statistics on income versus outlays in the decades up to 1950 show that households always ran annual deficits and so had to make hard decisions on how much to spend. No wonder working people lunched at the cheapest places possible, men often eating their bread, cold meats, and pickles for free at saloons for a nickel glass of beer.

Income played an important role in public dining. Since business activity was concentrated in urban areas, central cities usually, it is not surprising to find that changes in dining began there. In his book on the rise of middle-class dining, *Turning the Tables: Restaurants and the Rise of the American Middle Class, 1880–1920*, Andrew P. Haley theorizes class warfare and nationalism: the rising middle class consciously or otherwise drove snobby upper-class restaurants either out of business or to change to more middle-class tastes by exercising their market power and not patronizing them. Such places as Delmonico's with its voluminous French menus disappeared in favor of simpler, cheaper, and in many cases assimilated "foreign" dishes such as spaghetti and even chop suey.[20] A 1913 guide to New York City, discussing the grand French-style restaurants and hotels, complained that American food was hard to find, declaring that a hotelier (with a good restaurant in it) would make a fortune if only he built an

"American House . . . something quite removed from the aristocratic nomenclature that our modern generation of tavern-keepers have borrowed from Europe without the slightest sense of fitness."[21] Mark Twain in his *Tramp Abroad* mode would have agreed. The guide has even fewer good things to say about "grubby ethnic" eateries.

In fact there was no monolithic middle class, one reason being social fluidity based on income and on individual Americans' notions of just what the term meant. White-collar work was deemed "better" than manual labor by many Americans in the years around 1900. That would not change, somewhat, until the post-Second World War years. There is no better description of such social and economic differences than James T. Farrell's brilliant sequence of five novels about the O'Neill and O'Flaherty families set in Chicago between 1906 and the early 1920s. The often desperately poor working-class O'Neills are contrasted with their censorious lower middle-class relatives, the O'Flaherty family. What makes them different is not just that they have more money—the breadwinner, Uncle Al, is a fairly effective traveling shoe salesman and Aunt Margaret is a clerk at a good downtown hotel—but that the O'Flahertys think of themselves as members of a successful middle class. They can treat themselves to good dinners on the road and in the city. Al eats thick steak and pies, while Margaret (when she is not drinking herself into a self-pitying stupor at some bar) dines with her friends at decent, clean but not haute cuisine restaurants that were now common in downtown Chicago. No such luck for the down-and-out O'Neills, who are happy to eat hamburger and plenty of potatoes on good days, gruel on others, and snack at fast food stands.[22]

Margaret O'Flaherty was part of the new masses of women workers that grew in numbers from the late nineteenth century onward. A 1929 study described a hierarchy of women's jobs: domestic work was at the bottom, followed by factory work (some dirty and dangerous) and then sales (fin de siècle newspapers always had advertisements for experienced women salespeople for women's departments) and then ranges of office positions.[23] Businesses needed records and women became keepers of them. Once the first practical typewriter by Milwaukeean Christopher L. Sholes appeared in 1873, and was then standardized by the Underwood Typewriter Company of New York in 1895, typing became a much needed skill. Stenographers were also required for dictation along with clerks at various levels of skill, including personal secretaries later in the century. In 1900, more than a million clerical jobs needed to be filled; by 1920 that number was three million, 45 percent of them held by women. Usually young women trained in the nation's universal free high schools or the many commercial colleges that sprang up in cities. These women thought of themselves as belonging to the middle class. Downtown cities such as New York, Chicago, and San Francisco were packed with daytime workers: Chicago's Loop had seven thousand errand boys and ten thousand stenographers plus others.[24] Where were a respectable young woman and upright male office worker to eat?

As Harvey Levenstein observed, restaurateurs changed with the times to accommodate the needs of customers such as the new urban staffs for inexpensive meals in sanitary settings with decent nutritional values. Service had to be quick since lunch hours were typically thirty minutes.[25] A more nuanced hierarchy of dining establishments was soon to be found in America's cities and then smaller towns around the concept of lunchrooms. Boston was a center for them, as was Chicago, where in 1880 Herman H. Kohlsaat, who ran one of the country's largest commercial bakeries, founded a downtown "dairy lunch room" with fixed tables and swiveling chairs. Milk was thought to be wholesome and pure and was featured at the great 1893 Columbian Exposition's Dairy Pavilion. "Lucky" Charlie Weeghman started as a coffee boy at a popular Chicago Loop restaurant in the 1890s. Once he accumulated $2,800, he set off on his own to pioneer "one-armed" quick service dairy eating places. The term refers to chairs with one arm forming a small flat table like a school desk. He made a fortune, one place earning $11,000 a day in the 1920s. John Raklios, a Greek immigrant to Chicago, arrived penniless in 1901 and began his food career by selling apples in the street. Saving his money, he built a chain of white-tiled mainly one-armed lunch restaurants that were kept spotlessly clean and served reasonably priced food. By the 1920s he had more than thirty outlets, most of which were served by a central commissary. His advertising centered on fresh bread and desserts made in their own bakery and dishes such as cold cut platters (35 cents), frankfurters and spinach—as only they could make it, they declared—(30 cents), and frankfurters and potato salad for hot weather (25 cents).

Quick service places took on other names with somewhat different service and fare. John Kruger, who operated a smorgasbord restaurant in 1890s Chicago (the city had a large Scandinavian population), restyled his place a "Cafeteria." The name was simply a marketing ploy inspired by a trip to exotic Cuba, which was much in the news because of war. Meanwhile in 1899 Samuel and William Childs opened an eponymous lunch place on Cortland Street in Manhattan. They are credited with introducing the

Horn & Hardart Automat, Times Square, New York, *c.* 1939.

self-service line to restaurants. Later, in the twentieth century, the cafeteria and the serving line became intertwined, giving rise to a number of food service operations, from institutions to restaurant chains. Modern buffet outlets are an example and a return to the old smorgasbord concept: cheap and plentiful, if not high-quality.

Another lunchroom variant came to be called luncheonettes in the first decade of the twentieth century. The name implied lighter fare meant for those of more delicate sensibility, namely working or shopping women. A 1916 sales advertisement for Dows' Soda Shop at 3 Park Place in New York City, near the new Woolworth Building, listed a long Italian marble soda fountain top with soda-making equipment, a 16-ft marble lunch counter with plenty of storage space behind for milk, and luncheonette furnishing that included thirty round tables with chairs, three highboys, a serving counter, steam tables, and a refrigeration unit, among its assets.[26] Dow's was more elaborate than most, indeed the model for elaborate new classical-style fountains, but what they served was similar to other lunch-eonettes at the time.[27] Weeghman's was typical of these places providing dairy lunches in offering "crackers with milk or cream and milk toast, but also oatmeal or cereals such as shredded wheat, Force, Appetizo, grape nuts, and corn flakes."[28] Childs's menus around 1900 included oatmeal and milk, oatmeal and cream, rice and milk, graham crackers and milk, creamed chicken on toast, creamed soups such as clam chowder, stews, lots of egg dishes, and sandwiches at prices from 10 to 30 cents. In the course of time, luncheonettes came to mean small, simply appointed places with standup counters or a few tables that served little more than egg dishes, pancakes, soups, and sandwiches (often on toast) such as ham, tuna, grilled cheese, and bacon–lettuce–tomato, along with coffee, pie, and cakes.

In parallel fashion lunch counters moved to drug stores along with soda fountains. Lunch counters were actually the oldest of the fixed location quick service breed, dating to early railway stations in the 1850s, but had morphed into lunchrooms and cafes of various kinds. Walgreen's drug store, now a huge international chain, put a soda fountain in its second Chicago location in 1909 with great success. A few years later they added lunch counters serving luncheonette-style dishes, all made in the first five years by Mrs. Myrtle Walgreen herself. Five-and-dime general merchandise stores beginning with F. W. Woolworth (founded in 1879), followed by S. H. Kress & Co., S. S. Kresge Company, J. J. Newberry's, and G. C. Murphy Co. among others, opened lunch counters early in the twentieth century not only in cities but smaller towns throughout the United States. Fixed location diners often shaped like trolley or railway cars served similar fare, becoming iconic features of urban landscapes. Food preparation was simple, the equipment being a griddle or grill, a soup kettle, and refrigeration as befitted the food served.

Low-cost dining was an example of Horatio Alger's idea of upward social mobility, that is, capitalism from the bottom up. Serving more people with low profit margins was a way to make a lot more money than the old elite restaurants and hotel dining rooms. Unlike the latter, once systems were in place to assemble dishes, especially with central commissaries

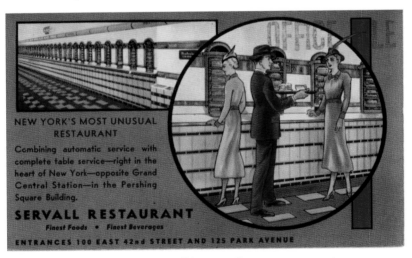

NEW YORK'S MOST UNUSUAL RESTAURANT

Combining automatic service with complete table service—right in the heart of New York—opposite Grand Central Station—in the Pershing Square Building.

SERVALL RESTAURANT
Finest Foods • Finest Beverages

ENTRANCES 100 EAST 42nd STREET AND 125 PARK AVENUE

Postcard view of the Servall Automatic Restaurant, c. 1930–45.

making the basics such as the always advertised fresh bread, skilled cooks and wait staffs were not required. The machine model that had emerged in America during the later nineteenth century took hold and still does. The famous and often mourned Automat was a prime example of a mechanized dining system. Established in Berlin as Quisisana in 1895, the system featured banks of glass doors with shelves that were replenished by a staff behind them. Customers put coins in slots that unlocked the door for them. Dishes were arranged in sections, from soups and salads to main dishes and desserts. Coffee and hot water poured from an ornate spigot set on a fountain basin. In this swift self-service operation, staff costs were minimalized and customers liked the idea that their food was minimally handled, though they did not see what went on behind the window banks. And it was cheap, most dishes costing a nickel, few more than a quarter. Philadelphia lunchroom owners Joseph Horn and Frank Hardart, the latter a German immigrant, saw the concept, liked it and imported it in 1902. New York got its first Automat in 1912, followed by some 36 during the next thirty years with units serving almost three-quarters of a million people daily. Art Deco in design, the décor fit perfectly with the machine ideal. Here was "democratic" food since people of all walks of life patronized Automats and it was long remembered as being fresh and good. Pot pies, chipped beef and noodles, macaroni and cheese, baked beans, creamed spinach, sandwiches of all kinds, pumpkin and other pies, rice pudding, cakes, and many others were on the menu. Also relying on a central commissary, the Automat is thought to be arguably a model for

Exterior of middle-class chain, Childs Restaurant, Washington, DC, 1917.

229

modern fast food outlets,[29] as indeed it was for food outlets depending on a long food and food-processing chain.

Still other kinds of restaurants that remain important parts of public dining arose from changes in food systems from the late nineteenth and early twentieth centuries. With large profits flowing, chains grew and some elaborated into having varied restaurants in their portfolios. John R. Thompson's Chicago-based chain, founded in 1891, was a small one-arm lunchroom chain that expanded to mid-priced day and evening service establishments. Thompson's later bought up the chain of John Raklios (he, like Weeghman, went bankrupt; see below) and then the somewhat upscale Henrici's, a Viennese-themed restaurant founded just after the Civil War. Childs' did the same, some of their restaurants elaborately decorated but still serving mid-priced dishes, though their sandwiches cost 20 cents in the 1920s compared to 10 cents at Weeghman's. Thompson's and Childs' were national chains with more than 110 units each around the country into the 1970s, before being bought out and disappearing. The concept lives on in "family" dining establishments, some corporate, others local places that are especially known in cities as Greek-owned family restaurants, the subject of gentle humor in popular culture from the 1920s to the present day.

As in the menu items shown above, Dario Toffenetti's restaurant chain is an example of the direction of American mid-level dining. In a familiar story, 21-year-old Toffenetti immigrated to the United States from his native northern Italy in 1910 and, after working in food sales and hotels, opened his own small restaurant in Chicago in 1914, eventually having eight in the city and a large, much-remembered one in New York's Times Square. Taking business classes at night at Northwestern University, he came to understand marketing and the new restaurant economy and his supply chains. Toffenetti's were not quick service cafeterias or fancy restaurants. With inexpensive breakfasts priced at 25 cents in the 1930s, and dinners such as hot roast ham with sweet potatoes at 75 cents, chicken à la king, corned beef hash, and open-faced roast beef sandwich covered in gravy, his clientele were assured of decent meals that they could afford. He is reported to have said in his Italian accent: "And the customers say to me, 'Dario, you serve too much food. I can't eat it all.'" In keeping with Americans' new interest in healthy dishes and the post-First World War fashion to be slim, however, salads and soups were always on the restaurants' menus, especially for lunch when they were patronized by women.

Toffenetti was a master of marketing language. His menu items were described in florid terms, saying that only a poet laureate could describe the

Interior of Poore Bros Cafeteria, Indiana, the descendant of early cafeterias with abundant cheap food.

glories of each dish. Today's mid-priced restaurant menus follow his hyperbolic lead. Among his signature dishes was strawberry shortcake, described as "tempting red translucent berries have arrived this morning to me made for you in the most magnificent of all desserts." Another signature dish was spaghetti served in a meat sauce, the recipe having been found "in the archives among the ruins of the ancient castle of the count of Bonpensler in Bologna," or created by Mrs. Toffenetti (his mother) from the finest semolina, "bountiful and delicious." One other food took a premier place on Toffenetti's menus: potatoes, specifically Idaho Burbank Russets. Having started life by selling baked potatoes to miners in the upper Midwest, he was a firm advocate of them. A single large baked potato with butter and a dash of paprika for 20 cents served as a meal in itself. It certainly was for poor folks in his time and Irish immigrants in the previous century, but the restaurateur made them into a reputable restaurant dish that, when baked and served in foil jackets with butter and sour cream, became a staple of mid-level restaurants into the twenty-first century.[30]

The Rise of the National Food System

Restaurants and home cooks now used fewer locally sourced ingredients, as national transportation systems allowed for specialized commodity production centers: California produce, Midwestern meats, Southern fruits and cottonseed oil, and coastal fish among them. Food processing corporations manufactured products that made cooking easier and cheaper for both restaurants that could count on pre-processed foods and at home.

Advertisement for the breakfast food Shredded Wheat and its associated biscuit, Triscuit, 1912. The plant was powered by electricity generated by Niagara Falls, giving the product the aura of modernity as well as hygiene.

Anyone could open a can of beans, condensed soup, or tomato sauce and many a lunch counter operator did, along with a loaf of sliced soft white bread. Simpler restaurant preparations were paralleled by home preparations as seen in newspaper and magazine columns, cookbooks, and corporate pamphlets. Cookbooks had always had doses of "foreign" and exotic dishes, and when Toffenetti opened his first restaurant some immigrant foods joined the standard American-British-West and Central European lexicon, but only as naturalized citizens.

Consider a lunch-counter staple, the melted cheese sandwich. The base was white wheaten bread. New wheat strains such as the hard winter Turkey reds and hard spring wheats produced bumper crops on the Bonanza farms of the newly opened western lands. Soft wheats were also grown where climates permitted. When crops failed from drought and cold, as they did in Kansas in the 1880s and across the west in 1917 (before the massive failures of the 1930s Dust Bowl), wheats were modified or new lands were opened up. There was a lot of it, some 360 lb of wheat per person in 1915.[31] Hard wheat made for the taste for finer milling led to the soft mushy loaves with a light crust that Americans know so well. This bread was made from mixtures of hard and soft flours developed for the baking industry, the wheat degerminated, bleached, and finely sifted at mills such as General Mills' plants in the Minnesota Twin cities. Sent out in barrels or sacks, it was then baked in large plants around the country. In 1920s Chicago alone a million loaves were claimed to have been used daily for a population of 2.7 million. White bread was cheap and flexible because it could be easily toasted for sandwiches and breakfasts (the pop-up toaster was invented in 1919). And Americans liked the gummy texture. When rural people recall poverty in pre-Second World War America they often speak of how much they wanted "store boughten bread" rather than their mothers' homemade loaves. This was as much about striving upward from poverty to modern middle-class status through consumption as it was about the flavor and texture of commercial bread.[32]

For the home market, bread bakers began wrapping loaves, the iconic loaf brand being the multi-colored bubble logo Wonder Bread created by the Taggart Baking Company of Indianapolis in 1921. Large baking conglomerates then began to buy up smaller companies to create virtual oligopolies. Continental Baking began life as Ward Baking in New York

A promotional piece from the state of Minnesota featuring its great wheatlands, *c.* 1910.

City in 1849, became United Bakeries in 1921, took its modern name in 1925, and bought up more companies including Taggart in 1926. It was not the first food corporation to expand this way. In 1906 the National Biscuit Company (Nabisco), formed by the merger of three national conglomerates, controlled 70 percent of the American market. Continental employed bread-slicing and packaging machines to transform Wonder Bread in 1930. The technology was perfected in 1928 by Otto Frederick Rohwedder in his Chillicothe, Missouri, bakery and his advertising may have been the source for the all-American phrase "the best thing since sliced bread." Continental also invented the even more famous Twinkie in 1930.[33] Gobbling up production in the form of companies or farms remains an ongoing process in the American food industry.

Cheesemakers were numerous and had been since the mid-nineteenth century. Every grocery store sold a generic yellow cheese that was simply called "American." Americans loved a creamed melted-cheese-on-toast dish called Welsh rarebit or rabbit. It is in every cookbook of the time and described during the First World War as a cheap protein substitute. Winsor McCay's newspaper cartoon strip "Dream of a Rarebit Fiend" became widely popular when introduced in 1904. Edwin S. Porter made a still amusing seven-minute film of the strip for the Edison Manufacturing Company in 1906. It is not surprising that a simplified and quickly made melted cheese sandwich would filter down to cheap restaurants. The now familiar American cheese was born in 1915, when the Canadian-born Chicago cheese merchant James L. Kraft patented a way to process lesser grade cheeses to extend their shelf life and create a product with a low melting point. By the 1920s Kraft sold some 40 percent of all cheese in the United States. Sold in blocks and sliced onsite, it became the standard for melted cheese sandwiches and, at the same time, firmed up Americans' taste in cheese to a soft melted somewhat tangy cheese.[34] Only the flat griddle in a lunch counter was needed to turn inexpensive food-corporation-made ingredients into an American classic.

Kraft sold an even further processed cheese called Velveeta in 1927 and created the *pièce de résistance* of spreadable soft cheese, Cheez Whiz, in 1952–3. Both were made for Americans' taste for thickly sauced dishes. The chicken à la king on Toffenetti's menu had become popular as a menu item and in home cookery a little before 1915. It descends from common fricassees with mushrooms, chopped sweet peppers or pimentos added and all thickened with cream.[35] Creamed preparations were made especially popular by the rage for chafing dish cookery that began in the last decades of the nineteenth century. Originally elegant dishes served in fine restaurants and elite dinner parties, they descended down the social scale to common restaurants and to ordinary home cooks. Creamed chipped beef on toast (alias sos to soldiers and sailors of the twentieth century for whom it was a mess-hall staple), creamed gravy on biscuits, especially in the South, fish croquettes in New England, and lots more were found everywhere. Manufacturers of canned foods put out recipes using branded products to make creamed dishes, among many others, fairly early. As an example, a 1917 recipe from Veribest, a division of Armour the meatpacker, for Creamed Corned-Beef au Gratin calls for its own brand of evaporated milk, butter (made from its own Wisconsin and New York dairies), and beef made in a double boiler (the equivalent of a chafing dish).[36] The beloved Quick Chicken à la King recipe was created when the Campbell Soup Company introduced its cream of mushroom soup.[37] Like a cream sauce, Velveeta and its relatives were formulated to top some other solid ingredient. They retain their smooth texture when melted so could be used to cover everything from some versions of Philadelphia cheesesteaks to an even soupier concoction dispensed with a pump to be put on tortilla chips. Served at public events as "nachos," these are a particularly commercial Americanized snack-food version of a Mexican-American dish created in the 1940s on the Texas border.[38] Whether cream or cheese, the idea of a thick goopy topping lives in the heart of American fare.

Armour's Veribest Package Foods

The convenience of ready-cooked foods to be served cold, or with a few minutes heating, is appreciated by all housekeepers. Veribest Package Foods are prepared by expert Armour chefs in Armour's sanitary kitchens and include many delicacies difficult and expensive to prepare in the home. They are not only time-savers, but add variety to the menu. The housewife with a shelf of Armour's Veribest Foods is protected against any emergency. The Veribest Foods sold under the Oval Label include so wide a choice that almost the entire menu, day after day, can be satisfactorily arranged from them.

Advertisement for Veribest Products, Armour & Co, *c.* 1917.

Dario Toffenetti sold so many baked potatoes over his 48 years in the business that he was given a special award from the Idaho Potato Commission. The restaurateur was a pioneer in co-branding, his hams labeled as Oscar Mayer, Louisiana strawberries, and potatoes from Idaho. These large potatoes could not have existed without the genetic manipulation of a particular kind of potato, the American idea of extensive agriculture, railroads, and large changes in the landscape. Luther Burbank, a brilliant if unorthodox plant breeder from Lancaster, Massachusetts, developed a floury firm-fleshed potato on his small farm in 1872 (after planting thousands of seeds) that came to be called russet Burbank. It became the parent of many other related varieties when transplanted to the west; there are at least eighteen russets developed by the University of Idaho School of Agriculture at present. It was further developed by the Sweet family near Carbondale, Colorado, and then spread to Washington, Canada, and Idaho, the latter about 1923.[39] Burbank himself moved to California where he made history creating numerous hybrids that are widely grown today, including the freestone peach and Santa Rosa.[40] A heavily mountainous state with high deserts, Idaho did not develop into a major commodity agricultural region until the passage of the Desert Land Act (the Carey Act) in 1894. Mormon settlers from Utah who had developed irrigation farming in that state in the 1850s had small-scale systems, but the federal bill called for major irrigation projects using waters from the Snake and other rivers. Once an extensive network of canals was dug, the state's volcanic soils proved to be perfect for potatoes—and sometimes catastrophic for the land through erosion.[41] Production rose dramatically in the later 1920s as the Idaho brand became well known, declined during the Great Depression of the 1930s and then zoomed up, making Idaho the fourth largest producer of potatoes at present. Most of these go to make French fries and some for mashing, since baked potatoes have fallen from restaurant menus in favor of these preparations.

On his list of longed-for American food, Mark Twain had this: "Fresh American fruits of all sorts, including strawberries which are not to be doled out as if they were jewelry, but in a more liberal way." Twain meant freshly picked, but by the 1880s fresh fruits and vegetables were pouring into America's cities from across the nation. The varied ecological zones of California lent themselves to monoculture production. In the north, the wide valleys were among the nation's first areas to adopt new harvesting machinery in the nineteenth century: California was already the eighth largest agricultural producing state by 1869, the year that the transcontinental railroad was finished.[42] One of the greatest engineering feats in American history, the railroad opened the east to California produce. Another marvel, the Panama Canal, was another major link in the new American food chain. In 1882 southern California's San Gabriel Valley had citrus orchards, almond and walnut production, pears, peaches, apricots, and, of course, grapevines. A citrus fair held that year in the new town of Riverside celebrated the produce of its 209,000 orange trees. Four years later the new railroads directly linking Chicago and small southern California towns like Los Angeles and Pasadena brought fruit in refrigerated cars to a huge Chicago Citrus Fair.[43] More was to follow:

> A torrent of other fruits poured eastward from California...Table grapes and raisins, apples, peaches, pears, plums, apricots, figs, and olives were all produced for the California market and then for eastern ones. In the 1890s the date industry began and nourished, especially after someone got shoots of the Deglet Noor. To the north, Washington and Oregon came to have many pear, apple, and cherry orchards and large raspberry plantations.[44]

More citrus and berries from Florida, citrus from Texas, blueberries from New Jersey and later sandy Michigan soils were grown on specialized acreage and shipped out over long distances. Peaches became big business: in Georgia an industry developed after the end of the plantation system, as peaches are suited to the well-drained clay soils of the fall line that runs between the state's Piedmont and Coastal Plain. In particular the firm-fleshed freestone Elberta peach, created between 1870 and 1875 by Samuel H. Rumph, was perfect for shipping, the first commercial shipment going to New York City in 1889.[45] By the later twentieth century, however, Georgia, although known as the "Peach State," was being out-produced by California twenty to one. More successful for Georgia from the later nineteenth century to the present has been the peanut. It became one of America's leading snack foods, being mentioned in the archetypal baseball song "Take Me Out to the Ballgame" (1908). Whether processed into peanut butter or oils, roasted, or raw, large shipments continue to be sent across the nation.[46]

Many other fruits and vegetables were to follow into urban central markets where they diffused into the food supply system. In the central produce markets of Chicago and New York, Dario Toffenetti picked up fresh strawberries for his shortcake dessert and retail market owners got their fresh food. From the later nineteenth century onward, story after story in newspapers describes or mentions the hectic activities around the markets and the people who worked there. Among them were individual vendors who came every day to buy small amounts of edible merchandise for sale on the city's streets. The vendors represent the other "half"—actually much more than half—of American food culture in the pre-Second World War era. An example is John Raklios, the erstwhile cafeteria mogul who had only $10 when he first came to the United States in 1901, as the *Chicago Daily Tribune* later noted: "He used part of this to buy bananas and chestnuts, which he sold downtown. But people didn't buy bananas or chestnuts, so he changed to apples. People bought them. Raklios saved most of his profits. In a few years he had $500."[47] A banana mania swept America in that period, fueled by cheap prices made possible by expanding monoculture in Central American countries, shipping technologies and ruthless exploitation of the peoples and politics of these "Banana Republics" by the United Fruit Company (now Chiquita Brands International, after a trademark devised for a famous 1940s advertising campaign) and the Standard Fruit and Steamship Company (now Dole Food Company).[48] Raklios's story and the behavior of unbridled corporate power represent main themes in American history.

Though Americans eat more bananas than apples each year (28 lb compared to 19 lb), apples have always been an all-American fruit. Ragged Dick would have said so because his regular snack and sometimes only meal was an apple. Apples came to the Americas with early European settlements where they mainly supplied juice to be made into the ubiquitous North American drink, cider. Apples spread across the continent, most famously seeded by the nurseryman John Chapman, alias Johnny Appleseed (1774–1845). Grown from seed, apples differentiate into new varieties easily because they are heterozygous plants; during the nineteenth century thousands of new types appeared across the country. With the rise of the large-scale nursery business in the mid- to later nineteenth century, Chapman's seeding model was discarded in favor of uniform apple-types bred by grafting. In Dick Hunter's time it would be hard to say what kind of apples he ate. In the years after 1900 many of the apples bought by street vendors came from Washington State, where by the 1920s irrigation systems and train routes had transformed the state's north central area into America's leading producer of apples. The region specialized in several varieties of the handsome, if cardboard-tasting, Delicious apples that are today the standard in the nation's supermarkets.[49] Photographs of impoverished men and women selling apples on city streets during the Great Depression show none other than Red Delicious apples.

NEW IMMIGRANTS

Like John Raklios, street vendors were poor and served the have-nots of urban America. And like both him and Dario Toffenetti, many were recent immigrants. As noted, the overwhelming majority of the millions who streamed into the United States between 1880 and 1920 came from eastern, southern, north and central Europe. Italians, mostly from south of Rome and Sicily, numbered more than five million. One-third returned after making enough money to purchase a farm or business back home; some of these food companies then shipped products such as olive oil to America. Two million Jews who fled pogroms and conscription in Russia, Poland, Ukraine, and Bessarabia found their way to America, most settling in large cities such as New York (still the world's largest Jewish city). Some 1.5 million Norwegians, Swedes, Finns, and Danes fled poverty and political difficulties to settle in the rural and urban upper Midwest. Greeks, mainly from the poorest upland regions of the Peloponnese, numbered about four hundred thousand in the same period. Poles, Bohemians (Czechs), Bulgarians, Hungarians, and Russians, as well as the ongoing German immigration, also helped to make this the era of perhaps the greatest mass movements in human history. One might suppose that given such large numbers there would have been many Chinese settling in the United States. Because of serious anti-Chinese sentiments in California about jobs, as well as nativist racism about what came to be called "the Yellow Peril," the state passed a series of laws restricting immigration. Federal exclusion laws followed in 1882, 1888, and 1892 (they were repealed in 1943, though cooks had been given a special exemption in 1915). Nonetheless existing Chinatowns remained and versions of Chinese, or rather Cantonese–Taishanese, foods entered mainstream American cuisine. So did others, but it took time.

Scholars have argued about the effects and meaning of this wave of immigration to American life. One line that applies to food is about integration or not: how did immigrants become ethnic Americans? Because many came through family connections—one member immigrated and became a founder—some traditional foodways remained within communities. Germans had the most powerful effect on American food from the mid-nineteenth century, as in lager beer, sausage culture, bread, sauerkraut. But if it comes to numbers of dining places, then one might argue for the Chinese. In the twenty-first century there are roughly 41,000 Chinese restaurants in America, a number far outstripping hamburger and mid-level restaurant chains. Most of them do not serve the more or less "authentic" (in style if not exactly ingredients) regional dishes that became popular in the late 1970s. Instead they are famous for two Americanized dishes: chop suey and chow mein. Both came from the Taishan region at the mouth of the Pearl River, a region from which many immigrated across the world. Like other immigrants the Chinese were poor, exploited as manual labor, and segregated into Chinatowns. But they did maintain family ties and built their communities. Since Chinese people were notoriously ethnocentric about their regional and local cuisines, they soon began importing ingredients that they could not find in America (soy sauce and dried fungus are examples) and began growing the kinds of vegetables they liked, such as cabbages of various kinds, long beans, bean sprouts, and many more. Often without wives, Chinese men ate in the small restaurants that opened in their enclaves.

Chop suey, or *shap sui*, is a standard dish meaning "mixed bits," or leftovers quickly stir-fried together with vegetables. Chow mein means literally "fried noodles," consisting of boiled wheat noodles that are fried and topped with other ingredients, even chop suey.[50] Chinese cooks made these dishes for working members of their communities. Around 1890 New Yorkers, especially the "Bohemian" crowd seeking new taste sensations, began going to Chinatown for these bargain dishes. The same happened in other cities such as Chicago, where cheap Chinese eateries opened in the red light district for louche clientele. Very soon thereafter a chop suey craze raced across the nation. Chop suey places opened in cities and towns everywhere and in so doing restaurateurs changed the composition of their dishes. Some places were large fancy restaurants that served American food such as steaks alongside what were thought of as exotic Cantonese dishes. Most were small Ma and Pa eateries such as are found in numerous small towns across the North American continent. Restaurateurs discovered that Americans ate far more meat than the

---

La Choy

In 1922 two entrepreneurs (one Korean, the other an American grocer) founded the La Choy company, headquartered in Detroit. Featuring canned vegetables topped with a can of thick sauce with meat, along with canned fried chow mein, the company sold Chinese-American products across the nation and it still does.

Italian Entrepreneurs

Though both macaroni and spaghetti were well known, Italian food was not mainstream American. A French chef, Alphonse Biardot, opened a successful canned soup and canned spaghetti plant in Jersey City in 1886, but it was hardly Italian. Earlier Italian immigrants had created food businesses, and in the later nineteenth century Ligurians settling in San Francisco founded a well-known fishing and restaurant community around Fisherman's Wharf. By the 1880s and '90s Italian farmers had built significant fruit and vegetable businesses in California's Central Valley, notably Marco Fontana's canning company Del Monte, a brand that retains a large place on America's store shelves. In New Orleans, where Sicilian immigration was high, the Vaccaro and D'Antoni families began produce businesses in 1867. Eventually and despite considerable prejudice by nativists they controlled a good deal of the import business, renaming their company the Standard Fruit Company (now Dole) in 1924. Planters Peanuts, incorporated in 1908 by the Venetian Amedeo Obici and Mario Peruzzi in Wilkes Barre, Pennsylvania, was another of many food companies with Italian immigrant origins.

Postcard view of the Savoy Inn, Freeport, New York, c. 1930–45.

Chinese, liked celery, and they wanted a lot of gravy on their dishes. So was born the heavy cornstarch-thickened sauces that grace Chinese-American fare. Popular cookbooks from the turn of the century onward have chop suey recipes, all the early ones calling for unthinkably high cornstarch to liquid ratios. Other Chinese-American dishes appeared in these restaurants such as General Tso's Chicken, battered deep fried chunks covered in a sweet sauce whose origins are in dispute, and the similar Orange Chicken. Chinese may not have much liked American cuisine but they knew what Americans liked.

Italians, mostly *contadini*, farmers, deprived of land and jobs settled in the crowded and impoverished neighborhoods of America's "Little Italys." There they made many of their vegetable-based dishes, pasta and bread. Many kept gardens in every bit of open space available to them where they raised tomatoes, eggplants, zucchini, garlic, fennel, and peppers. What they could not produce, Italians imported from home, including olive oil, cheeses, and wine. Dietary reformers such as Jane Addams, working through settlement houses, tried to Americanize Italians' diets for health reasons current at the time, but they failed because Italian women who did the cooking resisted any such attempts. What these Italian immigrants did discover was abundant meat. Meager though their incomes were, working mainly as non-unionized day laborers, meat was cheap enough to eat every day, as opposed to the twice a week or so regimen in Italy. The same holds for fish eaten especially on Fridays. In America the small meals of Italy became much larger and with more meat. Mounds of spaghetti covered in tomato sauce, surrounded by large meatballs, is a dish that no Italian then or now recognizes as native to their homeland.[51]

Italian food did not break out of its ethnic enclave to become "respectable" until the decade around 1900 when small spaghetti houses became popular among the literati and artists and then the general public. Red checked tablecloth places that served mounds of cheap spaghetti and meatballs, an American dish called "Veal Parmesan" and other hearty dishes accompanied by Chianti wine advanced upon the American dining scene.[52] Dario Toffenetti's copious plates of spaghetti—always effective for the restaurateur because of low food costs—were an example of the naturalization of immigrant fare. Pizza and regional Italian cuisine would come much later in the twentieth century.

East European, or Ashkenazi, Jews came to America to stay. They arrived in family groups often from the same shtetl or small towns of the Russian Pale of Settlement and settled in American urban versions of the

Pizza, once a simple Italian dish, morphed in America into a melted cheese
and pepperoni-laden extravaganza.

same. "Ghettos," as they were often called, were filled with tenements
packed with people who often came from the same region, Romania,
Galicia, and Lithuania among them. There were regional food differences among them but the basics, like the Yiddish language in its several
dialects, were much the same. Many observed kosher dietary laws so
shochets, kosher butchers, and rabbis who supervised the ritual purity of
food were important members of the communities. Jewish food shops
and delicatessens sporting hand-painted signs in Yiddish were features of
the urban landscape. Classic Jewish dishes were much the same as those
in the country where the Jewish communities lived. For instance *kishka*
is like east European blood and grain sausage (called *kiszka* in Polish),
the difference being that the Jewish version is beef intestine stuffed with
matzo meal, chicken or beef fat and spices. Lithuanian Jews, Litvaks, used
more sour cream in dishes than others. *Kugel*, kinds of noodle or potato
puddings, were made in regional variations as well, some with sugar and
raisins, others spicier. Eventually a kind of generalized Jewish cuisine arose
from contact among the Ashkenazi communities. Bagels and bialys, lox,
chicken soup with matzo balls, knishes (heavy filled savory pastries),
potato pancakes, blintzes with sour cream, gefilte fish, pickled green tomatoes and "Kosher" pickles, corned beef and pastrami, sweet hamantaschen,
and others became staples of delicatessens.[53] Many dishes moved into the
general urban food scene partly because Jewish delicatessens, especially
their sandwiches, became popular from the 1920s onward. Bagels are the

preeminent assimilated Jewish food. They entered the mainstream in the 1960s when frozen, pre-sliced and sold to supermarkets as a healthy food at a time when high carbohydrate diets were the rage. The modern industrially produced bread rounds are nothing like the originals that were made by craftsmen organized into guilds, but that is to be expected with mass culture.

One of the ways that the immigrants had an effect on American food has to do with poverty, the other side of the American food story. Studies of diets around 1900 show how meager diets of impoverished immigrants were. One in 1909 demonstrates that of all the immigrant and African American groups studied, 23 percent were underfed, most of them at the bottom of the wage scale such as day laborers and pieceworkers in the garment industry. Almost half the Russians, meaning Jews, were among the most food insecure.[54] Interestingly, Italians at all wage levels fared better than Russians because they normally spent much less on meat than on vegetables and pasta. It is a shocking tale that was ameliorated somewhat by cheap street food.

Street vending has always been a way for the poor to get into the greater economy, a way of eking out a meager living.[55] As cities grew in population and business activity in the latter nineteenth century, street vendors also grew in numbers. Any city street of the time was literally filled with hawkers selling everything from shoeshines to shoelaces, fruit, candy, peanuts, bagels on long sticks (in Jewish areas), and cooked foods, especially sausages. Vending platforms ranged from trays hung around the neck to pushcarts, carts with heating mechanisms, horse-drawn wagons, and then motorized vehicles. Food peddlers got into the business cheaply by buying their goods daily at the wholesale market and selling at low prices since they had few overheads. Their customers were mainly poor immigrants themselves, knowing little English and therefore confined to their own cultural and linguistic communities. The 1909 study showed that half the families with men, children, and women working outside the home ate meals out, lunches in particular. The white American families in the survey, as distinct from east and south Europeans and "coloreds," dined out more than others and we can imagine them patronizing luncheonettes and cafeterias. Those with lesser incomes such as laborers and garment workers spent about 6 percent of their small incomes on eating out. Where they ate was on the street, quick food from carts and wagons. Jews, Italians and Greeks, and Mexican-Americans in the southwest became the main players in this small-scale industry. In 1920s New York City as many as 60

Interior of a diner, Annapolis, Maryland, 1950s.

percent of vegetable and fruit sellers were Jews and almost all the rest were southern Italians, with similar numbers elsewhere in the country.

Raw produce was fairly easy to sell, cooked foods more complicated in the portable food venue industry. Lunch wagons appeared on city streets in 1872 when a street vendor named Walter Scott in Providence, Rhode Island, built his cart into a horse-drawn wagon and moved it to business areas. Mostly selling homemade pre-prepared sandwiches and pies, the wagon could serve large numbers quickly. The concept was much imitated and mutated. Enclosed "night owl" lunch wagons that patrons could enter appeared in the 1880s. They were America's first all-night eateries and so were to be found in theater and red light districts—yet more marks of developing urban life. By 1900, the T. H. Buckley company fitted their wagons with cooking gear, much like the fixed-location lunch counters.[56] Nothing fancy was served, only quick service dishes such as sandwiches, hot dogs, egg dishes, and plenty of coffee. The first mention of a hamburger sandwich appears in a night wagon in 1894.[57] Lunch wagons were and remained mainly working-class eating places as were their descendants, diners. And a good number were owned by now ethnic Americans.

Street food, fast food, portable food, and cheap food was the way into the American economic system for the new Americans of the age. They and their food were absorbed into American life in several ways, though street sellers were always on the periphery of the greater economic and social system. One way in was by moving up the economic ladder, John Raklios style. By around the First World War Italian and Greek retail vendors entered the wholesale fruit and vegetable business, often in competition with one another, and came to dominate the business by the 1920s. Greeks went heavily into the confection business, both as soda fountain owners and candy shop operators and as manufacturers. At one time almost all Midwestern sweet shop owners were Greeks trained by fellow Greeks in Chicago.[58] Almost every such place bore a cute American name, unlike a number of Greek-owned diners and corner restaurants, because they were selling sweets rather than regular nourishing fare.[59] Jews moved into meat processing, going from kosher operations to wider audiences as the opportunity arose. Hygrade, once a Jewish-owned New York City company, now in suburban Detroit as Ballpark Franks, New Jersey's Sabrett (a united Jewish- and Greek-owned company) and Chicago's Vienna Beef (Jewish) are examples. In this way street vendors became American middle class as they settled into fixed locations and began manufacturing units.

A second way that immigrant foods became American was through the popularity of street food. For instance, in the nineteenth century German pretzels of the large soft kind were common and remain popular on Philadelphia and New York streets, and are now featured items in several national food chains. Sandwiches composed of long crusty rolls loaded with cheeses and cold meats, made for Italian working men around 1900, later came to be popular in the 1920s and '30s. Big, hearty, and portable, they were called submarines, hoagies, or grinders among a host of other names, and were thoroughly Americanized by chains such as Subway, founded in the 1970s.[60]

One dish, however, is purely immigrant and an icon of American popular culture: the hot dog. Hot dogs began with the heavy German immigration of the mid- to later nineteenth century. Unlike Anglo and Irish-Americans, theirs was and is a sausage-centric food culture. Several German sausage varieties, namely frankfurters, wieners, knackwurst, and Thuringers, along with generic weisswurst and bratwurst, moved from German butcher shops and beer gardens (where they were served with beer and hearty bread) to the streets as early as the 1860s. Within a decade vendors were selling roasted and grilled sausages at public venues such as the newly built amusement parks, Coney Island the most famous, and sporting events. The long-standing connection between baseball and hot dogs dates to the 1890s. So ubiquitous were sausages at the time that they were given the joke name "hot dog." Part of the joke is that hot dogs were made from unsavory animal parts both by butchers and in the new large meatpacking plants in major cities. Certainly this is true of the giant meatpackers, who used big, fast chopping machines on odd animal parts to make cheap sausages. Sold in buns from at least the 1880s, one key to hot dogs' popularity was their low cost, usually 5 cents. They were food for the masses, cheap protein for working folks and as snacks for recreational crowds.

Germans were the earliest purveyors and vendors but Greeks, newly arrived in the first decade of the twentieth century, took up the hot dog business. Greek hot dog carts and stands proliferated across the country. In 1913, the whole of downtown Atlanta, Georgia, was filled with stands "as thick as fleas on a mongrel's back," according to a contemporary newspaper account. The oldest vendor, "Old" John Salas, had been on the main street since 1899 selling steamed pork and beef "weenies" or frankfurters topped with mustard, ketchup, and some sauerkraut. That style morphed into

Sabrett hot dog cart, New York City.

How the Hot Dog Got Its Name

Americans are noted for their wry, sometimes mordant, sense of humor. In the nineteenth and early twentieth centuries, sensibilities were rough by modern standards. Racial and ethnic stereotypes, cock fighting, and bloody bareknuckle boxing were all popular entertainments, and abattoirs were tourist attractions. And that is when America's iconic street food got its name: the hot dog. Sausage culture came to the United States with heavy German immigration in the mid-nineteenth century. Frankfurters, wieners, Thuringers, bratwurst, and other types were made by butchers in cities and towns across the nation. Jokes about what "mystery" meat went into the butchers' meat grinders came with them, along with comic German dialect songs. One of these is the 1864 "Die Deitcher's Dog," about the narrator's dog becoming sausage. Similar stories became popular fare for the rest of the century. At the same time, the words "red" and "hot" became staples of vaudeville songs, such as "There'll Be a Hot Time in the Old Town Tonight," the marching song of the Spanish–American War. Sometime around the late 1880s or 1890 someone put the two together to coin the jokey phrase "hot dog"; the analogous "red hot" was recorded a little earlier. The term took off, 1892 being the earliest use in a newspaper found so far. Americans loved it, connecting beloved doggies to an equally loved food. Iconography in the form of signs, postcards, and newspaper and magazine cartoons became ubiquitous and remains so across America.

southern slaw dogs. In Rhode Island and New Jersey Greek vendors added new toppings to the normal German-style mustard and onions. These were thin tomato-based sauces seasoned with cinnamon and nutmeg that resembled standard sauces used in Greek home cooking, hence dubbed chili sauce. The style spread across the country most famously in Michigan "coneys" and Cincinnati. Meanwhile Jews who were averse to eating pork, made all-beef ones. Called "Frankfurters" interchangeably with hot dogs, vendors sold them aggressively from carts, stands and to restaurants. Because of a popular notion that the label kosher meant cleaner, purer food—it did not—all-beef sausages became the standards in cities with large Jewish populations. In Chicago Italian and Greek vegetable stores located near Jewish street vendors provided ingredients for the city's signature style: pickle spears, tomato slices, pickled hot chili peppers, green relish (or piccalilli) added to chopped onions, mustard, and sometimes celery salt. Hot dogs done in any of these styles are a synthesis of immigrant foods and flavors melded in an all-American dish.[61]

Early on in the later nineteenth century and into the twentieth, while a number of ethnic dishes moved onto the common American menu, some remained as identifiers of the communities from which they sprang. Olive oil among Italians, borscht and chicken fat in Ashkenazi cuisine are but a few examples. That would always remain, though to lesser and lesser degrees as the twentieth century wore on and the old European immigrants became assimilated. Surely, the rising amounts of meat in immigrant diets informed these two processes, with immigrants eating a lot more of it and changing their food preparations to incorporate it. Another reason is that Americans came to accept newly incarnated immigrant food and the people themselves, although the latter came more slowly as lingering racism, anti-Semitism, and popular stereotypes of Italians as mobsters show.[62]

As Katherine Leonard Turner put it in her fine study of working-class foods, "American food after 1930 would never again be identified merely as the food of traditional, native-born, farming white Americans; it had been irrevocably marked by the street food, ethnic dishes, and 'fast food' that began with the working classes."[63]

RURAL AMERICA AT CENTURY'S END

While cities were changing American food, a large percentage of America's population was still rural. Most were in the farming industry whose numbers declined from 38 percent in 1900 to 18 percent in 1940, and about 2 percent in 2015. The changes in restaurants, urban eating habits, and products reached the market town to which all farms were attached, but not all at once. And since farmers often lacked income to buy new goods, especially during the many economic downturns the country suffered up to and including the Great Depression, older foodways remained the same: that is, self-sufficiency on the farm along with hunting, fishing, and gathering. In Mark Twain's food list he recalled his youth in small town Missouri: "Possum. Coon. Sliced tomatoes, with sugar or vinegar. Stewed tomatoes. Green corn, cut from the ear and

Deep Fried—Fair Food

One kind of food preparation transcends all class lines. As a nine-teenth-century critic said, Americans were addicted to the frying pan. The tradition lives on nowhere better than in America's fairs, places where deep frying has long been a fetish. For instance, one of the oldest pan fried foods, hush puppies or corn dodg-ers, became state fair specials in their southern homeland. When encasing a hot dog skewered on a stick and deep fried, likely at a Texas fair in the 1920s, they became the now ubiquitous corn dogs. Fried stick foods proliferated as fair favorites and can be found on street trucks as well. Other savory stick foods followed, including bacon dipped in chocolate (called a "muddy pig" at the Ohio State Fair), batter-dipped fish, patty sausage dipped in batter, pizza, battered macaroni and cheese, pickle slices, bat-tered Spam filled with faux cheese, sausage- and cheese-stuffed jalapeño poppers, Texas fried beer (encased in pretzel dough), fried butter balls and sticks, and Elvis on a Stick in Wisconsin (battered banana with peanut butter and bacon). At perhaps the supreme deep fried food event, the Minnesota State Fair, where 75 such dishes are served, Spaghetti and Meatballs on a Stick (spa-ghetti is mixed into a meatball, which is then cooked, battered, fried, skewered and rolled in marinara sauce) and Paneer on a

served with butter and pepper. Green corn, on the ear. Buttermilk. Iced sweet milk." Hamlin Garland and Willa Cather, poets of rural America, recognized this list at once. They also knew the hard work that went into feeding rural families, women's work.

Americans' standard image of farm life, much reinforced by depic-tions of it in popular culture, such as the "Stix Pix" so called by the movie trade paper *Variety* in the 1940s, is the Midwest. Although the farms were devoted to cash crops such as wheat and corn (and soybeans after the 1960s), farmers had to feed themselves from their own land. A typical farm of about 140 acres in the early to mid-twentieth century had gardens where staple vegetables were raised. Tomatoes, green beans, peas, corn, beets, potatoes, sweet potatoes, cabbages, peppers, lettuces, and spinach were all grown in rotation so that fresh products were available for much of the

Spear (deep-fried Indian-seasoned paneer cheese coated with a local craft beer batter and served with tomato garlic chutney) have recently appeared.

Sweet deep-fried dishes are much loved in American venues, starting with doughnuts in numerous forms, filled and plain, and crullers which are sold from street stands and trucks, especially for breakfast. Fried batters, especially the Pennsylvania Dutch themed funnel cakes made by pouring yeast or baking powder-raised batters into hot oil and serving with powdered sugar, and elephant ears (flat, round pastries) appear at almost all fairs and amusement parks. In recent years, Mexican-style buñuelos (fried dough balls) and churros (fried dough sticks sprinkled with sugar and cinnamon) have spread to carts, trucks, and fairs. Fried Coca-Cola is one recent creation, made by mixing coca-cola syrup with batter, deep frying it, and pouring more syrup on top of the final product. Sweet stick foods are common in many fairs. Among them are battered deep-fried chocolate cake, S'mores, banana splits, fresh fruits, Oreo cookies, Twinkies, candy bars (especially Snickers, Milky Way, Three Musketeers, Reese's Peanut Butter Cups, and Tootsie Rolls), and fried jelly beans in Massachusetts. In America almost nothing escapes deep hot oil and batter.

year. Surpluses were canned for the winter or, as in the case of cabbages, sliced, pickled in vinegar, and thus made into sauerkraut. Chopped mixed vegetables were made into piccalilli or chow chow. Fruits were widely grown, especially apples that could be stored in cellars over the winter. In season, berries were gathered from the roadsides and woods, as were wild herbs and mushrooms. Although Cather does not say it, the Bohemian Shimerdas knew all about mushrooms from the old country. If the family had cows—and many did—then milk, butter, and cream came from them almost year round. Chickens were omnipresent, eggs eaten almost every day. For those with pigs, killing time was late autumn and early winter, the animals rendered for lard and cooking fat, the meat salted for the winter or put into cold stores. Since farmers were often cash poor, women sold their surplus eggs, butter, and produce in local markets. Flour, sugar, a few spices, salt, and clothing plus a few luxury goods are what they got for their money. The image of well-fed, apple-cheeked children and hearty men and women is not misplaced, but it is not the full image of rural life.

By no means were all farmers so fortunate. In the South after the Civil War, once independent farmers and newly freed slaves were forced by necessity and landowners' guile into sharecropping. Farmers rented land in return for a portion, often a big one, of their crops. Most were impoverished as cotton production pushed into the uplands with new types adapted to the soils and climates. Laborers were deprived of land to raise food and the ability to keep enough money in order to purchase their own land. Cotton production increased greatly in the later nineteenth century under this system. Nutritional studies done at the turn of the nineteenth century show serious problems among sharecroppers both white and black, especially in the cotton lands. Seasonal shortages of protein in the winter and early spring were followed by outbreaks of pellagra in summer, the effects of the old hog-and-hominy diet. That disease comes from dependence on corn that has not been processed with lime and so lacks niacin vitamin B3.[64] Many Southern men were rejected as military draftees in both world wars because of the effects of poor nutrition. Similar studies of Mexican families along the Rio Grande show much the same, diets made up of corn and beans, 87 percent vegetarian but not especially

Fresh Mexican produce section in an American supermarket, including various chilies and cactus paddles.

The Corn Palace in Mitchell, South Dakota, decorated with whole ears of dried corn. It symbolizes American abundance that flowed from America's farms.

healthy.[65] Nonetheless these ingredients were the basis for the tacos and hot Mexican sauces that characterize Tex-Mex and Cal-Mex cuisine and, later, national corporate fast service chains.

Up to the Second World War both rural and urban Americans were stratified by income, race, class and thus by food. The urban poor scrambled and made do even though food prices fell through the nineteenth and early twentieth centuries. In rural areas sharecroppers, river fishermen, itinerant farm laborers, and farmers who could not make it in the new national food system ate as best they could. At least here they could hunt and gather. Twain's opossum and raccoon were supplemented by squirrel (to be made into the famous Brunswick Stew or Burgoo), fowl, fish, wild greens, nuts, and berries. These were the makings of African American "soul food." But it was never enough and so as urban economies expanded and new farm machinery and advances (an arguable word to some) in chemistry were introduced, people left the land for cities, themselves kinds of machines. Paradoxically, it would seem, Americans came to be better fed than any mass society in human history, or at least had the potential to be.[66]

NINE

What We Eat and Why (since 1945)

We must not forget that every farm is a factory, and that in every state there
are thousands of these factories which need our best thought
and effort to make them productive.

Every Farm is a Factory, International Harvester, 1916

Would I go back to the old farm life? No. Frozen food and
my microwave do just fine.

Ruth Parker, age 91 in 2008

The long evolution of American food became truly revolutionary after
the Second World War. The transformations of production, land
use, industrialization, and society discussed in the last chapter accelerated
with ever increasing speed during and after the twentieth century's world
conflicts. It is always tempting to suppose that current conditions are
the *inevitable* result of processes that happened in the past. Technology
is particularly amenable to this kind of interpretation, as Moore's Law
about computer chip speeds suggests. Some inevitability is real, such as
the fact that more than 350 parts per million of carbon dioxide molecules
in the atmosphere means global warming; we are now over 400 ppm.
Why this has happened and what, if anything, is to be done about it is
a matter of human actions. Choice comes from ideas and practices that,
once ingrained, become processes that to many people are the normal
way of doing things. For instance, the growth of business monopolies or
combines in the later nineteenth century might appear to be the inevitable
result of increasing efficiency in businesses. By 1900, six meat companies
controlled the American market, and small local producers merely hung
around the fringes of the economy. The Meat Trust was not inevitable,

but a series of policies carried out by a group of predatory business leaders who wanted to control all aspects of the market. Most of them truly believed that they had the moral right and obligation to do so. Even though trusts such as Standard Oil were broken up under federal law, the idea that size means efficiency remains ingrained in American thought. The application of new technologies is another such process. Oliver Evans's eighteenth-century flour mills did not inevitably lead to the massive Minneapolis milling industry, but the Brandywine laid foundations for them. Nor did gasoline-driven tractors themselves change the American landscape; perceptions about market-driven economies did. The story is long and complex. It is enough to say that the modern industrial food system is based on ideas and processes that originate in the American mind in the eighteenth and nineteenth centuries. Some of what happened is set out below.

Some change was due to the demands of global wars and what followed, the long-developing global economy that is unprecedented in human history. Even more, changes depended and still do on ideas.[1] Innovations in every aspect of physical life have led to more and arguably better food being available for the ever expanding human population. Ongoing from the eighteenth century, improvements in food production have made Americans "efficient" producers by standard definitions, and these techniques and ideas are spreading across the globe in the hope of feeding the burgeoning world population. Not that all people are well nourished: by some estimates 800

Waterloo (Iowa) Boy Milking Machine advertisement. The company was a pioneer in gasoline-powered tractors.

million out of 7.4 billion people suffer from chronic hunger. In the United States, the world's leading food exporter and among the top three or four food producers, 15 percent of households and 21 percent of children are food insecure. The United States is not alone in innovation; what has been historically American was the ability to act on new technological ideas, if not political ones.

SCIENCE IN THE KITCHEN

In 1892 Ella (Ervilla) Eaton Kellogg published the first edition of what would be one of the more influential vegetarian cookery manuals of the time, *Science in the Kitchen*. Her preface to the 1904 edition lays out her intention. Food was to take its place among the other new sciences:

> It is a singular and lamentable fact, the evil consequences of which are wide-spread, that the preparation of food, although involving both chemical and physical processes, has been less advanced by the results of modern researches and discoveries in chemistry and physics than any other department of human industry. Iron-mining, glass-making, even the homely art of brick-making, and many of the operations of the farm and the dairy, have been advantageously modified by the results of the fruitful labors of modern scientific investigators; but the art of cookery is at least a century behind in the march of scientific progress. The mistress of the kitchen is still groping her way amid the uncertainties of mediaeval methods, and daily bemoaning the sad results of the "rule of thumb."[2]

Mrs. Kellogg was the wife and work partner of Dr. John Harvey Kellogg. His Battle Creek Sanitarium (a neologism created by Kellogg) in Michigan was renowned as a health resort from the late 1870s to the 1920s. Kellogg was a pioneer in developing theories about how foods exactly affected human health and at the same time an entrepreneur typical of his era. He and his brother Will (and separately another Battle Creek resident, the businessman C. W. Post) more or less created the cold breakfast cereal business, thus changing America's eating habits.[3] Mrs. Kellogg sought to do the same but for different reasons. She devised the sanitarium's dietary plans using her experience to test her book's recipes. The goal was to improve Americans' physical and moral fiber by dietary means. She relied on her and her husband's scientific studies of food and body chemistry to show that certain ingredients or mixtures of them had deleterious effects on health and behavior. That morality and food choices sound like some modern dietary gurus' ideas and advice should not be surprising since morality of one sort or another has always tinged American theories of life.

Ideas have long lives. Some of Kellogg's came from the nineteenth-century reform movements such as public education, abolitionism, and temperance. Others were inherent in the evangelical religious movement called the Second Great Awakening, out of which came the Kelloggs' church, the millennialist Seventh Day Adventists. She founded a school of home economics and was an original member of the American Dietetic Association. The era also saw the beginnings of eugenics, which when combined with imperialism led to the conclusion that people in foreign lands, usually of color, were lesser folk than Europeans by breeding and diet. Kellogg's strictures on spicy food could be taken to mean that, but it was more likely she was concerned with moral uplift, with food as a key element in it (the leading advocate of African American rights Sojourner Truth was a guest at the sanitarium). These ideas began to change in the mid-1960s when a combination of new immigrants, foreign travel, and food writers brought food flavoring changes to wider American audiences. Nonetheless, despite her mixed bag of old and new ideas, Ella Kellogg was part of a larger moment in America's food history. It was a time when orderly scientific study, new chemical research, mechanical technologies, and ideas—economic, social, political, and cultural—came together to create the modern American food system.

Toward the end of *Science in the Kitchen* is a section called "The Fuel Value of Foods." It describes a new way of measuring nutrition, the calorie. Using a device called a calorimeter, the section shows a long list of foods with their caloric, or food energy, values. The American calorimeter was created by chemist Wilbur Olin Atwater who had trained in Germany with Europe's leading nutritional chemist Carl von Voit, a colleague of the pioneering chemist Justus von Liebig.[4] Atwater has been much discussed because of his influence on American diets and he had influential allies. Fellow chemist Ellen Swallow Richards, the first woman to receive a degree from the Massachusetts Institute of Technology, worked on similar problems, including ground-breaking studies of sanitation, and founded a cooking school to teach her methods. She was also a main force behind the new Home Economics Association.[5] Beginning in 1879, Mary A. Lincoln ran the New England Kitchen, which at its height taught physiology and hygiene, bacteriology, and chemistry along with actual cooking.[6] Like Richards, Lincoln was a popular speaker who inspired cooking schools and home economics school curricula across the nation, including the vegetarian Battle Creek school.

NEW FOOD SCIENCES

Chemistry was a leg upon which the Second Industrial Revolution stood. In recent times there has been much debate in the scientific community about how basic research may be divorced from technological application. That was not the case in Kellogg's era and for many decades afterward. From agriculture to food manufacturing technology, chemistry and physics, along with allied biological fields, remained at the core of modern food systems. As one of the leading companies in the field, E. I. du Pont de Nemours and Company, put it in a 1935 advertising line, "Better Things for Better Living . . . Through Chemistry." Later the slogan was reduced in popular parlance to "better living through chemistry." Meant to be a positive message about a benevolent corporation, it has been taken to apply to everything from drug-taking to an ironic comment on the prevalence of chemicals in agriculture and the environment. Popular sentiments about science have always been ambivalent.

Chemistry is logical, a compound's components described in the periodic table by symbols of each element. Their effects on human and other animals' bodies or land and water are all subject to testing in an orderly way. What characterizes systems is just that, order, plus interchangeability of parts/substances, organized and controlled by management techniques. Americans came to see machines or perhaps "gears and girders" as the symbols of the new ways of life, with efficiency as the watchword.[7] Frederick Winslow Taylor was the best-known prophet of efficiency. His time and motion studies, as described in his 1911 book *Principles of Scientific Management*, saw human workers as machines whose output could be maximized by doing one task on one machine, that is, an assembly line. Taylor studied every motion, stopwatch in hand, and developed timetables for each worker's actions.[8] Bosses including those in the newly formed Soviet Union loved Taylorism, as the system came to be called. As Mrs. Kellogg and the New Nutrition movement to which she was related saw it, the body was a machine that needed proper fuel to work correctly. Calories expressed as kilocalories and, later, kilojoules became measures not just of diet but of the optimum amount of work a human being could do efficiently. They, along with proteins, fats, carbohydrates, and vitamins (vitamins were not discovered until Casimir Funk's work in 1911), have remained indices of health and work ability in studies of populations past and present. The measures have particular relevance in American history for the study of African Americans living under plantation slavery as well as for urban industrial workers.[9]

The Factory as the Model of Efficiency

Efficiency means maximizing the energy use in systems, whether human or industrial. For instance in 1880 a bushel of corn took a worker four-and-one-half hours to produce and forty minutes in 1912; today an astounding two minutes yields double or triple the 1880 levels.[10] Purpose-designed machinery run by internal combustion engines (and electric motors) accounts for labor and energy saving. Consider that horses needed about 25 percent of the land for feed, unlike the much cheaper gasoline or diesel fuel. The greater the mechanical horsepower per hour, the greater the manufacturing and farming output. The output of products per hour rose sixfold from the 1880s to 1920.[11] Even when fewer workers were needed to plant and harvest in 1912, there was nothing like modern "precision" farming with planters and harvesters operated by one person using GPS and now satellite imaging devices to guide them to precisely the best uses of land and water. Henry Ford, who meshed men and machines on a continuous-flow assembly line, was the symbol of all the systems. As a young man, Michigan-born Ford visited the Chicago meatpacking plants (they were tourist attractions) where he saw animal disassembly lines in action. His assembly lines with men standing at single stations doing repetitive work were based on the Chicago model. So efficient were they that his original cars that sold for $950 in 1908 dropped in price to $269 by 1923. Ford's own diet followed his notion of the body as a machine. He is reported to have eaten hardly anything but various wild green weeds served as salads,

> or lightly boiled, or even stewed—and often appearing in sandwiches. There is nothing quite like a dish of stewed burdock, followed by a sandwich of soybean bread filled with milk weeds, to set a man up for an afternoon's work.

Healthy eating, as Mrs. Kellogg said, fueled the body.[12] Yet, Fordism, as it was called, was widely seen as dehumanizing, satirized by Charlie Chaplin in his movie *Modern Times* (1936), and more seriously (and melodramatically overwrought) in Fritz Lang's *Metropolis* (1927), to say nothing of Aldous Huxley's 1932 novel *Brave New World*, where it is society's official religion.

Mrs. Kellogg's Plain Food Manifesto
(from *Science in the Kitchen*)

Ella Eaton Kellogg was forthright in her convictions about the effects of bad food habits. For instance,

A more serious reason why high seasonings lead to intemperance, is in the perversion of the use of the sense of taste. (p. 31)

It is not strange that an appetite thus pampered in childhood becomes uncontrollable at maturity; for the step from gormandizing to intoxication is much shorter than most people imagine. The natural, unperverted taste of a child will lead him to eat that which is good for him. But how can we expect the children to reform when the parents continually set them bad examples in the matter of eating and drinking? (p. 32).

A traveler in Mexico, some time ago, described a favorite Mexican dish as composed of layers of the following ingredients: "Pepper, mustard, ginger, pepper, potato, ginger; mustard, pepper, potato, mustard, ginger, pepper." The common use of such a dish is sufficient cause for the great frequency of diseases of the liver among the Mexicans, noted by physicians traveling in that country. That the use of condiments is wholly a matter of habit is evident from the fact that different nations employ as condiments articles which would be in the highest degree obnoxious to people of other

Fordism, meaning mass production, was the triumph of American technology. Making the most products at the lowest cost per unit is usually applied to hard goods such as automobiles, but small grains and animal carcasses are analogues. Uniformity is a key concept in mass production, or as Henry Ford famously said, "Any customer can have a car painted any color that he wants so long as it is black." However, mass production or commodified farming was first applied to food production, from farm to food market to table. As discussed previously, a developed railroad infrastructure made this possible so that wheat from the western countries. For example, the garlic, so freely used in Russian cookery, would be considered by Americans no addition to the natural flavors of food; and still more distasteful would be the asafetida frequently used as a seasoning in the cuisine of Persia and other Asiatic countries. (pp. 30–31)

But the sense of taste was given us to distinguish between wholesome and unwholesome foods, and cannot be used for merely sensuous gratification, without debasing and making of it a gross thing. An education which demands special enjoyment or pleasure through the sense of taste, is wholly artificial; it is coming down to the animal plane, or below it rather; for the instinct of the brute creation teaches it merely to eat to live. (p. 31)

The cultivation of a taste for spices is a degradation of the sense of taste. Nature never designed that pleasure should be divorced from use. (p. 32)

The prevalent custom of loading the table with a great number of viands, upon occasions when guests are to be entertained in our homes, is one to be deplored, since it is neither conducive to good health nor necessary to good cheer, but on the contrary is so laborious and expensive a practice that many are debarred from social intercourse because they cannot afford to entertain after the fashion of their neighbors. (p. 33)

Imagine Mrs. Kellogg in a modern supermarket!

Bonanza farms using plowing and harvesting machines could be brought to milling centers such as Minneapolis. Pillsbury and other companies developed continuous flow-through flour milling using steel rollers and new bolting machinery.[13] Ford's model was food, Chicago's meatpacking plants. After the Civil War meat entrepreneurs such as Nelson Morris and Philip Armour established the Union Stockyards on Chicago's south side; Gustavus Swift arrived ten years later. Rail lines connected the city to the cattle-raising west and to markets in the east. The stockyards' business took off after Swift's engineers devised refrigerated rail cars that could carry dressed animal carcasses over long distances in all seasons. By 1900 the six corporations whose operations were located at the Stockyards manufactured 80 percent of America's meat. The actual numbers are staggering: roughly fourteen to eighteen million animals were slaughtered each year. Slaughtering, skinning, cutting, and other processes were labor-intensive, needing something like seventy men to kill and dress sixty cattle per hour (60,000 lb at roughly 1,000 lb per animal) in 1905.[14] Hard labor as it was, what made this production possible was the kind of mechanization that Henry Ford admired: bring the work to the worker, he said, using overhead trolleys.[15] Machinery invented in the 1870s made swifter processing possible. A large wheel upon which live pigs were chained by one leg, hoisted, and slaughtered or a slide system on which living creatures were hooked and sent down to meet their deaths by throat slitting were commented on by visitors to the abattoirs. The descriptions of screaming animals—pigs are sentient beings with self-awareness—the gushing blood and stench of slaughter are appalling to any sensible modern reader.[16] Within a few minutes a pig carcass was scalded, debristled, and sent on its way to be cut into hams, bacon, ribs, and other highly processed products (with lard a major extract) to be sold as cheaply as possible. Except for the inhumane slaughter style, much in production methods and speed remains the same.

The French novelist Paul Bourget, who visited Chicago for the 1893 Columbian Exposition, commented that though the scenes of death were disturbing, packinghouses were the embodiment of the new American order:

> We understood what these men require of a machine that for them prolongs, multiplies, perfects the acts of men. Once again we felt how much they have become refined in their processes of work, how they excel in combining with their personal effort the complication of machinery, and also how the least among them has a power of initiative, of direct vision and adjustment.[17]

Henry Ford thought much the same, only in an automobile factory parts were always uniform, while in meat production and agriculture constant adjustments had to be made. Companies sought uniformity in cuts and quality and were careful in instructing workers on proper techniques. That is less so in modern operations such as chicken production, where an average plant can hook live chickens to a conveyor belt, slaughter, pluck, and process them at a rate of fifteen thousand per hour. No artisanal cutting for

Herding cattle in stockyard, Montana, *c.* 1910.

the best quality is needed here, as it was in the old beef plants. Instead it is true mass production, cutting and boning out meat as fast as possible. Even inspection is automated, each bird passing under cameras for scrutiny, the imperfect ones removed for grinding as sausage ingredients or pet food.[18]

Mass Production

Mass production has a corollary: mass consumption. What could be more fully consumed than food? Increasingly, industries came into the hands of large corporations "with different departments to handle purchasing, production and marketing." Vertical integration it is called, exactly what Gustavus Swift and other meatpackers created. Separate plants for lard and oils, for the hundred or more pharmaceuticals made from animal glands, and later laboratories for food safety and nutritional values were all melded together.[19] Though some large companies such as Campbell's, Pillsbury, General Mills, and Heinz became household or even generic names for products (Kleenex for facial tissues is an example), there was plenty of room for smaller manufacturers and distributors.[20] Canning was a prime example of the production line. The history of canning has a large literature; suffice to say that modern steel rolling and tinning were developed by several companies at the end of the nineteenth century. Crimp sealing, so critical to the vacuum needed to preserve products, was done by machines invented by Charles M. Ams for the Max Ams Machine Company. In 1914 three billion cans poured off the producer's lines and by 1950 one in three products on supermarket shelves was in a can.[21]

Serried rows of colorful cans line supermarket shelves, the retail counterpart to rows of crops and fruit trees in fields. Shoppers plucking cans, bottles, or packages of food see only the labeled exteriors. Any knowledge of their production beyond this comes from films and video images showing rows of cans or bottles whizzing along metallic lines, filled by funnels, sealed, and sent off for cooking, packing, and shipping. "Untouched by human hands," went the marketing phrase, sometimes jokingly, to describe foods that were somehow uncontaminated by personal contact. This idea was and remains a reaction to numerous food adulteration scandals. Packages remedy that fear of corruption; they "promise, and usually deliver, predictability . . . you don't think about packages . . . you don't need to."[22] Consistency, uniformity, the hallmarks of industrial processes, sold factory foods to Americans. Nor were they wrong in the main, because the pre-packaged goods were usually safer than food sold in the old general stores that dominated the retail food trade before the rise of supermarkets. The National Biscuit Company is an example. Formed in 1898 by a merger of bakeries in the Midwest and east, the company created sealed-package biscuits that drove the old bulk-stored and unhygienic (as in mold and rot) cracker barrel out of business. It and others used new endless belt ovens that moved, baked, and packaged uniform products quickly. Nabisco's main product bore the brilliant name Uneeda Biscuit stamped on the cracker and boxes. With it and others, such as Shredded Wheat breakfast cereal, the company controlled 70 percent of the American market. Nabisco was a major player in the development of the idea of the supermarket with its myriad packaged items.[23]

Once public trust in brands was established by corporations that were distant from consumers in many ways, once factory-made food was regarded as safe, then something else happened, something magical. Raw materials went into one end of the factory and finished products came out of the other. Better living through whirring complex machines all inside a box, people were told. Or, perhaps the phrase ought to be: out of sight, out of mind. The passage of the Pure Food and Drug Act and Federal Meat Inspection Act in 1906 and the creation of the Food and Drug Administration did much to allay public fears about food safety. Long advocated by health reformers such as the government's chief chemist Harvey Washington Wiley, public outcries about foul meat were

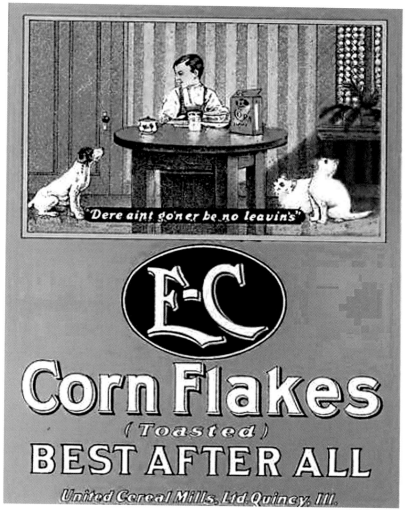

Advertisement for E-C Cornflakes, 1910. By this time central-factory-made breakfast foods were sold as children's fare, as they are today.

intensified in the same year by Upton Sinclair's exposé, *The Jungle*. Readers did not seem to get his message about the need for socialism, marveled the author, who famously said, "I aimed for the head and instead reached their stomach."

Yet, meat was to be one of those magical foods when transformed into sausages. Americans had long worried about meat quality, especially when made into sausages. Jokes about dogs going into butchers' grinding machines date to the mid-nineteenth century when grinders and powered choppers became common. But sausages, especially those called hot dogs or red hots in the 1890s, were generally cheap and popular. The new safety regulations helped. Chicago meat company Oscar Mayer promoted its German sausage-style Edelweiss brand as pure and became one of the first companies, if not the first, to embrace the new inspection rules. Oscar's yellow-banded sausages were meant to show quality of the kind associated with artisanal production. But in a mass market speed and quantity are critical to business success. In the 1939 World's Fair in New York, Swift and Company introduced a new production system "linking previously discrete production stages with conveyor belts . . . without hand labor."[24] Advances in processing led to completely integrated machines. In the late 1950s Oscar Mayer's research head Edward C. Sloan and a team created a system of chopping, stuffing, and new anaerobic plastic packaging that they called the "wiener tunnel" or "hot dog highway." Meat sent into large bowl choppers at one end came out as finished hot dogs in about an hour. Films made for advertising and schools show the wieners pouring out of the chutes at the amazing rate of ten thousand an hour. At almost the same time Ray Townsend of his eponymous company in Des Moines, Iowa, created the even more amazing Frank-A-Matic, which cascaded out of its metal mouth 36,000 frankfurters in an hour. The system Townsend invented remains the industry standard for the several billions of hot dogs consumed every year by Americans (and more worldwide).

Out of plain sight, grains, vegetables, and whole animals were stuffed into factories to end up on grocers' shelves, in bins and cold cases transformed into palatable food sold in attractive packages. Several ideas inherent in American food rose from the industrial food system. For one, absolute food prices and the amount of family income spent on food fell from the inception of industrialization. Though people at the lowest income levels spend about 20 percent of their income on food compared to 10 percent for middling income families and half that for the top 1 percent, these figures compare favorably with 1890–1900 levels of 40–50 percent on food.[25] In 2015 close to half these food expenditures for middling and upper incomes was on food eaten away from home; in 1890–1900 such expenditures were much less. Cheap fast food accounts for some restaurant turnover, but studies show that among children and adolescents, at least on average, only 12 percent of their daily caloric intake come from these outlets.[26] Though lower prices sound like a triumph of agricultural capitalism, the fact is that modern America's commodity foods receive heavy government subsidies, unlike in the pre-Great Depression era.

Then there is the much discussed loss of flavor and nutrients in processed foods. The demands of uniformity mean that varieties of plants and animals had to be pared down to a few. American white bread, soft, mushy, bland, and sliced (since 1928) for convenience, is an example. It is made from new power mixers churning hard and soft flours (like flours made for home use) bleached and fortified with vitamins to replace nutrients lost in milling. Commercial canners and agricultural universities experimented with varieties from early in the twentieth century to find the right product to be picked at the right time. Taste was not always the determinant.[27] Canned foods became routine because of price, safety, convenience, and prestige. Certainly they improved American nutrition by evening out seasonal foods and providing more vitamins. Studies of diets in impoverished parts of the United States during the Great Depression of the 1930s show that people at the bottom regarded canned foods as luxury items.[28] These commercial products took on their own flavors from the acid or sugar and salt mixtures in which they were marinated and from the tinned cans themselves. Modern cans have non-interactive plastic liners to counteract the transfer of metal flavors, but still canned green beans or peas taste nothing like fresh ones. Americans became acclimated to these particular flavors and textures to the chagrin of fresh food advocates. For generations American thought of green peas as soft, mushy green balls, not the al dente cooked aromatic seeds that they once were. Flavoring indifferent vegetables by mixture became common, perhaps the most famous being green bean casserole, developed by a home economist working for the Campbell soup company in the mid-1950s. It consists of canned green beans mixed with condensed cream of mushroom soup, some milk, soy sauce, and canned French-fried onions baked up for a half-hour. The green bean casserole remains a somewhat derisory symbol of Midwestern cookery.[29] If canned foods made for mainstream consumers were bland, so was fast food and so was much of popular culture. The television fare of the period is infamous for being anodyne. Fluxes of change in America, however, were hidden beneath the canned culture: there is a reason why Edmund McIlhenny's hot pepper sauce created on Avery Island in Louisiana in 1868 from tabasco chilies has been in business, and sold nationally, for so long.

THE LAND TRANSFORMED

Two more unseen elements of America's new food systems were and remain: what happened to the land, the original and changed biotas, and the true costs of food. Both are fundamental to the ongoing transformation of the American continent by scientific and mechanical innovation. They are also parts of historical changes in American society and policy decisions that arise from them, namely wars, immigration, urbanization and changes in the economy (including depressions), climate change, and cultural ideas among others.

Films about farming from around the world made from the teens of the twentieth century onward often showed legions of tractors on wide farms moving in formation. Pare Lorentz satirized the image in *The Plow that Broke the Plains* (1936); the Soviets, who theoretically believed in scientific systems of all kinds, gloried in it. The American internal combustion engine tractor was invented by Iowan John Froelich in 1892, who cobbled it together in a blacksmith shop. The next year his design was incorporated in his home state as the Waterloo Gasoline Traction Engine Company. Always small, the company was absorbed by John Deere in 1918, its machines the basis for the highly successful products of its new parent company.[30] The First World War created a boom in tractors because the United States government asked for massive increases in wheat production to feed the military and hungry people in Europe: "Wheat will win the war" went the slogan. Henry Ford heeded it in 1917 and began major assembly line production of his Fordson tractors. By 1920 he had sold a hundred thousand tractors, more than half of all units in the United States. Large machines, they were ideal for the broad wheatlands of the prairies and plains, but they were not usable in the kind of work needed on most farms. Row-crop farming needs tractors that can plow and cultivate rows of crops roughly 42 inches wide, that is, the width of a mule pulling a plow.[31] The Farmall created by International Harvester was just the thing. Introduced in the early 1920s, the tall, narrow tractor became the model for all of them including such rivals as Case, Massey-Harris, Deere, and Allis-Chalmers, the last of which introduced rubber wheels. Many more improvements were to follow, including those made by farmers, as celebrated by the John Deere Museum.

Apart from the tractor's crucial role in increasing productivity through power and efficiency, using it brought uniformity in farming. In 1967 John Noble Wilford, the distinguished science writer of the *New York Times*, wrote about his visit to a farm in Maryland. There he saw picking machines being used for tomatoes that had been especially developed to resist damage by such harvesting methods. Quoting an expert, Wilford predicted that food plants would be transformed: "Peach trees will be shaped like umbrellas and orange trees will grow in hedgerows. Heads of lettuce will be selected and packaged in fields."[32] Every one of the developing technologies bore fruit. Lettuce is picked, washed, and packaged in the field and is widely advertised as being fresher and presumably more tasty than older methods. Thirty-seven years later the same newspaper reported on machines used on orderly, perfectly spaced Florida citrus trees. Large machines armed with steel bristles shake each tree as they move along: "In under 5 minutes, the machines shake loose 36,000 pounds of oranges from 100 trees, catch the fruit and drop it into a large storage car."[33] Although 17 percent of the American labor force, non-citizen workers included, works in food production, labor-saving efficiency is impressive. In 1918 one farmer fed seven people, by 1967 the number of people fed increased to thirty, and in 2016 each American farmer provided food for 155 people across the planet.

Modifying plants to accommodate machinery is not new, since American farmers, seed merchants, and research institutions all developed new strains of plants to fit environmental conditions. In monocropping systems, however, plants and machines have now co-evolved in a positive feedback system. Both have deeply affected the landscapes in which they are set. As Deborah Fitzgerald pointed out, there is a large literature on the development of picking machines which are, after all, varieties of older harvesting mechanisms. Modern-style mechanical pickers really got started in the 1920s and '30s in cotton production with the inventions of John and Mack Rust.[34] But before that, rice farming was a model for industrialized production that profoundly transformed landscapes. Rice was a major crop

Modern cotton harvester.

of coastal Carolina plantations from their inception. It was a labor-intensive crop, planted in the traditional way, in waterlogged fields, and harvested by hand. After the Civil War Mississippi was home to traditional rice production that still required a lot of labor. In the 1880s entrepreneur Jabez Bunting Watkins from Kansas bought 1.5 million acres of prairie land in the Cajun lands of southwest Louisiana for development.[35] At the time local farmers were growing rice on small patches of land without benefit of irrigation. They called it "providence" rice, because the crop depended on sufficient rainfall to produce. Watkins, followed by other Midwesterners, brought Midwestern production techniques to the region. By early in the next century a number of irrigation canals had been dug and thousands of acres flooded for rice. Instead of harvesting in water, the new farmers drained the fields first and then put harvesting and binding machines on them. Production boomed: by 1899 the new fields produced almost three million barrels of rice compared to one million using traditional methods.[36] Irrigated rice production spread into Texas near Beaumont-Houston and especially into the Arkansas prairie after 1895 when Nebraska farmer William J. Fuller began irrigating and planting in the northeastern part of the state near Lanoke. Today Arkansas is the nation's leading rice producer with mechanization of the digging and maintenance of irrigation systems, of planting with drills, and large-scale harvesting and binding. These mechanisms not only transformed rural economies but changed the landscapes from the American prairie to seasonal rice paddies. The eighteenth- and nineteenth-century commentators on American agriculture and landscapes seen earlier would surely have loved the regularity of American farms such as this: the wilderness truly tamed.

Arkansas produces more than half of America's rice crop on 1.7 million acres of irrigated land. The rice comes from a half-dozen species, mostly medium and long grain, usually polished, enriched with vitamins, and sold under the trade name of a large cooperative called Riceland Foods.[37] Mrs. Kellogg tells us that white rice is easy to digest but contains few nutrients necessary for a healthy body. It has to be eaten with other nutritious foods to be fully utilized. Again, for her food was fuel for the body, but for commodity rice growers uniformity is important, partly because rices are grown for national markets and like other products are expected to look and be cooked in prescribed ways. Early "providence" rices were probably long-grain indicas but the exact strain is not clear. They did tend to break easily. A sturdier Japanese breed was introduced in 1895 but today most Arkansas and other southern rices are indicas. California, on the other hand, also grows a fair amount of short-grain, stickier japonicas called Calrose. Within the general rice species are numerous sub-types developed from both natural selection and by plant scientists. In Arkansas, for instance, something in the order of 41 rice cultivars are in use or development.[38] The point is to find just the right kind for maximum production within its environment. After milling, rice is graded by size, how many broken bits there are, texture, and moisture content, and then assigned grades from 1 to 6. The best "perfect" rice is the most uniform in grade and quality. Unlike Thai jasmine or Indo-Pakistani basmati rices (varieties that are grown in the United States with varied success), they are bland and have been since Mrs. Kellogg's day. Her dietary theories saw spicy food as akin to moral degradation. The words uniformity, consistency, and commodity are essential here.

Anyone who drives along the South Carolina and Georgia coast, such as the road between Charleston and Savannah, will notice wide fields along freshwater inlets going into the sea. Overgrown with lush grass, they look like perfect rice fields. They were once, but have not been used for rice since around 1911. There are now efforts to revive the crop related to the Carolina Gold Rice Foundation.[39] Once a foundation of the South Carolina slave plantation economy, fragrant, delicious Carolina rice was originally grown, harvested, and processed by hand. Indeed, people from the rice-growing regions of Africa were brought in specifically for the tasks. With a national market Carolina rice underwent mechanization in the form of steam-powered harvesting and milling, but the industry was not to last. The Civil War, hurricanes, and changing markets virtually killed Carolina Gold. The large machines developed for prairie "providence" rice were too heavy for the muddy fields of the southeastern coast; economy of scale created much cheaper and probably consistent products for American consumers. Only in the late 1990s were heirloom strains revived and some new hybrids developed for the commercial market, notably by Anson Mills.[40]

Similar stories can be told about landscapes across the continent, dating to Thomas Jefferson and George Washington's realization that their estates' lands had been denuded of nutrients, "worn out" in the popular phrase. The deeply eroded cotton lands of the Deep South were commented on almost from the start of the industry as it moved ever westward in the ante-bellum period.[41] Nor were these southern lands alone in ruined habitats. Oysters, especially *Crassostrea virginica*, which once appeared on menus of every quality restaurant and recipes for which were in every cookbook, virtually disappeared around the First World War due to human pollution along the east coast.[42] The same happened to San Francisco Bay oysters by the 1940s. Whole species were wiped out or close to it. Passenger pigeons,

Eroded land, Jackson, Mississippi, 1936.

whose numbers blacked out the sun when they flocked up, were killed by "sportsmen" in such numbers that they died out in 1914. American bison almost suffered the same fate, only to be rescued by conservationists, of whom President Theodore Roosevelt was a leader. They were replaced on the Great Plains by cattle, yet another kind of monocropping.

DROUGHT AND POLICY

The Dust Bowl is the best-known example of commercial farming's destructive effects on land. The shortgrass southern Great Plains is a region where, receiving on average 10 inches of rain a year, drought is an ever-present threat. As Pare Lorentz put it in the commentary to *The Plow that Broke the Plains*, "A high, treeless continent, without rivers, without streams . . . A country of high winds, and sun . . . and of little rain." Agricultural experts knew how fragile the land was: so did President Theodore Roosevelt who advocated massive irrigation projects. Crops had failed before when Bonanza farms went bust in the 1880s and '90s. Serious soil erosion at the rate of 5 billion tons a year had been observed in 1909 and 1928 studies.[43] Still, tractors combined with record rainfalls lured farmers to the land around 1910. Real estate agents and equipment salesmen did great business as farmers plowed money into land and machines. Initially, the investments paid off as wheat prices doubled in 1917 to $3.00 per bushel, later stabilized to $2.25 by the federal government.[44] Production doubled as more than 20 percent of America's crop went to European countries that were locked in war. But, after the war prices dropped by half and even worse, machines did their damage. Tractors pulling disk plows churned the thin soils that quickly dried out to dust in drought conditions. They came when after a decade-long drought immense clouds of dust rose from South Dakota farms and blew eastward in 1933. The next year dust clouds dropped 4 lb of dust per person on Chicago and reached the Atlantic seaboard. Three million ecological refugees poured out of the region, three-quarters of a million from Oklahoma. Deeply impoverished and hungry, they set out for California to work picking fruit and vegetables. Derisively called Oakies, their plight was told in John Steinbeck's wrenching *The Grapes of Wrath* (1939) and John Ford's 1940 movie of the same name. Urban Americans, by then almost 60 percent of the population, learned what an ecological disaster was and what agricultural policies, or lack of them, really meant.

The story has been told many times. One compelling argument says that capitalism had severed the links between people and land, in a way similar to how it alienates industrial workers from what they create. The race for money using the tools of finance and machines overcame common sense and expertise about what matters in what is now called sustainable farming. It was "the inevitable outcome of a culture that deliberately and

Lettuce workers, California 1937. During the Great Depression, migrant farm workers came from everywhere. The best known were "Okies" from the Oklahoma Dust Bowl memorialized in John Steinbeck's novel *The Grapes of Wrath* and by the Federal Farm Security Administration's photographers such as Dorothea Lange and Walker Evans.

self-consciously set itself that task of dominating and exploiting the land for all it was worth."[45] One might claim that beneath the urgencies of capitalism runs the stream of America's bucolic vision—nature uncorrupted, as perhaps Henry David Thoreau living at Walden Pond thought. On the other side is an argument that technology and science moves on in an inexorable logic. It was the machines that caused the Dust Bowl. Taken to an extreme one might think of opening a can as akin to summoning up Skynet, the soulless villain of the *Terminator* movie series. In truth, linking certain kinds of exploitative capitalism to reckless action also connects the Dust Bowl to slower-moving catastrophes. Two of many are draining the great mid-continent underground lake, the Ogallala Aquifer, to water lands that were devastated in the 1930s, and the loss of Midwestern top soils, now down to about 40 percent of 1800 levels or less in some places. American capitalism, or rather the people who ran and profited from it, was the cause of the other calamity of the time, the Great Depression. How to deal with these problems gave rise to regulatory systems that affect food production and what Americans eat to this day.

There are several schools of thought about what caused the Great Depression. The stock market collapse in October 1929 was the symbol of what was to come, but it was not the whole cause. Reckless speculation in stocks, bonds and real estate, failure of the monetary system, and a stringent tariff on imported goods have all been adduced as causes. Recently economists have looked to the explanation offered by Marriner Eccles, President Franklin Delano Roosevelt's chairman of the Federal Reserve. In a mass production system, mass consumption is necessary. If consumers do not have enough buying power then the whole system collapses.[46] Maldistribution of wealth, a disparity between the super-rich and the ordinary people over time, never worse than in 1929 or in 2016, destabilized the whole economy. The disparity was evident in the rural sector where poverty and debt of all kinds was rampant. From sharecroppers in the south to leveraged farmers in the Midwest and west, the underpinning of the "Roaring Twenties" was weaker than is often supposed. Recall that poor folks of both races ate meager hog and hominy diets.

Responding to the sight of long breadlines and soup kitchens for the unemployed and of farmers destroying food because it cost more to grow than its sale price, from 1933 the Roosevelt administration moved to deal with ecological and human tragedies. Among the agencies set up under the New Deal were those dealing with land reclamation and agriculture. The 1933 Agricultural Adjustment Act gave farmers price supports for basic crops—corn, wheat, cotton, rice, peanuts, tobacco, and milk—and paid to take land out of production. A later Agricultural Adjustment Act in 1938 replaced the AAA and included a crop insurance program. The Farm Security Act in 1935 and 1937 loaned money to tenant farmers and created farming cooperatives as a means of keeping impoverished farmers on the land. In 1936, Congress created the Soil Conservation Service, a program meant to save soils from further erosion. Tree planting, contour plowing, terracing, hybrid seeds, and fertilization worked well. Plains landscapes were changed and wheat production increased greatly during and after the Second World War. The related Civilian Conservation Corps sent young men to restore forests and parks that had been devastated by overcutting of timber and neglect. Put into effect immediately after Roosevelt took office, the decade-long program enrolled more than three million young men, planted some three billion trees, and restored hundreds of parks. It is likely that the CCC's military-style organization provided the organizational know-how that prepared the United States to quickly organize its military, including mass dining, for the Second World War.[47]

Food was a main front in the war on the Depression. To feed hungry Americans immediately, the 1933 Federal Surplus Relief Corporation bought up bulk food such as apples, canned beef, and cheese to be distributed through local relief organizations, some of which were informal social centers such as bars and taverns. The program has remained in one form or another to the present day, the best-known being school lunch programs.[48] A food stamp program in 1939 fell into disuse during the Second World War, but was revived in 1961 and expanded into several other programs to help children, despite opposition from conservative politicians. The Bureau of Home Economics, a government agency formed in 1923 and staffed by trained home economists, was tasked with teaching women on the effective use of these surplus or cheap foods. Pamphlets, classes, newspaper stories, and the now widespread radio were all vehicles by which home economists carried out their long-standing nutritional programs. Food corporations did the same since they wanted to sell the same canned and packaged products.[49] The trend was amplified during the First World War when the government set up the U.S. Food Administration in 1917 to feed the Allies in Europe and to supply American troops. Recommendations such as meatless days and using beans and cheese as protein sources were widely advertised as patriotic duties. The downside of the slogan "Food Will Win the War" was the great plow-up of the Great Plains.

In the 1920s the Bureau ran a radio program and related publication series called "Aunt Sammy's Kitchen." Like other characters invented by advertising agencies to sell product, such as Betty Crocker in 1924 and the real-life Nancy Green and her successors who were identified as Aunt Jemima, Aunt Sammy gave household tips and lots of recipes.[50] Aunt Sammy's suggested menus and recipes in 1931 are similar to recipes of earlier periods. Spring dinner menus include the likes of: fresh beef tongue, wilted dandelion greens, fried potato cakes, banana pudding; or curried fowl with carrots, flaky boiled rice, buttered asparagus, orange salad, apricot whip. These days apricot whip might be concocted with canned whipped cream, but here it is made with tapioca and fresh whipped cream in the manner of a pie filling. Aunt Sammy's recipes are a kind of bridge to the more simplified recipes of the post-Second World War era found in Betty Crocker or *Good Housekeeping* cookbooks, but they are archaic in the choice of ingredients such as tongue, now more an ethnic dish, and in their lack of brand names; gelatin, for instance, is generic and not the famous and ubiquitous Jell-O or Royal.

Only three years later, and under the new federal administration, the Bureau was issuing pamphlets such as "Canned Beef Recipes" (1934). The recipes are much plainer, almost as if telling the recipient of surplus food that they should not "put on airs."

> Browned hash.—To 1 quart mashed potatoes add 1 pint chopped canned beef, 1 finely chopped onion, and seasonings to taste, and mix thoroughly. Mold into flat cakes and fry slowly on both sides until crusty. Or spread the mixture in an even layer in a greased frying pan and cook slowly until well browned.

> Tamale pie.—Cook together 2 cups corn meal, 2 teaspoons salt, and 4 cups water to make a fairly thick mush. Mix 1 pint cut-up canned beef with 1 pint canned tomatoes, add a finely chopped onion, and salt and pepper to taste. Put a layer of mush in a greased baking dish or pan, add the meat mixture and cover with the rest of the mush. Bake in a moderate oven until hot through and lightly browned on top.[51]

Tamale pie was one of a number of non- or low-meat recipes issued by government agencies and food processors during the Second World War. It is a one-pot meal, much like stews or Kraft boxed macaroni and cheese, introduced in 1937 as a family dinner. At first glance tamale pie might be an example of Mexican or Mexican-American regional dishes becoming national, but it was not exactly. Tamales were common street food in American cities from the 1890s and likely they were not the proverbial "hot" tamales one might find in Mexico or the American southwest. In fact tamales were canned by Armour & Company at the time and advertised as "a novel Mexican delicacy." The pie is made with cornmeal "mush" like many Southern dishes, so if anything it is a poor folks' food, only made with industrial ingredients. The common man became a major theme in 1930s American popular culture with echoes of simple food for hardworking people running through it. No images are more poignant than those showing impoverished Southern tenant farmers in the 1938 documentary *The River*. A thin, haggard mother living with her family in a small shack cooks a one-pot meal for her children on a primitive stove. The scrawny children eat from tin plates, licking every drop of gravy from them. The narration asks why there is such poverty in the Mississippi Valley, the richest valley in the world.[52]

In times of need people make do. Farm families, people in small towns who had land around them or garden areas, grew as much as they could for personal consumption. Anecdotes are numerous about how city people went out on weekends to visit family and friends who were able to grow their own. Ruth Parker, who lived on a northern Illinois farm near the Iowa border, recalled that her mother grew carrots, turnips, cabbage, potatoes, onions, corn, cucumbers, kohlrabi, lettuce, and tomatoes. The family canned a lot, so they bought hardly anything at the store, just staples like

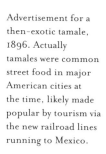

Advertisement for a then-exotic tamale, 1896. Actually tamales were common street food in major American cities at the time, likely made popular by tourism via the new railroad lines running to Mexico.

GMO-GM Foods

Americans have always worried about food safety. Processed foods, especially meat, have always drawn public attention. Following the publication of Rachel Carson's book *Silent Spring* (1962), the overuse of pesticides drew so much public, scientific, and governmental scrutiny that certain pesticides were banned. From the 1990s that concern began to shift to new technologies partly related to pest control: plants and animals that are genetically modified to fit the needs of farmers and food processors. Under the rubric of biotechnology, the terms genetically modified organisms (GMOs) and genetically engineered organisms (GEs) have been used interchangeably in the heated discussions about the new science and technology. They are not the same thing. The U.S. Department of Agriculture defines a GMO as: "A range of tools, including traditional breeding techniques, that alter living organisms, or parts of organisms, to make or modify products; improve plants or animals; or develop microorganisms for specific agricultural uses." That means traditional cross open-air pollination and breed selection to create new versions of an organism. Genetic engineering means "introducing, eliminating or rearranging specific genes using the methods of modern molecular biology, particularly those techniques referred to as recombinant DNA techniques." Golden rice whose genome has been modified to produce beta-carotene, a source of vitamin A, is an example.

The infamous Flavr Savr tomato was an early attempt to introduce a GE product to the general public. In an attempt to increase its shelf life, scientists had used the plant's own genes to inhibit the enzyme that breaks down its cell walls. Almost immediately critics said that fish genes had been introduced, labeling the tomato "Frankenfood," meaning that it was an unnatural hybrid of plant and animal and thus monstrous (never mind that the original in Mary Shelley's novel was anything but a monster). Actually the tomato was nothing of the kind but it was flavorless and thus failed. To date, no such GE foods have been made or sold directly to consumers. The big four genetically engineered crops at 90 percent or so are soybean, corn (the only GE crop grown in Europe), rapeseed (for canola oil), and cotton. All of these enter the food chain through animal feeds and oils, including cottonseed.

The debate about the effects of GE foods falls into several interrelated categories: the effects on human health of the genetic modification itself; the use of pesticides and their effects on humans, other plants, and animals; ownership and profit. Claims abound about increases in susceptibility to allergies, cancers, and pulmonary diseases, among others. Crops that have been modified, usually by *Bacillus thuringiensis* (Bt), are made to resist such pests as corn borers, cotton bollworm, pink bollworm, and the Colorado potato beetle. Other kinds of GE crops are resistant to glyphosate, a potent herbicide best known by its brand name, Roundup. That these plants abet monocropping and give rise to herbicide-resistant weeds (superweeds) is the case. As for ownership of GE organisms, companies such as Monsanto and DuPont claim to own the seeds they created down generations and aggressively sue for what they deem to be usage or patent infringements. They have been accused, not without reason but not entirely accurately, of putting profit before the general good in their various business and lobbying practices.

In 2016 the National Academies of Sciences, Engineering and Medicine issued a lengthy report based on a detailed study by a joint committee of reputable scientists on the issue of GMO-GE foods. Based on comparative studies from around the world among populations that eat foods with GE bases and those who do not, the report concluded that there is no convincing evidence that such modifications have any major impacts on human health. The report also concluded that GE plants save farmers time and money but they do not significantly increase crop yields. Nor is the world about to be overrun by GE crops, since only 12 percent of it is planted with such crops. Despite this convincing report the controversy rages on. As a result more and more American food companies are pledging not to use GMO-GE ingredients in their products and labeling them as such.

flour, sugar and coffee. Ruth and the family women gathered dandelion greens for salads and wild berries when in season. The family raised chickens and sold eggs in local markets, kept a cow for milk, and slaughtered and processed a hog in the winter. Except for some newer machinery (they did not have electricity until 1945), this late 1920s and '30s farm was much like those a century and a half before. However, when relatives came out from town on weekends they brought with them the much desired "store boughten bread."[53] "In hard times no one went hungry—we may have thought about food a lot, but no one starved," Ruth says. Of course, there were plenty of hungry people in cities and also in deeply impoverished parts of the South, especially among African Americans.

An estimated 80 percent of farmers and people in small towns raised food this way before the great farm consolidations of the 1970s. This kind of local–personal horticultural economy was not included in government statistics, but when another national emergency came gardens became government policy. As in the First World War, at the United States' entry into the Second World War the federal government asked Americans to plant gardens since so much food production was going to be sent to the millions of military personnel overseas. The federal and local programs were a great success. Vacant urban lots became mini-farms. In Chicago alone at least 7,000 tons of vegetables were produced in 1943. By the war's end in 1945 about 40 percent of America's vegetables came from these community gardens. If the currently fashionable locavorism has antecedents, it is in farm gardens and urban gardens. In some ways perhaps both kinds of horticulture were also ancestors of the now popular farmers' markets. They are also inspirations for the vegetable garden First Lady Michelle Obama planted at the White House in 2009.[54]

Newer Science and New Policies

Meanwhile, factory farming grew rapidly during and after the Second World War. A combination of science-chemical, biological-technology and economic policy decisions created new generations of Bonanza farms. One of the oldest techniques, hybridization, really took off in the 1930s with corn, wheat, rye, barley, and a relative newcomer, soybeans. Modified by traditional breeding and cross-breeding (not yet GMO) for specific landscapes and climate during the great drought of the period, production increased in time for the war effort in the next decade. Later hybridization was and still is linked to the application of

Corn and soybeans growing in a field, Morgan Road, Pittsfield Township, Michigan.

chemicals.[55] Farmers had always known about replenishing soils with organic matter, even if they did not know that the stuff was composed of chemicals that might be generated from non-organic substances. In the 1840s, chemist Justus von Liebig figured out what some of them were. Soil science developed in the later nineteenth century, a pioneer in the field being Eugene Hilgard, who worked in Mississippi and California. The fertilizer industry really began, however, when the German scientist Fritz Haber discovered in 1909 that nitrogen could be obtained from liquid ammonia. His process was perfected by Carl Bosch who worked for the German firm BASF. Fertilizer plants were established at the new Tennessee Valley Authority's hydroelectric dams in the late 1930s; many more were built after the Second World War. By the 1960s cheap nitrates combined with new non-organic pesticides doubled wheat production and raised corn sevenfold in North America.[56] They are still widely used despite environmental issues with field runoff, but to a far lesser extent in 2016 than thirty years before.

Fertilizers were not the only chemical revolution. Pesticides, herbicides, and fungicides were all developed in the same period. The most (in)famous is DDT (dichlorodiphenyltrichloroethane), invented by Nobel Prize winner Paul Hermann Müller in 1938. It was highly praised during the war because it was effective in killing disease-bearing insects such as mosquitos and lice. It was also sold as a household insecticide in a distinctive spray pump can under the brand name Flit. The catchphrase "Quick Henry, the Flit!" became part of popular culture before DDT's dangers to the environment and human health became widely known. Banned about 1970, DDT was replaced by many pesticides including the recently popular organically derived neonicotinoid family. Unfortunately these compounds seem to have shattered bee colonies and may be banned. Of the many herbicides used in agriculture, glyphosate is the most common. The best-known brand is the Monsanto Company's Roundup and to go with it the company created genetically modified (GMO) proprietary herbicide-resistant seed called Roundup Ready. Others have followed. Ninety percent of all soybeans and 60 percent of all corn are modified to resist glyphosate and therefore receive the largest doses of this compound.[57] Since both plants are at the base of the American food chain because of their use for animal feed and oils, much of the nation's food uses GMO products. Pesticides, herbicides, and modified seeds are a main reason for protests and the organic food movement.

The federal government has continued its close relationship to agriculture. Until the 1970s price crop supports, called parity, and other programs were employed to manage supply. The system worked to stabilize farm family ownership. As in manufacturing system-energy models, farm productivity increased as inputs, as economists like to say, fell in price and outputs jumped. Chemical prices declined by 75 percent and machinery cost 60 percent less between 1948 and 2011. Family farm income rose at comparable rates to that of industrial and white collar workers during what has been called the Golden Age of the middle class (1950s–70s). Marginal tax rates on upper incomes were high, but the benefits to Americans as a whole were palpable. Unionization, subsidies to agriculture, building a national infrastructure in the form of a new national highway system, along with massive government spending on education and the military, created the world's largest middle class. It was a class that spent its money on housing and hard goods such as automobiles, appliances, and television sets, and on travel, though less and less on food.[58] Government policy from the New Deal onward, no matter which political party was in power, promoted cheap food. Subsidies, price supports, tax policies, and more made it so for the consumer. To do otherwise would have had political consequences.

Agriculture was to change. Led by President Richard Nixon's Secretary of Agriculture, Earl Butz, in the 1970s Congress did away with the old subsidy system, replacing it with direct payments to farmers. His goal was massive production with a view toward export. "Plant from fence post to fence post," he said, "we'll export the surplus." For a while it worked as farmers invested heavily in machines, seed, and chemicals. Farmers were businessmen—not that they had not been before—but now in the new "free market" they had to be better versed in business practices. It was not to last. In the early 1980s prices dropped, high-interest loans had to be repaid, and farmers went broke. Cheap corn could be turned into corn syrup and ethanol by large agribusiness corporations who bought up more and more land. Corporations such as Cargill that handled grain exports benefited; small farmers not so much. An ongoing trend was accelerated: the number of farmers declined, the size of farms increased and so did specialization.[59] In 1900 most farms produced five commodity crops; in 2015 it was one. Like Henry Ford's Model T, one product seems to be the most efficient use of land.

Farms are everywhere, but many picturesque farmhouses and silos are empty, many a barn collapsing. Traveling through the countryside one sees dilapidated barns and run-down houses everywhere. Hundreds, thousands even, of small towns across America that fed on farming are now hollowed out, their main streets scenes of boarded-up buildings and few people. In a phrase, "industrialization has moved with a vengeance, filling farmyards with confinement systems that automatically control food, water, climate, and animal movement."[60] Concentrated animal feeding operations (CAFOs) are a fact and symbol of what has happened to farming. When farmers cannot make it economically or when they age out—the average age for a farmer is 55 and not going down—they sell up. Sometimes it is to larger farm operations but too often it is to developers. In the past thirty years 24 million acres of farmland have been paved over for suburban development. According to America's Farmland Trust, 91 percent of the country's fresh fruit and vegetables are grown at the edge of urban sprawl, much of that in California. In addition 13 million more acres are needed for Americans to meet the USDA's dietary recommended amounts of fruit and vegetables.[61] As America and the world urbanizes, food production must adapt itself to new conditions, as it always has, given the resources available.

Small-scale acquisition of food runs beneath the macroeconomics of commodity production. In similar ways, old methods of cookery that reflect standard American ingredients and tastes remain intact to the present day, although modified by "foreign" elements. Two themes that make up modern American food and foodways arise from these propositions. One is where people get their food and what they do with it; the second is what American cuisine is or what Americans seem to think it is. In city and town, small and large, Americans get their food from supermarkets. Large multi-department food stores rose in the 1920s in California based on the self-service model created by Clarence Saunders's Piggly Wiggly store in Memphis, Tennessee, in 1916. They spread across the country during the next decade, and after a lull in the Second World War blossomed into 38,015 stores with millions of dollars in sales. On average a store holds 42,214 items, although studies show that an average shopper buys only 260 items in a year.[62] Using the concept of food miles, the number of miles an item travels from production center to market, the best estimate for produce is 1,300–2000. The food chain has become longer than ever. In today's international marketplace a good number of items come from large producers overseas: Chilean grapes, Dutch greenhouse tomatoes, and plenty of Mexican produce joined the old imports bananas, pineapples, and coffee in almost every supermarket in the nation. Using large warehouses and trucking networks, factory farms have found the most efficient way to sell in high volumes.[63] The rise of farmers' markets from 1,755 in 1994 to 8,284 in 2014, as reported by the USDA, tests the distribution system, but these local markets are as yet a small fraction of the food system.

THE BLAND AND THE SPICY: CHANGES IN AMERICA

There is an argument for shoppers and cooks having fallen under the hegemony of the agribusiness and great food processing corporations, allegedly with the collusion of professional dieticians. Taylorism, the production line, and a narrowing of actual food choices in the sense of the same or similar products in different packaging are put forward as proof. Consumers have become "deskilled" in depth of knowledge of what food is, how it is raised, and in actual cooking techniques. Composed of standardized products, American processed food is bland even if there is some superficial knowledge of spicier ethnic food. Salt and sugar have replaced the taste of real food directly from the earth, while consumers are directed by advertising to become merely pawns of industry.[64] This is not just an academic exercise but is an argument made by many in the organic, farm to table, and heritage breeds movement. There is some truth in this verbal picture but it assumes that the actual taste of food and the meaning people attach to it have been drained away. Lots of evidence counters this argument, making American food a paradox, difficult to categorize.

Even at 260 items per shopper, any supermarket in the United States has a greater variety of products than in generations past, though much the same cuts of meat, packaged in varieties of new ways. Pre-sliced, nitrogen-flushed, plastic-packed cold meats in numerous styles are one example. Shoppers pick and choose just as they do in a farmers' market, just as they might have done in a Colonial marketplace where raw ingredients vied with bread and made pies. The pre-made meal sector is growing, with made-in-store dishes the new hot trend in supermarkets. Both are extensions of the original idea of canned and frozen foods. However, there is good evidence that Americans have opened their minds and taste buds to new food, flavors, and cooking techniques. Rather than "deskilling" on many levels, Americans' culinary skills have adapted to the new systems. One need only open a daily newspaper's food section, look through the "women's" magazines on supermarket checkout racks (or displayed in medical offices), or turn on a television to see people's interest in actual cooking. Since the 1990s cooking shows of many kinds have jammed the airwaves. Like the magazines, they range from the time-consuming cookery of the pioneering Julia Child and Jacques Pepin to the straightforward recipes of Martha Stewart and the simpler ones of Rachel Ray. The Food Network cable and satellite channel, combined with other cable and on-air networks, attracts between five and six million viewers every week. Much of the demographic for these shows is younger, including teenagers.[65] Cooking and exploration of new tastes is hardly dead.

Again, cooks are animals who adapt to their environments, milieus of all kinds, physical, social, and cultural. In a nation of immigrants, that means peoples from elsewhere who bring their own food cultures with them. Since they now live and eat in a country whose economy and culture is driven by consumption, then new foods and ways of preparation must appear in the public space: markets, restaurants, and street fare. Aside from recidivists who are a small fraction of the population and who become a political force from time to time, American ideology is that the country takes in immigrants and absorbs them into general culture. So it is with food, "absorbed" being the operative word. As discussed in Chapter Eight, the older European and Asian immigrants had more or less integrated by the 1950s. Community cookbooks, compiled by charitable organizations as fundraisers, are a good place to see this fusion in action. A recipe called "Taco Meatball Ring", printed in a cookbook put together for a church in Tennessee, McDonough County, Illinois, but taken originally from the September/October 1999 issue of *Country Woman* magazine, lists the ingredients as shredded Cheddar cheese, taco seasoning, ground beef, refrigerated crescent rolls, iceberg lettuce, tomatoes, onions, olives, jalapeno peppers, and optional sour cream and bottled or canned salsa. The directions call for cooked meatballs to be stuffed into the crescent rolls that are shaped into a ring, the center of which, after baking, is filled with the rest of the ingredients. The dish resembles the tamale pie of 1934 mentioned above, only more elaborate in the far richer 1990s when it was created. In the name and use of onions, tomatoes, jalapeno peppers, and flavorings (taco and salsa) there is a touch of Mexican cuisine, but it is an example of industrial food products put together, probably in a corporate test kitchen, for the home cook. She or he might even experiment with soy or sriracha sauce. With its wheat bread, beef, cheese, and iceberg (an American vegetable nationally marketed in 1896), it is an all-American dish and considered so by those who eat it.

Go to a supermarket almost anywhere today and there will be an "Ethnic Food" section. Invariably on the shelves will be several brands of soy and teriyaki sauces, tamari, bottles of prepared "stir-fry" sauce, sweet soy sauce, bead molasses, hot mustard sauce, hoisin sauce, duck sauce, plum sauce, oyster sauce, sesame oil, canned water chestnuts, dried Chinese mushrooms, Thai soft jasmine rice, Thai peanut sauce, Thai-inspired sriracha sauce, rice threads, coconut milk, several forms of "Middle Eastern" pilaf, couscous, Jamaican jerk sauce, a few curry pastes and sauces, a half-dozen Mexican hot sauces such as habanero sauces, an equal number of Mexican-style salsas, and stacks of both corn and wheat flour tortillas. Not only are the prepared sauces mentioned here sold, but so are vegetables and other ingredients that most American consumers once considered alien because the flavors were unfamiliar, or the food was thought to be frankly disgusting—try okra cooked to a gelatinous consistency in the upper Midwest, for example. In an essay on American food, the anthropologist Sidney Mintz added:

> consumers have learned about hummus, falafel, bagels, "designer" coffees, coriander, basil, arugula and radicchio, Jerusalem artichokes [a New World sunflower, by the way], jicama, quinoa, buckwheat groats, new rice varieties (jasmine, arborio, basmati), lactose-free milk, scones ... breads baked with ingredients such as tomatoes or olives, a staggering variety of capsicums, soy milk, tofu and dried soy products, previously neglected seafoods such

as monkfish, 'artificial' crabmeat (surimi), and many subtropical fruits, such as mangoes, soursops, red bananas, and star apples, and a dizzying number of packaged foods designed to relieve our worries, especially about fiber and fats.[66]

Do the varieties of foods mean the aforementioned opening of the American palate, though within limits, or food producers differentiating basically similar products to increase sales? Quinoa is similar enough to other whole grains as to be interchangeable, its marketing power coming from supposed health benefits. The answer is probably both, in a dialogue of culture and money.

Americans have become more culinarily multicultural than ever, though whether the general public is ready for the potent, rotted flavors of foods such as southeast Asian shrimp or anchovy pastes, Chinese preserved vegetables, or rotted bean curd, or really powerfully spiced kimchee, is doubtful. Hot sauces have become normalized, these kinds of fermented foods less so. Dining out is another matter. Of the more than 600,000 restaurants in the United States in 2014, almost 100,000 were Italian of which 71,000 were pizza places; 54,000 were Mexican (including chain stores), and 44,000 were Chinese.[67] In terms of numbers of diners per week, surveys show that 77 percent of Americans eat some form of ethnic food once a month when dining out, with millennials (age 18–34) being the most interested in new kinds of cuisine. Of these Italian is the number one "ethnic" cuisine in the United States in terms of frequency, but Mexican and Chinese are not far behind. Far down the list lie Thai, Japanese, Korean, Indian, and Middle Eastern. As *Nation's Restaurant News* observes, the food of the big three—Italian, Mexican, and Chinese—is so common as to be completely "American." Restaurant dining has changed dramatically in that a common Italian dish such as linguini in clam sauce is found in even chain "family" restaurants, but will hardly be made at home by American families. On the other hand, everyone eats pasta and tacos in some form or other.

Why change, aside from the natural human inclination to taste interesting things? The usual reasons proposed are foreign travel, which rose dramatically after the Second World War, and media such as television that brought vivid images of the world to Americans as never before. More important was an emphasis on multiculturalism in the nation's education after the 1960s.[68] Partly that was due to the Civil Rights movement of the 1950s and '60s and partly to immigration. As it did in the late eighteenth

Thai food has become integrated into American cuisine, like versions of Chinese before it, and is available at quick serve chains in shopping malls, airports, and similar venues.

and nineteenth centuries, immigration and settlement comes in two forms, internal and external. People coming to America is a story told many times over. More than a century ago what the Bohemian Shimerda family living in Nebraska ate was "ethnic" in that their preparations were not exactly the same as their neighbor Anglo-Americans. Like German fare, which arrived earlier, it was close enough to be quickly assimilated. The same holds for East Europeans, Ashkenazi Jews, Italians, and Greeks. The large Mexican populations of the west and southwest formed the basis for hybrid Cal-Mex and Tex-Mex dishes, while Chinese restaurateurs adapted their fare to American tastes. Chop suey is far more American than its Taishanese ancestor. In 1965 Congress passed the Hart–Celler Act, legislation that lifted quotas on national origins and raised limits on the numbers of people allowed into the country; another 1990 law raised the cap limits again. The effect was to allow in millions of immigrants from countries that were hitherto restricted, including Indians, Thais, Vietnamese, Koreans, Filipinos, Latin Americans, and Africans. The appearance of regional variations on Chinese cuisine, some under the name Szechuan-Mandarin (two different styles), in the late 1960s is one result. Another was the rise in the 1970s of Thai and, depending on the region, such as Minneapolis where Hmong were settled, Vietnamese and Laotian restaurants. Los Angeles' Koreatown expanded and became a culinary center, with Koreans also well known for operating newly popular Japanese restaurants. Based on the existing popularity of Chinese-American cuisine and, as discussed previously, the amount of newly introduced meat in their preparations, other Asian foods spilled out from restaurants and stores into the general American food inventory, hence their presence in supermarkets. With these cuisines came an interest in new flavors, especially hotter ones.

A simple explanation for the new interest in foreign or ethnic foods is that it arose from immigrant and groups living adjacent to one another and close to long-established American communities, as in earlier eras, mainly in cities. That is part of the story but not all. Of the hundreds of ethnic groups living in the United States only a few cuisines have crossed to the mainstream. None has been accepted in its totality, but rather in individual preparations. The new dishes had to have mainstream analogies: the most popular Thai dish by far is pad thai, in American terms a more flavorful chow mein. For some years experts in the food industry have predicted that South Asian cuisine will be the new "hot" cuisine. To date, no Indian or Pakistani cuisine in their many, many regional variations has achieved this. A few foods such as naan and some pulse preparations plus basmati rice are sold in supermarkets either frozen or packaged, but Indian–Pakistani style restaurants are minor players in the hospitality industry. South Asian immigration history is not the same as older groups, being relatively small and urban/suburban. Aside from north Indian tandoori preparations such as chicken, most dishes do not correspond to American fare, and the flavors may be just too dissimilar for comfort. Peruvian, Ethiopian, Persian, African (both north and sub-Saharan), and others are all represented by a few restaurants, mainly in large cities, but despite having interesting

General Tso's Chicken is a Westernized (and sweetened) Hunanese dish introduced in the 1970s and now universal in American Chinese restaurants.

Array of Asian food products widely available in supermarkets across the country.

cuisines are not widely known. Hummus and tahini yes, sheep's head no. Population density and proximity do matter and so does flavor and texture.

As we have seen previously, changes in foodways are a complex interaction among immigrants and the host culture, among generations, and are part of the mysterious ways of cultural change. The first is, again, fitting into a new physical and food environment. If one simply cannot get a food, say jackfruit, used in South Asian cuisine, then kohlrabi might do (the chop suey effect). Subjected to the stresses of modern working conditions, an immigrant family might take up American breakfast foods. Indeed, studies show exactly that among many groups. Cornflakes replaced congee, the West African staple fufu, south Indian idlis with sambar, or heavy, spicy meat dishes that Koreans used to eat as breakfasts. Nor can the allure of modern fast and snack foods be discounted as changing ethnic food habits. Hot dogs and hamburgers cross all ethnicities. At the same time, entrepreneurs imported foods from their native lands, set up shops and restaurants, and as discussed before, some of their foods filtered out into the larger American community. The next generation of ethnic families adapted to American ways, often melding family foods and the American ones they found at school or on the street. More than one teacher has been surprised to learn that their second- or third-generation Mexican-Americans know little about their grandmothers' cooking. Food is an important element of cultural acclimation. At the same time, "ethnic" dishes became denatured, acceptable to a broader American public, and finally became integrated into the industrial food system. After all, the succeeding generation of immigrants became Americans, and so, usually willingly and with enthusiasm, acculturated.

Of all the immigrant groups none were more important than Mexicans. After all, all of the southwest and California had once been Mexican. Mexican cuisine is regional, the northern iterations moving across the fluid southwestern and California borders.[69] The street market in San Antonio, Texas, in the nineteenth century became famous for its Chili Queens, while in California Mexican-Americans set up food stands and restaurants whose cuisine mirrored local ingredients and tastes. Now standard restaurant dishes such as enchiladas stuffed with meat or cheese, fried and covered in melted cheese and a mildly spicy sauce were staples. So were burritos, an American invention, and nachos. Internal immigrants to California from the 1920s onward, such as African Americans, discovered tacos as good cheap food and so did other migrants. During and after the Second World War the defense industry and military bases attracted Americans from across the nation who discovered the joy of Mexican food, especially tacos. In 1962 Glen Bell opened his first Taco Bell franchise based on the successful McDonald's. It featured deracinated tacos that had the virtue of being mostly salad and very cheap. Today the chain numbers more than five thousand outlets. At the same time salsa companies such as Pace and Old El Paso marketed bottled sauces made

Burritos, meaning "little donkeys," likely originated in the northern Mexican-American borderlands in the late 19th century. Using flour tortillas makes them amenable to a greater variety of international fillings. These upscale rolls are made with black beans popular in southern Mexico and quinoa from the Andean highlands.

Mexican tacos in infinite varieties are now American staples. These three iterations are steak, seafood, and chopped vegetable tacos.

to North American tastes. In 1991 salsas surpassed ketchup sales, as can be seen on grocers' shelves.

Mexicans and Mexican-Americans became internal migrants themselves when they moved northward to find jobs in industries and agriculture. For instance, northern Illinois has attracted some six hundred thousand (perhaps as many as a million counting undocumented people). As a result there is a vibrant Mexican food community with restaurants serving food that is close in kind and quality to the dishes of their home states, such as Guerrero and Michoacán. The same is happening in rural areas where agricultural workers have settled. Stores carrying Mexican

Taco stand, Maxwell Street Market, Chicago. The market began in the Jewish self-styled "ghetto" but changing demographics have made it Mexican, and one of the country's best.

Menu showing Mexican and Mexican American dishes commonly offered in the United States.

ingredients, bakeries, and taco stands have popped up. Much depends on how quickly the new immigrants rise economically because Americans' perceptions of "ethnic" foods are bound to class. Mexican tacos still have to overcome prejudice against the people who make them.

The longest-standing internal immigration has been among African Americans. Beginning with the First World War and ending in the 1970s, roughly six million people moved from the rural South to northern cities. Jim Crow laws, lynchings, and general prejudice drove black Americans out, while jobs in industry lured them in. The story of the migrants' food-ways, some of which have been called soul food, has been much discussed in terms of community identity and to some degree flavor.[70] Despite African Americans' enormous contribution to American food, this amalgam of Southern traditions has not really become mainstream American. Partly that is due to the regionality of the cuisines that compose it, Southern with specific flavors and textures, and partly it is due to racial and class barriers. Despite the breakdown of many cultural walls, as evidenced by the popularity of black urban music (starting with jazz in the teens of the twentieth century), most elements of soul food have not followed. Most white

Packaged products in a Hispanic–American supermarket with tortillas and tortilla chips.

Americans may not dive into plates of ham hocks, delectable long-cooked greens, chitterlings, and grits every day. What they do is fire up their grills for summer cooking and use some version of Southern-style barbecue sauce. Barbecue knows no race in the South with all of its regional styles. In northern cities barbecue popularity and styles arrived with black migration. The famous Kansas City versions originated in Memphis, Tennessee, and in Chicago, mostly from western Mississippi and Arkansas, following the second Great Migration in the post-Second World War era. As for dining out, the two main kinds of African American public eating places can be found almost everywhere: rib joints (many of the most celebrated black-owned) and chicken shacks. None is immune to corporate fast food. There are local places, but Kentucky Fried Chicken, Church's, and the New Orleans-style Popeye's dominate the market. Southern and soul-food related, like so much else in American food, they are not exactly models of regional food.

FAST FOOD

Ethnicity and locality should be considered with America's contribution to world cuisine, fast food. The type of products and service embodied in it reflect the themes of standardization and change, both mediated by American ideology and commercial culture. To people around the world the image of American food is enrobed in a yellow arch or fronted by a jolly Kentucky colonel. The theme song might be set to the all-American phrase "fast, clean, and cheap"—though less cheap than at the beginning. As seen in the last chapter, quick service food—fast food—runs deep in American food culture. From the early nineteenth century on, Americans ate fast, the speed increasing as the nation became an urban, industrialized society. Quick service restaurants of various kinds appeared in cities and towns in the late nineteenth and early twentieth centuries as functions of these changes. From diners to lunch counters, much of what they served was similar: sandwiches, hot dogs, hamburgers, egg dishes, corned beef hash (hence another term for cheap food, "hash house"), and plenty of coffee.

Perhaps it was inevitable that quick service food would follow the industrial model of production and sales: manufacturing and franchising operations. The ingredients for dishes served could be made in a central location and then sent to outlets that were uniform in cooking and service, all at low prices. The first of these operations appeared in Wichita,

Grocery store in Chicago's "Black Belt," 1940s.

Roadside fruit and snack stand, Ponchatoula, Louisiana, 1930s. An ancestor of today's
industrialized and uniform roadside fast-food chains.

Kansas, when diner owner Walter Anderson teamed up with real estate
agent Edgar Waldo "Billy" Ingram to create White Castle in 1921.[71] Kansas
was beef country, ground meat hamburgers a way to buy and sell locally
sourced cheaper meat. Anderson developed a way to cook his small squares
of meat quickly, infusing them and the buns with meat juices and chopped
onion flavors. Modeled on Chicago's crenelated Water Tower, only in anti-
septic white, the stores served cheap (5 cents) food quickly in an apparently
clean atmosphere. "Buy 'em by the sack," their advertising went. The concept was a success, the design even more so, with a string of imitators that
ranged from chains such as White Tower to local restaurants like Nick's
in Brookton, South Dakota, founded in 1929 with the motto "Buy 'em by
the bag." Steak 'n Shake, a hamburger chain founded in 1934 in Normal,
Illinois (with more than five hundred units in the u.s. and abroad), used
the variation "takhomasak" for the same idea. White Castle was a model
of efficiency and national uniformity within the context of American food
preferences. Freshly griddled beef merged with bread and coffee hit the
sweet spot and still does. For various reasons none of these chains dominated the fast food scene. White Castle's 480 outlets cannot match Burger
King's approximately 7,750 or McDonald's estimated 14,000 in the United
States, double that worldwide.

McDonald's and rivals like Carl's Jr. and Burger King perfected
the American fast food system. The story of how brothers Richard and

Maurice McDonald set up a highly efficient fast food serving system in their San Bernardino drive-in restaurant in 1948 has been told many times. So has the tale of Ray Kroc who turned it into the world's largest restaurant chain. Post-war southern California was changing rapidly from a region of citrus and avocado farms centered on small towns to the traffic-choked urban/suburban sprawl that it is today. Water had been brought to the dry region by (often corrupt) diversionary schemes in the 1920s; the federal government rained money on war industries during and after the war. The population grew rapidly along the new streets, roads and freeways. So did food outlets. In California's waxing car culture, drive-ins (likely invented by the A&W Root Beer chain in Lodi, California, in the early 1920s) with car-hops would seem just the thing. The McDonalds realized that speedy service was even better for people on the go. Now with a severely limited menu, they built an assembly line where one person did only one task to produce a standardized finished product. Pre-made beef patties were grilled by one person, another garnished and wrapped it, yet another made milkshakes, while French fries were another worker's task. Paper wrappers, trays, and plastic forks were all disposable (though not recycled), each customer who now lined up at a serving counter receiving a neat pre-set package. And the food was cheap at 15 cents a burger.[72]

Ray Kroc, who sold milkshake machines when he was not being a jazz musician, famously visited McDonald's in 1954 to sell his machines. Impressed by their operation, he persuaded the brothers to allow him to

Nick's Hamburgers, Brookton, South Dakota. A local place serving fresh locally sourced beef, but the building is in the White Castle chain style.

sell franchises. Kroc's first store, complete with golden arches, was opened in Des Plaines, Illinois, in 1955. Franchising was not new; the model works not only for food but fittingly for automobile dealerships. The company provided the products along with promotions and received moneys in return. Kroc was not the first to realize the import of the McDonald's system. Carl N. Karcher, who founded the Carl's Jr. chain (now owned by CKE along with Hardee's), and Matthew Burns and Keith G. Cramer, who formed the ancestor of Burger King, all saw the same thing and imitated it. The new national road system begun in the 1950s by the Eisenhower administration as a national defense initiative was made for the new fast food outlets, which proliferated to the detriment of local dining spots as the new highways bypassed older two-lane roads. Eventually fast food chains entered cities, replacing the old cafeterias, lunchrooms, and lunch counters. They could afford downtown rents; small operators could not. By the teens of the twenty-first century, fast food chains numbered more than 45,000 outlets in the United States alone, most of them franchised or owned by nineteen companies.

What these places sold was and largely remains American food: meat and potatoes, savory, juicy, salty, griddled, or grilled for flavor, accompanied by a sweet milk-based or soft drink. The places were clean, the food cheap enough to allow customers to buy several. McDonald's original menu was simply these: hamburgers, cheeseburgers, French fries, malts, and soft drinks. Consistency in product and flavor has always been a selling point for the fast food chains, under the correct assumption that people wanted the same things wherever they happened to buy them. How to differentiate oneself in a competitive market has always been a question. Burger King's predecessor Insta-Burger King had virtually the same menu as its rivals, but in 1957 introduced the larger Whopper, since in America more is always better. That became a quarter-pounder in the 1980s and soon all the chains were selling bigger hamburgers. Burger King's Original Chicken Sandwich was soon matched by others, its BK Chicken Tenders created to match McDonald's Chicken Nuggets. The competition goes on, salad by salad, healthier alternatives by alternatives or, conversely, monster calorie-heavy sandwich by even more heart-unhealthy sandwich. Yet there is a kind of gourmetship in fast food. People long remember McDonald's French fries because they were cooked in beef fat (replaced with vegetable oils as a health measure). Besides being told by advertising which burger place is better than the others, regular consumers know the differences in flavors. Regular surveys by newspapers and food journals rate the food at

Menu of ABC
Restaurants, Ohio
Turnpike, 1956.

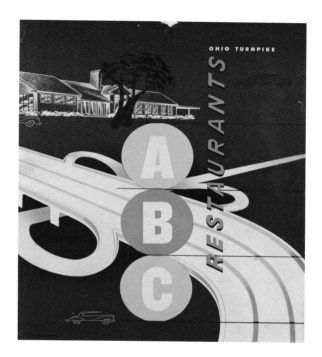

ABC RESTAURANT & COFFEE SHOP

TOMATO JUICE .15 .25   GRAPEFRUIT JUICE .15 .25

ORANGE JUICE .15 .25   GRAPE JUICE .15 .25

FRESH FRUIT CUP .30   SHRIMP COCKTAIL .65

HALF GRAPEFRUIT .25

SOUP DU JOUR
CUP .20   BOWL .35

CHILI CON CARNE .45   ALA
CARTE   DINNER

CHEF'S SUGGESTIONS

BAKED SOUTHERN HASH   .90   1.40
Buttered Lima Beans, Pickled Beets

BRAISED BEEF STEW EN-CASSEROLE   1.10   1.60
Cole Slaw

CHICKEN FRICASSEE OVER NOODLES   1.25   1.75
Buttered Lima Beans, Whipped Potatoes

FRIED SEA SHORE DINNER, SHRIMP, PERCH, SCALLOPS,
TARTER SAUCE   1.35   1.85
French Fried Potatoes, Cole Slaw

HOT MEAT LOAF SANDWICH   .75
Whipped Potatoes, Gravy

COMPLETE DINNER INCLUDES CHOICE
OF SOUP OR JUICE .20 DESSERT .20
AND .10 BEVERAGE

DESSERTS

FRUIT JELLO WITH WHIPPED CREAM .25 ICE CREAM .20
SHERBETS .20   LAYER CAKE .20 APPLE .20 OTHER PIES .25
HALF GRAPEFRUIT .25

ABC Ohio Turnpike
Specials, 1956. Now
disappeared from high-
ways and most byways,
the dishes are a mélange
of local home cooking
and an imitation of
the national Howard
Johnson's fried seafood
platters.

the chains, especially the hamburgers. Those at Los Angeles-based In and Out and the new East Coast-based Shake Shack are always at the top, to the chagrin of their rivals.

Hot dogs and hamburgers are among the most industrial of foods. Hamburger chains abound, not so with hot dogs. Only the California-based Wienerschnitzel and the new Dog Haus can claim to be national/regional hot dog chains, though their menus are wide. A&W and much later Dog n Suds tried basing their stores on hot dogs but never succeeded. Nathan's of Coney Island's franchises have withered from highs in the 1990s. Why this very American street food has not come under the hand of chain stores is a complex question. Perhaps it is that from their beginning as street food in the late nineteenth century, hot dogs have ramified into many regional and local styles, their differences celebrated by local communities and widely noted in the press.[73] Across America local manufacturers make sausages for their particular markets. At hot dog venues toppings of every kind, often adjusted by the individual customer to their own taste, vary widely. Hamburgers have recently been undergoing a similar transformation, especially when in the hands of chefs who have become interested in them and hot dogs. People eating them are not automatons. They know a lot about flavors and textures and even the unhealthy ingredients of some products. The food chain from animals to factory may be in the hands of a relatively few restaurant and processing companies but absolute hegemony, not the cultural kind at least, does not work. Not that fast food chains are not trying. In the 1970s Burger King rolled out the slogan "Have it Your Way" as a way to sell custom-topped burgers, to be matched a few years later by the computer company Apple, Inc.'s famous "1984" advertisement that touted the individuality of its products and customers. In the 2010s Sonic, which operates drive-ins across the country, began selling hot dogs with regional toppings. Since the company descends from a drive-in root beer stand in Shawnee, Oklahoma, that likely served Cincinnati chili dogs, it was a natural extension of their history. They are still fast food with standard toppings but changed from the bland hot dogs found at gas stations and convenience stores.

Fast food chains notwithstanding, what Americans eat and what they think about what they eat has been changing, especially from the 1990s onward. The industrial model of consistent food products made in factories, whose processes are unseen but whose safety is assured, is one. Low prices conquer all. A second model looks toward foods produced locally, preferably sustainably, whose flavors, theoretically, are not only from the land but are more varied than the national products. Any historical survey of American

Soft, fresh pretzels have been a street food since Colonial days, the Philadelphian ones especially famous. Like other such foods they are sold in chain stores, this one in a shopping mall.

food takes it as fact that there were regional cuisines or at least regional foods prepared in ways unique to the regions. Mark Twain observed that in his famous gustatory wish list. There are several ways to consider this. Terroir is one. It means foods whose flavors are based on the particular soil and bedrock of the locale from which it comes.[74] The argument is that once outside of the constraints of factory food, Americans understand varied tastes not only on the palate but that identify with local cultures. Smell and taste as identifiers of place are well known, as in the poet Archestratus of Gela's dictum in the fourth century BCE that if anyone wants the best culinary experience they have to eat the thing in its natural place. One might say that about Nathan's Famous Hot Dogs on the Coney Island boardwalk.

Reactions to Industrialized Food

Memory or maybe nostalgia is another idea about locality that has a pull upon current American food. Heirloom foods are an example. Heirloom plants are generally "varieties that are capable of being pollen fertilized and that existed before the 1940s when industrial farming spread in North America and the variety of species grown commercially was significantly reduced."[75] Heirlooms come from seeds saved from one year to the next, some successfully grown the next year, some not. They are genetic

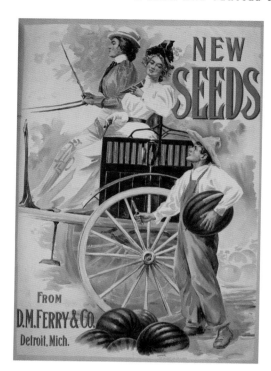

New seeds catalogue, *c.* 1890,
from a major seed company
that created new varieties.

memories of species that appeared in specific places (terroirs) that survive
because diligent gardeners or arborists kept them alive in seed form, if
not always as living plants. They are also parts of collective memory, perhaps of places as they once were and certainly within families who were
attached to the land where heirlooms grew. Large numbers of tomato and
apple varieties appeared or were propagated in the nineteenth century,
a kind of golden age of variations. Nineteenth-century seed catalogues
show lots of other plants, from cabbages to beans. Each had specific
flavors and textures, even if not grown in its native soils. They still do.

Heirloom tomatoes and to some degree apples have become "hot"
in the food world. Not only will any farmers' market in the country have
heirloom tomatoes (and, if you are lucky, apples) but such tomatoes are
now sold in supermarkets. That means larger farms using seeds from commercial growers. Home gardeners will find 54 heirloom tomatoes in the
W. Atlee Burpee & Co catalogue, some organic, others conventional.
Visit a garden center in season and there will be pots of already growing
heirlooms, usually Brandywines. Does this mean that corporations have
coopted folk food? Advertisers have played on American nostalgia when
the times seemed right, as in the 1980s when Ronald Reagan was president

and it was "Morning in America." Perhaps, or maybe commercial heirlooms are an example of people using what is available to them in their own ways. Whether this kind of heirloom evokes a sense of place in the customer is doubtful, rather here is greater interest in flavors that differ from standard hybrids such as the Big Boy. Biting into a crisp tart-sweet Stayman-Winesap apple, however, knowing that it was developed in 1866 by Dr. Joseph Stayman of Leavenworth, gives one a sense of the American heartland worthy of a Willa Cather story.

All of this relates to the aforementioned term "sustainability." It is much used by advocates of smaller-scale, often organic farming or horticulture, to mean not adding agricultural inputs such as "artificial" fertilizers but instead using only what was originally in and on the land. It sounds good, but is ambiguous because no matter what is planted, it is not the original version. Nor is the climate or the soil that is changed by what has been planted. In an experiment famous among agricultural scientists, Alexander C. Magruder of Oklahoma A&M University planted a test plot of several acres of wheat in 1892. That soil has been replanted year after year with wheat to this day without the addition of external nutrients or being allowed to go fallow. The plot produced 20 bushels of wheat at the beginning and still does. Other plots had nitrogen added to see if yields increased. Today normal wheat yields nearby are 27.6 bushels. The original plot's soil has deteriorated but yield has not for one reason: new strains of wheat are planted each year. New devices have made it possible for farmers to check the amount of nitrogen in each plant so that the least amount can

Locally grown apples at a farmers' market.

Junk Foods

Junk foods are defined as having "high calories and little nutritional value." They include candy, salted snacks, fried fast food, and sugar-laced or high-fructose-corn-syrup-loaded soft drinks. Junk foods are widely thought to be unhealthy because taken in large amounts they encourage obesity, exacerbate diseases such as diabetes, and syndromes like attention deficit disorder. The term often overlaps with "fast food" and "snacks," though food in these categories can also be nutritious or benign in the form of nuts, peanuts, and even plain popcorn. Few critics can complain about fast food chain salads, though there are plenty of problems with the ways that the ingredients are grown and labor conditions in picking and processing. Before the early twentieth century:

> No fast food chains existed, and neither did hamburgers, hot dogs, pizza, Hershey bars, Snickers, french fries, potato chips, Oreos, or Nachos; none of these foods became important until almost the mid-twentieth century . . .

The first commercially successful junk food was Cracker Jack, created by Frederick and Louis Rueckheim. The major reason for its success was advertising. Within a decade of its national launch in 1896, Cracker Jack quickly became the most popular confection in America, and by 1916 it was the best-selling confection in the world. Others followed Cracker Jack's lead, and Americans began to buy branded confections.

> [The company] launched advertising campaigns that targeted children with toys, claimed healthful contents of Cracker Jack, and promulgated grand slogans. These

be precisely added to boost production.[76] That is, no matter how heirloom the plant, it is not the original eaten by the first farmers to plant it. The flavors will never be exactly the same; terroir is only a snapshot of taste at a given time—it is not forever. With few exceptions such as wild persimmons or paw paws, everything has been manipulated to suit changing campaigns were so successful that they were emulated by other fast food and junk food manufacturers.[77]

America's most famous candy companies—Wrigley, Hershey, Tootsie Roll, Mars, Curtiss, Just Born, Brach's, Goldenberger—were all founded between the 1890s and 1920s. Of the various types of salted snacks, potato chips are counted as a major dietary villain. Chips were not new when commercial manufacture began in the late nineteenth century: Mary Randolph has a recipe for chips in her 1828 cookery book. In 1926 Laura Scudder founded the first successful packaged chips company in Monterey Park, California, and in 1938 Herman Lay of Dorset, Ohio, added potato chips to his snack food line using new waxed glassine bags to retain freshness. After 1950 manufacturers learned how to salt and flavor their chips and the industry boomed.

Today Americans eat more than 4 lb of potato chips a year, consumed by 83 percent of households:

Studies had demonstrated that almost 75 percent of Americans derived at least 20 percent of calories from snacks. Snacking has replaced meals for many Americans. By the beginning of the twenty-first century, Americans annually consumed almost $22 billion of salted nuts, popcorn, potato chips, pretzels, corn chips, cheese snacks, and other salty snacks.[78]

Governments and health agencies have tried to curb snack food consumption through public campaigns and taxes. New York City famously tried to limit the sizes of soft drinks sold, but met with considerable public resistance. So far, reduction in junk food consumption is largely voluntary.

regional and local conditions. It is application of human ingenuity, in this case new fertilization technologies, an environmentally sensitive approach to commodity production, and we are the better for it.

Locality of food implies a sense of authenticity which, in turn, relates to the question of whether there is an American cuisine. Mark Twain

Advertisement for a
seed company selling its
developed corn seed,
Sweetheart of the Corn,
1911.

thought so in its plurality, others not because, among other reasons, the
concept of national cuisines is a construct. There is no single "Chinese" or
"Mexican" cuisine but lots of regional and local ones. The idea of a national
cuisine is used as social and personal identification, as in "we know our-
selves because of what we eat and how we eat it." It is political in a number
of ways such as the United States' "hamburger politics" in its international
relations: everyone in the world wants to be authentically American by
eating our fast food. And in the world of commerce nationality and
authenticity are marketing tools. From food products to restaurants, the
label "authentic" is common and obviously still effective. Whether the
many Mexican-style restaurants that claim authenticity actually reflect a
particular Mexican regional or local terroir is unlikely. While the sauces
may be made from imported chilies and other ingredients or the cooking
techniques are much the same as in Mexico, the flavors, much less the
ambience, cannot replicate the original. Authentically Mexican-North
American, reflecting the immigrant experience of settling in, might be a
better term. Packaged foods are even more removed from original food
cultures. A packaged food like Rice-a-Roni, a boxed rice–pasta–dried
soup mix advertised as a "San Francisco treat," was invented in the city in
the late 1950s by an Italian family, but it can hardly be a real taste of that
famous culinary city. Georgia peaches, Florida oranges, and Washington

State apples are all geographical designations that are more marketing tools than marks of distinctive flavor. Maybe the frozen string beans picked and packed in California's Central Valley are authentically American and even offer a taste of place—American factory style.

If America's food is so commodified in its sourcing, production and reproduction in the form of nationally distributed recipes, can there be regional cuisines? Most would be in the South. David S. Shields posits that Southern cookery as distinct from others dates to the Reconstruction period and has political implications. His work on low-country cookery in the Carolinas mirrors John Martin Taylor's cookery book that digs into this distinctive Creole cuisine, which he found more heavily African than others. But standard cookbooks have many non-indigenous recipes.[79] In "What Is Southern?" the celebrated chef Edna Lewis identified close to fifty dishes as distinct to the region. Shields and others, such as chef Joe Randall of Savannah, Georgia, are trying to revive low-country cookery through heirloom rice, shrimp, benne seeds, corn, and other ingredients that almost disappeared. In the words of one food scholar:

> Lewis's own perspective is that her southern is not so much refined as old-fashioned, in danger of "passing from the scene" unless deliberately preserved. It is hard to disagree with her. In our time, much of Lewis's lovely southern—turtle soup with turtle dumplings, baked snowbirds, braised mutton, wild pig with pork liver and peanut sauces, potted squab with the first wild greens, and fig pudding—can only be cooked as historical reenactment.[80]

The most famous example of continuous regional culinary tradition is in New Orleans where the distinctive European–African–Native American Creole exists near the equally unique Cajun. Dishes such as versions of jambalaya and gumbo, crawdads, Gulf Coast seafood (when not covered in slicks from oil spills), and beignets among others are paradigmatic. They have been mixed together in New Orleans restaurants and commercialized in cans and dried mixes, but at least some dishes are still made at home, especially in Cajun country, as a means of retaining local culture—along with music, of course.

Regional cuisines hardly exist if that means coming directly from their place of origin and cooked distinctively. There are plenty of local ones: maple syrup from Vermont, French Russet apples from the Maine coast, American persimmons in the Midwest, Illinois pecans, Alabama mussels, Washington State Olympia oysters, and more. But these do not make regional culinary cultures on their own. Local eating habits might differ, such as the famous "meat and three" restaurant menus of the south or diners on the east coast, taco stands in the southwest and even Sonoran hot dogs around Tucson, Arizona. Older cuisines that date from the days when America was far more rural, before the large internal migrations (try finding a central Texas accent in Dallas or local Georgian in Atlanta), have to be revived; terroir must be established and protected to exist. They are delicious museums, as antique as the commentary by Mark Twain.

American food in the twenty-first century cannot escape its history, but people are trying. Americans created a continent-wide food system on the factory model. If every single American did not actually build it, their demand, influenced by marketing or not, did. Now a majority of consumers are more interested than ever in what they eat as evidenced by labeling: people read labels while standing in supermarket aisles. Mrs. Kellogg would be happy, especially since her husband's products are still on grocers' shelves. By and large they do heed the advice of experts on nutrition, unless they are snacking (hence America's vast junk food industry). Meat consumption has declined as flexitarian eating has grown, especially among the millennial generation. And Americans are more adventurous about new tastes and textures. For instance, spice consumption has risen steadily to more than 1 billion lb a year, more than 50 percent of it in the "hot" category. But aside from meat consumption, these elements carry on from older ways. Contrary to the idea that they like blandness, Americans have always enjoyed some spice, whether horseradish, mustard, or even in some places hot peppers. They have also liked mash-ups of food traditions into something new. Modern food trucks often specialize in these, such as Roy Choi's Kogi Taco Truck with its kimchee hot dogs in Los Angeles, versions of the much earlier Chicago-style hot dogs. Only the ethnic ingredients have changed. Or consider Buffalo wings (from the Anchor Bar in Buffalo, New York, in the 1960s), a widely popular bar food and now a fast food chain that consists of deep-fried chicken wings smeared with a spicy hot sauce. It might actually be African American with hints of Jamaica, New Orleans, and even Asia—in short a creole dish. The American food system might be national with uniformity/consistency at its base, but it is what people do with American food in their own unique ways that keeps it as varied as it is and always has been.

Kosher Sushi, Jewel Foods, Chicago, showing the cultural mash-up in an urban setting.

CODA

At the beginning and end of the story of America's food is its land and waters. From the scientific and human perspectives, both are complicated stories as witnessed by the mountainous literature on the subjects. Both have been stressed, as witness the depleted lands of the northeast and South and the Dust Bowl. As an Illinois farmer said, "I'm upset because we take and we take and we take from nature, and we never bother to put back."[81] Bad as it has been, it is likely worse is to come.

In 2002 a new geological term came into public use:

> For the past three centuries, the effects of humans on the global environment have escalated. Because of these anthropogenic emissions of carbon dioxide, global climate may depart significantly from natural behaviour for many millennia to come. It seems appropriate to assign the term "Anthropocene" to the present, in many ways human-dominated, geological epoch.[82]

Among the causes Paul Crutzen described were large amounts of methane produced by cattle, deforestation for cattle and agriculture, massive destruction of fish and their habitats, a sixteen-fold increase in energy use over the last century resulting in large amounts of sulfur dioxide release, the use of more nitrogen fertilizer in farming than can be utilized by plants, leading to considerable runoff, and, of course, fossil fuel burning. The result is not only global warming that has changed the planet's climate, but

> We spread our manmade ecosystems, including "megaregions" with more than 100 million inhabitants, as landscapes characterized by heavy human use—degraded agricultural lands, industrial wastelands, and recreational landscapes—become characteristic of Earth's terrestrial surfaces."[83]

We are, as in the title of a celebrated book, in the sixth geological extinction.[84]

Much of this has to do with agriculture, though by estimate America's sprawling urban areas account for some 65 percent of global climate change. No matter, prolonged droughts in California and the southwest, torrential summer rains in the Midwest and southeast, have affected millions of acres of farmland. Almost all water resources in these regions have been depleted by lack of winter snowpacks in the mountains, while water tables are being drained rapidly. Even the great mid-continent underground sea, the Ogallala

Aquifer, is being drained. Although the figure is disputed by the beef industry, the best estimate of water used in beef production is about 2,400 gallons per pound, including the crops used for feed, and that does not count the millions of pounds of nitrogen fertilizer and pesticides used. Access to and usage of water has always been an issue in the west, for example in California's Sacramento River and Central Valley. Whether California's industrial-scale farmers can change their production methods with more droughts in sight is an open question. And by some estimates North America's wheat production will move ever northward into northern Canada to follow the water sources that will more reliably originate in Alaska during this century.

Never before in human history has so much food been produced as in the United States. "We feed the world" is the catchphrase used by many a large-scale farmer. To quote Pare Lorentz, we plowed the land and fed the world, but at what a cost. Monocropping, soil loss, and industrial use of animals are among the many problems in America's farmlands. A recent series of articles in the *Chicago Tribune* detail what can only be described as the horrors of industrial-scale pork production.[85] The cruelty of jamming thousands of pigs into sheds, hogs living their whole lives in gestation crates unable to even turn around, and rough treatment by workers is akin to Upton Sinclair's *The Jungle*, only experienced by these sentient animals. The problem of tens of thousands of gallons of hog waste breaking their containment dams is common. About half a million fish are killed every year from river and stream pollution and the smell is unbearable to neighbors. Punishment is hardly ever levied against large-scale operators because of weak legal authority and the power of farm lobbies. None of these stories is new; Iowa, America's top pork producer, has had so many waste spills that they hardly make news. Such is the price of cheap pork chops and spareribs for the backyard barbecue and the bacon craze that infects America at the moment.

It is not that farmers are not stewards of the land; they are. There are simply fewer and fewer of them as they age out of the business and the economic pressure to produce as much as possible is great. Middle-sized farms make up about 40 percent of all farms, but because of the need to make a living, pay off bank loans for expensive machinery, and all the other costs of doing business, they usually plant single crops and then have to sell to agribusinesses.[86] Others under contract to raise animals are also pressed to produce maximum quantities for the least cost; chickens and pigs are the most egregious examples. There are other food producing models. A third way of how Americans think about food is a scaled-down model, one that may or may not

Animal Welfare, Ethical Eating

According to a report from *Meat and Poultry*, an industry news-letter, "A 2013 American Humane Association poll showed 89 percent of consumers surveyed stated they were very concerned about animal welfare with 74 percent willing to pay more for humanely raised meat, dairy and eggs. Participants of the survey also ranked humanely raised food the highest in importance over organic, natural and antibiotic-free." Another survey, by *Vegetarian Times*, indicates that 3 percent of, or more than seven million, Americans live on plant-based diets but that 10 percent of Americans say that they follow a mostly vegetable-based or flexitarian diet. A far smaller number follow a fully vegan eating regimen. Besides animal welfare, other reasons given were concerns for the planet's environment (the fact of global warming) and personal health. A large majority of the respondents were people under 30–35, the cohort called millennials. Ideas about the American food system have been changing rapidly.

Ethical eating, meaning renouncing cruelty to non-human animals, goes back to the nineteenth century. The modern iteration took root with the philosopher Peter Singer's 1975 book *Animal Liberation*. His argument, called "speciesism," says that animals suffer like humans and ought not to be exploited (suffer) for our gustatory pleasure: they have rights, as do people. The book and the argument have given rise to a vast literature on the matter. Numerous scientific studies show many species of non-human animals are intelligent (able to understand and solve problems, and make tools) and have awareness

be organic. If they were to become truck farmers who sell in farmers' markets and to retail stores that stock local produce, then a living can be made. Many organic farmers do so and at the same time husband their land using organic fertilizers, crop rotation, and proper animal care. This sounds good, nostalgic even, and successful farmers such as Dan Barber (also a chef) have made a go of it. In reality, with the nation and the world increasingly urbanized, few young of self or cognition. Jane Goodall's work with chimpanzees is a celebrated example, but animal ethologists have shown similar attributes in animals from porpoises to pigs, dogs, birds, and even octopi. Reports in the media including large numbers of television shows and documentaries with wide viewership have reinforced humane ideas about our relationships to animals. Organizations devoted to animal welfare and animal rights, from the moderate Humane Society to the activist People for the Ethical Treatment of Animals, have also swayed public opinion. Most important in changing the climate of opinion is social media, where stories from animal rescue to farm sanctuaries speak to a mostly younger participatory audience.

As the poll shows, the effects of changing attitudes are seen in the food industry. Almost every large retailer, from Walmart to SUPERVALU and Aldi, is pledging to switch entirely to cage-free eggs by the 2020s as opposed to battery chickens. Producers are swearing off gestation crates for pigs, and leaders in the humane treatment movement like Temple Grandin, the subject of a feature film, are celebrated for their work. The original question remains: do animals have the right not to suffer and be used as food? A middle ground has become popular. If animals are treated humanely, such as being raised in pastures and allowed to mature for long periods, then diners' consciences are cleared. The inevitable development of laboratory-made protein from animal tissue might eventually put an end to the meat part of the question—dairy still entails killing calves and lambs. The first broad-scale marketing of such meat is scheduled for 2020.

people want to do the kind of labor that small-scale farming entails. Nor is it likely that people will want to pay higher prices for everyday foods. Inexpensive food is a cornerstone of the food and political system and not likely to change soon. More expensive "organic" food—the designation is not rigid—remains at under 10 percent of sales, though rising a bit. Surprisingly most of the organic produce sold in supermarkets is lettuce.

Can farmers, in Donald Worster's phrase, create an "agroecosystem, which, as the name suggests, is an ecosystem reorganized for agricultural purposes—a domesticated ecosystem"?[87] Iowa State University scientists, for instance, have persuaded a group of Iowa farmers to recreate patches of natural prairie amid their crop fields as ways of controlling soil loss and reducing the massive runoff of nutrient pollution.[88] The experiment is a successful example of an agroecosystem, but whether farmers will take land out of production is still a question. American farming is a major part of the nation's GDP. Exports such as soybeans and meats will not be deliberately diminished. American farmers do feed the world, as the industry has long proclaimed. The answer lies in science and technology. Today 81 million acres of land produce the same amount of corn as 228 million acres did in the 1950s. Similar figures work for wheat, soybeans, cotton, and cows. These results have been achieved using less low to no-till cropping and fewer fertilizers and pesticides, the latter becoming safer to beneficial insects with the banning of neonicotinoids.[89]

In 2017 major food processor General Mills partnered with the Land Institute of Kansas to use and further develop Kernza, a modified wheatgrass. A perennial that does not have to be reseeded every year like conventional wheat, Kernza lives on after harvest, taking large amounts of carbon from the atmosphere. It also sinks deep roots into the ground, cutting erosion by up to 87 percent, and it needs far less artifical fertilizer than ordinary wheat. Other wild perennials are also in development in what is likely to be a revolution in farming.[90]

And for those who worry about animal slaughter and suffering, to say nothing of environmental impact, emerging technology at Maastricht University in the Netherlands and other laboratories will soon produce animal fibers (muscle) that, when scaled up for the market, will be sold at reasonable cost: hamburgers without the cow.[91] The future of American food is varied from small to large scale. The changing climate, degraded land, and population pressure require what humans have always done: use ingenuity. As Rachel Laudan puts it:

> What we need is an ethos that comes to terms with contemporary, industrialized food, not one that dismisses it . . . Such an ethos, and not a timorous Luddism, is what will impel us to create the matchless modern cuisines appropriate to our time.[92]

References

ONE: The Land

1 Richard Barsam, *Nonfiction Film: A Critical History* (Bloomington, IN, 1973, rev. 1992), p. 166.

2 William Cronon, *Changes in the Land: Indians, Colonists and the Ecology of New England* (New York, 1983, rev. 2003), pp. 26–7.

3 Albert Perry Brigham, *Geographic Influences in American History* (New York, 1903), p. 180.

4 Stephen S. Birdsall and John Florin, *An Outline of American Geography: Regional Landscapes of the United States* (Washington, DC, 1990).

5 *The River* (1938), written and dir. Pare Lorentz. Documentary for U.S. Farm Resettlement Administration.

6 R. J. Mitchell and S. L. Duncan, "Range of Variability in Southern Coastal Plain Forests: Its Historical, Contemporary, and Future Role in Sustaining Biodiversity," *Ecology and Society*, XIV/1 (2009), p. 17; www.ecologyandsociety.org, accessed January 16, 2017.

7 Frederick Law Olmsted, *The Cotton Kingdom: A Traveller's Observations on Cotton and Slavery in the American Slave States. Based upon Three Former Volumes on Journeys and Investigations by the Same Author [1852–1854]* (New York, 1861), pp. 150–51ff.

8 *The Plow that Broke the Plains* (1936), written and dir. Pare Lorentz. Documentary for U.S. Farm Resettlement Administration.

9 The best-known of these museums is in Petersburg, Kentucky; see www.creationmuseum.org.

10 Bootie Cosgrove-Mather, "Poll: Creationism Trumps Evolution," CBS News, November 22, 2004, www.cbsnews.com.

11 Timothy Gardner, "More Americans Believe World is Warming, New Reuters/Ipsos Poll Shows," *Inside Climate News*, September 16, 2011, https://insideclimatenews.org.

12 Brian Romans, "Ghostly Image Reveals Ice Age Rivers," *Wired*, October 4, 2010, www.wired.com.

13 Peter U. Clark and Alan C. Mix, "Ice Sheets and Sea Level of the Last Glacial Maximum," *Quaternary Science Reviews*, XXI/1–3 (2002), pp. 1–7; Kurt Lambeck, Yusuke Yokoyama, and Tony Purcell, "Into and Out of the Last Glacial Maximum: Sea-level Change during Oxygen Isotope Stages 3 and 2," *Quaternary Science Reviews*, XXI/1–3 (2002), pp. 343–60.

14 Fray Joseph de Acosta, *Historia Natural y Moral de las Indias* [1590], vol. II (Madrid, 1894), p. 240.

15 On Mormon-Indian origins, see Simon G. Southerton, *Losing a Lost Tribe:*

Native Americans, DNA, and the Mormon Church (Salt Lake City, 2004); and on the intellectual environment of Joseph Smith's times, see Richard L. Bushman, *Joseph Smith and the Beginnings of Mormonism* (Urbana, IL, 1984).

16 John McIntosh, *The origin of the North American Indians with a faithful description of their manners and customs, both civil and military, their religions, languages, dress, and ornaments: to which is prefixed a brief view of the creation of the world . . . concluding with a copious selection of Indian speeches, the antiquities of America, the civilization of the Mexicans, and some final observations on the origin of the Indians* (New York, 1844).

17 Brian Fagan, *The First North Americans: An Archaeological Journey* (London, 2011), p. 26.

18 David J. Meltzer, *The First Peoples in a New World: Colonizing Ice Age America* (Berkeley, CA, 2009), pp. 254–5.

19 "Artifacts in Texas Predate Clovis Culture by 2,500 years, New Study Shows," *ScienceDaily*, March 25, 2011, www.sciencedaily.com.

20 Jennie Cohen, "Native Americans Hailed from Siberian Highlands, DNA Reveals," *History in the Headlines*, January 26, 2012, www.history.com.

21 David Reich et al., "Reconstructing Native American Population History," *Nature*, CDLXXXVIII (July 11, 2012), pp. 370–74.

22 Nicholas Wade, "Earliest Americans Arrived in Waves, DNA Study Finds," *New York Times*, July 11, 2012.

23 Meltzer, *The First Peoples in a New World*, p. 330.

24 Cronon, *Changes in the Land*, pp. 3–18.

25 Paul Martin, "The Discovery of America," *Science*, CLXXIX (1973), pp. 969–74; Paul Martin, "Prehistoric Overkill: The Global Model," in Paul S. Martin and Richard Klein, *Quarternary Extinctions: A Prehistoric Revolution* (Tucson, AZ, 1984), pp. 354–403.

26 Meltzer, *The First Peoples in a New World*, pp. 255–74.

27 Shepherd Krech III, *The Ecological Indian: Myth and History* (New York, 1999).

28 Michael E. Harkin, introduction to *Native Americans and the Environment: Perspectives on the Ecological Indian*, ed. Michael E. Harkin (Lincoln, NE, 2007).

29 Especially see James Fenimore Cooper, *The Last of the Mohicans* [1826], intro. by Richard Slotkin (New York, 1968).

30 Washington Irving, *A History of New-York from the Beginning of the World to the End of the Dutch Dynasty, by Diedrich Knickerbocker* [1809], author's revised edn. (New York, 1848), p. 39.

31 Fagan, *The First North Americans*, pp. 98–9.

32 Dan Flores, "Wars over Buffalo Stories versus Stories on the Northern Plains," in *Native Americans and the Environment*, ed. Harkin, p. 160.

33 Alfred W. Crosby, *The Columbian Exchange: Biological and Cultural Consequences of 1492* (Westport, CT, 1972), p. 18.

34 Fagan, *The First North Americans*, p. 41.

35 Alice Ross, "Native American Foods," in *The Oxford Encyclopedia of Food and Drink in America*, ed. Andrew F. Smith, 2nd edn. (New York, 2013), II, pp. 644–60.

36 Stuart Struever and Felicia Antonelli Holton, *Koster: Americans in Search of their Prehistoric Past* (Garden City, NY, 1979), pp. 120ff. on pecans and hickory.

37 Peter Bellwood, *First Farmers: The Origins of Agricultural Societies* (Malden, MA, 2005), p. 176.

38 Ross, "Native American Foods," p. 684.

39 Bellwood, *First Farmers*, p. 176.

40 Biloine Whiting Young and Melvin J. Fowler, *Cahokia, the Great Native American Metropolis* (Urbana, IL, 1999), pp. 319–22.

41 Antoine-Simon Le Page du Pratz, *The History of Louisiana: Or of the Western Parts of Virginia and Carolina: Containing a Description of the Countries that Lie on Both Sides of the River Mississippi: with an Account of the Settlements, Inhabitants, Soil, Climate, and Products* [1758] (London, 1774), pp. 326–31.

42 Thomas E. Emerson and R. Barry Lewis, eds., *Cahokia and the Hinterlands: Middle Mississippian Cultures of the Midwest* (Urbana, IL, 2000), pp. 423–4.

43 Cronon, *Changes in the Land,* p. 41.

44 Ibid., p. 45.

45 Kristina M. Crawford, "Daily Bread: Prehistoric Cooking Features in the Northern Sacramento Valley, California," MA thesis, California State University, Chico, 2011.

46 C. J. Sapart et al., "Natural and Anthropogenic Variations in Methane Sources during the Past Two Millennia," *Nature*, CDXC (October 2012), pp. 85–8.

47 William Ruddiman, *Plows, Plagues, and Petroleum: How Humans Took Control of Climate* (Princeton, NJ, 2005), pp. 132–40.

48 Decolonizing Diet Project Blog, www.decolonizingdietproject.blogspot.com, accessed September 6, 2014.

TWO: Colonial America

1 Lorenzo Veracini, "Settler Colonialism: Career of a Concept," *Journal of Imperial & Commonwealth History*, XLI/2 (June 2013), pp. 313–33.

2 Peter Martyr d'Anghiera, *De orbe novo*, I–III [1511–16], trans. Richard Eden as *The Decades of the Newe Worlde or West India* (London, 1550), p. 252. For a later translation with notes and introduction, see that by Francis Augustus MacNutt, 2 vols. (New York, 1912).

3 Matthew Restall, *Seven Myths of the Spanish Conquest* (New York, 2003), pp. 27–43.

4 Of all the vast literature on the interchange of transoceanic foodstuffs beginning in the late fourteenth century, Alfred Crosby's *The Columbian Exchange: Biological and Cultural Consequences of 1492* (Westport, CT, 1972) remains the iconic work.

5 Trudy Eden, "Food, Assimilation, and the Malleability of the Human Body in Early Virginia," in *A Centre of Wonders: The Body in Early America*, ed. Janet Moore Lindman and Michele Lise Tarter (Ithaca, NY, 2001), pp. 29–39.

6 As in Jared Diamond's classic, *Guns, Germs, and Steel: The Fates of Human Societies* (New York, 1997).

7 The Americas are an exception to the dead marsupial rule. The Virginia opossum is native with wide geographical distribution partly based on its own omnivorous feeding behavior and partly because they have adapted to humans. They thrive on leftover human food and even ride railcars from their southern habitats to northern cities where they flourish.

8 Luis Millones Figueroa, "The Staff of Life: Wheat and 'Indian Bread' in the New World," *Colonial Latin American Review*, XIX/2 (August 2010), pp. 301–22.

9 William H. McNeill, "How the Potato Changed World History," *Social Research*, LXVI (1999), pp. 69–83.

10 Alfred W. Crosby, *Germs, Seeds and Animals: Studies in Ecological History* (Armonk, NY, 1993), pp. 10–11.

11 Ralph Lane, letter to Richard Hakluyt, September 3, 1585; quoted in Richard Hakluyt, *The Principal Narrations, Traffics, Voyages, and Discoveries of the English Nation* (London, 1598–1600); repr. in Arthur Barlowe, *The First Voyage to Roanoke, 1584*, Old South Leaflets 92 ([Boston, MA,] 1898), p. 18; available at www.docsouth.unc.edu, accessed January 17, 2017.

12 "Florida Cracker Cattle," in The Livestock Conservancy, www.albc-usa.org, accessed February 8, 2015. See also Virginia Dejohn Anderson, *Creatures of Empire: How Domestic Animals Transformed Early America* (New York, 2004).

13 See Bruce Kraig, "Pigs," in *The Oxford Encyclopedia of Food and Drink in America*, ed. Andrew F. Smith, 2nd edn. (New York, 2013), II, pp. 836–40.

14 See Crosby, *The Columbian Exchange*, pp. 80ff. for a discussion of the introduction of the horse in North America. See also R. B. Cunninghame Graham, *The Horses of the Conquest*, ed. Robert Moorman Denhardt (Norman, OK, 1949).

15 Crosby, *Germs, Seeds and Animals*, p. 55. See Pekka Hämäläinen, "The Rise and Fall of Plains Indian Horse Cultures," *Journal of American History* (December 2003), pp. 833–62 for a compelling contrary view.

16 Hämäläinen, "The Rise and Fall of Plains Indian Horse Cultures," p. 844. See also Andrew C. Isenberg. *The Destruction of the Bison: An Environmental History, 1750–1920* (Cambridge, 2001).

17 See "Human Microbiome Project," www.commonfund.nih.gov, May 15, 2016, for the ongoing National Institutes of Health's project to identify and categorize these organisms according to species and function.

18 Diamond, *Guns, Germs, and Steel*. See also William H. McNeill's classic study, *Plagues and People* (New York, 1976).

19 For the mechanisms of trans-species infections, see Greg Brennan et al., "Adaptive Gene Amplification as an Intermediate Step in the Expansion of Virus Host Range," *PLOS Pathogens*, X/3 (March 2014), www.plospathogens.org, accessed January 17, 2017.

20 Nathan D. Wolfe, Claire Panosian Dunavan, and Jared Diamond, "Origins of Major Human Infectious Diseases," *Nature*, CDXLVII (May 17, 2007), p. 281.

21 For a good discussion of malaria, see Charles C. Mann, *1493: Uncovering the New World Columbus Created* (New York, 2011), pp. 99–155.

22 McNeill, *Plagues and People,* pp. 9–10.

23 See Stephen T. Smiley, "Immune Defense against Pneumonic Plague," *Immunological Reviews*, CCXXV/1 (October 2008), pp. 256–71, www.ncbi.nlm.nih.gov.

24 Paul Kelton, *Epidemics and Enslavement: Biological Catastrophe in the Native Southeast, 1492–1715* (Lincoln, NE, 2007).

25 Ibid., pp. 137–57.

26 Gerald N. Grob, *The Deadly Truth: A History of Disease in America* (Cambridge, MA, 2009), p. 57. See also Elizabeth A. Fenn, *Pox Americana: The Great Smallpox Epidemic of 1775–82* (New York, 2001) for ongoing equal opportunity diseases among Europeans and Indians.

27 Ferdinand Braudel, *The Structures of Everyday Life: The Limits of the Possible* [1973], trans. Siân Reynold (New York, 1982), pp. 190–99.

28 As noted by Sir Fulke Greville in his *Life of Sir Philip Sidney, Etc.* [1652], fore-word by Nowell Smith (London, 1907), p. 97: "We conquered France, more by such factions & ambitious assistances, than by any odds of our Bows, or Beef-eaters, as the French were then scornfully pleas'd to terme us." Also cited in *Oxford English Dictionary*, "beef eater."

29 Sophie Coe, "A Tale of Two Banquets," in *Oxford Symposium on Food and Cookery 1991: Public Eating: Proceedings*, ed. Harlan Walker (London, 1992), pp. 61–6.

30 Enrique Rodríguez Alegría, "Eating Like an Indian: Negotiating Social Relations in the Spanish Colonies," *Current Anthropology*, XLVI/4 (August/October 2005), p. 557.

31 *William Byrd's Natural History of Virginia or The Newly Discovered Eden*, ed. and trans. Richard C. Beatty and William J. Mulloy (Richmond, VA, 1940). This book was probably written by the contemporary naturalist John Lawson. Lawson's own book, *A New Voyage to Carolina; Containing the Exact Description and Natural History of That Country: Together with the Present State Thereof. And a Journal of a Thousand Miles, Travel'd Thro' Several Nations of Indians. Giving a Particular Account of Their Customs, Manners, &c.* (London, 1709), pp. 17–19, contains his comments on pigs.

32 Bernard Bailyn, *The Barbarous Years* (New York, 2012), pp. 46–7.

33 Ibid., pp. 94–5.

34 Ibid., p. 308.

35 Eden, *The Decades of the Newe Worlde*, p. 233.

36 Cronon, *Changes in the Land*, pp. 40–41.

37 Cited in Rebecca Earle, "'If You Eat Their Food . . .': Diets and Bodies in Early Co-lonial Spanish America," *American Historical Review*, CXV/3 (June 2010), p. 703.

38 See Ruddiman, *Plows, Plagues, and Petroleum* and Franz X. Faust, Cristóbal Gnecco, Hermann Mannstein, and Jörg Stamm, "Evidence for the Postconquest Demographic Collapse of the Americas in Historical CO_2 Levels," *Earth Interactions*, X/11 (May 2006), http://journals.ametsoc.org, accessed January 18, 2017.

39 Braudel, *Structures*, pp. 78ff.; Geoffrey Parker, *Global Crisis: War, Climate Change and Catastrophe in the Seventeenth Century* (New Haven, CT, 2013), chap. 1 for summary.

40 Parker, *Global Crisis*, pp. 359–60.

41 David W. Stahle, Malcolm K. Cleaveland, Dennis B. Blanton, Matthew D. Ther-rell, and David A. Gay, "The Lost Colony and Jamestown Droughts," *Science*, n.s., CCLXXX/5363 (April 24, 1998), pp. 564–7; Bailyn, *Barbarous Years*, pp. 146–7.

42 Thomas Hariot, *A Briefe and True Report of the New Found Land of Virginia* [1588]; Eng. trans. in Richard Hakluyt, *The Principall Navigations, Voiages, and Discoveries of the English Nation* (London, 1589); separate repr. (New York, 1871), available at www.docsouth.unc.edu, accessed March 3, 2014.

43 Joseph Stromberg, "Starving Settlers in Jamestown Colony Resorted to Eating a Child," www.smithsonianmag.com, April 30, 2013.

44 *Bradford's History of Plymouth Plantation, 1606–1646*, ed. William T. Davis (New York, 1908); also see James Deetz and Patricia Scott Deetz, *The Times of Their Lives: Life, Love, and Death in Plymouth Colony* (New York, 2000).

45 Cronon, *Changes in the Land*, p. 45.

46 Jorge Cañizares-Esguerra, "How Derivative was Humboldt? Microcosmic

Nature Narratives in Early Modern Spanish America and the (Other) Origins of Humboldt's Ecological Sensibilities," in *Colonial Botany: Science, Commerce, and Politics in the Early Modern World*, ed. Londa Schiebinger and Claudia Swan (Philadelphia, 2004), pp. 148–65.

47 Cronon, *Changes in the Land*, pp. 105–26.

48 Peter [Pehr] Kalm, *Travels into North America*, trans. John Reinhold Forster, 2 vols. (London, 1773), pp. 226–7, available at www.americanjourneys.org; cited in Richard J. Hooker, *Food and Drink in America: A History* (Indianapolis, 1981), p. 53. Kalm was appalled at the Native Americans' habit of letting dogs lie in bed with them at night and the consequent onslaught of fleas, among many other "strange" things he had to endure.

49 Luis Millones Figueroa, "The Staff of Life: Wheat and 'Indian Bread' in the New World," *Colonial Latin American Review*, XIX/2 (August 2010), p. 315; Earle, "'If You Eat Their Food,'" p. 697.

50 Millones Figueroa, "The Staff of Life," p. 314.

51 Earle, "'If You Eat Their Food,'" p. 704.

52 Rodríguez-Alegría, "Eating Like an Indian," pp. 563–5.

53 Rachel Laudan and Jeffery M. Pilcher, "Chiles, Chocolate, and Race in New Spain: Glancing Backward to Spain or Looking Forward to Mexico?" *Eighteenth Century Life*, XXIII (May 1999), pp. 59–70.

54 Karen Hess, introduction to facsimile edition of Amelia Simmons, *American Cookery* (Bedford, MA, 1996), p. xv.

55 Hariot, *A Briefe and True Report*, pp. 15–16.

56 Ebenezer Cook, *The Sot-weed Factor: Or, a Voyage to Maryland, a Satyr* (London, 1708; repr. New York, 1865); Hooker, *Food and Drink in America*, p. 38.

57 Sandra L. Oliver, *Food in Colonial and Federal America* (Westport, CT, 2005), p. 22.

THREE: Immigrants: The Things They Brought with Them and Found

1 Reuben Gold Thwaites, ed., *Travels West of the Alleghanies: Made in 1793–96 by André Michaux; in 1802 by F. A. Michaux; and in 1803 by Thaddeus Mason Harris, M.A.* (Cleveland, 1904). Incidentally, the elder Michaux may have been an agent of the infamous Citizen Genêt (Edmond-Charles Genêt) a French envoy to the United States in 1793 who compromised American neutrality and was accused of fomenting a French-style revolution in the Florida border region.

2 Ibid., p. 178.

3 David Hackett Fischer, *Albion's Seed: Four British Folkways in America* (Oxford and New York, 1989), p. 17.

4 Ibid. See Introduction for the book's main themes.

5 Bernard Bailyn, *The Barbarous Years* (New York, 2012), p. 424. Also see Allan Kulikoff, "Capitalism in the Core, Barbarism in the Periphery?" *Reviews in American History*, XXXII (2014), pp. 207–12.

6 *American Husbandry: Containing an Account of the Soil, Climate, Production and Agriculture, of the British Colonies in North-America and the West-Indies; With Observations on the Advantages and Disadvantages of Settling in Them, Compared with Great Britain and Ireland*, vol. I (London, 1775), p. 46. The author of *American Husbandry* was probably England's greatest authority on the North

American colonies, Richard Oswald (1705–1784), who had lived in Virginia and helped broker the peace settlement between the new United States and Great Britain. The book used letters of a South Carolina planter, John Lewis Gervais (1741–1798). See Robert Scott Davis, "The Mystery Book and the Forgotten Founding Father," *Journal of the American Revolution*, July 17, 2014, https://all-thingsliberty.com.

7 Sarah F. McMahon. "A Comfortable Subsistence: The Changing Composition of Diet in Rural New England, 1620–1840," *William and Mary Quarterly*, 3rd ser., XLII/1 (January 1985), pp. 26–65.

8 Amelia Simmons, *American Cookery, or the art of dressing viands, fish, poultry, and vegetables, and the best modes of making pastes, puffs, pies, tarts, puddings, custards, and preserves, and all kinds of cakes, from the imperial plumb to plain cake: Adapted to this country, and all grades of life*, 2nd edn., see intro by Karen Hess to the Applewood Books reprint (Albany, NY, 1796); this is the first edition fully authorized by Simmons herself.

9 Kelly O'Leary, "The Flouring of Early New England: Wheat and its Function in the Loaves and Lives of Colonial Americans," MA thesis, Boston University, 2010.

10 South Carolina, among many other places, was similar; see G. D. Bernheim, *History of the German Settlements and of the Lutheran Church in North and South Carolina* (Philadelphia, 1872), p. 267.

11 Willa Cather's prairie trilogy, especially *My Ántonia* (1918).

12 Marianne S. Wokeck, "German and Irish Immigration to Colonial Philadelphia," Symposium on the Demographic History of the Philadelphia Region, 1600–1860, *Proceedings of the American Philosophical Society*, CXXXIII/2 (1989), pp. 128–43. See also Farley Grubb, "German Immigration to Pennsylvania, 1709 to 1820," *Journal of Interdisciplinary History*, XX/3 (Winter 1990), pp. 417–36 for a good analysis on family and social status of German immigrants.

13 See Rosalind J. Beiler, "German-Speaking Immigrants in the British Atlantic World, 1680–1730," *OAH Magazine of History*, XVIII/3 (April 2004), pp. 19–22 for a discussion of religious dissenters in Germany and why they came to America.

14 Carl Theo. Eben, trans., *Gottlieb Mittelberger's Journey to Pennsylvania in the Year 1750 and Return to Germany in the Year 1754, Containing not only a Description of the Country According to its Present Condition, but also a Detailed Account of the Sad and Unfortunate Circumstances of Most of the Germans that Have Emigrated, or are Emigrating to that Country* (Philadelphia, 1898), p. 64.

15 Ibid., p. 65.

16 Eliza Smith, *The Compleat Housewife: Or, Accomplish'd Gentlewoman's Companion* (London, 1727); Hannah Glasse, *The Art of Cookery Made Plain and Easy* (London, 1747), rev. Alexandria, VA, 1805, facsimile with foreword by Karen Hess (Boston, MA, 1997).

17 William Woys Weaver, *Sauerkraut Yankees: Pennsylvania Dutch Foods and Foodways*, 2nd edn. (Mechanicsburg, PA, 2002). This is a groundbreaking translation and interpretation of *Die Geschickte Hausfrau* (1848) with additional materials from nineteenth-century German cookbooks. See also William Woys Weaver, *As American as Shoofly Pie: The Foodlore and Fakelore of Pennsylvania Dutch Cuisine* (Philadelphia, 2013).

18 André Michaux, in Thwaites, ed., *Travels West of the Alleghanies*, p. 184.

19 John S. C. Abbott. *The Adventures of the Chevalier De La Salle and his Companions, in their Explorations of the Prairies, Forests, Lakes, and Rivers, of the New World, and their Interviews with the Savage Tribes, Two Hundred Years Ago* (New York, 1875).

20 P.F.X. De Charlevoix, SJ, *History and General Description of New France* (1761), trans. John Gilmary Shea, 6 vols. (New York, 1866), V, p. 283.

21 "The Coureur de Bois," www.chroniclesofamerica.com, accessed March 3, 2015.

22 Sandra L. Oliver, *Food in Colonial and Federal America* (Westport, CT, 2005), pp. 179–80.

23 [François-Marie] Perrin du Lac, *Travels through the two Louisianas and among the savage nations of the Missouri also in the United States, along the Ohio and the adjacent provinces in 1801, 1802, & 1803: with a sketch of the manners, customs, character, and the civil and religious ceremonies of the people of those countries* (London, 1807), p. 47.

24 Patricia Cleary, "Contested Terrain Environmental Agendas and Settlement Choices in Colonial St. Louis," in *Common Fields: An Environmental History of St. Louis*, ed. Andrew Hurley (St. Louis, 1997), pp. 71–2.

25 Christopher Morris, *The Big Muddy: An Environmental History of the Mississippi and Its Peoples, from Hernando De Soto to Hurricane Katrina* (New York, 2012), pp. 48–68.

26 Ibid., pp. 59–61.

27 Stanley Dry, "A Short History of Gumbo," Southern Foodways Alliance, www.southernfoodways.org, accessed April 5, 2015.

28 François-André Michaux, in Thwaites, ed., *Travels West of the Alleghanies*, pp. 304–5.

29 Johann Martin Bolzius, "Reliable Answer to Some Submitted Questions Concerning the Land Carolina," ed. and trans. Klaus G. Loewald, Beverly Starika, and Paul S. Taylor, *William and Mary Quarterly*, 3rd ser., 14 (April 1957), pp. 257–9.

30 Alexander Falconbridge, *An Account of the Slave Trade on the Coast of Africa* (London, 1788), pp. 21–2.

31 Robert L. Hall, "Food Crops, Medicinal Plants, and the Atlantic Slave Trade," in *African American Foodways*, ed. Anne L. Bower (Urbana, IL, 2007), pp. 18–44.

32 See Anne B. Yentch, "Excavating the South's African American Food History," in Bower, ed., *African American Foodways*, pp. 59–98.

33 Johannes de Laet, *Neiuwe Wereldt* (1625), cited in Oliver A. Rink, *Holland on the Hudson: An Economic and Social History of Dutch New York* (Ithaca, NY, 1986), p. 24.

34 For the best recent account of how New Netherlands evolved, see Jaap Jacobs, *New Netherland: A Dutch Colony in Seventeenth-century America* (Leiden, 2005). Also see Albert E. McKinley, "The English and Dutch Towns of New Netherland," *American Historical Review*, VI/1 (1900), pp. 1–18.

35 Adriaen van der Donck, *A Description of the New Netherlands* (1655–6), trans. Jeremiah Johnson (New York, 1841). The best translation is Adriaen van der Donck, *A Description of New Netherland*, ed. Charles T. Gehring and William A. Starna, trans. Diederik Willem Goedhuys (Lincoln, NE, 2008).

36 Peter G. Rose, "Dutch Food in Life and Art," *Culinary Historians of New York Newsletter*, XVI/1 (Fall 2002), pp. 1–4. Peter G. Rose is the author of the excellent translation and interpretation of *Die Verstandige Kock* (1665) as *The Sensible Cook: Dutch Foodways in the Old and the New World* (Syracuse, NY, 1998).

37 Washington Irving, *A History of New-York from the Beginning of the World to the End of the Dutch Dynasty, by Diedrich Knickerbocker* [1809], author's revised edn. (New York, 1848), Book III, Chapter III, p. 161.

38 Washington Irving, "The Legend of Sleepy Hollow," in *The Sketch Book of Geoffrey Crayon, Gent.* (London, 1820).

39 François-André Michaux, in Thwaites, ed., *Travels West of the Alleghanies*, p. 152.

40 Thaddeus Mason Harris, *The Journal of a Tour into the Territory Northwest of the Alleghany [sic] Mountains, Made in the Spring of the Year 1803: With a Geographical and Historical Account of the State of Ohio* (Boston, 1805), pp. 52–3.

41 Ibid., pp. 59–60.

FOUR: Technology and Land

1 Walt Whitman, "The Song of the Broad-axe" (1856), in *Leaves of Grass* (Philadelphia, 1900), cantos 1 and 9.

2 Neil McKendrick, "The Commercialization of Fashion," in Neil McKendrick, John Brewer, and J. H. Plumb, *The Birth of a Consumer Society: The Commercialization of Eighteenth-Century England* (Bloomington, IN, 1982), p. 53.

3 A.T.H. Breen, "An Empire of Goods: The Anglicization of Colonial America, 1690–1776," *Journal of British Studies*, XXV/4 (1986), p. 477.

4 François-André Michaux, in Reuben Gold Thwaites, ed., *Travels West of the Alleghanies: Made in 1793–96 by André Michaux; in 1802 by F. A. Michaux; and in 1803 by Thaddeus Mason Harris, M.A.* (Cleveland, 1904), p. 182.

5 Sally L. Duncan, "Leaving it to Beaver," *Environment*, XXVI/3 (April, 1984), pp. 41–5, and Lina E. Polvi and Ellen Wohl, "The Beaver Meadow Complex Revisited: the Role of Beavers in Post-glacial Floodplain Development," *Earth Surface Processes and Landforms*, XXXVII/3 (March 2012), pp. 332–46.

6 Quoted in Daniel P. Barr, *Unconquered: The Iroquois League at War in Colonial America* (Westport, CT, 2006), p. 33.

7 Walter Scott Dunn, *Frontier Profit and Loss: The British Army and the Fur Traders, 1760–1764* (Westport, CT, 1998), p. 52.

8 David E. Nye, *America as Second Creation: Technology and Narratives of New Beginnings* (Cambridge, 2003), p. 5.

9 Ibid., pp. 44ff.

10 Steven A. Rosen, *Lithics after the Stone Age: A Handbook of Stone Tools from the Levant* (Walnut Creek, CA, 1997), p. 161. Rosen cites experiments using Neolithic axes versus metal tools and shows that for trees of 10 cm circumference there was little difference in cutting abilities.

11 Henry Kauffman, *The American Axe: A Survey of their Development and their Makers,* (Brattleboro, VT, 1972, repr. Morgantown, PA, 2007), p. 23. See also Nye, *America as Second Creation*, p. 44.

12 Rev. Francis Higginson, *New-Englands Plantation* (London, 1630), repr. in *New-Englands Plantation with The Sea Journal and Other Writings* (Cambridge, MA, 1908), pp. 110–11.

13 Samuel Parker inventory in "The Plymouth Colony Archive Project: Analysis of Selected Probate Inventories," www.histarch.illinois.edu, accessed 8 April, 2015.

14 Judith A. McGaw, "Agricultural Tool Ownership," in *Early American Technology: Making and Doing Things from the Colonial Era to 1850*, ed. Judith A. McGaw

(Chapel Hill, NC, and London, 1994), pp. 328–57.

15 James T. Lemon, "The Agricultural Practices of National Groups in Eighteenth-century Southeastern Pennsylvania," *Geographical Review*, LVI/4 (October 1966), p. 469.

16 Ibid., pp. 478–9.

17 McGaw, "Agricultural Tool Ownership," p. 355.

18 Andrew Smith, *Potato: A Global History* (London, 2011), and many more studies.

19 Whitman, "The Song of the Broad-axe," canto 12.

20 William Byrd of Westover, *The Westover Manuscripts: Containing the History of the Dividing Line betwixt Virginia and North Carolina; A Journey to the Land of Eden, A.D. 1733; And a Progress to the Mines. Written from 1728 to 1736, and now first Published* (Petersburg, VA, 1841), p. 129, available at www.docsouth.unc.edu, accessed January 20, 2015.

21 Robert B. Gordon, *American Iron, 1607–1900* (Baltimore, 1996), p. 14.

22 T. K. Derry and Trevor I. Williams, *A Short History of Technology: From the Earliest Times to A.D. 1900* (Oxford, 1960), pp. 140ff.

23 "The First Century of the Republic (Second Paper): Mechanical Progress," *Harper's New Monthly Magazine*, L/296 (January 1875), p. 72; available at http://ebooks.library.cornell.edu, accessed January 20, 2017.

24 Michael Williams, *Deforesting the Earth: From Prehistory to Global Crisis* (Chicago, 2002), pp. 172ff. See also Arthur Standish, "New Directions of Experience to the Commons Complaint, for the planting of Timber and Firewood, invented by Arthur Standish" (London, 1613), who among other writers of Elizabethan and Jacobean England decried deforestation.

25 Derry and Williams, *A Short History of Technology*, pp. 3–4.

26 William Rosen, *The Most Powerful Idea in the World: A Story of Steam, Industry, and Invention* (New York, 2010), pp. 154–7.

27 Thomas J. Misa, *Leonardo to the Internet: Technology and Culture from the Renaissance to the Present* (Baltimore, 2004), pp. 84–6.

28 Gordon, *American Iron*, pp. 20–21.

29 Byrd, *The Westover Manuscripts*, p. 127.

30 Williams, *Deforesting the Earth*, p. 316.

31 Byrd, *The Westover Manuscripts*, p. 139.

32 Mrs. Mary Randolph, *The Virginia House-wife, or Methodical Cook* (Washington, DC, 1824); facsimile reprint, ed. Karen Hess (Columbia, SC, 1984), p. 167.

33 Carl Bridenbaugh, *The Colonial Craftsman* (New York, 1950), p. 61.

34 Henry Wadsworth Longfellow, "The Village Blacksmith," in *Ballads and Other Poems* (Cambridge, MA, 1842 [1840]), pp. 99–102.

35 Nye, *America as Second Creation*, p. 103.

36 Peter D. McClelland, *Sowing Modernity: America's First Agricultural Revolution* (Ithaca, NY, 1997), pp. 206–12.

37 Eugene S. Ferguson, "On the Origin and Development of American Mechanical 'Know-How,'" *Midcontinent American Studies Journal*, III/2 (Fall 1962), pp. 3–26.

38 Nye, *America as Second Creation*, p. 59.

39 There are many histories of mills. See Terry Reynolds, *Stronger than a Hundred Men: A History of the Vertical Water Wheel* (Baltimore, 1983, repr. 2002); Oliver Evans's book on mills was in use for some fifty years and remains a marvel of engineering description: Oliver Evans, *The Young Mill-wright and Miller's Guide:*

Illustrated by Twenty-eight Descriptive Plates and a Description of an Improved Merchant Flour Mill with Engravings by C. and O. Evans, Engineers (Philadelphia, 1795) and many subsequent editions. David Macaulay, *Mill* (New York, 1983), brilliantly illustrates how old mills worked.

40 George Branson, "Early Flour Mills in Indiana," *Indiana Magazine of History*, XXII/1 (March 1926), pp. 20–27.

41 Richard Leslie Hills, *Power from Wind: A History of Windmill Technology* (Cambridge, 1996), pp. 236–60.

42 Arthur G. Peterson, "Flour and Grist Milling in Virginia: A Brief History," *Virginia Magazine of History and Biography*, XLIII/2 (1935), p. 100.

43 Bill Pensack, "Colonial Pennsylvania Mills," *Building Community: Medieval Technology and American History*, www.engr.psu.edu, accessed April 4, 2015.

44 G. Terry Sharrer, "The Merchant-millers: Baltimore's Flour Milling Industry, 1783–1860," *Agricultural History*, LVI/1, Symposium on the History of Agricultural Trade and Marketing (January 1982), pp. 138–50.

45 For a good description of mills and milling, see Theodore R. Hazen, "The History of Flour Milling in Early America," www.angelfire.com, accessed April 6, 2015.

46 Andrew F. Smith, *Eating History: Thirty Turning Points in the Making of American Cuisine* (New York, 2009), pp. 5–10; Coleman Sellers Jr., "Oliver Evans and his Inventions," *Journal of the Franklin Institute*, 122 (July 1886), pp. 2–4, available at https://todayinsci.com, accessed January 22, 2017. The most complete study is Greville Bathe and Dorothy Bathe. *Oliver Evans: A Chronicle of Early American Engineering* (Philadelphia, 1935).

47 Brooke Hindle, "The Exhilaration of Early American Technology," in *Early American Technology: Making and Doing Things from the Colonial Era to 1850*, ed. Judith A. McGaw (Chapel Hill, NC, 1994), pp. 40–67.

FIVE: Old Hickory's Big Cheese

1 Washington Irving, *A Tour on the Prairies* (New York, 1832), pp. 221–2.

2 John K. Howat, introduction to *American Paradise: The World of the Hudson River School* (New York, 1988).

3 Kris Lackey, "Eighteenth-century Aesthetic Theory and the Nineteenth-century Traveler in Trans-Allegheny America: F. Trollope, Dickens, Irving and Parkman," *American Studies*, XXXII/1 (1991), pp. 33–48. This is an excellent study of Romantic literary imagery among three very diverse writers.

4 David Garrick and George Colman the elder, *The Clandestine Marriage* (London, 1766), 2.2.

5 Charles Dickens, *American Notes for General Circulation* (London, 1842), p. 133.

6 Ralph Waldo Emerson, *Journals and Miscellaneous Notebooks of Ralph Waldo Emerson*, VII: *1838–1842*, ed. A. W. Plumstead and Harrison Hayford (Cambridge, MA, 1969), p. 268.

7 Charles Sellers, *The Market Revolution: Jacksonian America, 1815–1846* (New York, 1991).

8 Richard R. John, review of *The Market Revolution: Jacksonian America, 1815–1846,* by Charles Sellers, *New England Quarterly*, XLVI/2 (June 1993), pp. 302–5.

9 Jay Monaghan and William Hall, "From England to Illinois in 1821: The Journal

of William Hall," *Journal of the Illinois State Historical Society*, XXXIX/1 (March 1946), pp. 21–67, pp. 44–5.

10 Ibid., p. 46.

11 Ibid., p. 55.

12 Milo Milton Quaife, ed., *Growing Up with Southern Illinois, 1820 to 1861: From the Memoirs of Daniel Harmon Brush* (Chicago, 1944), p. 27.

13 Ibid., p. 47.

14 Helen Walker Linsenmeyer, *Cooking Plain: Illinois Country Style*, foreword by Bruce Kraig (Carbondale, IL, 1976, repr. 2011).

15 Quaife, *Growing Up*, p. 44.

16 A. Jeff Bremer, "Frontier Capitalism Market Migration to Rural Central Missouri, 1815–1860," in *Southern Society and Its Transformations, 1790–1860*, ed. Susanna Delfino, Michele Gillespie, and Louis M. Kyriakoudes (Columbia, MO, 2011), pp. 78–100.

17 Richard Lyman Bushman, "Markets and Composite Farms in Early America," *William and Mary Quarterly*, LV/3 (July 1998), pp. 351–74.

18 Timothy Flint, *Recollections of the Last Ten Years, Passed in Occasional Residences and Journeyings in the Valley of the Mississippi, from Pittsburg and the Missouri to the Gulf of Mexico, and from Florida to the Spanish Frontier: in a Series of Letters to the Rev. James Flint, of Salem, Massachusetts* (Boston, 1826), p. 104.

19 Sellers, *Market Revolution*, pp. 15–16. See also Carole Shammas, "How Self-sufficient Was Early America?" *Journal of Interdisciplinary History*, XIII/2 (Autumn 1982), pp. 247–72.

20 See Harry L. Watson, "Slavery and Development in a Dual Economy: The South and the Market Revolution," in *The Market Revolution in America: Social, Political, and Religious Expressions, 1800–1880*, ed. Melvyn Stokes and Stephen Conway (Charlottesville, VA, 1996), pp. 43–73.

21 Angela Lakwete, *Inventing the Cotton Gin: Machine and Myth in Antebellum America* (Baltimore, 2003).

22 Alan L. Olmstead and Paul W. Rhode, *Creating Abundance: Biological Innovation and American Agricultural Development* (Cambridge, 2008), pp. 98–133.

23 The pioneering interpretation of this view of the slave system is Kenneth M. Stampp, *The Peculiar Institution: Slavery in the Ante-Bellum South* (New York, 1956).

24 Sellers, *Market Revolution*, p. 32.

25 John C. Harriman, ed., "'Most Excellent—far fam'd and far fetch'd Cheese': An Anthology of Jeffersonian Era Poetry," *American Magazine and Historical Chronicle*, II/2 (1986–7), pp. 1–26, available at http://clements.umich.edu, accessed May 16, 2015; see also Nancy Siegel, "Cooking Up American Politics," *Gastronomica*, VIII/3 (Summer 2008), pp. 53–61 for a discussion of political recipes, images and expressions.

26 Harriman, "'Most Excellent," p. 6.

27 Ibid., p. 13 (from an article by "Republicanus" in the *Western Star* [Stockbridge, MA], 1801).

28 Jeffrey L. Pasley, "The Cheese and the Words: Popular Political Culture and Participatory Democracy in the Early American Republic," in *Beyond the Founders: New Approaches to the Political History of the Early American Republic*, ed. Jeffrey L. Pasley, Andrew W. Robertson, and David Waldstreicher (Chapel Hill, NC,

2004), pp. 32–56. Richard Zacks, *The Pirate Coast: Thomas Jefferson, the First Marines, and the Secret Mission of 1805* (New York, 2005).

29 James Parton, *The Life of Andrew Jackson*, 3 vols. (New York, 1860), III, p. 323.

30 "A Splendid Present," *Genesee Farmer and Gardener's Journal* [Rochester, NY], V, no. 42 (October 17, 1835), pp. 330–31; Parton, *The Life of Andrew Jackson*, III, p. 626.

31 N. P. Willis, *Loiterings of Travel*, vol. I (London, 1840), pp. 125–6. The best modern description of Jackson's cheese is Robert Remini, *Andrew Jackson*, III: *The Course of American Democracy (1833–1845)* (New York, 1984), pp. 393–4.

32 See Mark R. Cheathem, *Andrew Jackson, Southerner* (Baton Rouge, LA, 2013), an excellent discussion of Jackson's background in not so exactly rural South Carolina and the ideas that informed his life and actions.

33 "Agriculture," *Andrew Jackson's Hermitage: Home of the People's President*, http:// thehermitage.com, accessed June 6, 2015.

34 Menu from Brigg's House, January 1, 1859 in the menu collection, Chicago History Museum.

35 From an historic dinner put on in Jackson, Tennessee, in October 2009, cited in "American Presidents' Food Favorites," *The Food Timeline*, www.foodtimeline. org, accessed June 6, 2015.

36 William Parker Cutler, Julia Perkins Cutler, E. C. Dawes, and Peter Force, eds. *Life, Journals and Correspondence of Rev. Manasseh Cutler, LL.D.* (Cincinnati, 1888), p. 154. See also Catherine Allgor, *A Perfect Union: Dolley Madison and the Creation of the American Nation* (New York, 2013), pp. 73–4.

37 See Barbara G. Carson, *Ambitious Appetites: Dining, Behavior, and Patterns of Consumption in Federal Washington* (Washington, DC, 1990). This is a well-known and fine study of the meaning of food for the political and social elites in America.

38 For a summary of ideas see the fine essay: Thomas B. Latner, "Preserving 'the natural equality of rank and influence': Liberalism, Republicanism, and Equality of Condition in Jacksonian Politics," in *The Culture of the Market: Historical Essays*, ed. Thomas L. Haskell and Richard F. Teichgraeber III (Cambridge, 1993), pp. 189–230.

39 Rob Bryer, "Americanism and Financial Accounting Theory—Part 1: Was America Born Capitalist?" *Critical Perspectives on Accounting*, XXIII (2012), pp. 511–55. See also the classic work Alan Kulikoff, *The Agrarian Origins of American Capitalism* (Charlotte, NC, 1992).

40 "President Jackson's Veto Message Regarding the Bank of the United States; July 10, 1832," available at http://avalon.law.yale.edu, accessed June 15, 2015.

41 Charles Woodmason, *The Carolina Backcountry on the Eve of the Revolution: The Journal and Other Writings of Charles Woodmason, Anglican Itinerant*, ed. Richard J. Hooker (Charlotte, NC, 1953), p. 34.

42 Frances Trollope, *Domestic Manners of the Americans* (London, 1832), p. 50.

43 Ibid., pp. 36–7.

44 Capt. J. E. Alexander, *Transatlantic Sketches, Comprising Visits to the Most Interesting Scenes of North and South America and the West Indies* (Philadelphia, 1833), p. 269.

45 John F. Kasson, *Rudeness and Civility: Manners in Nineteenth-century Urban America* (New York, 1991), p. 186. See also Trollope's novel *The Refugee in*

America, 3 vols. (London, 1833) for commentaries on the "celerity" with which Americans downed their fried chicken and beef-steaks.

46 Dickens, *American Notes*, p. 121.

47 Trollope, *Domestic Manners*, p. 130.

48 Ibid.

49 Alexis de Tocqueville, letter to Ernest de Chabrol, June 9, 1831, in *Selected Letters on Politics and Society*, ed. Roger Boesche (Berkeley, CA, and Los Angeles, 1986), p. 39.

50 Trollope, *Domestic Manners of the Americans*, p. 325.

51 Nelson F. Adkins, "James Fenimore Cooper and the Bread and Cheese Club," *Modern Language Notes,* XLVII/2 (February 1932), pp. 71–9.

52 Paul Kindstedt, *Cheese and Culture: A History of Cheese and its Place in Western Civilization* (White River Junction, VT, 2012) has a good discussion of early American cheese and production.

53 Sally McMurry, "Women's Work in Agriculture: Divergent Trends in England and America, 1800 to 1930," *Comparative Studies in Society and History*, XXXIV/2 (April 1992), pp. 248–70, 257. Cheese is a large element of this fine study.

54 "The Dairy: Process of Cheese Making," *Genesee Farmer and Gardener's Journal*, V, no. 31 (August 1, 1835), pp. 242–3; V, no. 32 (August 8, 1835), p. 253.

55 H. E. Erdman, "The 'Associated Dairies' of New York as Precursors of American Agricultural Cooperatives," *Agricultural History*, XXXVI/2 (April 1962), pp. 82–90, 84.

SIX: Grass and Animals

1 Walt Whitman, *Specimen Days & Collect* (Philadelphia, 1882–3), p. 109.

2 Ibid., p. 268.

3 Ed Folsom, "Whitman's Crunching Cow," *Whitman's Manuscript Drafts of "Song of Myself,"* http://bailiwick.lib.uiowa.edu, accessed January 4, 2016.

4 Katharine M. Rogers, *Pork: A Global History* (London, 2012), p. 84. For example, see Juliet Corson's commentary on dangers of pork in *The "Home Queen" World's Fair Souvenir Cook Book: two thousand valuable recipes on cookery and household economy, menus, table etiquette, toilet, etc. contributed by over two hundred World's Fair lady managers, wives of governors and other ladies of position and influence* (Chicago, 1893), pp. 98ff.

5 Loyal Durand Jr., "The Migration of Cheese Manufacture in the United States," *Annals of the Association of American Geographers*, LXII/4 (December 1952), pp. 263–70.

6 Lewis Cecil Gray, assisted by Esther Katherine Thompson, *History of Agriculture in the Southern United States to 1860*, 2 vols. (Washington, DC, 1933), I, p. 205.

7 Vaclav Smil, *Energy in World History* (Boulder, CO, 1994), p. 1.

8 William S. Curran and Dwight D. Lingenfelter, "Johnsongrass and Shattercane Control: An Integrated Approach" (2016), http://extension.psu.edu, accessed January 24, 2017; National Agricultural Library, "Johnsongrass," www.invasivespeciesinfo.gov, accessed July 2, 2015; Carleton R. Ball and Arthur H. Leidigh, "Milo as a Dry Land Grain Crop," U.S. Department of Agriculture, Farmers' Bulletin 322 (Washington, DC, 1908); "Sorghum Introduction," *Gramene*, http://archive.gramene.org, accessed July 3, 2015.

9 Anne Rodiek, "Hay for Horses: Alfalfa or Grass?" in Proceedings, 31st California Alfalfa & Forage Symposium, December 12–13, 2001, www.alfalfa.ucdavis.
   edu, accessed January 24, 2017.

10 E. L. Jones, "Creative Disruptions in American Agriculture, 1620–1820," *Agricultural History*, XLVIII/4 (October 1974), p. 525.

11 Elizabeth A. Kellogg, "Evolutionary History of the Grasses," *Plant Physiology*,
   CXXV (2001), pp. 1198–205. On new theories of the origins of grasses in the
   Cretaceous period see: Vandana Prasad, Caroline A. E. Strömberg, Habib Alimohammadian, and Ashok Sahni, "Dinosaur Coprolites and the Early Evolution
   of Grasses and Grazers," *Science*, CCCX/5751 (November 18, 2005), pp. 1177–80.

12 Virginia Scott Jenkins, *The Lawn: A History of an American Obsession* (Washington, DC, 1994), p. 11.

13 Charles Morrow Wilson, *Grass and People* (Gainesville, FL, 1961), pp. 4–5.

14 William Cronon, *Changes in the Land: Indians, Colonists and the Ecology of New
   England* (New York, 1983, rev. 2003), p. 144; David R. Montgomery, *Dirt, the
   Erosion of Civilizations* (Berkeley, CA, 2007, rev. 2012), p. 89; Christopher Gras-
   so, "The Experimental Philosophy of Farming: Jared Eliot and the Cultivation of
   Connecticut," *William and Mary Quarterly*, L/3 (July 1993), pp. 502–28.

15 Wilson, *Grass and People,* pp. 2–3. Charles V. Piper and Catherine M. Bort,
   "The Early Agricultural History of Timothy," *Journal of the American Society of
   Agronomy*, VII/1 (January–February 1915), pp. 1–14. See also "The History of
   Timothy Grass Hay," 2009, www.estyranch.com, accessed January 24, 2017, for a
   good short summary and, for a technical description, Daniel G. Ogle, Loren St.
   John and Derek J. Tilley, "Plant Guide for Timothy (*Phleum pretense*)," https://
   plants.usda.gov, accessed March 18, 2011.

16 Wilson, *Grass and People*, pp. 181–3; H. A. Fribourg, D. B. Hannaway, and C. P.
   West, eds., *Tall Fescue for the Twenty-first Century*, Agronomy Monographs 53
   (Madison, WI, 2009); available at http://forages.oregonstate.edu, accessed June
   30, 2015.

17 Michael J. Christensen and Christine R. Voisey, "Tall Fescue—Endophyte Sym-
   biosis," in Fribourg, Hannaway, and West, eds., *Tall Fescue for the Twenty-first
   Century*, pp. 251–72.

18 Gray, *History of Agriculture*, II, p. 823; Jenkins, *The Lawn*, p. 12.

19 Alfred W. Crosby, *Ecological Imperialism: The Biological Expansion of Europe,
   900–1900* (Cambridge, 1986, rev. 2004), p. 153.

20 George P. Marsh, *The Earth as Modified by Human Action: A Last Revision of
   Man and Nature* (New York, 1874), pp. 72–3.

21 Michael P. Russelle, "Alfalfa: After an 8,000-year journey, the 'Queen of Forages'
   stands poised to enjoy renewed popularity," *American Scientist*, LXXXIX/3 (May–
   June 2001), pp. 252–3.

22 U.S. Borax, Inc.,"Borax: The Twenty Mule Team," www.scvhistory.com, accessed
   June 5, 2015.

23 Russelle, "Alfalfa," pp. 258–61.

24 Larry Holzworth, Jeff Mosley, Dennis Cash, David Koch, and Kelly Crane,
   "Dryland Pastures in Montana and Wyoming: Species and Cultivars, Seeding
   Techniques and Grazing Management," *Montana State University Extension
   Service*, rev. Fall 2003, www.animalrange.montana.edu, accessed January 25, 2017.

25 Department of Ecology, State of Washington, "Non-native, Invasive, Freshwater

Plants," www.ecy.wa.gov, accessed July 2, 2015.

26 Corey L. Gucker, "Euphorbia esula," Fire Effects Information System. U.S. Department of Agriculture, Forest Service, Rocky Mountain Research Station, Fire Sciences Laboratory (2010), www.fs.fed.us, accessed August 2, 2015.

27 Luke Runyon, "The Long, Slow Decline of the U.S. Sheep Industry," *Harvest Public Media* (October 8, 2013), www.harvestpublicmedia.org, accessed January 26, 2017; and National Agricultural Statistics Service, "Overview of the United States Sheep and Goat Industry," August 9, 2011, http://usda.mannlib.cornell. edu, accessed August 30, 2015.

28 Mrs. Child (Lydia Maria Child), *The Frugal Housewife* (Boston, 1829), 12th edn. as *The American Frugal Housewife* (Boston, 1832).

29 Alan L. Olmstead and Paul W. Rhode, *Creating Abundance: Biological Innovation and American Agricultural Development* (Cambridge, 2008), p. 284.

30 Mrs. Lettice Bryan, *The Kentucky Housewife* (Cincinnati, 1839, repr. 2001), p. 28.

31 G. E. Fussell, "The Size of English Cattle in the Eighteenth Century," *Agricultural History*, III/4 (1929), pp. 160–81.

32 Olmstead and Rhode, *Creating Abundance*, pp. 288–9.

33 George F. Lemmer, "The Spread of Improved Cattle through the Eastern United States to 1850," *Agricultural History*, XXI/2 (1947), p. 80.

34 Marleen Felius, Marie-Louise Beerling, David S. Buchanan, Bert Theunissen, Peter A. Koolmees, and Johannes A. Lenstra, "On the History of Cattle Genetic Resources," *Diversity*, VI/4 (2014), pp. 705–50, available at www.mdpi.com, accessed July 7, 2015.

35 Joan E. Grundy, "The Hereford Bull: His Contribution to New World and Domestic Beef Supplies," *Agricultural History Review*, L/1 (2002), pp. 69–88; M. R. Montgomery, *A Cow's Life: The Surprising History of Cattle, and How the Black Angus Came to Be Home on the Range* (New York, 2004).

36 Emily Jane McTavish, Jared E. Decker, Robert D. Schnabel, Jeremy F. Taylor, and David M. Hillisa, "New World Cattle Show Ancestry from Multiple Independent Domestication Events," *Proceedings of the National Academy of Sciences*, CX/15 (2013), pp. E1398–E1406, available at www.pnas.org, accessed January 26, 2017.

37 J. Frank Dobie, *The Longhorns* (Austin, TX, 1980), pp. 41–2.

38 Paul C. Henlein, "Cattle Driving from the Ohio Country, 1800–1850," *Agricultural History*, XXVIII/2 (1954), pp. 83–95; Paul C. Henlein, "Shifting Range-Feeder Patterns in the Ohio Valley before 1860," *Agricultural History*, XXXI/1 (1957), pp. 1–12.

39 Lester A. Hubbard and Kenly W. Whitelock, ed., "The Apex Boarding House," *Ballads and Songs from Utah* (Salt Lake City, 1961), p. 435.

40 Dobie, *The Longhorns*, p. 38.

41 Joseph G. McCoy, *Historic Sketches of the Cattle Trade of the West and Southwest* (Kansas City, MO, 1874).

42 William T. Hornaday, *Our Vanishing Wild Life: Its Extermination and Preservation* (New York, 1913), p. 180. See also Stefan Bechtel, *Mr. Hornaday's War: How a Peculiar Victorian Zookeeper Waged a Lonely Crusade for Wildlife that Changed the World* (Boston, 2012).

43 Raymond B. Becker, *Dairy Cattle Breeds, Origins and Development* (Gainesville, FL, 1973), p. 95.

44 Olmstead and Rhode, *Creating Abundance,* p. 334.

45 Ibid., p. 339; Becker, *Dairy Cattle Breeds,* pp. 204ff. 309ff. See also Anne Mendelson, *Milk: The Surprising Story of Milk through the Ages* (New York, 2008), pp. 39–40.

46 Wisconsin Milk Marketing Board, "2015 Dairy Data: A Review of the Wisconsin Dairy Industry," available at http://docplayer.net, accessed January 26, 2017.

47 Olmstead and Rhode, *Creating Abundance,* p. 349.

48 Norman K. Risjord, "From the Plow to the Cow: William D. Hoard and America's Dairyland," *Wisconsin Magazine of History,* LXXXVIII/3 (Spring 2005), pp. 40–49.

49 Fred Bateman, "Improvement in American Dairy Farming, 1850–1910: A Quantitative Analysis," *Journal of Economic History,* XXVIII/2 (June 1968), pp. 255–73.

50 Ibid., p. 257; Olmstead and Rhode, *Creating Abundance,* pp. 347–50.

51 Don P. Blayney, "The Changing Landscape of U.S. Milk Production," USDA Statistical Bulletin no. 978, June 2002, http://usda.mannlib.cornell.edu, accessed September 24, 2015.

SEVEN: The Rise of Machines

1 Willa Cather, *My Ántonia* (Boston, 1918. repr. Mineola, NY, 2011), p. 62.

2 Bertrand Russell, *The Conquest of Happiness* (London, 1930), p. 152.

3 Hamlin Garland, "Boy Life on the Prairie, IV: Between Hay an' Grass," *American Magazine* [Brooklyn], VIII/2 (June 1888), p. 149; "Boy Life on the Prairie, V: Meadow Memories," *American Magazine,* VIII/3 (July 1888), p. 297.

4 Deborah Fitzgerald, *Every Farm a Factory: The Industrial Ideal in American Agriculture* (New Haven, CT, 2003), p. 5.

5 Wayne G. Broehl, *John Deere's Company: A History of Deere & Company and Its Times* (New York, 1984), p. 252. Deere's may not have been the first steel plow; a blacksmith named John Lane in Freeport, Illinois, had made one about 1834, also out of an old saw blade but using a different production method. See E. L. Bogart and C. M. Thompson, *The Centennial History of Illinois,* IV: *The Industrial State 1870–1893* (Springfield, IL, 1920), p. 226.

6 Patrick J. Furlong, "James Oliver," *Indiana Historical Society,* www.indianahistory.org, accessed December 6, 2014.

7 Leo Rogin, *The Introduction of Farm Machinery in its Relation to the Productivity of Labor in the Agriculture of the United States during the Nineteenth Century* (Berkeley, CA, 1931), pp. 68–72.

8 Follett L. Greeno, ed., *Obed Hussey, Who, of All Inventors, Made Bread Cheap* (Rochester, NY, 1912), pp. 56–67.

9 Frederick Law Olmsted, *A Journey in the Seaboard Slave States; With Remarks on Their Economy* (New York, 1856), p. 42. The great landscape architect Olmsted loathed slavery and most of the people who lived upon it.

10 William T. Hutchinson, *Cyrus Hall McCormick,* 2 vols. (New York, 1930–35).

11 Clarence H. Danhof, *Change in Agriculture: The Northern United States, 1820–1870* (Cambridge, MA, 1969), p. 238.

12 Bureau of the Census, *Historical Statistics of the United States, 1789–1945: A Supplement to the Statistical Abstract of the United States* (Washington, DC, 1949), E 181–195 (pp. 88–9, 106).

13 Rogin, *The Introduction of Farm Machinery,* p. 91.

14 Bureau of the Census, *Historical Statistics of the United States. Colonial Times to 1970,* 2 vols. (Washington, DC, 1970), K 445–485 (pp. 500–501).

15 Joseph Wickham Roe, *English and American Tool Builders* (New Haven, CT, 1916), p. 1.

16 David Hounshell, *From the American System to Mass Production, 1800–1932: The Development of Manufacturing Technology in the United States* (Baltimore, 1984), pp. 32–43.

17 Roe, *English and American Tool Builders,* pp. 206–7.

18 Vaclav Smil, *Energy in World History* (Boulder, CO, 1994), p. 86.

19 Anna N. Greene, "War Horses, Equine Technology in the American Civil War," in *Industrializing Organisms: Introducing Evolutionary History,* ed. Susan Schrepfer and Philip Scranton (New York, 2004), p. 146.

20 Smil, *Energy in World History,* p. 91.

21 Reynold M. Wik, "Steam Power on the American Farm, 1830–1880," *Agricultural History,* XXV/4 (1951), p. 182.

22 Ibid., p. 184.

23 Hart-Parr company of Charles City, Iowa, advertisement in *The American Thresherman,* May 1906, p. 38.

24 Carrie A. Meyer, "The Farm Debut of the Gasoline Engine," *Agricultural History,* LXXXVII/3 (Summer 2013), pp. 287–313. Meyer's book *Days on the Family Farm: From the Golden Age through the Great Depression* (Minneapolis, 2007) is an excellent account of the transition from horse-powered farming to tractors on a northern Illinois farm.

25 Fitzgerald, *Every Farm a Factory,* pp. 3, 91–105.

26 Eugene V. Smalley, "The Flour-mills of Minneapolis," *Century Illustrated Monthly Magazine,* XXXII (Sept. 1886), pp. 39–40; cited in David B. Danbom, "Flour Power: The Significance of Flour Milling at the Falls," *Minnesota History,* LVIII/5–6 (2003), p. 272.

27 Guy A. Lee, "The Historical Significance of the Chicago Grain Elevator System," *Agricultural History,* XI/1 (1937), pp. 16–32; see also David Witter, "Grain of Truth: Taking Stock of the Relics of Chicago's Era as the World's 'Stacker of Wheat,'" *New City,* June 2, 2010, www.newcity.com, accessed January 24, 2016.

28 Yūjirō Hayami and Vernon W. Ruttan, *Agricultural Development: An International Perspective* (Baltimore, 1971, rev. 1985) and Vernon W. Ruttan and Yujiro Hayami, "Toward a Theory of Induced Institutional Innovation," *Journal of Development Studies,* XX (1984), pp. 302–23.

29 Edgar Lee Masters. *Spoon River Anthology* (New York, 1916), p. 156.

30 Damian Alan Pargas. "In the Fields of a 'Strange Land': Enslaved Newcomers and the Adjustment to Cotton Cultivation in the Antebellum South," *Slavery and Abolition,* XXXIV/4 (2013), pp. 562–78, discusses picking gender and picking skills required by plantation owners and their hired overseers.

31 Alan L. Olmstead and Paul W. Rhode, *Creating Abundance: Biological Innovation and American Agricultural Development* (Cambridge, 2008), pp. 98–133.

32 Henry Carey Baird, *Protection of Home Labor and Home Productions Necessary to the Prosperity of the American Farmer* (New York, 1860).

33 Julius Rubin, "The Limits of Agricultural Progress in the Nineteenth-century South," *Agricultural History,* XLIX/2 (1975), pp. 362–73.

34 Paul W. Rhode, "Do Crops Shape Culture? Contrasting Cotton and Wheat in Nineteenth-Century North America," in Barbara Hahn, Tiago Saraiva, Paul W. Rhode, Peter Coclanis, and Claire Strom, "Does Crop Determine Culture?" *Agricultural History*, LXXXVIII/3 (Summer 2014), pp. 407–39.

35 See, among a voluminous literature, Sam B. Hilliard, "Pork in the Ante-bellum South: The Geography of Self-sufficiency," *Annals of the Association of American Geographers*, LIX/3 (1969), pp. 461–80 and Beth Blonigen, "A Re-examination of the Slave Diet," Thesis, College of St. Benedict/St. John's University, 2004.

36 Mrs. A. M. Collins, *Mrs. Collins' Table Receipts: Adapted to Western Housewifery* (New Albany, IN, 1851, repr. as *The Great Western Cook Book or Table Receipts, Adapted to Western Housewifery* (New York, 1857); Philomelia Ann Maria Antoinette Hardin, *Every Body's Cook and Receipt Book: But More Particularly Designed for Buckeyes, Hoosiers , Wolverines, Corncrackers , Suckers, and All Epicures Who Wish to Live with the Present Times* (Cleveland, 1842).

37 Andrew F. Smith, ed., *Centennial Buckeye Cook Book* (Columbus, OH, 2000), pp. x–xiii.

38 Mrs. T.J.V. Owen, *Mrs. Owen's Illinois Cook Book* (Springfield, IL, 1871).

39 Ruth Schwartz Cowan, *More Work for Mother: The Ironies of Household Technologies from the Open Hearth to the Microwave* (New York, 1983), pp. 53–60.

40 Ibid.

41 Mrs. W. W. Brown, compiler, *The Illinois Cook Book; from Recipes Contributed by The Ladies of Paris, and Published for the Benefit of Grace (Episcopal) Church* (Claremont, NH, 1881).

42 For the an illustrated discussion of the baroque style of dress, see Natalie Ferguson, "A Brief History of the Dolly Varden Dress Craze," in *A Frolic through Time*, August 23, 2008, http://zipzipinkspot.blogspot.com, accessed January 26, 2016.

43 For a brief summary and pictures of early beaters, see "Early Rotary Egg Beaters," in *Home Things Past*, August, 2012, www.homethingspast.com. These are among many patented beaters and mixers, one of which is a commercial device patented by the African American inventor Willis Johnson in 1884.

44 "Improvement in Can Openers," Letters Patent No. 105,346, dated July 12, 1870, http://patentimages.storage.googleapis.com.

45 See Anne Mendelson's essay on class distinctions in nineteenth-century New York food: "Goodbye to the Marketplace: Food and Exclusivity in Nineteenth-century New York," in *The American Bourgeoisie: Distinction and Identity in the Nineteenth Century*, ed. Julia B. Rosenbaum and Sven Beckert (New York, 2011).

46 Victor S. Kennedy and Linda L. Breisch, "Sixteen Decades of Political Management of the Oyster Fishery in Maryland's Chesapeake Bay," *Journal of Environmental Management*, CLXIV (1983), pp. 153–71.

47 Mrs. S. T. Rorer, *Philadelphia Cook Book: A Manual of Home Economies* (Philadelphia, 1886).

48 The only major study of Mrs. Rorer is Emma Seifrit Weigley, *Sarah Tyson Rorer, the Nation's Instructress in Dietetics and Cookery* (Philadelphia, 1977).

49 Cowan, *More Work for Mother*, pp. 92–4; Susan Strasser, *Never Done: A History of American Housework* (New York, 2000), pp. 109–24.

50 Garland, "Boy's Life on the Prairie, VI: Melons and Early Frosts," *American Magazine*, VIII/6 (October 1888), p. 716.

51 Cather, *My Ántonia*, p. 60.

EIGHT: What We Ate and Why (to 1945)

1 Horatio Alger, Jr., *Ragged Dick; or Street Life in New York with the Boot Blacks* (Boston, 1868).

2 Laurence J. Malone, "Rural Electrification Administration," EH.net, https://eh.net, accessed June 6, 2015.

3 Andrew F. Smith, *Hamburger: A Global History* (London, 2008), pp. 25–37.

4 John F. Love, *McDonald's: Behind the Arches* (New York, 1986, rev. 1995).

5 Mark Twain (Samuel L. Clemens), *A Tramp Abroad* (Hartford, CT, 1880).

6 See Andrew Beahrs, "Twain's Feast: 'The American' at Table," *Gastronomica: The Journal of Food and Culture*, VII/2 (Spring 2007), pp. 26–34, and Andrew Beahrs, *Twain's Feast: Searching for America's Lost Foods in the Footsteps of Samuel Clemens* (New York, 2010) for fine discussions of the dishes and their varied meanings.

7 Twain, *A Tramp Abroad*, pp. 239–41.

8 Andrew Beahrs, "Mark Twain: Writer, Humorist, Locavore," *The Atlantic*, July 14, 2010, www.theatlantic.com.

9 Twain, *A Tramp Abroad*, pp. 236–7.

10 New York Public Library menu collection, http://menus.nypl.org. For Delmonico's glorious history as a dining place and influence on American cookery, see Judith Choate and James Canora, *Dining at Delmonico's: The Story of America's Oldest Restaurant* (New York, 2008). This is one of several histories and cookery books about and from the restaurant, notably chef de cuisine Charles Ranhoffer's *The Epicurean* (New York, 1894).

11 Ranhoffer, *The Epicurean*.

12 Major W. Shepherd, *Prairie Experiences in Handling Cattle and Sheep* (London, 1884), p. 12.

13 David M. Potter, *People of Plenty: Economic Abundance and the American Character* (Chicago, 1954), p. 118.

14 Robert M. Collins, "David Potter's People of Plenty and the Recycling of Consensus History," *Reviews in American History*, XVI/2 (1988), p. 330; Amy Bentley, "American Abundance Examined: David M. Potter's People of Plenty and the Study of Food," *Digest: An Interdisciplinary Study of Food and Foodways*, 15 (1995), pp. 20–24. On the idea and marketing of abundance there is no better study than Jackson Lears, *Fables of Abundance: A Cultural History of Advertising in America* (New York, 1994).

15 C. W. Gesner, "Concerning Restaurants," *Harper's New Monthly Magazine*, XXXII/191 (April 1866), pp. 591–4.

16 William Grimes, *Appetite City: A Culinary History of New York* (New York, 2009), pp. 81–3.

17 Margery W. Davies, *Woman's Place is at the Typewriter: Office Work and Office Workers, 1870–1930* (Philadelphia, 1982), p. 57.

18 Michael L. Dolfman and Denis M. McSweeney, *100 Years of U.S. Consumer Spending: Data for the Nation, New York City, and Boston*, BLS Report 991 (Washington, DC, 2006), www.bls.gov, accessed April 13, 2016.

19 Estelle M. Stewart and J. C. Bowen, *History of Wages in the United States from Colonial Times to 1928: Revision of Bulletin No. 499 with Supplement, 1929–1933*, Bulletin of the United States Bureau of Labor Statistics No. 604 (Washington, DC, 1934).

20 Andrew P. Haley, *Turning the Tables: Restaurants and the Rise of the American Middle Class, 1880–1920* (Chapel Hill, NC, 2011).

21 Edward Hungerford, *The Personality of American Cities* (New York, 1913), p. 51.

22 James T. Farrell's series comprises *A World I Never Made* (1936), *No Star is Lost* (1938), *Father and Son* (1940), *My Days of Anger* (1943), and *The Face of Time* (1953); all repr. with an introduction by Charles Fanning (Urbana, IL, and Chicago, 2007–8).

23 Grace L. Coyle, "Women in the Clerical Occupations," *Annals of the American Academy of Political and Social Science*, CXLIII/1 (May 1929), pp. 180–87.

24 Dominick Pacyga, *Chicago: A Biography* (Chicago, 2009), p. 101.

25 Harvey Levenstein, *Revolution at the Table: The Transformation of the American Diet* (New York and Oxford, 1988), pp. 183–93.

26 *New York Times*, March 12, 1916. See John A. Jackle and Keith A. Sculle, *Fast Food: Roadside Restaurants in the Automobile Age* (Baltimore, 1999) for a discussion of soda fountains and quick service restaurants.

27 For a fuller history of soda fountains and their importance in American culture, see Anne Cooper Funderburg, *Sundae Best: A History of Soda Fountains* (Madison, WI, 2002).

28 Jan Whitaker, "Quick Lunch," *Gastronomica*, IV/1 (Winter 2004), pp. 69–73. For more on the subject, see also Whitaker's site "Restaurant-ing through History," https://restaurant-ingthroughhistory.com, accessed April 1, 2016.

29 Lorraine B. Diehl and Marianne Hardart, *The Automat: The History, Recipes, and Allure of Horn & Hardart's Masterpiece* (New York, 2002); and Carolyn Hughes Crowley, "Meet Me at the Automat," *Smithsonian* (August 2001), pp. 22–4, available at www.smithsonianmag.com, accessed March 30, 2016.

30 Grimes, *Appetite City,* pp. 49–51; Bruce Kraig, "Toffenetti, Dario," in Carol Haddix, Bruce Kraig, and Colleen Taylor Sen, *The Encyclopedia of Chicago Food* (Urbana, IL, forthcoming).

31 "Wheat Data—All Years," Economic Research Service, United States Department of Agriculture, www.ers.usda.gov, accessed February 2, 2017. See also Alan L. Olmstead and Paul W. Rhode, *Creating Abundance: Biological Innovation and American Agricultural Development* (Cambridge, 2008), pp. 17–63 for a discussion of climate, geography, and pests in the American wheat belt.

32 Abigail Carroll, *Three Squares: The Invention of the American Meal* (New York, 2013), pp. 153–4. For a discussion of the social meaning of white bread, see Aaron Bobrow-Strain, *White Bread: A Social History of the Store-bought Loaf* (Boston, 2012).

33 Carolyn Wyman, *Better than Homemade: Amazing Foods that Changed the Way We Eat* (Philadelphia, 2004).

34 Anne Bucher and Melanie Villines, *The Greatest Thing since Sliced Cheese: Stories of Kraft Foods Inventors and their Inventions* (Northfield, IL, 2005).

35 Barry Popik and Andrew F. Smith, "Chicken à la King," in *The Oxford Encyclopedia of Food and Drink in America*, ed. Andrew F. Smith, 2nd edn. (New York, 2013), I, p. 371.

36 Jean Prescott Adams, *The Business of Being a Housewife* (Chicago, 1917).

37 Martha Esposito Shea and Mike Mathis, *Campbell Soup Company* (Mount Pleasant, SC, 2002), p. 7. See also Douglas Collins, *America's Favorite Food: The Story of Campbell Soup Company* (New York, 1994).

38 Raymond Sokolov, "The Search for the Perfect Nacho," *Wall Street Journal*, February 4, 2006.

39 Paul C. Bethke et al., "History and Origin of Russet Burbank (Netted Gem), a Sport of Burbank," *American Journal of Potato Research,* 91 (2014), pp. 594–609.

40 See Jane S. Smith, *The Garden of Invention: Luther Burbank and the Business of Breeding Plants* (New York, 2009) for the best recent survey of Burbank's life and work.

41 Mark Fiege, *Irrigated Eden: The Making of an Agricultural Landscape in the American West* (Seattle, 2009), pp. 3–10, 86–96.

42 Leo Rogin, *The Introduction of Farm Machinery in its Relation to the Productivity of Labor in the Agriculture of the United States during the Nineteenth Century* (Berkeley, CA, 1931), p. 120.

43 H.H. [Helen Jackson], "Outdoor Industries in Southern California," *The Century Illustrated Monthly Magazine*, XXVI/6 (October 1883), p. 810.

44 Hooker, *Food and Drink in America*, p. 232.

45 "The Georgia Peach History," University of Georgia College of Agricultural and Environmental Sciences, 2015, http://caes2.caes.uga.edu, accessed February 2, 2017; Thomas H. McHatton, "History of the Georgia Peach Industry," Master of Horticulture Thesis, Michigan State University, 1921.

46 Andrew F. Smith, *Peanuts: The Illustrious History of the Goober Pea* (Urbana, IL, 2002).

47 "Ex-Millionaire John Raklios Jailed for Debt," *Chicago Daily Tribune*, August 1, 1939.

48 James Wiley, *The Banana: Empires, Trade Wars, and Globalization,* (Lincoln, NE, 2008) and Dan Koeppel, *Banana: The Fate of the Fruit that Changed the World* (New York, 2008).

49 R. Thomas Schotzko and David Granatstein, *A Brief Look at the Washington Apple Industry: Past and Present* (Pullman, WA: Washington State University, 2004). Chapman, breeds and the business are discussed in William Kerrigan's excellent study, *Johnny Appleseed and the American Orchard: A Cultural History* (Baltimore, 2012).

50 Andrew Coe, *Chop Suey: A Cultural History of Chinese Food in the United States* (New York and Oxford, 2009), p. 160. See also Anne Mendelson, *Chow Chop Suey: Food and the Chinese American Journey* (New York, 2016), for the best discussion of Chinese food and identity to date.

51 Hasia R. Diner, *Hungering for America: Italian, Irish, and Jewish Foodways in the Age of Migration* (Cambridge, MA, 2001). Mark Zanger, "Italian American Food," in *Oxford Encyclopedia of Food and Drink in America*, ed. Smith, I, pp. 345–55.

52 For how ethnic dishes emerged from their original enclaves, see Donna Gabaccia, *We Are What We Eat: Ethnic Food and the Making of Americans* (Cambridge, MA, 2000). See also Krishnendu Ray, *The Ethnic Restaurateur* (London and New York, 2016), pp. 87–93.

53 Diner, *Hungering for America*, p. 345.

54 Robert Coit Chapin, *The Standard of Living among Workingmen's Families in New York City* (New York, 1909), pp. 123–61. For excellent discussions of these topics see also Robert Dirks, *Food in the Gilded Age: What Ordinary Americans Ate* (Baltimore, 2016).

55 Carolyn Eastwood, *Chicago Jewish Street Peddlers* (Chicago, 1991); Bruce Kraig

and Colleen Taylor Sen, eds., *Street Food around the World: An Encyclopedia of Food and Culture* (Santa Barbara, CA, 2012), rev. as *Street Food: Everything You Need to Know about Open-air Stands, Carts, and Food Trucks across the Globe* (Evanston, IL, 2017), pp. xix–xxii.

56 Richard J. S. Gutman, *The American Diner, Then and Now* (Baltimore and London, 1993).

57 "Hungry People—the Nocturnal Sandwich Wagon," *Chicago Tribune*, April 15, 1894. Thanks to Andrew F. Smith for pointing this out.

58 Ann Flesor Beck, "Greek Immigration to, and Settlement in, Central Illinois, 1880–1930," PhD diss., University of Illinois at Urbana-Champaign, 2014.

59 Thomas Burgess, *Greeks in America: An Account of their Coming, Progress, Customs, Living, and Aspirations* (Boston, 1913), p. 38, discusses how Greek lunch countermen moved along into third-class chop houses and even second-class restaurants.

60 See Barry Popik, "Hoagie (sandwich)," *The Big Apple*, June 10, 2009, www.barrypopik.com, accessed December 10, 2014; and Jackle and Sculle, *Fast Food: Roadside Restaurants*, pp. 170–71.

61 Bruce Kraig, *Hot Dog: A Global History* (London, 2009), and Bruce Kraig and Patty Carroll, *Man Bites Dog: Hot Dog Culture in America* (Lanham, MD, 2012).

62 Ray, *The Ethnic Restaurateur*, pp. 70–71; and Diner, *Hungering for America*, pp. 48–53.

63 Katherine Leonard Turner, *How the Other Half Ate: A History of Working Class Meals at the Turn of the Century* (Berkeley, CA, and Los Angeles, 2014), p. 7.

64 Jack Temple Kirby, *The Mockingbird Song: Ecological Landscapes of the South* (Chapel Hill, NC, 2006).

65 Dirks, *Food in the Gilded Age*, p. 90.

66 Ibid., pp. 4–9.

NINE: What We Eat and Why (since 1945)

1 As more or less celebrated by Ralph Waldo Emerson in his 1847 essay "Self-reliance," in *Essays by Ralph Waldo Emerson*, ed. Edna H. L. Turpin (New York, 1907) and recently by Dierdre McCloskey in her trilogy of books on the American economy ending with *Bourgeois Equality: How Ideas, Not Capital or Institutions, Enriched the World* (Chicago, 2016).

2 Ella Eaton Kellogg, *Science in the Kitchen* (Battle Creek, MI, 1892, 4th edn. 1904).

3 The story is well summarized in Andrew F. Smith's *Eating History: Thirty Turning Points in the Making of American Cuisine* (New York, 2009), pp. 141–54. See also Hillel Schwartz, *Never Satisfied: A Cultural History of Diets, Fantasies and Fat* (New York, 1986), pp. 181–9, for a discussion of the machinery. Kellogg's treatments, including constant enemas with yogurt, are hilariously satirized in T. Coraghessan Boyle, *The Road to Wellville* (New York, 1993).

4 Jessica J. Mudry, *Measured Meals: Nutrition in America* (Albany, NY, 2009), pp. 31–2, belongs to a large literature on Atwater and his influence on American history. See also Warren Belasco's discussion of caloric needs and changes in recommendations over time in *Meals to Come: The Future of American Food* (Berkeley, CA, 2006), pp. 69–73.

5 Laura Shapiro, *Perfection Salad: Women and Cooking at the Turn of the Century* (New York, 1986), rev. with an Afterword (Berkeley, CA, and Los Angeles, 2008), pp. 37–42ff.

6 Ibid., p. 65.

7 Alan Trachtenberg, *The Incorporation of America: Culture and Society in the Gilded Age* (New York, 1982) and Cecilia Tichi, *Shifting Gears: Technology, Literature, Culture in Modernist America* (Chapel Hill, NC, 1987), cited by Thomas P. Hughes, *American Genesis* (New York, 1989), pp. 184–5.

8 Hughes, *American Genesis*, pp. 188–202.

9 Richard H. Steckel, "A Peculiar Population: The Nutrition, Health, and Mortality of American Slaves from Childhood to Maturity," *Journal of Economic History*, XLVI/3 (1986), pp. 721–4.

10 Praveen Ghanta, "List of Foods by Environmental Impact and Energy Efficiency," *The Oil Drum*, March 2, 2010, www.theoildrum.com, accessed February 6, 2017; Field to Market: The Alliance for Sustainable Agriculture, "Environmental and Socioeconomic Indicators for Measuring Outcomes of On-Farm Agricultural Production in the United States," 3rd edn., December 2016, http://fieldtomarket.org.

11 Robert J. Gordon, *The Rise and Fall of American Growth* (Princeton, NJ, 2016), pp. 269–70.

12 Sidney Olson, *Young Henry Ford: A Picture History of the First Forty Years* (Detroit, 1963), p. 29.

13 Charles R. Morris, *The Dawn of Innovation* (New York, 2012), pp. 274–84; Sigfried Giedion, *Mechanization Takes Command* (New York, 1948) is a seminal book about mass production showing the triumph of the assembly line in several food products such as meat and bread.

14 Roger Horowitz, *Putting Meat on the American Table: Taste, Technology, Transformation* (Baltimore, 2006), p. 39.

15 Henry Ford, with Samuel Crowther, *My Life and Work* (New York, 1923), pp. 80–81.

16 See Stephen F. Eisenman, *The Cry of Nature: Art and the Making of Animal Rights* (London, 2016) for a thoughtful and heart-rending discussion based on eyewitness accounts. Rudyard Kipling was one of them, saying in his *American Notes* (New York, 1899) of his 1889 visit that all Englishmen went to the stockyards to witness the dreadful, if necessary, slaughter. There is no more shocking description than Upton Sinclair's *The Jungle* (New York, 1906), which is essential reading.

17 Paul Bourget, *Outre-mer: Impressions of America* (London, 1895), p. 127.

18 Carroll Pursell, *Technology in Postwar America: A History* (New York, 2007), pp. 889–90.

19 Susan Strasser, *Never Done: A History of American Housework* (New York, 2000), pp. 26–7; Rudolf Alexander Clemen, *The American Livestock and Meat Industry* (New York, 1923), pp. 347–78.

20 See Glenn Porter and Harold C. Livesey, *Merchants and Manufacturers* (Baltimore, 1971), pp. 166–79 on the fruit distribution by such companies as the Boston Fruit Company and United Fruit.

21 Arthur I. Judge, ed., *Souvenir of the 7th Annual Convention of the National Canners' and Allied Associations, Baltimore, Feb'y 2 to 7, 1914* (Baltimore, 1914),

pp. 95–6; Smith, *Eating History*, pp. 70–71.

22 Thomas Hine, *The Total Package: The Evolution and Secret Meanings of Boxes, Bottles, Cans, and Tubes* (Boston, 1995), pp. 3–4. Chapter 3 "Trusting the Package" (pp. 46–80) is an excellent summary of how consumers were taught how to trust brand names.

23 William Cahn, *Out of the Cracker Barrel: The Nabisco Story from Animal Crackers to Zuzus* (New York, 1971). This remains the standard telling of the company's early history. See also Giedion, *Mechanization Takes Command*, pp. 191–200.

24 Horowitz, *Putting Meat on the American Table*, p. 91. For hot dog history and popular culture, see Bruce Kraig, *Hot Dog: A Global History* (London, 2009), and Bruce Kraig and Patty Carroll, *Man Bites Dog: Hot Dog Culture in America* (Lanham, MD, 2012).

25 Bureau of Labor Statistics, "Consumer Expenditures—2014," September 3, 2015, www.bls.gov.

26 Sundeep Vikraman, Cheryl D. Fryar, and Cynthia L. Ogden, "Caloric Intake from Fast Food among Children and Adolescents in the United States, 2011–2012," *National Center for Health Statistics*, NCHS Data Brief, no. 213 (September 2015), www.cdc.gov/nchs.

27 As an example of the thousands of such experiments carried out to the present day, see A. N. Hume, *Trials with Commercial Varieties of Canning Peas*, South Dakota State University Agricultural Experiment Station, Bulletin 221 (Brookings, SD, 1927), available at www.openprairie.sdstate.edu, for a study of ten kinds of commercial pea; see Giedion, *Mechanization Takes Command*, pp. 196–9 on white or "bubblegum" bread.

28 John W. Bennett, Harvey L. Smith, and Herbert Passin, "Food and Culture in Southern Illinois: A Preliminary Report," *American Sociological Review*, VII/5 (1942), pp. 645–60; see also Richard J. Hooker, *Food and Drink in America: A History* (Indianapolis, 1981), p. 213, on the popularity of canned goods in the newly settled west.

29 James A. Thorson, *Tough Guys Don't Dice* (New York, 1989) gives this dish as a staple of easy cookery for supposedly uninterested cooks.

30 Robert C. Williams, *Fordson, Farmall, and Poppin' Johnny: A History of the Farm Tractor and its Impact on America* (Urbana, IL, 1987), pp. 15–16, 287–313.

31 Ibid, p. 88.

32 John Noble Wilford, "Food is Redesigned to Suit Machines," *New York Times*, August 23, 1967. See also Andrew F. Smith, *Souper Tomatoes: The Story of America's Favorite Food* (New Brunswick, NJ, 2000) for the story of how the Campbell Soup Company mechanized its California soup tomato harvests. Modern tomato harvesters and sorters can handle a ton in fifteen minutes. See James F. Thompson and Steven C. Blank, "Harvest Mechanization Helps Agriculture Remain Competitive," *California Agriculture*, LIV/3 (May–June 2000), pp. 51–6.

33 Eduardo Porter, "In Florida Groves, Cheap Labor Means Machines," *New York Times*, March 22, 2004; Pursell, *Technology in Postwar America*, pp. 90–93.

34 Deborah Fitzgerald, *Every Farm a Factory: The Industrial Ideal in American Agriculture* (New Haven, CT, 2003), p. 14; Donald Holley, "Mechanical Cotton Picker," EH.net, June 16, 2003, https://eh.net.

35 Pete Daniel, *Breaking the Land: The Transformation of Cotton, Tobacco, and Rice Cultures since 1880* (Urbana, IL, 1986), pp. 41–5.

36 Ibid., pp. 46–50.

37 J. T. Hardke, "Trends in Arkansas Rice Production, 2014," in *B. R. Wells Arkansas Rice Research Studies 2014*, ed. R. J. Norman and K.A.K. Moldenhauer (Fayetteville, AR, 2014), pp. 11–22.

38 Jarrod Hardke and Terry Siebenmorgen, "Rice Grades," in *Arkansas Rice Production Handbook*, ed. Jarrod Hardke (Little Rock, AR, [2013]), pp. 163–5.

39 David S. Shields, *Southern Provisions: The Creation and Revival of a Cuisine* (Chicago, 2015), pp. 229–53.

40 Anson Mills, "What We Do—And Why We Do It," www.ansonmills.com, accessed February 6, 2017.

41 David R. Montgomery, *Dirt, the Erosion of Civilizations* (Berkeley, CA, 2007, rev. 2012), pp. 151–3.

42 B. J. Rothschild, J. S. Ault, P. Goulletquer, and M. Héral, "Decline of the Chesapeake Bay Oyster Population: A Century of Habitat Destruction and Overfishing," *Marine Ecology Progress Series*, III (August 1994), pp. 28–39; Hooker, *Food and Drink in America*, pp. 312–13.

43 David Montgomery, *Dirt, the Erosion of Civilizations*, p. 151.

44 George Montgomery, "Wheat Price Policy in the United States," *Farm Foundation, Increasing Understanding of Public Problems and Policies* (Oak Brook, IL, 1953), pp. 25–70.

45 Donald Worster, *Dust Bowl: The Southern Plains in the 1930s* (New York, 1979, rev. 2004), p. 4. See also Jeffrey K. Stine, "A Sense of Place: Donald Worster's 'Dust Bowl,'" *Technology and Culture*, XLVIII/2 (2007), pp. 377–85.

46 Michael Lind, *Land of Promise: An Economic History of the United States* (New York, 2012), pp. 271–5.

47 Among the massive literature on New Deal programs, see T. H. Watkins, *The Hungry Years: A Narrative History of the Great Depression in America* (New York, 2000) for a lyrical account as seen from the perspective of working people. Studs Terkel's great *Hard Times: An Oral History of the Great Depression* (New York, 1986) is the go-to book for a "history from the bottom up."

48 Gordon W. Gunderson, *National School Lunch Program: Background and Development*, Food and Nutrition Service 63 (Washington, DC, 1971).

49 Jane Ziegelman and Andy Coe, *A Square Meal: A Culinary History of the Great Depression* (New York, 2016). This is an excellent study of food during the Depression and the results of government programs.

50 Ruth Van Deman and Fanny Walker Yeatman, *Aunt Sammy's Radio Recipes Revised*, Bureau of Home Economics (Washington, DC, 1931); Laura Shapiro, *Something from the Oven: Reinventing Dinner in 1950s America* (New York, 2004), pp. 190–95; Susan Marks, *Finding Betty Crocker: The Secret Life of America's First Lady of Food* (New York, 2010) has selected recipes; Jackson Lears, *Fables of Abundance: A Cultural History of Advertising in America* (New York, 1994), pp. 383–5.

51 "Canned Beef Recipes," Bureau of Home Economics, U.S. Department of Agriculture in Cooperation with the Federal Surplus Relief Corporation (Washington, DC, 1934).

52 *The River* (1938), written and dir. Pare Lorentz, 31 minutes. Documentary for U.S. Farm Resettlement Administration. See Nancy Isenberg, *White Trash: The 400-year Untold History of Class in America* (New York, 2016), pp. 206–30 for an excellent discussion of attitudes toward the poor and government policies during

Great Depression.

53 Interview with Ruth Parker, age 91, June 2008.

54 David M. Tucker, *Kitchen Gardening in America: A History* (Ames, IA, 1993) is a general history of the subject with some attention to Victory Gardens.

55 Alan L. Olmstead and Paul W. Rhode, *Creating Abundance: Biological Innovation and American Agricultural Development* (Cambridge, 2008), pp. 396–7.

56 David Montgomery, *Dirt, the Erosion of Civilizations*, pp. 185–98; "Wheat Data," *Amber Waves* (Washington, DC, 2016), www.ers.usda.gov. See also Vaclav Smil, *Enriching the Earth: Fritz Haber, Carl Bosch, and the Transformation of World Food Production* (Cambridge, MA, 2004).

57 Jorge Fernandez-Cornejo et al., "Pesticide Use in U.S. Agriculture: 21 Selected Crops, 1960–2008," *United States Department of Agriculture, Economic Information Bulletin 124* (May 2014), www.ers.usda.gov. For soybeans see Christine M. Du Bois, "Changing Soy Production and Consumption in the United States," in *The World of Soy*, ed. Christine M. Du Bois, Chee-Beng Tan, and Sidney Mintz (Urbana, IL, 2008), pp. 208–33.

58 Gordon, *The Rise and Fall of American Growth*, pp. 540–43; Lind, *Land of Promise*, pp. 346–7.

59 Tom Philpott, "A Reflection on the Lasting Legacy of 1970s USDA Secretary Earl Butz," *Grist*, February 8, 2008, http://grist.org, accessed February 6, 2017.

60 Fitzgerald, *Every Farm a Factory*, p. 189; Carolyn Dimitri, Anne Effland, and Neilson Conklin, "The 20th Century Transformation of U.S. Agriculture and Farm Policy," *United States Department of Agriculture, Economic Information Bulletin Number 3* (June 2005).

61 American Farmland Trust, "Farming on the Edge: The Nation's Best Farmland in the Path of Development," 2015, www.farmland.org.

62 Food Marketing Institute, "Supermarket Facts," 2015, www.fmi.org.

63 Smith, *Eating History*, p. 179.

64 JoAnn Jaffe and Michael Gertler, "Victual Vicissitudes: Consumer Deskilling and the (Gendered) Transformation of Food Systems," *Agriculture and Human Values*, 23 (2006), pp. 143–62. This is a good summary of the argument with a fine bibliography. See also the excellent collection of essays in Warren Belasco and Philip Scranton, eds., *Food Nations: Selling Taste in Consumer Societies* (New York, 2002), and Eric Schlosser, *Fast Food Nation: The Dark Side of the All-American Meal* (Boston, 2001).

65 The best survey to date is Kathleen Collins, *Watching What We Eat: The Evolution of Television Cooking Shows* (New York, 2009). See also Nancy A. Walker, *Shaping Our Mothers' World: American Women's Magazines* (Jackson, MS, 2000), pp. 177–88.

66 Sidney Mintz, *Tasting Food, Tasting Freedom: Excursions into Eating, Culture, and the Past* (Boston, 1996), p. 116.

67 Bret Thorn, "Survey: Italian Remains Most Popular Ethnic Cuisine: Consumption Highest in the Northeast," *Nation's Restaurant News*, August 28, 2015, www.nrn.com; "The Mexican Restaurant Industry Landscape: A Popular Choice for Cinco de Mayo and All Year Long," *CHD Expert*, April 29, 2014, www.chd-expert.com. See also Krishnendu Ray, *The Ethnic Restaurateur* (London and New York, 2016), pp. 64–6.

68 The process of how multicultural education, travel, and popular culture is

affected by the fringe or percolates upward, especially by younger generations, is well told by Warren Belasco in *Appetite for Change: How the Counterculture Took on the Food Industry, 1966–1988* (New York, 1989).

69 Jeffrey M. Pilcher, *Planet Taco: A Global History of Mexican Food* (New York, 2012); Sahar Monrreal, "'A novel, spicy delicacy': Tamales, Advertising, and Late 19th-century Imaginative Geographies of Mexico," *Cultural Geographies*, 15 (2008), pp. 449–70.

70 An early and influential study is Tracy N. Poe, "The Origins of Soul Food in Black Urban Identity: Chicago, 1915–1947," *American Studies International*, XXXVII/1 (1999): pp. 4–17. More recent books include Adrian Miller, *Soul Food: The Surprising Story of an American Cuisine, One Plate at a Time* (Charlotte, NC, 2013) and Frederick Douglass Opie, *Hog and Hominy: Soul Food from Africa to America* (New York, 2013).

71 John A. Jackle and Keith A. Sculle, *Fast Food: Roadside Restaurants in the Automobile Age* (Baltimore, 1999), pp. 100–103.

72 Eric Schlosser's *Fast Food Nation* is a good description of how the system worked and how it changed American food—for the worse.

73 Ibid., pp. 111–32 for commentary on flavors; for regional hot dogs and the cultures from which they rise, see Kraig and Carroll, *Man Bites Dog*.

74 Amy Trubek, *A Taste of Place: A Cultural Journey into Terroir* (Berkeley, CA, and Los Angeles, 2008), pp. 195–222.

75 Jennifer A. Jordan, *Edible Memory: The Lure of Heirloom Tomatoes and Other Forgotten Foods* (Chicago, 2015), p. 24.

76 Jayson Lusk, *Unnaturally Delicious: How Science and Technology Are Serving Up Super Foods to Save the World* (New York, 2016), pp. 123–9.

77 Andrew F. Smith, *Junk Food and Fast Food: An Encyclopedia of What We Love to Eat*, 2nd edn (Santa Barbara, CA, 2006), vol. II, p. 67.

78 Ibid., p. 636.

79 John Martin Taylor, *Hoppin' John's Lowcountry Cooking: Recipes and Ruminations from Charleston and the Carolina Coastal Plain* (New York, 1992, rev. 2012).

80 Stephen Schmidt, "When Did Southern Begin?" Manuscript Cookbooks Survey, November 2015, www.manuscriptcookbookssurveycom, accessed February 6, 2017; Edna Lewis, "What Is Southern?" *Gourmet Magazine* (January 2008), www.gourmet.com, accessed February 6, 2017.

81 Leland Ponton, quoted in David Jackson and Gary Marks, "Pig Waste Poisons Rural Waterways," *Chicago Tribune*, August 7, 2016, p. 10.

82 Paul J. Crutzen, "Geology of Mankind," *Nature*, CDXV (3 January 2002), p. 23.

83 Paul J. Crutzen and Christian Schwägerl, "Living in the Anthropocene: Towards a New Global Ethos," *Yale Environment 360*, January 24, 2011, available at http://e360.yale.edu, accessed February 6, 2017; see also Henning Steinfeld et al., *Livestock's Long Shadow*, Food and Agriculture Organization of the United Nations (Rome, 2006).

84 Elizabeth Kolbert, *The Sixth Extinction: An Unnatural History* (New York, 2014).

85 "The Price of Pork," *Chicago Tribune*, www.chicagotribune.com, accessed February 6, 2017; a good account of the system is Ted Genoways, *The Chain: Farm, Factory, and the Fate of Our Food* (New York, 2014).

86 Dan Barber, *The Third Plate: Field Notes on a New Cuisine* (New York, 2014), pp. 221–8.

87 Donald Worster, "Transformations of the Earth: Toward an Agroecological Per-spective in History," *Journal of American History*, LXXVI/4 (1990), pp. 1087–1106.

88 Darryl Fears, "Iowa Farmers Eye Prairie Renaissance," *Chicago Tribune*, August 12, 2016.

89 Jayson Lusk, "Industrial Farms Have Gone Green," *New York Times*, September 25, 2016; Lusk, *Unnaturally Delicious*, pp. 192–3.

90 "Cascadian Farm Partners to Help Scale-Up Kernza®," https://landinstitute. org/cascadian-farm-partners-kernza, accessed March 3, 2017; S. Whelchel and E. P. Berman, "Paying for Perennialism: A Quest for Food and Funding," *Issues in Science and Technology*, XXVIII/1 (Fall 2011), pp. 63–76, accessed March 8, 2017; David Van Tassel and Lee DeHaan, "Wild Plants to the Rescue," *American Scientist*, CI/3 (May–June 201), p. 218.

91 Lusk, *Unnaturally Delicious*, pp. 107–18.

92 Rachel Laudan, "A Plea for Culinary Modernism: Why We Should Love New, Fast, Processed Food," *Gastronomica: The Journal of Critical Food Studies*, 1/1 (Winter 2001), pp. 36–44, available at www.rachellaudan.com, accessed February 6, 2017.

Bibliography

Acosta, Fray Joseph de, *Historia Natural y Moral de las Indias* [1590], vol. II (Madrid, 1894)

Adams, Jean Prescott, *The Business of Being a Housewife* (Chicago, 1917)

Adkins, Nelson F., "James Fenimore Cooper and the Bread and Cheese Club," *Modern Language Notes*, XLVII/2 (February 1932), pp. 71–9

Alger, Horatio, Jr., *Ragged Dick; or Street Life in New York with the Boot Blacks* (Boston, 1868)

Allgor, Catherine, *A Perfect Union: Dolley Madison and the Creation of the American Nation* (New York, 2013)

American Farmland Trust, "Farming on the Edge: The Nation's Best Farmland in the Path of Development," 2015, www.farmland.org

Anderson, Virginia Dejohn, *Creatures of Empire: How Domestic Animals Transformed Early America* (New York, 2004)

Anonymous, *American Husbandry: Containing an Account of the Soil, Climate, Production and Agriculture, of the British Colonies in North-America and the West-Indies; With Observations on the Advantages and Disadvantages of Settling in Them, Compared with Great Britain and Ireland,* vol. I (London, 1775)

Anson Mills, "What We Do—And Why We Do It," www.ansonmills.com, accessed February 6, 2017

Bailyn, Bernard, *The Barbarous Years* (New York, 2012)

Baird, Henry Carey, *Protection of Home Labor and Home Productions Necessary to the Prosperity of the American Farmer* (New York, 1860)

Ball, Carleton R., and Arthur H. Liedigh, "Milo as a Dry Land Grain Crop," U.S. Department of Agriculture, Farmers' Bulletin 322 (Washington, DC, 1908)

Barber, Dan, *The Third Plate: Field Notes on a New Cuisine* (New York, 2014)

Barr, Daniel P., *Unconquered: The Iroquois League at War in Colonial America* (Westport, CT, 2006)

Barsam, Richard, *Nonfiction Film: A Critical History* (Bloomington, IN, 1973, rev. 1992)

Bateman, Fred, "Improvement in American Dairy Farming, 1850–1910: A Quantitative Analysis," *Journal of Economic History*, XXVIII/2 (June 1968), pp. 255–73

Bathe, Greville, and Dorothy Bathe, *Oliver Evans: A Chronicle of Early American Engineering* (Philadelphia, 1935)

Beahrs, Andrew, *Twain's Feast: Searching for America's Lost Foods in the Footsteps of*

Samuel Clemens (New York, 2010)

——, "Twain's Feast: 'The American' at Table," *Gastronomica: The Journal of Food and Culture*, VII/2 (Spring 2007), pp. 26–34

——, "Mark Twain: Writer, Humorist, Locavore," *The Atlantic*, July 14, 2010, www.theatlantic.com

Beatty, Richmond C., and William J. Mulloy, ed. and trans., *William Byrd's Natural History of Virginia or The Newly Discovered Eden* (Richmond, VA, 1940)

Bechtel, Stefan, *Mr. Hornaday's War: How a Peculiar Victorian Zookeeper Waged a Lonely Crusade for Wildlife that Changed the World* (Boston, 2012)

Beck, Ann Flesor, "Greek Immigration to, and Settlement in, Central Illinois, 1880–1930," PhD diss., University of Illinois at Urbana-Champaign, 2014

Becker, Raymond B., *Dairy Cattle Breeds, Origins and Development* (Gainesville, FL, 1973)

Beiler, Rosalind J., "German-speaking Immigrants in the British Atlantic World, 1680–1730," OAH *Magazine of History*, XVIII/3 (April 2004), pp. 19–22

Belasco, Warren, *Appetite for Change: How the Counterculture Took on the Food Industry, 1966–1988* (New York, 1989)

——, *Meals to Come: The Future of American Food* (Berkeley, CA, 2006)

Belasco, Warren, and Philip Scranton, eds., *Food Nations: Selling Taste in Consumer Societies* (New York, 2002)

Bellwood, Peter, *First Farmers: The Origins of Agricultural Societies* (Malden, MA, 2005)

Bennett, John W., Harvey L. Smith, and Herbert Passin, "Food and Culture in Southern Illinois: A Preliminary Report," *American Sociological Review*, VII/5 (1942), pp. 645–60

Bentley, Amy, "American Abundance Examined: David M. Potter's *People of Plenty* and the Study of Food," *Digest: An Interdisciplinary Study of Food and Foodways*, XV (1995), pp. 20–24

Bernheim, G. D., *History of the German Settlements and of the Lutheran Church in North and South Carolina* (Philadelphia, 1872)

Bethke, Paul C., et al., "History and Origin of Russet Burbank (Netted Gem), a Sport of Burbank," *American Journal of Potato Research*, XCI (2014), pp. 594–609

Birdsall, Stephen S., and John Florin, *An Outline of American Geography: Regional Landscapes of the United States* (Washington, DC, 1990)

Blayney, Don P., "The Changing Landscape of U.S. Milk Production," USDA Statistical Bulletin no. 978, June 2002, http://usda.mannlib.cornell.edu, accessed January 26, 2017

Blonigen, Beth, "A Re-examination of the Slave Diet," Thesis, College of St. Benedict/St. John's University, 2004

Bobrow-Strain, Aaron, *White Bread: A Social History of the Store-bought Loaf* (Boston, 2012)

Bogart, E. L., and C. M. Thompson, *The Centennial History of Illinois*, IV: *The Industrial State 1870–1893* (Springfield, IL, 1920)

Bolzius, Johann Martin, "Reliable Answer to Some Submitted Questions Concerning the Land Carolina," ed. and trans. Klaus G. Loewald, Beverly Starika, and Paul S. Taylor, *William and Mary Quarterly*, 3rd ser., XIV (April 1957), pp. 223–61

Bourget, Paul, *Outre-mer: Impressions of America* (London, 1895)

Boyle, T. Coraghessan, *The Road to Wellville* (New York, 1993)

Branson, George, "Early Flour Mills in Indiana," *Indiana Magazine of History*, xxii/1 (March 1926), pp. 20–27

Braudel, Ferdinand, *The Structures of Everyday Life: The Limits of the Possible* [1973], trans. Siân Reynold (New York, 1982)

Breen, A.T.H., "An Empire of Goods: The Anglicization of Colonial America, 1690–1776," *Journal of British Studies*, xxv/4 (1986), pp. 467–99

Bremer, A. Jeff, "Frontier Capitalism Market Migration to Rural Central Missouri, 1815–1860," in *Southern Society and Its Transformations, 1790–1860*, ed. Susanna Delfino, Michele Gillespie, and Louis M. Kyriakoudes (Columbia, MO, 2011), pp. 78–100

Brennan, Greg, et al., "Adaptive Gene Amplification as an Intermediate Step in the Expansion of Virus Host Range," *PLOS Pathogens*, x/3 (March 2014), www.plospathogens.org, accessed January 17, 2017

Bridenbaugh, Carl, *The Colonial Craftsman* (New York, 1950)

Brigham, Albert Perry, *Geographic Influences in American History* (New York, 1903)

Broehl, Wayne G., *John Deere's Company: A History of Deere & Company and Its Times* (New York, 1984)

Brown, Mrs. W. W., compiler, *The Illinois Cook Book; from Recipes Contributed by The Ladies of Paris, and Published for the Benefit of Grace (Episcopal) Church* (Claremont, NH, 1881)

Bryer, Rob, "Americanism and Financial Accounting Theory—Part 1: Was America Born Capitalist?" *Critical Perspectives on Accounting*, xxiii (2012), pp. 511–55

Bucher, Anne, and Melanie Villines, *The Greatest Thing since Sliced Cheese: Stories of Kraft Foods Inventors and their Inventions* (Northfield, IL, 2005)

Bureau of Labor Statistics, "Consumer Expenditures—2014," September 3, 2015, www.bls.gov

Burgess, Thomas, *Greeks in America: An Account of their Coming, Progress, Customs, Living, and Aspirations* (Boston, 1913)

Bushman, Richard L., *Joseph Smith and the Beginnings of Mormonism* (Urbana, IL, 1984)

Bushman, Richard Lyman, "Markets and Composite Farms in Early America," *William and Mary Quarterly*, lv/3 (July 1998), pp. 351–74

Byrd, William, of Westover, *The Westover Manuscripts: Containing the History of the Dividing Line betwixt Virginia and North Carolina; A Journey to the Land of Eden*, A.D. *1733; And a Progress to the Mines. Written from 1728 to 1736, and now first Published* (Petersburg, VA, 1841), p. 129, available at www.docsouth.unc.edu, accessed January 20, 2017

Cahn, William, *Out of the Cracker Barrel: The Nabisco Story from Animal Crackers to Zuzus* (New York, 1971)

Cañizares-Esguerra, Jorge, "How Derivative was Humboldt? Microcosmic Nature Narratives in Early Modern Spanish America and the (Other) Origins of Humboldt's Ecological Sensibilities," in *Colonial Botany: Science, Commerce, and Politics in the Early Modern World*, ed. Londa Schiebinger and Claudia Swan (Philadelphia, 2004), pp. 148–65

"Canned Beef Recipes," Bureau of Home Economics, U.S. Department of Agriculture in Cooperation with the Federal Surplus Relief Corporation (Washington, DC, 1934)

Carroll, Abigail, *Three Squares: The Invention of the American Meal* (New York, 2013)

Carson, Barbara G., *Ambitious Appetites: Dining, Behavior, and Patterns of Consumption in Federal Washington* (Washington, DC, 1990)

Cather, Willa, *My Ántonia* (Boston, 1918. repr. Mineola, NY, 2011)

Chapin, Robert Coit, *The Standard of Living among Workingmen's Families in New York City* (New York, 1909)

Charlevoix, P.F.X. de, SJ, *History and General Description of New France* (1761), trans. John Gilmary Shea, 6 vols. (New York, 1866)

Cheathem, Mark R., *Andrew Jackson, Southerner* (Baton Rouge, LA, 2013)

Child, Mrs. (Lydia Maria Child), *The Frugal Housewife* (Boston, 1829), 12th edn. as *The American Frugal Housewife* (Boston, 1832)

Choate, Judith, and James Canora, *Dining at Delmonico's: The Story of America's Oldest Restaurant* (New York, 2008)

Clark, Peter U., and Alan C. Mix, "Ice Sheets and Sea Level of the Last Glacial Maximum," *Quaternary Science Reviews*, XXI/1–3 (2002), pp. 1–7

Cleary, Patricia, "Contested Terrain Environmental Agendas and Settlement Choices in Colonial St. Louis," in *Common Fields: An Environmental History of St. Louis*, ed. Andrew Hurley (St. Louis, 1997), pp. 71–2

Clemen, Rudolf Alexander, *The American Livestock and Meat Industry* (New York, 1923)

Coe, Andrew, *Chop Suey: A Cultural History of Chinese Food in the United States* (New York and Oxford, 2009)

Coe, Sophie, "A Tale of Two Banquets," in *Oxford Symposium on Food and Cookery 1991: Public Eating: Proceedings*, ed. Harlan Walker (London, 1992), pp. 61–6

Cohen, Jennie, "Native Americans Hailed from Siberian Highlands, DNA Reveals," *History in the Headlines*, January 26, 2012, www.history.com

Collins, Mrs. A. M., *Mrs. Collins' Table Receipts: Adapted to Western Housewifery* (New Albany, IN, 1851), repr. as *The Great Western Cook Book or Table Receipts, Adapted to Western Housewifery* (New York, 1857)

Collins, Douglas, *America's Favorite Food: The Story of Campbell Soup Company* (New York, 1994)

Collins, Kathleen, *Watching What We Eat: The Evolution of Television Cooking Shows* (New York, 2009)

Collins, Robert M., "David Potter's *People of Plenty* and the Recycling of Consensus History," *Reviews in American History*, XVI/2 (1988), pp. 321–35

Cook, Ebenezer, *The Sot-weed Factor: Or, a Voyage to Maryland, a Satyr* (London, 1708; repr. New York, 1865)

Cooper, James Fenimore, *The Last of the Mohicans* [1826], intro. by Richard Slotkin (New York, 1968)

Corson, Juliet, *The "Home Queen" World's Fair Souvenir Cook Book: Two thousand valuable recipes on cookery and household economy, menus, table etiquette, toilet, etc. contributed by over two hundred World's Fair lady managers, wives of governors and other ladies of position and influence* (Chicago, 1893)

Cosgrove-Mather, Bootie, "Poll: Creationism Trumps Evolution," CBS News, November 22, 2004, www.cbsnews.com

Cowan, Ruth Schwartz, *More Work for Mother: The Ironies of Household Technologies from the Open Hearth to the Microwave* (New York, 1983)

Coyle, Grace L., "Women in the Clerical Occupations," *Annals of the American Academy of Political and Social Science*, CXLIII/1 (May 1929), pp. 180–87

Crawford, Kristina M., "Daily Bread: Prehistoric Cooking Features in the Northern Sacramento Valley, California," MA thesis, California State University, Chico, 2011

Cronon, William, *Changes in the Land: Indians, Colonists and the Ecology of New England* (New York, 1983, rev. 2003)

Crosby, Alfred W., *The Columbian Exchange: Biological and Cultural Consequences of 1492* (Westport, CT, 1972)

——, *Ecological Imperialism: The Biological Expansion of Europe, 900–1900* (Cambridge, 1986, rev. 2004)

——, *Germs, Seeds & Animals: Studies in Ecological History* (Armonk, NY, 1993)

Crowley, Carolyn Hughes, "Meet Me at the Automat." *Smithsonian* (August 2001), pp. 22–4

Crutzen, Paul J., "Geology of Mankind," *Nature*, CDXV (3 January 2002), p. 23

——, and Christian Schwägerl, "Living in the Anthropocene: Towards a New Global Ethos," *Yale Environment 360*, January 24, 2011, available at http://e360.yale.edu, accessed February 6, 2017

Curran, William S., and Dwight D. Lingenfelter, "Johnsongrass and Shattercane Control: An Integrated Approach" (2016), http://extension.psu.edu, accessed January 24, 2017

Cutler, William Parker, Julia Perkins Cutler, E. C. Dawes, and Peter Force, eds., *Life, Journals and Correspondence of Rev. Manasseh Cutler, LL.D.* (Cincinnati, 1888)

"The Dairy: Process of Cheese Making," *Genesee Farmer and Gardener's Journal*, v/31 (August 1, 1835), pp. 242–3; v/32 (August 8, 1835), p. 253

Danhof, Clarence H., *Change in Agriculture: The Northern United States, 1820–1870* (Cambridge, MA, 1969)

Daniel, Pete, *Breaking the Land: The Transformation of Cotton, Tobacco, and Rice Cultures since 1880* (Urbana, IL, 1986)

Davies, Margery W., *Woman's Place is at the Typewriter: Office Work and Office Workers, 1870–1930* (Philadelphia, 1982)

Davis, Robert Scott, "The Mystery Book and the Forgotten Founding Father," *Journal of the American Revolution*, July 17, 2014, https://allthingsliberty.com

Davis, William T., ed., *Bradford's History of Plymouth Plantation, 1606–1646* (New York, 1908)

Deetz, James, and Patricia Scott Deetz, *The Times of Their Lives: Life, Love, and Death in Plymouth Colony* (New York, 2000)

Department of Ecology, State of Washington, "Non-native, Invasive, Freshwater Plants," www.ecy.wa.gov, accessed July 2, 2015

Derry, T. K., and Trevor I. Williams, *A Short History of Technology: From the Earliest Times to A.D. 1900* (Oxford, 1960)

Dickens, Charles, *American Notes for General Circulation* (London, 1842)

Diehl, Lorraine B., and Marianne Hardart, *The Automat: The History, Recipes, and Allure of Horn & Hardart's Masterpiece* (New York, 2002)

Dimitri, Carolyn, Anne Effland, and Neilson Conklin, "The 20th Century Transformation of U.S. Agriculture and Farm Policy," *United States Department of Agriculture, Economic Information Bulletin Number 3* (June 2005)

Diner, Hasia R., *Hungering for America: Italian, Irish, and Jewish Foodways in the Age of Migration* (Cambridge, MA, 2001)

Dirks, Robert, *Food in the Gilded Age: What Ordinary Americans Ate* (Baltimore, 2016)

Dobie, J. Frank, *The Longhorns* (Austin, TX, 1980)

Dolfman, Michael L., and Denis M. McSweeney, *100 Years of U.S. Consumer Spending: Data for the Nation, New York City, and Boston*, BLS Report 991 (Washington, DC, 2006), www.bls.gov, accessed February 1, 2017

Donck, Adriaen van der, *A Description of New Netherland*, ed. Charles T. Gehring and William A. Starna, trans. Diederik Willem Goedhuys (Lincoln, NE, 2008)

Dry, Stanley, "A Short History of Gumbo," Southern Foodways Alliance, www.southernfoodways.org, accessed April 5, 2015

Du Bois, Christine M., "Changing Soy Production and Consumption in the United States," in *The World of Soy*, ed. Christine M. Du Bois, Chee-Beng Tan, and Sidney Mintz (Urbana, IL, 2008), pp. 208–33

Duncan, Sally L., "Leaving it to Beaver," *Environment*, XXVI/3 (April, 1984), pp. 41–5

Dunn, Walter Scott, *Frontier Profit and Loss: The British Army and the Fur Traders, 1760–1764* (Westport, CT, 1998)

Durand, Loyal, Jr., "The Migration of Cheese Manufacture in the United States," *Annals of the Association of American Geographers*, LXII/4 (December 1952), pp. 263–70

Earle, Rebecca, "'If You Eat Their Food . . .': Diets and Bodies in Early Colonial Spanish America," *American Historical Review*, CXV/3 (June 2010), pp. 688–713

Eastwood, Carolyn, *Chicago Jewish Street Peddlers* (Chicago, 1991)

Eben, Carl Theo., trans., *Gottlieb Mittelberger's Journey to Pennsylvania in the Year 1750 and Return to Germany in the Year 1754, Containing not only a Description of the Country According to its Present Condition, but also a Detailed Account of the Sad and Unfortunate Circumstances of Most of the Germans that Have Emigrated, or are Emigrating to that Country* (Philadelphia, 1898)

Eisenman, Stephen F., *The Cry of Nature: Art and the Making of Animal Rights* (London, 2016)

Emerson, Ralph Waldo, *Journals and Miscellaneous Notebooks of Ralph Waldo Emerson*, VII: *1838–1842*, ed. A. W. Plumstead and Harrison Hayford (Cambridge, MA, 1969)

——, "Self-Reliance," in *Essays By Ralph Waldo Emerson*, ed. Edna H. L. Turpin (New York, 1907)

Emerson, Thomas E., and R. Barry Lewis, eds., *Cahokia and the Hinterlands: Middle Mississippian Cultures of the Midwest* (Urbana, IL, 2000)

Erdman, H. E., "The 'Associated Dairies' of New York as Precursors of American Agricultural Cooperatives," *Agricultural History*, XXXVI/2 (April 1962), pp. 82–90

Evans, Oliver, *The Young Mill-Wright and Miller's Guide: Illustrated by Twenty-eight Descriptive Plates and a Description of an Improved Merchant Flour Mill with Engravings by C. and O. Evans, Engineers* (Philadelphia, 1795)

Fagan, Brian, *The First North Americans: An Archaeological Journey* (London, 2011)

Falconbridge, Alexander, *An Account of the Slave Trade on the Coast of Africa* (London, 1788)

Farrell, James T., *A World I Never Made* (Urbana, IL, 1936, repr. 2007)

Faust, Franz X., Cristóbal Gnecco, Hermann Mannstein, and Jörg Stamm, "Evidence for the Postconquest Demographic Collapse of the Americas in Historical CO_2 Levels," *Earth Interactions*, X/11 (May 2006), http://journals.ametsoc.org, accessed January 18, 2017

Fears, Darryl, "Iowa Farmers Eye Prairie Renaisssance," *Chicago Tribune*, August 12, 2016

Felius, Marleen, Marie-Louise Beerling, David S. Buchanan, Bert Theunissen, Peter A. Koolmees, and Johannes A. Lenstra, "On the History of Cattle Genetic Resources," *Diversity*, VI/4 (2014), pp. 705–50

Fenn, Elizabeth A., *Pox Americana: The Great Smallpox Epidemic of 1775–82* (New York, 2001)

Ferguson, Eugene S., "On the Origin and Development of American Mechanical 'Know-how,'" *Midcontinent American Studies Journal*, III/2 (Fall 1962), pp. 3–26

Ferguson, Natalie, "A Brief History of the Dolly Varden Dress Craze," in *A Frolic through Time*, August 23, 2008, http://zipzipinkspot.blogspot.com, accessed January 28, 2017

Fernandez-Cornejo, Jorge, et al., "Pesticide Use in U.S. Agriculture: 21 Selected Crops, 1960–2008," *United States Department of Agriculture, Economic Information Bulletin 124* (May 2014), www.ers.usda.gov

Fiege, Mark, *Irrigated Eden: The Making of an Agricultural Landscape in the American West* (Seattle, 2009)

Field to Market: The Alliance for Sustainable Agriculture, "Environmental and Socioeconomic Indicators for Measuring Outcomes of On-farm Agricultural Production in the United States," 3rd edn., December 2016, http://fieldtomarket.org

Fischer, David Hackett, *Albion's Seed: Four British Folkways in America* (Oxford and New York, 1989)

Fitzgerald, Deborah, *Every Farm a Factory: The Industrial Ideal in American Agriculture* (New Haven, CT, 2003)

Flint, Timothy, *Recollections of the Last Ten Years, Passed in Occasional Residences and Journeyings in the Valley of the Mississippi, from Pittsburg and the Missouri to the Gulf of Mexico, and from Florida to the Spanish Frontier: in a Series of Letters to the Rev. James Flint, of Salem, Massachusetts* (Boston, 1826)

Flores, Dan, "Wars over Buffalo Stories versus Stories on the Northern Plains," in *Native Americans and the Environment: Perspectives on the Ecological Indian*, ed. Michael E. Harkin (Lincoln, NE, 2007)

Food Marketing Institute, "Supermarket Facts," 2015, www.fmi.org

Ford, Henry, with Samuel Crowther, *My Life and Work* (New York, 1923)

Fribourg, H. A., D. B. Hannaway and C. P. West, eds., *Tall Fescue for the Twenty-first Century*, Agronomy Monographs 53 (Madison, WI, 2009); available at http://forages.oregonstate.edu, accessed January 24, 2017

Funderburg, Anne Cooper, *Sundae Best: A History of Soda Fountains* (Madison, WI, 2002)

Furlong, Patrick J., "James Oliver," *Indiana Historical Society*, www.indianahistory.org, accessed December 6, 2014

Gabaccia, Donna, *We Are What We Eat: Ethnic Food and the Making of Americans* (Cambridge, MA, 2000)

Garland, Hamlin, *Boy Life on the Prairie* (New York, 1899), rev. edn. of articles from *American Magazine* [Brooklyn], VIII (1888)

Garrick, David, and George Colman, the elder, *The Clandestine Marriage* (London, 1776)

Genoways, Ted, *The Chain: Farm, Factory, and the Fate of Our Food* (New York, 2014)

"The Georgia Peach History," University of Georgia College of Agricultural and Environmental Sciences, 2015, http://caes2.caes.uga.edu, accessed February 2, 2017

Gesner, C. W., "Concerning Restaurants," *Harper's New Monthly Magazine*, XXXII/191 (April 1866), pp. 591–4

Ghanta, Praveen, "List of Foods by Environmental Impact and Energy Efficiency," *The Oil Drum*, March 2, 2010, www.theoildrum.com, accessed February 6, 2017

Giedion, Sigfried, *Mechanization Takes Command* (New York, 1948)

Glasse, Hannah, *The Art of Cookery Made Plain and Easy* (London, 1747), rev. Alexandria, VA, 1805, facsimile with foreword by Karen Hess (Boston, MA, 1997)

Gordon, Robert B., *American Iron 1607–1900* (Baltimore, 1996)

Gordon, Robert J., *The Rise and Fall of American Growth* (Princeton, NJ, 2016)

Graham, R. B. Cunninghame, *The Horses of the Conquest*, ed. Robert Moorman Denhardt (Norman, OK, 1949)

Grasso, Christopher, "The Experimental Philosophy of Farming: Jared Eliot and the Cultivation of Connecticut," *William and Mary Quarterly*, L/3 (July 1993), pp. 502–28

Gray, Lewis Cecil, assisted by Esther Katherine Thompson, *History of Agriculture in the Southern United States to 1860*, 2 vols. (Washington, DC, 1933)

Greene, Anna N., "War Horses, Equine Technology in the American Civil War," in *Industrializing Organisms: Introducing Evolutionary History*, ed. Susan Schrepfer and Philip Scranton (New York, 2004), pp. 143–65

Greeno, Follett L., ed., *Obed Hussey, Who, of All Inventors, Made Bread Cheap* (Rochester, NY, 1912)

Greville, Sir Fulke, *Life of Sir Philip Sidney, Etc.* [1652], foreword by Nowell Smith (London, 1907)

Grimes, William, *Appetite City: A Culinary History of New York* (New York, 2009)

Grob, Gerald N., *The Deadly Truth: A History of Disease in America* (Cambridge, MA, 2009)

Grubb, Farley, "German Immigration to Pennsylvania, 1709 to 1820," *Journal of Interdisciplinary History*, XX/3 (Winter 1990), pp. 417–36

Grundy, Joan E., "The Hereford Bull: His Contribution to New World and Domestic Beef Supplies," *Agricultural History Review*, L/1 (2002), pp. 69–88

Gucker, Corey L., "Euphorbia esula," Fire Effects Information System. U.S. Department of Agriculture, Forest Service, Rocky Mountain Research Station, Fire Sciences Laboratory (2010), www.fs.fed.us, accessed January 26, 2017

Gunderson, Gordon W., *National School Lunch Program: Background and Development*, Food and Nutrition Service 63 (Washington, DC, 1971)

Gutman, Richard J. S., *The American Diner, Then and Now* (Baltimore and London, 1993)

H.H. [Helen Jackson], "Outdoor Industries in Southern California," *The Century Illustrated Monthly Magazine*, XXVI/6 (October 1883), pp. 803–20

Haley, Andrew P., *Turning the Tables: Restaurants and the Rise of the American Middle Class, 1880–1920* (Chapel Hill, NC, 2011)

Hall, Robert L., "Food Crops, Medicinal Plants, and the Atlantic Slave Trade," in *African American Foodways*, ed. Anne L. Bower (Urbana, IL, 2007), pp. 18–44

Hämäläinen, Pekka, "The Rise and Fall of Plains Indian Horse Cultures," *Journal of American History*, XC/3 (December 2003), pp. 833–62

Hardin, Philomelia Ann Maria Antoinette, *Every Body's Cook and Receipt Book: But More Particularly Designed for Buckeyes, Hoosiers , Wolverines, Corncrackers , Suckers, and All Epicures Who Wish to Live with the Present Times* (Cleveland, 1842)

Hardke, J. T., "Trends in Arkansas Rice Production, 2014," in *B. R. Wells Arkansas Rice Research Studies 2014*, ed. R. J. Norman and K.A.K. Moldenhauer (Fayetteville, AR, 2014), pp. 11–22

Hardke, Jarrod, and Terry Siebenmorgen, "Rice Grades," in *Arkansas Rice Production Handbook*, ed. Jarrod Hardke (Little Rock, AR, [2013]), pp. 163–5

Harkin, Michael E., ed., *Native Americans and the Environment: Perspectives on the Ecological Indian* (Lincoln, NE, 2007)

Harriman, John C., ed., "'Most Excellent—far fam'd and far fetch'd Cheese': An Anthology of Jeffersonian Era Poetry," *American Magazine and Historical Chronicle*, II/2 (1986–7), pp. 1–26

Harris, Thaddeus Mason, *The Journal of a Tour into the Territory Northwest of the Alleghany [sic] Mountains, Made in the Spring of the Year 1803: With a Geographical and Historical Account of the State of Ohio* (Boston, 1805)

Hayami, Yūjirō, and Vernon W. Ruttan, *Agricultural Development: An International Perspective* (Baltimore, 1971, rev. 1985)

Hazen, Theodore R., "The History of Flour Milling in Early America," www.angelfire.com, accessed April 6, 2015

Henlein, Paul C., "Cattle Driving from the Ohio Country, 1800–1850," *Agricultural History*, XXVIII/2 (1954), pp. 83–95

——, "Shifting Range-Feeder Patterns in the Ohio Valley before 1860," *Agricultural History*, XXXI/1 (1957), pp. 1–12

Hess, Karen, introduction to facsimile edition of Amelia Simmons, *American Cookery* (Bedford, MA, 1996)

Higginson, Rev. Francis, *New-Englands Plantation* (London, 1630), repr. in *New-Englands Plantation with The Sea Journal and Other Writings* (Cambridge, MA, 1908)

Hilliard, Sam B., "Pork in the Ante-bellum South: The Geography of Self-sufficiency," *Annals of the Association of American Geographers*, LIX/3 (1969), pp. 461–80

Hills, Richard Leslie, *Power from Wind: A History of Windmill Technology* (Cambridge, 1996)

Hindle, Brooke, "The Exhilaration of Early American Technology," in *Early American Technology: Making and Doing Things from the Colonial Era to 1850*, ed. Judith A. McGaw (Chapel Hill, NC, 1994), pp. 40–67

Hine, Thomas, *The Total Package: The Evolution and Secret Meanings of Boxes, Bottles, Cans, and Tubes* (Boston, 1995)

"The History of Timothy Grass Hay," 2009, www.estyranch.com, accessed January 24, 2017

Holley, Donald, "Mechanical Cotton Picker," EH.net, June 16, 2003, https://eh.net

Holzworth, Larry, Jeff Mosley, Dennis Cash, David Koch, and Kelly Crane, "Dryland Pastures in Montana and Wyoming: Species and Cultivars, Seeding Techniques and Grazing Management," *Montana State University Extension Service*, rev. Fall 2003, www.animalrange.montana.edu, accessed January 25, 2017

Hooker, Richard J., *Food and Drink in America: A History* (Indianapolis, 1981)

Hornaday, William T., *Our Vanishing Wild Life: Its Extermination and Preservation* (New York, 1913)

Horowitz, Roger, *Putting Meat on the American Table: Taste, Technology, Transformation* (Baltimore, 2006)

Hounshell, David, *From the American System to Mass Production, 1800–1932: The Development of Manufacturing Technology in the United States* (Baltimore, 1984)

Howat, John K., introduction to *American Paradise: The World of the Hudson River School* (New York, 1988).

Hubbard, Lester A., and Kenly W. Whitelock, eds., "The Apex Boarding House," *Ballads and Songs from Utah* (Salt Lake City, 1961)

Hughes, Thomas P., *American Genesis* (New York, 1989)

Hume, A. N., *Trials with Commercial Varieties of Canning Peas*, South Dakota State University Agricultural Experiment Station, Bulletin 221 (Brookings, SD, 1927)

Hungerford, Edward, *The Personality of American Cities* (New York, 1913)

Hutchinson, William T., *Cyrus Hall McCormick*, 2 vols. (New York, 1930–35)

Irving, Washington, *A History of New-York from the Beginning of the World to the End of the Dutch Dynasty, by Diedrich Knickerbocker* [1809], author's revised edn. (New York, 1848)

——, *A Tour on the Prairies* (New York, 1832)

——, "The Legend of Sleepy Hollow," in *The Sketch Book of Geoffrey Crayon, Gent.* (London, 1820)

Isenberg, Andrew C., *The Destruction of the Bison: An Environmental History, 1750–1920* (Cambridge, 2001).

Isenberg, Nancy, *White Trash: The 400-year Untold History of Class in America* (New York, 2016)

Jackle, John A., and Keith A. Sculle, *Fast Food: Roadside Restaurants in the Automobile Age* (Baltimore, 1999).

Jackson, David, and Gary Marks, "Pig Waste Poisons Rural Waterways," *Chicago Tribune*, August 7, 2016

Jacobs, Jaap, *New Netherland: A Dutch Colony in Seventeenth-century America* (Leiden, 2005)

Jaffe, JoAnn, and Michael Gertler, "Victual Vicissitudes: Consumer Deskilling and the (Gendered) Transformation of Food Systems," *Agriculture and Human Values*, XXIII (2006), pp. 143–62

Jenkins, Virginia Scott, *The Lawn: A History of an American Obsession* (Washington, DC, 1994)

John, Richard R., review of *The Market Revolution: Jacksonian America, 1815–1846*, by Charles Sellers, *New England Quarterly*, XLVI/2 (June 1993), pp. 302–5

Jones, E. L., "Creative Disruptions in American Agriculture, 1620–1820," *Agricultural History*, XLVIII/4 (October 1974), pp. 510–28

Jordan, Jennifer A., *Edible Memory: The Lure of Heirloom Tomatoes and Other Forgotten Foods* (Chicago, 2015)

Judge, Arthur I., ed., *Souvenir of the 7th Annual Convention of the National Canners' and Allied Associations, Baltimore, Feb'y 2 to 7, 1914* (Baltimore, 1914)

Kalm, Peter [Pehr], *Travels into North America*, trans. John Reinhold Forster, 2 vols. (London, 1773)

Kasson, John F., *Rudeness and Civility: Manners in Nineteenth-century Urban America* (New York, 1991)

Kauffman, Henry, *The American Axe: A Survey of their Development and their Makers* (Brattleboro, VT, 1972, repr. Morgantown, PA, 2007)

Kellogg, Elizabeth A., "Evolutionary History of the Grasses," *Plant Physiology*, CXXV (2001), pp. 1198–1205

Kellogg, Ella Eaton, *Science in the Kitchen* (Battle Creek, MI, 1892, 4th edn. 1904)

Kelton, Paul, *Epidemics and Enslavement: Biological Catastrophe in the Native Southeast, 1492–1715* (Lincoln, NE, 2007)

Kennedy, Victor S., and Linda L. Breisch, "Sixteen Decades of Political Management of the Oyster Fishery in Maryland's Chesapeake Bay," *Journal of Environmental Management*, CLXIV (1983), pp. 153–71

Kerrigan, William, *Johnny Appleseed and the American Orchard: A Cultural History* (Baltimore, 2012)

Kindstedt, Paul, *Cheese and Culture: A History of Cheese and its Place in Western Civilization* (White River Junction, VT, 2012)

Kipling, Rudyard, *American Notes* (New York, 1899)

Kirby, Jack Temple, *The Mockingbird Song: Ecological Landscapes of the South* (Chapel Hill, NC, 2006)

Koeppel, Dan, *Banana: The Fate of the Fruit that Changed the World* (New York, 2008)

Kolbert, Elizabeth, *The Sixth Extinction: An Unnatural History* (New York, 2014)

Kraig, Bruce, *Hot Dog: A Global History* (London, 2009)

——, "Pigs," in *The Oxford Encyclopedia of Food and Drink in America*, ed. Andrew F. Smith, 2nd edn. (New York, 2013), II, pp. 836–40

——, "Toffenetti, Dario," in Carol Haddix, Bruce Kraig, and Colleen Taylor Sen, *The Encyclopedia of Chicago Food* (Urbana, IL, forthcoming)

——, and Patty Carroll, *Man Bites Dog: Hot Dog Culture in America* (Lanham, MD, 2012)

——, and Colleen Taylor Sen, eds., *Street Food around the World: An Encyclopedia of Food and Culture* (Santa Barbara, CA, 2012), rev. as *Street Food: Everything You Need to Know about Open-Air Stands, Carts, and Food Trucks across the Globe* (Evanston, IL, 2017)

Krech, Shepherd, III, *The Ecological Indian: Myth and History* (New York, 1999)

Kulikoff, Allan, *The Agrarian Origins of American Capitalism* (Charlotte, NC, 1992)

——, "Capitalism in the Core, Barbarism in the Periphery?" *Reviews in American History*, XLII (2014), pp. 207–12

Lackey, Kris, "Eighteenth-century Aesthetic Theory and the Nineteenth-century Traveler in Trans-Allegheny America: F. Trollope, Dickens, Irving and Parkman," *American Studies*, XXXII/1 (1991), pp. 33–48

Lakwete, Angela, *Inventing the Cotton Gin: Machine and Myth in Antebellum America* (Baltimore, 2003)

Lambeck, Kurt, Yusuke Yokoyama, and Tony Purcell, "Into and Out of the Last Glacial Maximum: Sea-level Change during Oxygen Isotope Stages 3 and 2," *Quaternary Science Reviews*, XXI/1–3 (2002), pp. 343–60

Latner, Thomas B., "Preserving 'the natural equality of rank and influence': Liberalism, Republicanism, and Equality of Condition in Jacksonian Politics," in *The Culture of the Market: Historical Essays*, ed. Thomas L. Haskell and Richard F. Teichgraeber III (Cambridge, 1993), pp. 189–230

Laudan, Rachel, "A Plea for Culinary Modernism: Why We Should Love New, Fast, Processed Food," *Gastronomica: The Journal of Critical Food Studies*, I/I (Winter 2001), pp. 36–44, available at www.rachellaudan.com, accessed February 6, 2017

——, and Jeffery M. Pilcher, "Chiles, Chocolate, and Race in New Spain: Glancing Backward to Spain or Looking Forward to Mexico?" *Eighteenth Century Life*, XXIII (May 1999), pp. 59–70

Lears, Jackson, *Fables of Abundance: A Cultural History of Advertising in America* (New York, 1994)

Lee, Guy A., "The Historical Significance of the Chicago Grain Elevator System," *Agricultural History*, XI/I (1937), pp. 16–32

Lemmer, George F., "The Spread of Improved Cattle through the Eastern United States to 1850," *Agricultural History*, XXI/2 (1947), pp. 79–93

Lemon, James T., "The Agricultural Practices of National Groups in Eighteenth-century Southeastern Pennsylvania," *Geographical Review*, LVI/4 (October 1966), pp. 467–96

Le Page du Pratz, Antoine-Simon, *The History of Louisiana: Or of the Western Parts of Virginia and Carolina: Containing a Description of the Countries that Lie on Both Sides of the River Mississippi: with an Account of the Settlements, Inhabitants, Soil, Climate, and Products* [1758] (London, 1774)

Levenstein, Harvey, *Revolution at the Table: The Transformation of the American Diet* (New York and Oxford, 1988)

Lewis, Edna, "What Is Southern?" *Gourmet Magazine* (January 2008), www.gourmet.com, accessed February 6, 2017

Lind, Michael, *Land of Promise: An Economic History of the United States* (New York, 2012)

Linsenmeyer, Helen Walker, *Cooking Plain: Illinois Country Style*, foreword by Bruce Kraig (Carbondale, IL, 1976, repr. 2011)

Longfellow, Henry Wadsworth, "The Village Blacksmith," in *Ballads and Other Poems* (Cambridge, MA, 1842 [1840]), pp. 99–102

Lorentz, Pare, writer and dir., *The River* (1938), 31 minutes. Documentary for U.S. Farm Resettlement Administration

——, *The Plow that Broke the Plains* (1936), 25 minutes. Documentary for U.S. Farm Resettlement Administration

Love, John F., *McDonald's: Behind the Arches* (New York, 1986, rev. 1995)

Lusk, Jayson, "Industrial Farms Have Gone Green," *New York Times*, September 25, 2016

——, *Unnaturally Delicious: How Science and Technology Are Serving Up Super Foods to Save the World* (New York, 2016)

Macaulay, David, *Mill* (New York, 1983)

McClelland, Peter D., *Sowing Modernity: America's First Agricultural Revolution* (Ithaca, NY, 1997)

McCloskey, Dierdre, *Bourgeois Equality: How Ideas, Not Capital or Institutions, Enriched the World* (Chicago, 2016)

McCoy, Joseph G., *Historic Sketches of the Cattle Trade of the West and Southwest* (Kansas City, MO, 1874)

McGaw, Judith A., "Agricultural Tool Ownership," in *Early American Technology: Making and Doing Things from the Colonial Era to 1850*, ed. Judith A. McGaw (Chapel Hill, NC, and London, 1994), pp. 328–57

McHatton, Tomas H., "History of the Georgia Peach Industry," Master of Horticulture Thesis, Michigan State University, 1921

McIntosh, John, *The origin of the North American Indians with a faithful description of their manners and customs, both civil and military, their religions, languages, dress, and ornaments: to which is prefixed a brief view of the creation of the world . . . concluding with a copious selection of Indian speeches, the antiquities of America, the civilization of the Mexicans, and some final observations on the origin of the Indians* (New York, 1844)

McKendrick, Neil, "The Commercialization of Fashion," in Neil McKendrick, John Brewer, and J. H. Plumb, *The Birth of a Consumer Society: The Commercialization of Eighteenth-Century England* (Bloomington, IN, 1982), pp. 35–99

McKinley, Albert E., "The English and Dutch Towns of New Netherland," *American Historical Review*, VI/1 (1900), pp. 1–18

McMahon, Sarah F., "A Comfortable Subsistence: The Changing Composition of Diet in Rural New England, 1620–1840," *William and Mary Quarterly*, 3rd ser., XLII/1 (January 1985), pp. 26–65

McMurry, Sally, "Women's Work in Agriculture: Divergent Trends in England and America, 1800 to 1930," *Comparative Studies in Society and History*, XXXIV/2 (April 1992), pp. 248–70

McNeill, William H., "How the Potato Changed World History," *Social Research*, LXVI (1999), pp. 69–83

——, *Plagues and People* (New York, 1976)

McTavish, Emily Jane, Jared E. Decker, Robert D. Schnabel, Jeremy F. Taylor, and David M. Hillisa, "New World Cattle Show Ancestry from Multiple Independent Domestication Events," *Proceedings of the National Academy of Sciences*, CX/15 (2013), pp. E1398–E1406, available at www.pnas.org, accessed January 26, 2017

Malone, Laurence J., "Rural Electrification Administration," EH.net, https://eh.net, accessed June 6, 2015

Mann, Charles C., *1493: Uncovering the New World Columbus Created* (New York, 2011)

Marks, Susan, *Finding Betty Crocker: The Secret Life of America's First Lady of Food* (New York, 2010)

Marsh, George P., *The Earth as Modified by Human Action: A Last Revision of Man and Nature* (New York, 1874)

Martin, Paul, "The Discovery of America," *Science*, CLXXIX (1973), pp. 969–74

——, "Prehistoric Overkill: The Global Model," in Paul S. Martin and Richard Klein, *Quarternary Extinctions: A Prehistoric Revolution* (Tucson, AZ, 1984), pp. 354–403

Masters, Edgar Lee, *Spoon River Anthology* (New York, 1916)

Meltzer, David J., *The First Peoples in a New World: Colonizing Ice Age America* (Berkeley, CA, 2009)

Mendelson, Anne, "Goodbye to the Marketplace: Food and Exclusivity in Nineteenth-century New York," in *The American Bourgeoisie: Distinction and*

Identity in the Nineteenth Century, ed. Julia B. Rosenbaum and Sven Beckert (New York, 2011)

——, *Milk: The Surprising Story of Milk through the Ages* (New York, 2008)

Meyer, Carrie A., *Days on the Family Farm: From the Golden Age through the Great Depression* (Minneapolis, 2007)

——, "The Farm Debut of the Gasoline Engine," *Agricultural History*, LXXXVII/3 (Summer 2013), pp. 287–313

Miller, Adrian, *Soul Food: The Surprising Story of an American Cuisine, One Plate at a Time* (Charlotte, NC, 2013)

Millones Figueroa, Luis, "The Staff of Life: Wheat and 'Indian Bread' in the New World," *Colonial Latin American Review*, XIX/2 (August 2010), pp. 301–22

Mintz, Sidney, *Tasting Food, Tasting Freedom: Excursions into Eating, Culture, and the Past* (Boston, 1996)

Misa, Thomas J., *Leonardo to the Internet: Technology & Culture from the Renaissance to the Present* (Baltimore, 2004)

Mitchell, R. J., and S. L. Duncan, "Range of Variability in Southern Coastal Plain Forests: Its Historical, Contemporary, and Future Role in Sustaining Biodiversity," *Ecology and Society*, XIV/1 (2009), p. 17

Monaghan, Jay, and William Hall, "From England to Illinois in 1821: The Journal of William Hall," *Journal of the Illinois State Historical Society*, XXXIX/1 (March 1946), pp. 21–67

Monrreal, Sahar, "'A novel, spicy delicacy': Tamales, Advertising, and Late 19th-century Imaginative Geographies of Mexico," *Cultural Geographies*, XV (2008), pp. 449–70

Montgomery, David R., *Dirt, the Erosion of Civilizations* (Berkeley, CA, 2007, rev. 2012)

Montgomery, George, "Wheat Price Policy in the United States," *Farm Foundation, Increasing Understanding of Public Problems and Policies* (Oak Brook, IL, 1953), pp. 25–70

Montgomery, M. R., *A Cow's Life: The Surprising History of Cattle, and How the Black Angus Came to Be Home on the Range* (New York, 2004)

Morris, Charles R., *The Dawn of Innovation* (New York, 2012)

Morris, Christopher, *The Big Muddy: An Environmental History of the Mississippi and Its Peoples, from Hernando De Soto to Hurricane Katrina* (New York, 2012)

Mudry, Jessica J., *Measured Meals: Nutrition in America* (Albany, NY, 2009)

National Agricultural Library, "Johnsongrass," www.invasivespeciesinfo.gov, accessed July 2, 2015

Nye, David E., *America as Second Creation: Technology and Narratives of New Beginnings* (Cambridge, 2003)

Ogle, Daniel G., Loren St. John, and Derek J. Tilley, "Plant Guide for Timothy (*Phleum pretense*)," https://plants.usda.gov, accessed March 18, 2011

O'Leary, Kelly, "The Flouring of Early New England: Wheat and its Function in the Loaves and Lives of Colonial Americans," MA thesis, Boston University, 2010

Oliver, Sandra L., *Food in Colonial and Federal America* (Westport, CT, 2005)

Olmstead, Alan L., and Paul W. Rhode, *Creating Abundance, Biological Innovation and American Agricultural Development* (Cambridge, 2008)

Olmsted, Frederick Law, *A Journey in the Seaboard Slave States; With Remarks on Their Economy* (New York, 1856)

——, *The Cotton Kingdom: A Traveller's Observations on Cotton and Slavery in the American Slave States. Based upon Three Former Volumes on Journeys and Investigations by the Same Author [1852–1854]* (New York, 1861)

Olson, Sidney, *Young Henry Ford: A Picture History of the First Forty Years* (Detroit, 1963)

Opie, Frederick Douglass, *Hog and Hominy: Soul Food from Africa to America* (New York, 2013)

Owen, Mrs. T.J.V., *Mrs. Owen's Illinois Cook Book* (Springfield, IL, 1871)

Pacyga, Dominick, *Chicago: A Biography* (Chicago, 2009)

Pargas, Damian Alan, "In the Fields of a 'Strange Land': Enslaved Newcomers and the Adjustment to Cotton Cultivation in the Antebellum South," *Slavery and Abolition*, XXXIV/4 (2013), pp. 562–78

Parker, Geoffrey, *Global Crisis: War, Climate Change and Catastrophe in the Seventeenth Century* (New Haven, CT, 2013)

Parton, James, *The Life of Andrew Jackson*, 3 vols. (New York, 1860)

Pasley, Jeffrey L., "The Cheese and the Words: Popular Political Culture and Participatory Democracy in the Early American Republic," in *Beyond the Founders: New Approaches to the Political History of the Early American Republic*, ed. Jeffrey L. Pasley, Andrew W. Robertson, and David Waldstreicher (Chapel Hill, NC, 2004), pp. 32–56

Pensack, Bill, "Colonial Pennsylvania Mills," *Building Community: Medieval Technology and American History*, www.engr.psu.edu, accessed April 4, 2015

Perrin du Lac, [François-Marie], *Travels through the two Louisianas and among the savage nations of the Missouri also in the United States, along the Ohio and the adjacent provinces in 1801, 1802, & 1803: with a sketch of the manners, customs, character, and the civil and religious ceremonies of the people of those countries* (London, 1807)

Peterson, Arthur G., "Flour and Grist Milling in Virginia: A Brief History," *Virginia Magazine of History and Biography*, XLIII/2 (1935), pp. 97–108

Philpott, Tom, "A Reflection on the Lasting Legacy of 1970s USDA Secretary Earl Butz," *Grist*, February 8, 2008, http://grist.org, accessed February 6, 2017

Pilcher, Jeffrey M., *Planet Taco: A Global History of Mexican Food* (New York, 2012)

Poe, Tracy N., "The Origins of Soul Food in Black Urban Identity: Chicago, 1915–1947," *American Studies International*, XXXVII/1 (1999), pp. 4–17

Polvi, Lina E., and Ellen Wohl, "The Beaver Meadow Complex Revisited: The Role of Beavers in Post-glacial Floodplain Development," *Earth Surface Processes and Landforms*, XXXVII/3 (March 2012), pp. 332–46

Popik, Barry, "Hoagie (Sandwich)," *The Big Apple*, June 10, 2009, www.barrypopik.com, accessed December 10, 2014

——, and Andrew F. Smith, "Chicken à la King," in *The Oxford Encyclopedia of Food and Drink in America*, ed. Andrew F. Smith, 2nd edn. (New York, 2013), I, p. 371

Porter, Eduardo, "In Florida Groves, Cheap Labor Means Machines," *New York Times*, March 22, 2004

Porter, Glenn, and Harold C. Livesey, *Merchants and Manufacturers* (Baltimore, 1971)

Potter, David M., *People of Plenty: Economic Abundance and the American Character* (Chicago, 1954)

Prasad, Vandana, Caroline A. E. Strömberg, Habib Alimohammadian, and Ashok
    Sahni, "Dinosaur Coprolites and the Early Evolution of Grasses and Grazers,"
    Science, cccx/5751 (November 18, 2005), pp. 1177–80
Pursell, Carroll, *Technology in Postwar America: A History* (New York, 2007)
Quaife, Milo Milton, ed., *Growing Up with Southern Illinois, 1820 to 1861: From the
    Memoirs of Daniel Harmon Brush* (Chicago, 1944)
Randolph, Mrs. Mary, *The Virginia House-wife, or Methodical Cook* (Washington,
    DC, 1824); facsimile reprint, ed. Karen Hess (Columbia, SC, 1984)
Ranhoffer, Charles, *The Epicurean* (New York, 1894)
Ray, Krishnendu, *The Ethnic Restaurateur* (London and New York, 2016)
Reich, David, et al., "Reconstructing Native American Population History,"
    Nature, CDLXXXVIII (July 11, 2012), pp. 370–74
Remini, Robert, *Andrew Jackson*, III: *The Course of American Democracy (1833–1845)*
    (New York, 1984)
Reynolds, Terry, *Stronger than a Hundred Men: A History of the Vertical Water Wheel*
    (Baltimore, 1983, repr. 2002)
Rhode, Paul W., "Do Crops Shape Culture? Contrasting Cotton and Wheat in
    Nineteenth-century North America," in Barbara Hahn, Tiago Saraiva, Paul W.
    Rhode, Peter Coclanis, and Claire Strom, "Does Crop Determine Culture?"
    Agricultural History, LXXXVIII/3 (Summer 2014), pp. 407–39
Rink, Oliver A., *Holland on the Hudson: An Economic and Social History of Dutch
    New York* (Ithaca, NY, 1986)
Risjord, Norman K., "From the Plow to the Cow: William D. Hoard and Ameri-
    ca's Dairyland," *Wisconsin Magazine of History*, LXXXVIII/3 (Spring 2005), pp.
    40–49
Rodiek, Anne, "Hay for Horses: Alfalfa or Grass?" in Proceedings, 31st California
    Alfalfa & Forage Symposium, December 12–13, 2001, www.alfalfa.ucdavis.edu,
    accessed January 24, 2017
Rodríguez-Alegría, Enrique, "Eating Like an Indian: Negotiating Social Relations
    in the Spanish Colonies," *Current Anthropology*, XLVI/4 (August/October
    2005), pp. 551–73
Roe, Joseph Wickham, *English and American Tool Builders* (New Haven, CT, 1916)
Rogers, Katharine M., *Pork: A Global History* (London, 2012)
Rogin, Leo, *The Introduction of Farm Machinery in its Relation to the Productivity
    of Labor in the Agriculture of the United States during the Nineteenth Century*
    (Berkeley, CA, 1931)
Romans, Brian, "Ghostly Image Reveals Ice Age Rivers," *Wired*, October 4, 2010,
    www.wired.com
Rorer, Mrs. S. T., *Philadelphia Cook Book: A Manual of Home Economies* (Philadel-
    phia, 1886)
Rose, Peter G., "Dutch Food in Life and Art," *Culinary Historians of New York
    Newsletter*, XVI/1 (Fall 2002), pp. 1–4
——, trans. and ed., *The Sensible Cook: Dutch Foodways in the Old and the New
    World* (Syracuse, NY, 1998)
Rosen, Steven A., *Lithics after the Stone Age: A Handbook of Stone Tools from the
    Levant* (Walnut Creek, CA, 1997)
Rosen, William, *The Most Powerful Idea in the World: A Story of Steam, Industry, and
    Invention* (New York, 2010)

Ross, Alice, "Native American Foods," in *The Oxford Encyclopedia of Food and Drink in America*, ed. Andrew F. Smith, 2nd edn. (New York, 2013), II, pp. 644–60

Rothschild, B. J., J. S. Ault, P. Goulletquer, and M. Héral, "Decline of the Chesapeake Bay Oyster Population: A Century of Habitat Destruction and Overfishing," *Marine Ecology Progress Series*, III (August 1994), pp. 28–39

Rubin, Julius, "The Limits of Agricultural Progress in the Nineteenth-century South," *Agricultural History*, XLIX/2 (1975), pp. 362–73

Ruddiman, William, *Plows, Plagues, and Petroleum: How Humans Took Control of Climate* (Princeton, NJ, 2005)

Runyon, Luke, "The Long, Slow Decline of the U.S. Sheep Industry," *Harvest Public Media* (October 8, 2013), www.harvestpublicmedia.org, accessed January 26, 2017

Russell, Bertrand, *The Conquest of Happiness* (London, 1930)

Russelle, Michael P., "Alfalfa: After an 8,000-year journey, the 'Queen of Forages' stands poised to enjoy renewed popularity," *American Scientist*, LXXXIX/3 (May–June 2001), pp. 252–3

Ruttan, Vernon W., and Yujiro Hayami, "Toward a Theory of Induced Institutional Innovation," *Journal of Development Studies*, XX (1984), pp. 302–23

Sapart, C. J., et al., "Natural and Anthropogenic Variations in Methane Sources during the Past Two Millennia," *Nature*, CDXC (October 2012), pp. 85–8

Schlosser, Eric, *Fast Food Nation: The Dark Side of the All-American Meal* (Boston, 2001)

Schmidt, Stephen, "When Did Southern Begin?" Manuscript Cookbooks Survey, November 2015, www.manuscriptcookbookssurveycom, accessed February 6, 2017

Schotzko, Thomas, and David Granatstein, *A Brief Look at the Washington Apple Industry: Past and Present* (Pullman, WA, 2004)

Schwartz, Hillel, *Never Satisfied: A Cultural History of Diets, Fantasies and Fat* (New York, 1986)

Sellers, Charles, *The Market Revolution: Jacksonian America, 1815–1846* (New York, 1991)

Sellers, Coleman, Jr., "Oliver Evans and his Inventions," *Journal of the Franklin Institute*, 122 (July 1886), pp. 2–4, available at https://todayinsci.com, accessed January 22, 2017

Shammas, Carole, "How Self-sufficient Was Early America?" *Journal of Interdisciplinary History*, XIII/2 (Autumn 1982), pp. 247–72

Shapiro, Laura, *Perfection Salad: Women and Cooking at the Turn of the Century* (New York, 1986), rev. with an Afterword (Berkeley, CA, and Los Angeles, 2008)

——, *Something from the Oven: Reinventing Dinner in 1950s America* (New York, 2004)

Sharrer, G. Terry, "The Merchant-Millers: Baltimore's Flour Milling Industry, 1783–1860," *Agricultural History*, LVI/1, Symposium on the History of Agricultural Trade and Marketing (January 1982), pp. 138–50

Shea, Martha Esposito, and Mike Mathis, *Campbell Soup Company* (Mount Pleasant, SC, 2002)

Shepherd, Major W., *Prairie Experiences in Handling Cattle and Sheep* (London, 1884)

Shields, David S., *Southern Provisions: The Creation and Revival of a Cuisine* (Chicago, 2015)

Siegel, Nancy, "Cooking Up American Politics," *Gastronomica*, VIII/3 (Summer 2008), pp. 53–61

Simmons, Amelia, *American Cookery, or the art of dressing viands, fish, poultry, and vegetables, and the best modes of making pastes, puffs, pies, tarts, puddings, custards, and preserves, and all kinds of cakes, from the imperial plumb to plain cake: Adapted to this country, and all grades of life*, 2nd edn. (Albany, NY, 1796)

Sinclair, Upton, *The Jungle* (New York, 1906)

Smil, Vaclav, *Energy in World History* (Boulder, CO, 1994)

——, *Enriching the Earth: Fritz Haber, Carl Bosch, and the Transformation of World Food Production* (Cambridge, MA, 2004)

Smiley, Stephen T., "Immune Defense against Pneumonic Plague," *Immunological Reviews*, CCXXV/1 (October 2008), pp. 256–71

Smith, Andrew F., *Eating History: Thirty Turning Points in the Making of American Cuisine* (New York, 2009)

——, *Hamburger: A Global History* (London, 2008)

——, *Peanuts: The Illustrious History of the Goober Pea* (Urbana, IL, 2002)

——, *Potato: A Global History* (London, 2011)

——, *Souper Tomatoes: The Story of America's Favorite Food* (New Brunswick, NJ, 2000)

——, ed., *The Oxford Encyclopedia of Food and Drink in America*, 2nd edn., 3 vols. (New York, 2013)

——, *Centennial Buckeye Cook Book* (Columbus, OH, 2000)

Smith, Eliza, *The Compleat Housewife: Or, Accomplish'd Gentlewoman's Companion* (London, 1727)

Smith, Jane S., *The Garden of Invention: Luther Burbank and the Business of Breeding Plants* (New York, 2009)

Sokolov, Raymond, "The Search for the Perfect Nacho," *Wall Street Journal*, February 4, 2006

"Sorghum Introduction," *Gramene*, http://archive.gramene.org, accessed July 3, 2015

Southerton, Simon G., *Losing a Lost Tribe: Native Americans, DNA, and the Mormon Church* (Salt Lake City, 2004)

"A Splendid Present," *Genesee Farmer and Gardener's Journal* [Rochester, NY], V/42 (October 17, 1835), pp. 330–31

Stahle, David W., Malcolm K. Cleaveland, Dennis B. Blanton, Matthew D. Therrell, and David A. Gay, "The Lost Colony and Jamestown Droughts," *Science*, n.s., CCLXXX/5363 (April 24, 1998), pp. 564–7

Stampp, Kenneth M., *The Peculiar Institution: Slavery in the Ante-bellum South* (New York, 1956)

Standish, Arthur, "New Directions of Experience to the Commons Complaint, for the planting of Timber and Firewood, invented by Arthur Standish" (London, 1613).

Steckel, Richard H., "A Peculiar Population: The Nutrition, Health, and Mortality of American Slaves from Childhood to Maturity," *Journal of Economic History*, XLVI/3 (1986), pp. 721–4

Steinfeld, Henning, et al., *Livestock's Long Shadow*, Food and Agriculture Organization of the United Nations (Rome, 2006)

Stewart, Estelle M., and J. C. Bowen, *History of Wages in the United States from Colonial Times to 1928: Revision of Bulletin No. 499 with Supplement, 1929–1933*, Bulletin of the United States Bureau of Labor Statistics No. 604 (Washington, DC, 1934)

Stine, Jeffrey K., "A Sense of Place: Donald Worster's 'Dust Bowl,'" *Technology and Culture*, XLVIII/2 (2007), pp. 377–85

Strasser, Susan, *Never Done: A History of American Housework* (New York, 2000)

Struever, Stuart, and Felicia Antonelli Holton, *Koster: Americans in Search of their Prehistoric Past* (Garden City, NY, 1979)

Taylor, John Martin, *Hoppin' John's Lowcountry Cooking: Recipes and Ruminations from Charleston and the Carolina Coastal Plain* (New York, 1992, rev. 2012)

Terkel, Studs, *Hard Times: An Oral History of the Great Depression* (New York, 1986)

Thompson, James F., and Steven C. Blank, "Harvest Mechanization Helps Agriculture Remain Competitive," *California Agriculture*, LIV/3 (May–June 2000), pp. 51–6

Thorn, Bret, "Survey: Italian Remains Most Popular Ethnic Cuisine: Consumption Highest in the Northeast," *Nation's Restaurant News*, August 28, 2015, www.nrn.com

Thorson, James A., *Tough Guys Don't Dice* (New York, 1989)

Thwaites, Reuben Gold, ed., *Travels West of the Alleghanies: Made in 1793–96 by André Michaux; in 1802 by F. A. Michaux; and in 1803 by Thaddeus Mason Harris, M.A.* (Cleveland, 1904)

Tichi, Cecilia, *Shifting Gears: Technology, Literature, Culture in Modernist America* (Chapel Hill, NC, 1987)

Tocqueville, Alexis de, *Selected Letters on Politics and Society*, ed. Roger Boesche (Berkeley, CA, and Los Angeles, 1986)

Trachtenberg, Alan, *The Incorporation of America: Culture and Society in the Gilded Age* (New York, 1982)

Trollope, Frances, *The Refugee in America*, 3 vols. (London, 1833)

——, *Domestic Manners of the Americans* (London and New York, 1832)

Trubek, Amy, *A Taste of Place: A Cultural Journey into Terroir* (Berkeley, CA, and Los Angeles, 2008)

Tucker, David M., *Kitchen Gardening in America: A History* (Ames, IA, 1993)

Turner, Katherine Leonard, *How the Other Half Ate: A History of Working Class Meals at the Turn of the Century* (Berkeley, CA, and Los Angeles, 2014)

Twain, Mark (Samuel L. Clemens), *A Tramp Abroad* (Hartford, CT, 1880)

Van Deman, Ruth, and Fanny Walker Yeatman, *Aunt Sammy's Radio Recipes Revised*, Bureau of Home Economics (Washington, DC, 1931)

Vikraman, Sundeep, Cheryl D. Fryar, and Cynthia L. Ogden, "Caloric Intake from Fast Food among Children and Adolescents in the United States, 2011–2012," *National Center for Health Statistics*, NCHS Data Brief, no. 213 (September 2015), www.cdc.gov/nchs

Wade, Nicholas, "Earliest Americans Arrived in Waves, DNA Study Finds," *New York Times*, July 11, 2012

Walker, Nancy A., *Shaping Our Mothers' World: American Women's Magazines* (Jackson, MS, 2000)

Watkins, T. H., *The Hungry Years: A Narrative History of the Great Depression in America* (New York, 2000)

Watson, Harry L., "Slavery and Development in a Dual Economy: The South and the Market Revolution," in *The Market Revolution in America: Social, Political, and Religious Expressions, 1800–1880*, ed. Melvyn Stokes and Stephen Conway (Charlottesville, VA, 1996), pp. 43–73

Weaver, William Woys, *Sauerkraut Yankees: Pennsylvania Dutch Foods and Foodways*, 2nd edn. (Mechanicsburg, PA, 2002)

——, *As American as Shoofly Pie: The Foodlore and Fakelore of Pennsylvania Dutch Cuisine* (Philadelphia, 2013)

Weigley, Emma Seifrit, *Sarah Tyson Rorer, the Nation's Instructress in Dietetics and Cookery* (Philadelphia, 1977)

"Wheat Data—All Years," Economic Research Service, United States Department of Agriculture, www.ers.usda.gov, accessed February 2, 2017

Whitaker, Jan, "Quick Lunch," *Gastronomica*, IV/1 (Winter 2004), pp. 69–73

Whitman, Walt, "The Song of the Broad Axe," in *Leaves of Grass* (Philadelphia, 1900).

——, *Specimen Days & Collect* (Philadelphia, 1882–3)

Wik, Reynold M., "Steam Power on the American Farm, 1830–1880," *Agricultural History*, XXV/4 (1951), pp. 181–6

Wiley, James, *The Banana: Empires, Trade Wars, and Globalization* (Lincoln, NE, 2008)

Wilford, John Noble, "Food is Redesigned to Suit Machines," *New York Times*, August 23, 1967

Williams, Michael, *Deforesting the Earth: From Prehistory to Global Crisis* (Chicago, 2002)

Williams, Robert C., *Fordson, Farmall, and Poppin' Johnny: A History of the Farm Tractor and its Impact on America* (Urbana, IL, 1987)

Willis, N. P., *Loiterings of Travel*, 3 vols. (London, 1840)

Wilson, Charles Morrow, *Grass and People* (Gainesville, FL, 1961)

Witter, David, "Grain of Truth: Taking Stock of the Relics of Chicago's Era as the World's 'Stacker of Wheat,'" *New City*, June 2, 2010, www.newcity.com, accessed January 27, 2017

Wokeck, Marianne S., "German and Irish Immigration to Colonial Philadelphia," Symposium on the Demographic History of the Philadelphia Region, 1600–1860, *Proceedings of the American Philosophical Society*, CXXXIII/2 (1989), pp. 128–43

Wolfe, Nathan D., Claire Panosian Dunavan, and Jared Diamond, "Origins of Major Human Infectious Diseases," *Nature*, CDXLVII (May 17, 2007), p. 281

Woodmason, Charles, *The Carolina Backcountry on the Eve of the Revolution: The Journal and Other Writings of Charles Woodmason, Anglican Itinerant*, ed. Richard J. Hooker (Charlotte, NC, 1953)

Worster, Donald, *Dust Bowl: The Southern Plains in the 1930s* (New York, 1979, rev. 2004)

——, "Transformations of the Earth: Toward an Agroecological Perspective in History," *Journal of American History*, LXXVI/4 (1990), pp. 1087–1106

Wyman, Carolyn, *Better than Homemade: Amazing Foods that Changed the Way We Eat* (Philadelphia, 2004)

Yentch, Anne B., "Excavating the South's African American Food History," in *African American Foodways*, ed. Anne L. Bower (Urbana, IL, 2007), pp. 59–98.

Young, Biloine Whiting, and Melvin J. Fowler, *Cahokia, the Great Native American Metropolis* (Urbana, IL, 1999)

Zanger, Mark, "Italian American Food," in *The Oxford Encyclopedia of Food and Drink in America*, ed. Andrew F. Smith, 2nd edn. (New York, 2013), I, pp. 345–55

Ziegelman, Jane, and Andy Coe, *A Square Meal: A Culinary History of the Great Depression* (New York, 2016)

Acknowledgements

To my friends and colleagues in the world of food history who have helped me in writing this book, both directly and indirectly, I offer my deep gratitude. They are too many to enumerate, so forgive the omissions; they are not meant to displease. My special thanks to Andrew F. Smith and Rachel Laudan for reading the manuscript and for their suggestions about content—and for their encouragement. My many conversations over the past quarter-century with Andy have powerfully shaped many of my ideas about American food history. The same appreciation goes out to my long-time friends and collaborators on other books, Colleen Taylor Sen and Carol Haddix: ours is a mutual support writing group. Patty Carroll, also a book collaborator, has taught me more about art and American popular culture than I can say. Doing projects and programs has given me lots of ideas and material that have gone into this book. Gerry Rounds, Eleanor Hanson, Wanda Bain, Elizabeth Carlson (alias Miss Ellie), Cathy Kaufman, Anne Mendelson, Andy Coe, and Chris Koetke of Kendall College are among the many from whom I learned a lot. I am only sorry that all of our old friends are not here to continue our dialogues—over a good meal. My thanks, also, to my sons, Robert Kraig, Theodore Kraig, and Michael Kraig, for pointing me to ideas and sources about American culture, labor and environmental and educational issues. Every one of our gatherings has been stimulating.

My profound thanks go to the organizers of and participants in the Oxford Symposium on Food and Cookery. It was here, beginning many years ago with a presentation on a then unsavory subject, that I became interested in American food and its deep roots in American culture.

Last, because this book has taken so long to finish—if that's the word for an endless subject—my thanks to Michael Leaman for his patience. To the editorial and production people at Reaktion Books, my thanks for your excellent work in producing this book. It's been a pleasure.

Photo Acknowledgements

The author and the publishers wish to express their thanks to the below sources of illustrative material and/or permission to reproduce it.

Agricultural Research Service (ARS): p. 269; Luigi Anzivino: p. 24; The British Library: p. 233; Dwight Burdette: p. 281; Commission for Environmental Cooperation: p. 14; Daderot: p. 21 (Natural History Museum of Utah); Dimus: p. 44; Florida Cracker Cattle Association: p. 47; Freeimages: pp. 78 (Justyna Cilulko), 245 (Robert Burress); iStockphoto: pp. 291 (nata_vkusidey), 292 top (rez-art), 293 (Marchiez); The J. Paul Getty Museum, Los Angeles: p. 171; Bruce Kraig: pp. 26, 35, 190, 195, 207, 209, 231, 247, 252, 253, 288, 290, 292 bottom, 294, 297, 301, 303; Library of Congress, Washington, DC: pp. 18, 31, 50, 51, 76, 108, 116, 121, 123, 127, 141, 145, 147, 155, 164, 182, 183, 186, 188, 189, 193, 194, 229, 272, 295, 296; Max Pixel: p. 289; Miami University Libraries – Digital Collections: pp. 187, 232; Missouri History Museum: p. 72; Morguefile: pp. 106, 177 (Sgarton); NASA: p. 48 (KSC); National Gallery of Art, Washington, DC: pp. 65, 86, 103, 178; New York Public Library: pp. 119, 133, 152, 218, 219, 273, 299, 302; courtesy Michelle Podkowa: p. 67; photo courtesy Colleen Taylor Sen: p. 309; Smithsonian American Art Museum, Washington, DC: p. 29; Smithsonian National Museum of American History, Washington, DC: p. 117; Forest & Kim Starr: p. 157; courtesy Estate of Ben Steele: pp. 173, 174; John Sullivan: p. 243; U.S. Department of Agriculture: p. 57; U.S. Fish and Wildlife Service: p. 12; Virginia Historical Society: p. 55; The Walters Art Museum, Baltimore: p. 85; Western Heritage Center (Montana): pp. 175, 210, 263.

Index

Page numbers in *italics* indicate illustrations